FIRST FIGHTS IN FALLUJAH

FIRST FIGHTS IN FALLUJAH

Marines During Operation *Vigilant Resolve*, in Iraq, April 2004

LIEUTENANT COLONEL DAVID E. KELLY,
USMC, RETIRED

CASEMATE
Philadelphia & Oxford

Published in the United States of America and Great Britain in 2023 by
CASEMATE PUBLISHERS
1950 Lawrence Road, Havertown, PA 19083, USA
and
The Old Music Hall, 106–108 Cowley Road, Oxford OX4 1JE, UK

Hardcover Edition: ISBN 978-1-63624-318-4
Digital Edition: ISBN 978-1-63624-319-1

A CIP record for this book is available from the British Library

Printed and bound in the United Kingdom by CPI Group (UK) Ltd, Croydon, CR0 4YY
Typeset in India by DiTech Publishing Services

For a complete list of Casemate titles, please contact:

CASEMATE PUBLISHERS (US)
Telephone (610) 853-9131
Fax (610) 853-9146
Email: casemate@casematepublishers.com
www.casematepublishers.com

CASEMATE PUBLISHERS (UK)
Telephone (0)1226 734350
Email: casemate-uk@casematepublishers.co.uk
www.casematepublishers.co.uk

All images are official photos by Lt Col David E. Kelly, USMC, Ret., unless otherwise stated.

Contents

Dedication

This book is dedicated to three groups who played roles in allowing me to serve as a Marine field historian during a critical time in Iraq in 2004:

First, Colonel John Ripley, head of the Marine Corps History Division, who approved my deployment to Iraq. Also, Colonel Nick Reynolds, reserve head of the Field History detachment, who asked me to participate in the effort to record the words of the Marines in Iraq in early 2004. Members of the Field History detachment who deployed during the opening phase of Operation *Iraqi Freedom* in 2003 paved the way for me and Major John Piedmont.

Next, the Marines and Navy personnel of the 1st Marine Expeditionary Force (IMEF) who made me welcome to meet with them and record their stories. From MEF staff to infantry squad Marines, I was able to meet with individuals at all levels who were part of the early 2004 fighting in Fallujah, Iraq. Their pride in their actions was inspiring.

Finally, my family who supported me in my desire to deploy as a field historian four years after my retirement from the Marine Corps Reserve. My wife Terrie Kelly and daughters Donna Kelly Romero and Rosie Kelly Sullivan supported me when I wanted to serve in uniform once again. They also encouraged my later years-long efforts to write this book in order to make known the bravery and dedication of the Marines and sailors I met.

David E. Kelly, Lieutenant Colonel, USMC, Retired

Preface

Along with Major John Piedmont, I was one of two Marine Corps field historians sent to Iraq in the spring of 2004. We were both Reserve officers called to active duty. Our Letter of Instruction, the official document that outlined our mission, was clear: to travel throughout the Marine Area of Responsibility in Iraq, and conduct field history interviews with Marines and sailors. We had no quotas to meet. We did not attach to any individual unit. This allowed us the freedom to meet with Marines at all ranks and staff levels, to try and flesh out official reports with the words of these Marines. Future researchers and historians may find this information invaluable as they reconstruct the events in Iraq during 2004.

What made our work possible was the cooperation that we met at every level of command in IMEF. The command gave us access to meet with Marines in every part of Iraq. Use of the military internet and landline phone systems allowed us to inform units that we were in-bound, and gave them time to select key individuals for us to interview. As the senior member of the field history team, I created a matrix of all of the major command elements under IMEF, and attempted to visit each command at least once during our five-month deployment.

My deployment began with a commercial flight into Kuwait to Camp Wolverine, and I made arrangements with the Marine Liaison Office there to fly into Iraq. Once in Iraq, I began my work as a field historian.

I have arranged the material here in the most understandable way, as interviews were conducted at different times and in different camps. This was due to the challenges of the travel to meet and speak with Marines throughout Al Anbar province. After combining my interview notes and transcriptions, I have attempted to create a sense of the actions and thoughts of these Marines who were the first to fight in Fallujah and adjacent areas starting in March and April 2004.

Introduction

The Marines interviewed in this book include those from 2nd Battalion 1st Marines (2/1), 2nd Battalion 2nd Marines (2/2), 1st Battalion 5th Marines (1/5), the 3rd Amphibious Tractor Battalion, 1st Tank Battalion, and elements of the 3rd Marine Air Wing (III MAW). The book is organized to present the events as described by the participants, from high-ranking aviation officers to Marine infantrymen. This gives the reader first-hand accounts of some of the events of April 2004 in Fallujah, Iraq, at the start of Operation *Vigilant Resolve*. The language is sometimes raw, and has none of the limits of official after-action reports often used to write citations for valor.

Once deployed to Iraq, I quickly learned to make contact with key personnel from units scattered all over Al Anbar province. Close combat in Fallujah encompassed many different Marine units.

I have selected the interviews for this book from the 190 that I conducted. These Marines fought in different parts of Fallujah and the surrounding areas. Some of the notable actions include: a Marine using a laser scope to detect the origin of a sniper in a minaret; combat in the streets; clearing buildings and whole neighborhoods of insurgents; helicopter pilots and crewmen flying close air support missions and being fired at; and, finally, actions by a Marine Staff NCO to save a squad in a building surrounded by enemy fighters. The Marines in this squad had to leave a burning Amtrac, and hold off a large number of enemy. They fought attacking fighters as they ran out of ammunition, while waiting for a Quick Reaction Force (QRF) to relieve them. A stroke of luck prevented the rescue from becoming a disaster.

Ingenuity, teamwork, and pride in each other was a hallmark of every Marine I met. Even the most junior of them had a mature understanding of their actions, and an awareness of limits on them for political reasons.

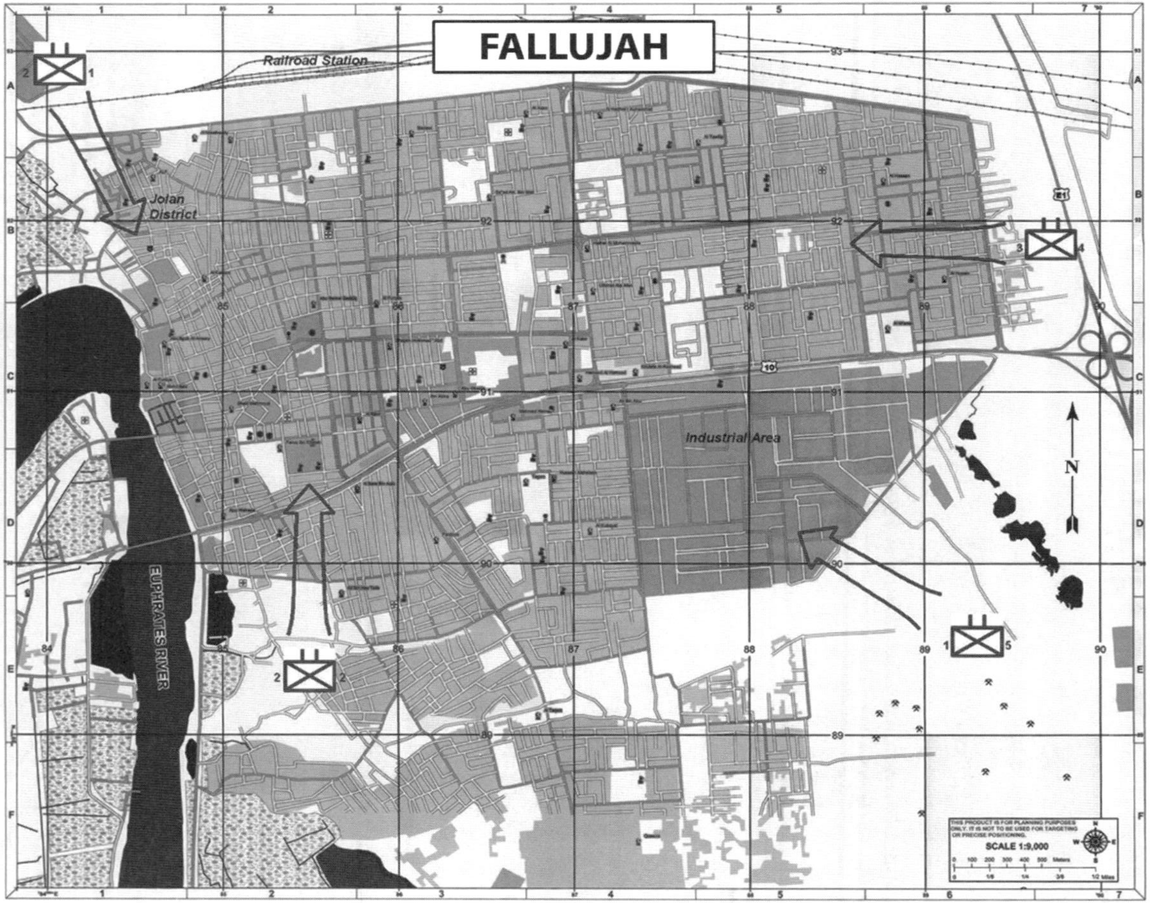

Map of Fallujah, Operation *Vigilant Resolve. (US Marines in Iraq 2004–2005: Into the Fray)*, by LtCol Kenneth W. Estes, USMC, Retired, History Division

CHAPTER ONE

Deployment to Iraq, Learning the Lay of the Land

During my final preparations for travel to Iraq, the situation throughout that country had deteriorated rapidly. An event in Fallujah was the catalyst. As the 1st Marine Expeditionary Force (IMEF) was assuming responsibility for operations from the U.S. Army in the Al Anbar province of Iraq, a bloody ambush in the city of Fallujah would cause the MEF's plans to be altered by direction of the National Command Authority in Washington, DC. Early on March 31, a small convoy of trucks escorted by two private security vehicles was ambushed traveling through Fallujah. Four Blackwater Security contractors were killed by overwhelming gunfire, their bodies dragged from the vehicles, beaten, set on fire, and then hung on a bridge over the Euphrates River. The images were soon seen on world-wide media. The initial response by the Marines was to first methodically seek out the leaders of the atrocity, then begin the process of rebuilding the city. By the time I arrived in Baghdad on April 11, the decision had been made by authorities in Washington to surround Fallujah and begin forcible entry into the city to destroy enemy positions. Fighting had already ramped up before I got to Camp Fallujah, several miles east of the city.

My deployment began with a commercial flight into Kuwait, where I stayed at Camp Wolverine, and made arrangements with the Marine Liaison Office to fly into Iraq. At the camp, the other Marine officers I traveled with (Major Troy Daniels and Major Will Mayberry of the Enduring Freedom Combat Assessment Team, EFCAT) spent two days getting ready to fly up to Baghdad, Iraq, on a KC-130 transport plane.

Flight into Iraq, Saturday April 10, 2004

On Saturday morning we dressed, ate breakfast, returned to our tent and waited for a possible call to the flight line. All of our gear was packed up, just in case we lucked out and got onto a flight. As the names were called, we were not on the flight list. But one Army detachment had 60 individuals traveling together, and there were only 20 spots available on the flight. Their senior sergeant said that he would wait until all of his soldiers could travel on the same flight. That opened up seats on the plane for us, so we were on our way out of the tent, loading our gear onto a small bus that would take us to the flight line.

Near the flight line, an Air Force loadmaster stacked our gear onto a large pallet and strapped it down, and we finally boarded the KC-130 and found nylon strap seats for the one and a half hours or so we'd be on the plane. We boarded the plane at 0730, and had to wait for about an hour for a South Korean general and his entourage to embark. We took off at about 0830 and headed north for Iraq.

This was my first time on one of these turboprop-driven airplanes in over 25 years, and it was just as uncomfortable as I remembered. The flight was uneventful, but I made the first of many preflight "Acts of Contrition" (a Roman Catholic prayer asking God for forgiveness) as we lifted off. I would say this prayer on every flight I would make over the next four months.

Our first indication that we were about to land at Baghdad was when the plane made a sharp banking movement. The sunlight from the small windows on the plane played across our faces, alternately putting each face in bright light and then plunging them into shadow. This banking motion continued as we started the sharp corkscrew descent into Baghdad International Airport. I had read about the need for this type of descent due to insurgents attacking several planes last year with man-packed surface-to-air rockets, but this was a jarring reminder of where we now were. This was Baghdad!

The plane landed smoothly, and we taxied to a section of the airport with several green military tents. The plane was very noisy, and the heat of Iraq hit my face like an open oven as the back ramp opened. The sunlight was blinding. Very sharp and bright. The combination was overpowering. I put on my sunglasses and tried to get used to the blasting heat. A forklift lifted the baggage pallet off the plane, and as I got my gear, I could hear explosions in the distance. There were also a couple of trails of black smoke going up to the sky. It looked like the smoke was coming from a source outside the perimeter of the airport. This reminded me of many war movies that I have seen over the years. Except that it was so real and I was watching it live!

I went into one of the tents by the loading area with the two majors, and we asked how we would get from here to Camp Fallujah. Until March 2004, the most common way of going to Fallujah from Baghdad was to hop a ground supply convoy. However, this April had witnessed a huge upsurge in violence against coalition forces. There were many attacks on convoys, bases, and any type of military movement. We would have to try to hop a helicopter flight, and none were scheduled or available today.

Majors Landry, Mayberry and I hopped a bus to Camp Flexible, a section of the airport with many tents available for transient units and individuals like us. Along the way, we picked up a couple of more Marines who were also headed to Camp Fallujah and places beyond: Lieutenant Justin L. McDonald, Staff Sergeant Christopher Bauer, and Lieutenant Mike Griesl. We found a nice empty air-conditioned tent with a plywood floor. We assembled aluminum cots that were stacked inside the tent to make a sleeping area for ourselves. Using his Iridium satellite phone, Will Mayberry attempted to call into the EFCAT staff at Camp Fallujah (at that time it was more commonly called MEK, for Mujahedin-E Kalq), but could not get through. Troy Landry hopped a ride back to the Marine liaison area on the far side of the airport to see what we could do about getting transportation from here. By late afternoon we had requests pending at both Marine and Army aviation channels, but saw we weren't going anywhere today, so we got some sleep, then walked to the nearby mess hall, which was only about a half mile away.

This camp and mess hall were on the edge of the airport, with the road that circled inside the airport on one side, and a cement or cinderblock wall about 15 feet high on the other side. The wall formed the boundary of the airport grounds. It was about 500 meters from the road to the wall.

While we were traveling, we never missed a chance to eat at a mess hall, mainly because we did not know where we might be in only a few hours, and didn't know how long it might be before we had another meal. Food at the chow hall at Camp Flexible was really good. Every meal had a choice of at least two meat portions, bread or rolls, sometimes a salad, lots of vegetables, milk, coffee, juices, soda and water, fresh fruits and ice cream novelties. Soldiers, Marines, and local civilian contract drivers ate here. A big concern at every eating facility I would encounter over here would be field sanitation, and all personnel had to wash hands at sinks just outside the entrance to every dining facility. Some facilities had personnel watching the line of people coming into the mess hall and would check to ensure that everyone had washed his or her hands.

Camp Flexible offered other comforts besides chow. Near our tent was a large MWR (morale, welfare, recreation) tent. Inside, soldiers and Marines watched videos on a large television screen, and another section of the tent held about a dozen computers with internet access. My little group signed up to use the computers, and I emailed to my wife Terrie to say that I had landed safely in Baghdad and was waiting for transportation to Camp Fallujah. I didn't give specifics about any of the arrangements, as this was an operational security issue: Unsecured internet messages can be scanned for intelligence purposes by anyone with the equipment and knowledge, so all email out of here had to be closely self-monitored.

After evening chow, I put on my PT (Physical Training) gear and shower shoes, and brought my shaving kit to walk to a small grouping of shower tents nearby. The tents were a temporary shower structure, made of wood, plastic tubing, and rubberized canvas, but at least it provided someplace to wash off the grit.

Firefight by the Wall

Sunday April 11, 2004, was Easter Sunday. I was not near a chapel, and only spoke of it at the time in that it was so strange to be in such a foreign place on Easter. The tent mates, now numbering six, walked to the dining trailers for breakfast, and Major Mayberry and Lieutenant Chieslo got on the Iridium phone to try to make transportation arrangements out of here. They found out that it would be Monday or Tuesday at the earliest before we could get moving out of this camp, since ground convoys out of Baghdad had been suspended due to the ongoing upsurge in violence in Iraq.

At noon, we walked over to the chow hall for another meal, and I was just about finishing up when there was a short series of loud explosions from outside. Immediately everyone in the mess hall moved quickly out of the building.

What was happening? Were we under some kind of attack? I was one of a small group of transients, and we had no prearranged place to go, or SOP (Standard Operating Procedure) to follow. Along with the two majors, I followed the crowd outside of the dining building, and crouched behind cement barriers by the roadside.

The noises were coming from the other side of the airport wall, about 150 meters from where we were. We could hear automatic gunfire, and a few more explosions, but there were no rounds coming in our direction. Now I could clearly understand the need to always wear a flak jacket and helmet here! After about a half hour, the explosions subsided, and we made our way back to our tent area, still cautious, and staying on the roadway side of tents and barriers.

All along the walls were guard towers manned by soldiers with 240G machine guns and M16s. These towers were spaced several hundred yards apart. However, we could not see over the walls, and could not know what kind of attack had happened outside the fence. Later we learned that there had been perhaps an RPG (rocket-propelled grenade) fired towards the airport, along with some small arms fire, but that the Army had a mechanized QRF move into the area just outside of the airport's walls and clear it of any threat.

After about 45 minutes things were quiet, so I went back into the MWR tent and again sent a message home that everything was quiet here. Well, at the exact time I wrote the message it was quiet!

I also found that bottled water was available everywhere on the camp. When leaving a mess hall, I got into the habit of grabbing a cold bottle, and ensured that I was properly hydrated all the time. It was not yet deadly hot over here as it was still only April, but I had been warned about heat problems when late spring and summer would arrive.

That afternoon Major Landry met up with Staff Sergeant Johnson from the G4 of IMEF, and went with him to try to firm up transportation out of here. Troy would work Army and Marine aviation and see who could get us out first.

Monday April 12, 2004

I went with the two majors for morning chow at about 0800. Things were quiet today at the camp, and Troy again went to work on getting transportation to Camp Fallujah. He discovered that a nearby Marine unit was making a run to the AAFES (Army Air Force Exchange) on the other side of the airport at 1300 today, so we planned to go along.

At 1300 we hopped on board a 7-ton truck and got to see a lot of the airport, many of the buildings still in great disrepair. The Exchange was in a large, warehouse-type building. It did not have air conditioning. Items for sale were mostly personal comfort items like shaving gear, underwear, soaps and snacks, but I was surprised to see things like folding chairs, personal DVD players, and fans available. Outside the Exchange was an area with a small Burger King franchise selling burgers and fries along with canned sodas. There was also an area where local Iraqi merchants were allowed to sell souvenir-type stuff—carvings, boxes, etc. I met a Catholic chaplain (Captain Grudz) who was buying a folding chair there, and would later meet up with him when Major John Piedmont interviewed him at Camp Fallujah.

At 1700 I went to chow, figuring that I would probably be here for several more days. However, at 1800, Troy Landry let us know that we would be getting picked up on a Marine helo flight Tuesday night at 2200. We had to make our way to LZ (Landing Zone) Griffin, somewhere on the grounds of the airport.

So we put the request for Army transportation on hold, and made plans to find out how to get to LZ Griffin.

Flight to Fallujah, Tuesday April 13, 2004

After chow I packed up my gear and got ready to leave later. Major Mayberry and I walked across the airport road to examine several large concrete bunkers that had been hit by precision-guided weapons. We were trying to figure out if these large bunkers were hit during the war in 1991 or in 2003. At either rate, the bombs/missiles had found their marks, penetrating several meters of concrete to collapse the insides of these constructions. If any planes had been inside, they would have been destroyed or damaged beyond repair. As we explored, we felt a definite change in the atmosphere at the airport. It had been hot on arrival in Baghdad this weekend, and now it was getting humid.

I received an email from Major Piedmont, who had gotten to Iraq several weeks ahead of me. He would be away from Camp Fallujah for several days, but gave me points of contact at EFCAT for when I finally got there.

After noon chow, I walked with Majors Landry and Mayberry over to the wall where the fighting had taken place on Easter Sunday. We climbed up a guard tower (Observation Post 7) and spoke with the soldiers on duty there. I took pictures of a burned-out farmhouse along with a burned car, and the soldiers gave us their version of what they had heard about the fight. Even at this point, I could see the importance of waiting until all the facts were in. Neither of these two soldiers had seen the fight, and their version was not an eyewitness account.

At 15:15, Lieutenant McDonald came into the tent and said that he had gotten us a ride to LZ Griffin this afternoon. All of us in the tent packed up our gear, and dragged/carried it across the dirt and gravel in the tent area to a road to meet up with an Army 7-ton truck. I had trouble climbing onto the truck bed. Was I that out of shape? Were my flak jacket and helmet weighing me down? I didn't remember having trouble climbing onto the back of a truck when I was a captain. I found out that the 7-ton trucks have a cargo bed that is much higher than the old trucks that were in use many years ago when I was with an infantry company. One of the soldiers helped boost me, the old lieutenant colonel, onto the back of the truck. I grabbed onto the top of a piece of sheet metal that had been roughly cut and made into a sort of armor, cutting my hand as I got boosted aboard the truck.

The truck dropped us off at a large tarmac area with two helo LZ zones marked on it. We six Marines in this group staged our sea bags and cases and sat in the growing dusk. Two stray dogs sniffed at the edge of the LZ.

While waiting at the LZ, I got to talking to Lieutenant McDonald and Staff Sergeant Bauer. They had just recently gone through a lot. Both were assigned to Marine Wing Support Group (MWSS 374) at Al Taqaddum, and while riding on a convoy to Baghdad International were in the middle of a running ambush/firefight. The lieutenant said that it was a 5-mile-long running ambush. Both had shot at insurgents who were attempting to kill them during this action. It was a harrowing tale, but they both talked about it with the excitement of someone who was in a big football game. My regret was that I did not yet have any of my interview gear (digital camera and voice recorder). These were waiting for me at Camp Fallujah. I made a note of where these two Marines were stationed, and hoped to do a full interview if I could get to their camp. (I never did get to catch up with them.)

We now had some time before the helo would get here, and had seen a chow hall on our drive here. I was the senior Marine in the group, and even though there was no formal chain of command, I was the guy who could make decisions for our little group. I sent a few of the group to go get chow, and waited until they got back so the rest could eat. To get to the chow hall, we passed by the lake with Saddam Hussein's "Water Palace" (Al Faw Palace). Once all had eaten, we again took turns leaving a few people at a time to watch our gear as the others went to inspect the large palace.

We walked across a bridge to the large ocher-colored palace. It sat on a man-made lake, and was being used by coalition forces as a sort of command post. Inside I took photos of the huge central chandelier, the marble walls, terrazzo floors, brass fixtures and dark wood doors. The place spoke of great extravagance. I had not yet seen any of the "real" Iraq, but I knew that Saddam had built many such large palaces all over the country. I became one of an unknown number of American military personnel who sat for a picture in a large throne chair at the palace! An Army lieutenant colonel who worked at the palace saw us, and asked if we would like to see Saddam's bedroom. On the way he showed us damage to the walls, and how, despite the ostentatious surfaces in the building, beneath it was shoddy construction and fills. At the bedroom, he explained that a U.S. precision-guided weapon had hit the room and destroyed everything inside it. Too bad that the Iraqi dictator was not inside that night, I thought.

As it grew dark, I walked with several of the Marines and made my way back to the LZ. After dark, trucks and Humvees dropped off several groups of soldiers who also waited for helo transportation. Each group stayed in separate areas around the perimeter of the LZ.

We listened for the sound of helos approaching. When we first heard the faint noises, we packed up our gear as the helos approached with all lights out. There were no aviation signal lights, and no light on board the helos. As each helo approached for a landing, I could see a luminous ring of static electricity formed by the rotors.

Unfortunately, the first pair of helos were Army Blackhawks, which picked up several soldiers. The next pair that arrived later were also Blackhawks. This continued throughout the evening. We were expecting Marine CH-46 choppers. As 2200 approached we were hopeful that our helos would be arriving. But 2200 came and went, more Blackhawks came and went, and still no Marine helos. By about 0130 on Wednesday morning, I thought that the best thing for us to do was to grab some sleep, and hope for the best. If the helos didn't show tonight, we would find someplace to stay tomorrow and work on transportation again. We were near the chow hall and near landline phones. So I pulled out my sleeping bag, took off my boots, and lay down with my 9mm pistol inside my bag, right next to me. The other Marines in the LZ did the same.

Camp Fallujah, Iraq, Wednesday April 14, 2004

Sometime later, the very loud sound of two CH-46 helos approaching quickly jolted me from a deep sleep. I was groggy, as was everyone else at the LZ, but reflexes took over and I got up instantly and started to scramble to get my boots on and gear packed up. All six Marines there on the tarmac surface reacted the same way. The prop wash from the helos blew our loose gear all over, and we ran to gather it all up. I was afraid that the helos would leave without us if we took too long getting ready to board them. However, the crew could clearly see us. I soon found out that they had night-vision goggles. The crew chief ran over to us and asked if we were headed to MEK (also known as Camp Fallujah). We had to shout to communicate with each other because of the whine of the helo jet engines and rotors whirling.

The chief pointed to the back ramp of the lead helo, and everyone in the zone helped one another to carry our gear onto the birds.

I looked at my watch—it was about 0300. The helos were supposed to be here about five hours earlier. But they were here now and we would be on our way.

We put our gear in the center rear of the bird and moved forward and sat in nylon seats facing the center of the helo. I reached for the safety belt and hooked it up. I looked across the cabin in the dim light and could see the faces of Majors Landry and Mayberry. They looked the way I felt—jolted into an unfamiliar setting, facing we knew not what. My eyes were open wide, and I looked out of the Plexiglas windows. As soon as all gear was stowed the ramp partially closed, the engines roared louder and the craft lifted off the ground. Once clear of the ground, the rear of the bird lifted higher and we were on our way as it swooped out of the landing zone.

All of us had often been on board helos for military exercises, but this time it was for real. This sense of reality was driven home when two enlisted crewmen moved to the front of the helos and "charged" the machine guns at each of the two front hatches. The third crew member sat by one of the hatches and crouched as he peered out, sighting with his M16. All three constantly scanned the ground, looking for ground fire or anything suspicious as we flew away from the city of Baghdad. I was nervous as we flew. Would we get hit by small arms fire from the ground? What if a missile was fired at us? How long would we be flying?

As we flew away from Baghdad we skirted many well-lit towns and villages that we could see in the distance. Most of the ground below was black in the night. The flight lasted about 30 nerve-wracking minutes. The helos arrived at the MEK in the early morning darkness. I carried my gear off the helo onto a sandy landing zone under a starlit, black night. Even though it had been 25 years since my last ride on a Marine helo, my training from long ago kicked in, like riding a bike. I still knew how to exit, to help the others off-load our gear, and where to go to get away from the rotors. The CH-46 I rode on was just about identical to the ones I rode as a captain when I was with Echo Company, 2/25, a Reserve infantry company back in the 1980s.

A Marine captain from the MHG (Marine Headquarters Group) met us at the LZ at Camp Fallujah and helped us move our gear onto a small Nissan bus. The bus drove a few minutes in complete darkness and took us to a stucco building to try to find where we should stay. The captain then took us to a series of tents known as the "Bug" looking for some of the EFCAT Marines who would have rooms for us. The Bug was a multi-million-dollar mobile command post, with areas for computer workstations, presentation areas, phone connections, a portable electrical system and air-conditioning system. It had been used in 2003 during the invasion of Iraq, and recently as the IMEF COC (1st Marine Expeditionary Force—Combat Operations Center). This was a headquarters control area, and usually some member of the EFCAT team would be there at all times. EFCAT also had a group of rooms for sleeping quarters for incoming members. Unfortunately, no one was expecting us to arrive at this late/early hour and no one was there to meet us.

The captain finally had the driver of the bus take us to an area that had two large tents for transient personnel. The three of us found three cots, dropped our gear, unrolled our sleeping bags, and went right to sleep on the cots. Later that morning, members of the EFCAT team, along with major Piedmont, came and woke us up, and took us to a billeting area.

IMEF Morning Briefing, Friday April 16, 2004

I attended my first IMEF COC Watch Change Brief in a large cement building across from the base theater building. The COC was a large room with about eight rows of desktop computers, and each Staff section had personnel manning desks to keep track of all phases of operations in Iraq, especially in Al Anbar province. The Marines at these computers were usually senior enlisted or staff-level officers (majors, lieutenant colonels and colonels). The MEF had responsibility from Fallujah out to the Syrian border, and up to Ramadi, basically the Sunni Triangle of Iraq where most of the trouble was then happening in this country.

A lot of what was presented to IMEF Commanding General James Conway, USMC, went right over my head. There were the names of unfamiliar places, dozens of Marine units and activities, PowerPoint presentations from various staff sections, photo imagery, and so on. At the front of the hall was a large screen that each section used to present its report. All of this info was then available to those with access to the Secret SIPRNET network (which now included me). In the coming weeks I learned to understand much of what was presented at these Watch Change Briefs. Today, much of it was a "fire hose on a flat rock" as far as what I could absorb.

Journal entry for today: "I'm overwhelmed right now!"

Speaking of journal entries, one of the big parts of my job as field historian was to keep a daily journal. This document became a part of the official record of my work here. It also helped me to review all events that I would see, and make a daily plan of goals, both short and long term.

As often as I could I attended briefings at IMEF, regimental (RCT1) headquarters, and different battalion headquarters. These meetings also allowed me to meet many of the officers in different units, and make arrangements to meet with their Marines. With SIPRNET internet access, I also read briefings to get a picture of developing significant events.

After a week or two into my deployment, I had established a matrix of units that the Field History team should get to see. Some of my interviews were at units stopping in at Camp Fallujah, or using the camp as their main base. For these I would make contact with key personnel in a variety of ways. Sometimes I would ask to speak with a staff officer or commander after a briefing at the IMEF COC, other times at RCT1 briefings. I also made contacts with officers via email, where I could give a concise outline of the Field History program, and ask for opportunities to meet with Marines for interviews. For meetings with Marines at Camp Taqaddum, Al Assad, or other distant outposts, email was our main method to set up interviews. This approach enabled both Major Piedmont and me to make the best use of our time when we visited these Marines.

Transportation to a unit could be as simple as walking a few hundred meters to units working out of various areas of Camp Fallujah. The camp was a good size—several miles square—and had a shuttle van service running throughout the day. If the target unit was on the opposite side of the camp, Piedmont and I would catch a ride. Other times we would make arrangements to meet with a staff officer from a unit and hitch a ride to their position. For the remote camps and bases, we made arrangements to travel by helicopter. These longer trips involved a lot more planning, and events could often disrupt the best plans to meet with Marines at some units. Travel time also varied greatly, as a helo lift to a camp only 30 minutes away by air could take a whole night to achieve due to operational constraints on the air assets. Helos did not run on a strict schedule, and many times we waited hours in the dark at the helo LZ at Camp Fallujah until our requested helo arrived.

When we arrived at a unit, we would do our in-person introductions with our contact person, and then separately meet with Marines there. When we returned to our desk area on Camp Fallujah, we would compare notes then do our reports separately. One result is that all of the Marines presented in this book are those who I personally met, and I have included my notes and daily journals when reviewing and writing up these encounters.

CHAPTER TWO

Marine Tankers and Trackers

Saturday April 17, 2004

I began at my second IMEF COC Watch Change Brief. I attended as many of these briefs as I could while that facility was in use and open to non-MEF staff like me. Later, I attended briefings at Division and RCT1's COC, or various battalion headquarters to get an overview of events and plans. I also had access to the military SIPRNET, a Secret Protocol internet network. The briefs and online updates gave me updates on ongoing events and plans.

After this brief, I went to the RCT1 (Regimental Combat Team 1) morning brief in an adjacent building. The XO (executive officer), Lieutenant Colonel Mike Lee, was presiding because Commanding Officer Colonel John A. Toolan was elsewhere. This briefing, Secret in nature, gave an overview of events in neighboring Fallujah at that time. A ceasefire of sorts was still in effect in the city, and negotiations ongoing. RCT1 was aggressively keeping watch over any efforts to enter or leave the city of Fallujah.

May 11, 2004

Major Piedmont and I sat in on today's RCT1 brief, then met up with Captain Vennig, commanding officer of Alpha Company, 3rd Tracs (3rd Amphibious Tractor Battalion). We had earlier spoken with him about interviews with his Marines. He had some of them lined up for us to interview at his CP (command post), just across a sand berm outside of my billeting area.

* * *

Sergeant Gilbert Guadalupe Alcantar

Assistant Section Leader, Alpha Company, 3rd Amphibious Tractor Battalion

Sergeant Gilbert Guadalupe Alcantar was an assistant section leader wounded by shrapnel when an RPG round hit the engine compartment of his AAV (Amphibious Assault

Vehicle, also known as an Amtrac) in the city of Fallujah in mid April. Eventually I interviewed many of the Marines involved in a different action with another Bravo Company trac inside the city of Fallujah in April 2004, including the infantry Marines who were riding in that other Amtrac, the tank Marines who came to their rescue, and the infantry company commander, Captain Jason Smith of Bravo Company, 1/5, who led the Quick Reaction Force during that rescue mission.

At the time of the interview, Sergeant Alcantar was serving as an admin clerk while he recovered from combat wounds received in Fallujah. He enlisted in 1997 on the delayed entry program, and graduated from boot camp in 1998. He made two deployments to Okinawa and was later involved in Operation *Iraqi Freedom 1* (OIF1) from January to July 2003. He was on the Marine boxing team for two months prior to deployment to Iraq in 2003. As an assistant section leader with Alpha Company, 3rd Amtrac Battalion, he normally rides up front in one of the cupolas of an Amtrac during operations.

Sergeant Alcantar said that the company learned in October 2003 that they would return to Iraq. "We got rid of Marines that weren't going to have enough time to come out here and started picking from Bravo Company, Charlie Company, Echo Company, Marines who volunteered to come out here or who had enough time.

"We were told that we'd be using vehicles [Amtracs] from Delta Company. We put armor on them. Then we were told that we wouldn't be using these vehicles. We started to do more of foot patrols, infantry squad patrols, we did convoy security ops, did a lot of SASO [Security and Stability Operations] training."

"Once we got into Iraq, we were a QRF for a while, and we were originally on Humvees. For our first mission we were out there with Humvees to the Thar Thar Bridge, counter-mortar, counter-rocket missions out there in Humvees with heavy guns on them." After this action, around April 4, the company got its Amtracs to use to go out into Fallujah.

The company's current AAVs came off MPS (Maritime Pre-Positioning Shipping), with an advance party sent to get the vehicles ready for transport into Iraq aboard U.S. Army HETS (Heavy Equipment Transporter System) vehicles from Camp Udari in Kuwait.

On April 4, the company got back onto its tracs: "We trackers were glad to be back on tracs." About half of his platoon got their tracs ready to go the cloverleaf east of Fallujah as part of a blocking force from April 4 to 8. "Then we got a mission to go to TCP 7 (Traffic Control Point 7) to link up with Bravo Company, 1/5, from April 9 to 11. We used our Mark 19s [40mm belt-fed grenade launcher] for supporting fires, they give a quicker response." He said that enemy shooters in Fallujah were firing mortars and occasional rockets at Marines in the cordon, and it was hard to see where the fire was coming from.

"On April 12, we pushed forward [west] on Route Violet to the Bravo Company CP to be closer to Fallujah. I went to talk to Sergeant Lynn, and we attached two of our four vehicles [tracs] to Bravo Company, 2nd Platoon, 1/5. We were supposed to go into a defilade position to support by fire. While we were linking up with 2nd Platoon, out from the corner of my eye I saw muzzle flashes, it was probably getting close to 1700 now, and I looked over there and saw infantry firing back at the [gun]fire coming from the houses, probably about four or five hundred meters down an alleyway. Finally the [infantry] lieutenant got done talking with my driver and he said we needed to go pick up those infantry pinned down who could not make it back. We needed to pick 'em up, and we were gonna go from there."

When they went to pick up the infantry platoon (from Bravo Company) that was pinned down inside the city they reached them and put down the Amtrac's ramp. Sergeant Alcantar gave one good burst from his .50 cal machine gun before it jammed up. He then engaged with his Mark 19, but that also jammed on him as well.

"We were still taking small arms fire so we got all the infantry loaded in there, I told the driver to punch out and get us out of that because there was no need for us to take a pop shot or anything… from something bigger. So he drove around and we had no idea where we were going…" He finally got radio contact with someone on the cordon and told them that both his weapons were jammed and he needed to pull back and clear the jams. "I had Corporal Reyes drive us back to where Sergeant Lynn had passed us the word, and that was about a 100, 150-meter back-track we had to do."

After he cleared his weapon, a Marine in the TC (Trac Commander's position) told him that he needed comm with his Bravo 2, his platoon commander. Sergeant Alcantar got on the radio with the lieutenant and learned that he might be needed for another mission. Another Amtrac Marine had radioed that he was taking his Amtrac into the city, which was not a good idea, one big trac moving into a hostile city. "He said he had headed south about four blocks and he was headed west already and he was continuing west. At this point I knew he was on his own."

The Marine in the TC told Alcantar that he needed to go out there into the city, because there were Marines there. The narrow streets made it difficult to maneuver into the city. "I used my turret viewer [a vision block—not the sight] to see where I was going. I saw two insurgents run in front of me."

He could see two insurgents running, one from left to right, and one running from north to south, and Alcantar was getting ready to engage them with his turret gun, when within a split second:

"I heard a pop, and then a big loud explosion. What it was, the pop, was an RPG piercing my vehicle and the explosion was the RPG blowing up in my engine compartment. The engine compartment was about three, four feet to my left inside my vehicle. Inside the turret we have a thin piece of sheet metal that goes around it, that splits the turret from the engine, and the RPG blast blew that up, sent shrapnel through my leg, the thigh area, sir. The thin sheet metal that was on the turret ripped a couple gashes outta my left leg, above my kneecap."

Sergeant Alcantar now had leg wounds from the shrapnel in the turret.

"I was in a daze for a while, probably about a second or two." He said that the whole series of events happened in a few seconds, from spotting the insurgents to the RPG explosion.

"I tell my driver to get us out of there, Corporal Reyes knew we were hit. The infantry starts engaging out the cargo hatches we had open. I believe they had about three SAWs [Squad Automatic Weapons]. They were up top, and still taking small arms fire. They're engaging. I then tried to move around in the turret. My trousers caught inside the turret from where the blast had exploded, so I had to pull my trousers off of it, ripping a small part of them. Then a flame starts coming from the engine compartment into the turret.

"We were now headed east, 'cause when I got hit we were facing south, I got hit and I started heading east. We were leaving and still taking small arms. The flames started getting higher, and, up to about waist level in the turret, and I'm holding myself up, with my turret hatch at a 90-degree angle, I can stand up, and I had my arms like this out of the turret. And I was pretty much trying to kick the flames out, or do whatever I can to move around 'cause my trousers were on fire for a while, by my left cargo pocket, but that was put out. We probably had to backtrack about 400 to 500 meters.

"We made it all the way back to Route Violet, probably about 10 meters from Route Violet from where Staff Sergeant Lynn had told us we had to be going. The vehicle pretty much quit on us, right there. I pulled off my yoyo cord off my comm helmet, hopped out of the turret and jumped off the front of the vehicle."

The vehicle was near Route Violet and Route Michigan. Alcantar thought that the area was clear, so he said, "I started running, and I started taking small-arms fire from behind us. I can see it from the floor, just scrapings and dust coming up. So I then rolled over. I didn't get too far in his direction [Staff Sergeant Lynn], by a berm." Alcantar rolled toward the berm and then saw how his leg was bleeding.

"I looked back up at my vehicle and there was infantry just started getting out of the vehicle and they start running towards this one building that they had already cleared. So I run back towards them. I saw my crew chief of the vehicle, Corporal Reyes, and I did not see the crewman, PFC Boise." Alcantar let Reyes know that he was okay, and Reyes noticed Sergeant Alcantar's leg, and that he was limping at that time. "I saw that everything was fine, they were putting out the fire on the vehicle."

Sergeant Alcantar then got into a Humvee and a Corpsman from Bravo 1/5 gave him medical treatment at an aid center at the cloverleaf. He also had minor facial burns, and his eyebrows were burned off. His eyelids had burns from when he closed his eyes during the blast in the Amtrac. He described some of the burns as relatively minor, like sunburn. An ambulance then took him to Bravo Surgical at Camp Fallujah at about 1800 that day. He had X-rays and they checked his wounds. His vital signs were good. He had some shrapnel in the leg and abdomen but there was no nerve or ligament damage in his leg. Very soon, his ops chief, Gunnery Sergeant Brown, came to see Sergeant Alcantar and check on his status.

Alcantar said that the time frame, from when he got the order to move his Amtrac to when he got hit, was very short. He first moved into action at about 1700, and by 1745 was at Bravo Surgical. He had to wait until about 2200 to get into surgery to have his wounds cleaned. He was not an urgent case.

"The next day I had a couple people come visit me, Master Sergeant Vargas, our Company Gunny and First Sergeant Smith."

The medical staff lent Sergeant Alcantar an Iridium satellite phone so that he could make a phone call home and let them know that he was doing good.

"I did find that the other vehicle that was attached to me, Corporal [Kevin T.] Kolm, had a KIA. I couldn't believe it. I found out that Corporal Kolm's vehicle went into the city with the lieutenant who was supposed to tell us where to go. They headed into the city and they got into a real bad place there. A lot of RPGs. Corporal Kolm didn't make it. He was killed in action. The driver of the vehicle [Corporal Puckett] made it out."

Sergeant Alcantar was discharged from Bravo Medical on crutches on April 15. For ten days he was allowed to relax and recover. By April 23, he was off crutches, and was now getting his wound dressing changed daily. He was glad that he could stay and finish it out with the rest of the Marines in his company.

I asked him to compare *OIF1* last year and *OIF2* this year. He said that he has a different job this year, and now the action stops and starts. Last year his unit was on full alert at all times, and there was a fast tempo. This year it was more stop and start for the Amtrac Marines. Since they were now working as Amtrackers again, "The training that we did [SASO and infantry ops] did not get us ready for what we wound up doing here." He remarked that the new Marines in the unit relied on the veterans, and that the Trackers were glad to be back in their vehicles again.

* * *

Captain Michael Dale Skaggs

Commanding Officer, Charlie Company, 1st Tank Battalion

Prior to 2004, the last time that Marine Corps tanks were involved in heavy urban combat was at Hue City, Vietnam in 1968. In Fallujah, Captain Skaggs' tank crews quickly learned to work closely with supported infantry units to destroy obstacles and bunkers, and provide close fire support from machine guns and main tank guns. They also coordinated with infantry Marines with the newly installed "grunt phones" enabling those Marines to speak directly with tank crews in the heat of battle. One of his challenges was providing logistical support to his tank platoons and sections that had been attached to different infantry units that surrounded Fallujah and were spread across western Iraq.

I met up with Captain Skaggs on May 12, 2004 after the RCT1 morning briefing. His CP was adjacent to the Amtrac Company's, on the other side of a large sand berm outside my billeting area. He served in the USMC Reserves from 1987 to 1997, was an 0311 (Infantryman), then a combat engineer during activation for *Desert Storm* in Saudi Arabia. After college he was a teacher for a year, and later a police officer for a couple of years. He completed OCS (Officer Candidate School) in 1997, and became an armor officer with 1st Tanks. During the initial invasion of Iraq in 2003, he was a student at the Marine Corps company-level professional school, the Expeditionary Warfare School (EWS), at Quantico, Virginia.

"All of us [young captains] thought that we would all be going. We thought that if the war started in the spring, we'd graduate in May, and we'd all be going." Thirty of his EWS classmates were sent to serve in OIF1. The war ended in April, and the rest were not called up. He said that those who did not go were greatly disappointed at not going to Iraq in 2003, feeling that they had missed the opportunity of a career.

But he and many of his classmates went out to the Fleet, where many soon learned that they would be sent to operations in Iraq.

In September 2003 he became commanding officer of Charlie Company, and had his Marines start tank training leading to a Combined Arms Exercise. "In about October we learned that we were selected to go to Iraq." It was a new company (half were new Marines). Starting in December 2003 the company got SASO training with the rest of the 1st Marine Division, but they couldn't get units to train with tanks. The tankers got a lot of cultural and language training, and convoy security in Humvees.

"We arrived here in Kuwait around the 1st of March, we were down in Kuwait… for a couple of weeks, and we were tasked with our first convoy security deal which was bringing up about 150 Humvees that were offloaded from the Norway caves. In March 2004, Charlie Tank Company provided security for a 150-Humvee convoy moving from Kuwait into Iraq. So our first convoy task was a very big one."

The convoy went from Udari, Kuwait up to what was then called FOB (Forward Operating Base) St.-Mère Église (currently called Camp Fallujah). It made it all the way up without a single incident. "When we got here we were immediately put to work on convoy security [for RCT1]."

One platoon returned from convoy security on Humvees, and got the word to move out in their tanks. They made the transition seamlessly. "The whole company was ready in about an hour, ready to roll out the gate." Captain Skaggs believed that was the day that the American contractors from Blackwater Security were killed.

When the violence escalated, especially in Fallujah, in late March and early April 2004, the tankers transitioned into using their tanks once again.

"On April 5 several platoons were sent off to different battalions. One platoon was sent out to 7th Marines way out to the west, and one platoon, 2nd Platoon, was sent to 1st Battalion 5th Marines [1/5], and my headquarters section and 1st Platoon was sent to 2nd Battalion 1st Marines [2/1]."

This created a problem: How to logistically support the various platoons that were scattered over the AO (Area of Operations) in Al Anbar province. A platoon is made up of four tanks. Of the 100 Marines in Skaggs' company, 60 are support personnel. "It became quite a challenge to support these platoons that were scattered all over the Area of Operations.

"My tank and my XO's tank were used as a tank section." His talented master sergeant formed a combat train to support the platoons throughout the fighting battle space. He went out through unsecured territory to support the platoons in the battle space around Fallujah.

Skaggs' 2nd Platoon, with 1/5 south of Fallujah, received lots of battle damage. It was in a mostly industrial area, more open. An RPG caused a mobility kill of one tank. The engine was hit and the tank had to be dragged to a more secure area for repairs. There were no injuries to any of his Marines in that tank. His tankers patched it up, replaced the engine, and had it back in the fight the next day. "The infantry that was with them had a tendency to stay a little bit behind them, about 100 meters."

The 1st Tank Platoon was in the Jolan area of the city.

"I was with my 1st Platoon, who was with 2/1, north of Fallujah, for the first ten days. They saw their fair share of action up there. Their platoon sergeant [Gunnery Sergeant Popaditch] was blinded [in his right eye] by an RPG that hit his tank. His helmet is what saved his life. Shrapnel penetrated the side of his skull and severed the optic nerve in his right eye, shutting the eye off forever. He was evacuated to Baghdad, to Germany, and then home. A great man, just a testament to him." Popaditch was currently working in the 3 Shop (Operations Section of the 1st Tank Battalion, an administrative job) back in the States. "The rest of his crew was wounded, too. His loader, his gunner, also received some shrapnel."

Another crew whose tank had transmission problems took over the hastily repaired tank and went back into the fight. "This crew go into a tank that had blood all over it, all over the instrument panel, and drove it away, right back into the fight." Tanks were saving Marine lives during the fight, as Humvees and Amtracs were too vulnerable in the city.

"The enemy had three-man hunter-killer teams. They were aggressive, but lacked military skills." Skaggs said that the enemy had trouble hitting moving targets more than 100 meters away. Usually they would try to get within 50 meters of a tank to fire an RPG, and this was where the Marine infantry played a role in protecting the tanks by taking out the RPG teams.

Captain Skaggs said that his tank crewmen adapted to conditions in city fighting. "The laser range finders (on the tanks) do not work at less than 200 yards, so my guys did work-arounds. Main [tank] guns used precision fire to destroy strong points. We used the MPAT OR [obstacle-reducing round] for the first time in combat. The technique we used was to hit the foundation of a building or courtyard walls." He explained that the rounds would penetrate courtyard walls and hit the building beyond them. They hit strong points with barricaded enemy machine gunners without causing a huge amount of collateral damage such as would be caused by an air strike.

He found that the most interesting thing about current operations was "doing things that you didn't prepare for." His tank Marines had trained for SASO, and wound up doing tank-infantry operations in an urban setting. "We never had a single day of MOUT [Military Operations in Urban Terrain] training prior to coming here. But that's what we did [here] for nearly a month straight."

He said that the tank-infantry phone that was recently installed on the Marine tanks has been great for communication between the infantry and the tankers. The last time there was a tank-infantry phone was on the M48 tanks. Now infantrymen could again walk up to the back of a tank and coordinate with the crew. "It was very useful. It could also hook into the tank's radio, so an infantry commander could talk right back to his battalion on that phone." The power amps on the tank radio give it great range, much greater than the man-packed radios with an infantry unit.

On May 10, his tank company was used as a regimental reserve (Quick Reaction Force) during the ride by General Mattis into Fallujah. It consisted of his tank company, an infantry platoon, and a platoon of Army engineers. They were positioned in an assembly area immediately behind the Fallujah Liaison Team building outside of the city. "We had rehearsed at length what we were going to do if we had to go into the city to relieve that convoy if it got hit." General Mattis' ride went without incident, and fortunately the QRF was not called upon that day.

Task Force 3/4 (a temporary combat formation based around 3rd Battalion 4th Marines—3/4—with attached combat forces from other Marine units) also had a couple of infantry companies and tanks from Bravo Company standing by in case of any problems in the city during the ride.

He described one insurgent attack: "Echo Company, 2/1, had pushed out a salient into the city, with one of their platoons in an outpost and it was attacked by several hundred enemy fighters. It began with a barrage of 50 RPGs. It went from there. They took a lot of casualties, really, they were surrounded, cut off, the salient had been cut off. There were only two tanks up there. It was a staff sergeant's section and that staff sergeant took those tanks and relieved that cut-off platoon, destroyed a good number of the enemy and allowed that platoon to withdraw, and was the hero of that day."

Captain Skaggs described his role as company commander as like that of a watchmaker. He has gotten them ready and they operate on their own. He worked hard to form his Marines into a team as he prepared them to come over here. Two of his lieutenants have been recommended for the Bronze Star. One first lieutenant (Lieutenant Benjamin Adams) led a platoon to rescue the crew and infantry of a burning Amtrac while they were under fire. This denied the enemy a propaganda incident and retrieved the body of the dead Marine who was still inside the destroyed Amtrac. Another of his lieutenants (Lieutenant Troy Sayler) saw a noncombatant (an old Iraqi man) shot in crossfire, then drove his tank into the middle of a firefight, and rescued the old man while under enemy fire.

Captain Skaggs said that, "The ghosts of Iwo Jima must certainly be celebrating, knowing that their legacy is still here. These Marines are no different than those days. The exact same bolt of cloth, just a different fight. Generation X, or whatever, has had no effect on our Marines, at least not in combat."

Captain Skaggs was very proud of all of his Marines. He ensured that every one of his Marines received rifles for this deployment, and some grumbled because their T/O (Table of Organization and Equipment) weapon is a 9mm pistol. But given the varied combat and convoy experiences so far, they have been grateful to have their rifles with them. Captain Skaggs himself found himself off his tank in one situation, and had to use his own rifle to defend himself.

"I am very proud of these Marines. I can't imagine having a greater group of men, you know, fifty years ago, a hundred years ago, it doesn't matter. They're the same kids. Americans will do what needs to be done if you put them in those circumstances. It's very refreshing, for sure."

* * *

Lieutenant Benjamin Scott Adams

Platoon Commander, 2nd Platoon, Charlie Company, 1st Tank Battalion

During the heavy mid-April fighting in Fallujah, Marine tanks were called upon for myriad missions by several infantry units. At one point after five days of non-stop operations, Adams had to request that his Marines be given some time to rest so that they could get some much-needed sleep. For days his tanks survived mortar and RPG fire inside the city. He led a section of tanks as part of a QRF to rescue a surrounded squad of Marines from Bravo Company 1/5 who were holding off an enemy force of over 100 fighters. A last-minute decision saved him from firing his main tank gun at the building where the Marines were holed up.

Captain Skaggs introduced me to his 2nd Platoon commander, Lieutenant Benjamin Adams. In March 2002 Adams completed the Marine Officers' Basic School in Quantico, VA. After armor training at Fort Knox, he joined 1st Tank Battalion, taking over his platoon in July 2003.

Adams described the missions that he and his Marines trained for: SASO and convoy escort in Humvees. "We did this type of operations in our first two to three weeks here in Iraq. I was a convoy commander, never really thought I'd be in my tanks based on the current situation in Iraq when we landed," he said. His convoys were uneventful. His platoon was to be the regimental reserve, and he was told that he should get used to being a convoy commander.

Several days after that, he was told to get his tanks ready to join 1/5 and participate in the siege of Fallujah.

"Then around April 3–4, we got a 'short fuse' notice to get ready for tank operations in Fallujah. We had 16 hours of planning time, and my Marines got their tanks ready. We didn't do the rehearsals or things that we normally do. Time was not on our side." His tanks moved to go with 1/5, and his tankers were excited to be in their tanks for the fight.

Tanks led the way on April 4, and they closed the road with their tanks at the cloverleaf east of Fallujah. There are about six lanes of traffic on the highway there. They placed signs warning drivers to stay away from this coalition checkpoint. At about 0300 traffic began to approach the cloverleaf and they had to fire warning shots at approaching vehicles.

Lieutenant Adams described another incident where a dump truck approached the position, slowed at the warning sign, then sped up to about 40 miles per hour, heading straight towards his tanks.

"At that point I had to make a tough call; we were given intel that the enemy was using dump trucks to conduct operations, to have enemy in the back to pop up as they came past a convoy and shoot at them. They also were attempting to run off road blocks with dump trucks. At that point, they were close to about 100 meters from my tanks, I gave the command to fire 'coax' [coaxial machine gun rounds]. All my tanks fired coax into the driver's side of the dump truck, [which] stopped approximately 75 meters north of my position. It showed hostile intent."

Soon his Marines were being hit with mortar fire and RPG rounds. They were not sure if there would be an IED in the back of the truck. Adams described how enemy mortars were registered right on his position. Engineers set up obstacles, and one of his Marines was wounded during the fire that first night.

"Around that day [April 5] we started receiving mortar fire on our position. It seemed to be 120s [120mm mortars] landing. As I was reaching up to shut my cupola I had a mortar go off right in front of my tank. A piece of shrapnel flew up, hit me in the head, pretty much knocked me out for about 20 minutes. I wasn't unconscious but I was stunned to the point where I really couldn't think clearly." They couldn't back up at the time, as engineers were still working in the area improving the position.

Finally, around April 7 or 8 they got orders to move down south to support "Apache" Company 1/5, and take part in an advance in the southern part of Fallujah from east to west. "We made contact every day." Adams' platoon was attached to different units of 1/5, at one time to a CAAT (Combined Anti-Armor Team) platoon that got into an ambush. "That was our first really big firefight, close quarters."

During the two-and-a-half-hour firefight, his tanks systematically fired their guns at enemy buildings. For some Marines the first time firing the main gun was during that fight. "That was really the first time the insurgents could see what the tanks could do." The tanks won new respect from the insurgents. "After that, they [the insurgents] would pretty much melt away anytime we showed up." Also, the infantry Marines saw for the first time what the tanks could do for them.

He described minarets that were believed to be used by the insurgents as observation posts for mortars and sniper positions, and how some insurgents made daring attacks that some Marines felt must have been enhanced with the use of drugs.

His tank was disabled by RPG fire on Route Violet in Fallujah. It rolled out of the kill zone, and the rest of his platoon had to come and rescue it: "Tanks are vulnerable in the rear." Over five or six RPG rounds had previously hit his tank without serious damage, and dozens of rounds fired at him missed. Lieutenant Adams said that the RPG gunners were very poor shots.

Adams said that during this time, he began to feel that some of the enemy fighters were motivated by more than just Jihad. "They were very, very daring." He said that at one time, an insurgent with an AK 47 came within 20 feet of his tank, and was shooting at its right ballistic skirt. The tank's .50 caliber machine gun could not traverse towards the insurgent, so he had his gunner aim the tank's main gun to engage him. The insurgent did not move as the gun aimed at him, but continued to sit there and shoot at the tank. Adams felt that some of the insurgents seemed to be under the influence of some sort of drugs.

On another occasion, two insurgents with an RPG stood about 30 meters away, and made no move away from the tank as the main gun traversed and engaged them with a HEAT (High-Explosive Anti-Tank) round.

"With Apache, I stayed with them for about four or five days. My platoon was split up into sections at that point. During that time with Apache we had many missions, we responded to medevac."

At this point I was looking through my notes, and was unsure just what Apache Company was. I asked Lieutenant Adams to explain. He answered, "Apache is Alpha Company 1/5." They got the name because they were on the front line for the battalion's push into Fallujah from east to west. They went into the city of Fallujah with the armor.

"We were always on high alert. In fact, my platoon didn't sleep for the first five, six days we were out there. It was a real problem. Towards the sixth day I had to talk to the colonel [Lieutenant Colonel Byrne], pretty much just telling him my platoon just couldn't go on, probably another day. My driver was falling asleep and I couldn't wake him up."

Adams said that the battalion wanted to use the tanks around the clock because of their weapons capabilities.

"But it came to a point that we just had to get rest." That night the Apache company commander pulled the tanks back and posted guards so that the tankers could get some essential and much-needed rest.

"Another mission we got. We had a little problem with mortars for the first weeks of this thing. They had mortar positions all over the city. One of our missions, because we have our optical capability, we are able to see a very long range and engage at a long range." In the southern part of Fallujah, the tankers engaged mortar teams observing 1/5 from the tops of buildings there. "That was very successful. They [the insurgents] didn't really understand our capabilities at that point."

They also had other missions, including rescuing an infantry platoon from Bravo Company that was caught inside of Fallujah, bringing out the wounded lieutenant along with the stranded Marines, and supporting patrols by overwatching fire. They also shot at mortar teams using the tank optics. Tank-infantry integration was constantly improving as the different units worked together.

"Around the 13th of April was our most significant firefight that we had."

It went very wrong to start with. Adams' platoon was at Route Michigan. Bravo Company 1/5 had pushed west and two Amtracs had been sent about 150 meters to bring resupply to the infantry platoon. An infantry commander (Lieutenant Ayres) in an Amtrac decided to pursue the enemy into narrow streets. Adams theorized that the enemy had studied our tactics, and designed a trap to lure an aggressive Marine unit. "The enemy was obviously waiting for the Amtracs (in order) to ambush them."

The infantry platoon commander's Amtrac continued to pursue the enemy fighters and made a wrong turn (headed west, when it should have gone east). It became heavily engaged and was disabled by an RPG round. About 15 infantry Marines then took cover in a building.

"At that point they called us into the city as part of the QRF. We led the way. As there's always friction in every situation, they gave us the wrong coordinates. We went to the wrong place in the city initially."

Initially they looked for smoke coming from the burning trac. Adams said that the Amtrac was at least three clicks away from where it was supposed to be. The enemy anticipated the QRF and had placed hasty obstacles—cars—in the streets. The tanks were able to run over the cars. "The whole time we were receiving massive amounts of fire… The tanks weren't made for this type of environment, but they learned as they went along."

"Finally got to the burning trac. Whole time receiving a lot, a lot of fire. And, uh, we didn't know where the friendly units were. We immediately cordoned off the trac, there were the remains of Marines inside. We didn't want pictures of insurgents jumping up and down on top of a tank, pulling out charred bodies. We prepared to fight. We set in there, we were immediately surrounded by strong points, continued to take heavy, heavy RPG fire, small arms fire, machine gunfire. We began engaging enemy strong points.

"Every building there's probably seven to eight insurgents, each room, shooting at us, taking turns shooting at us. We [Adams and his platoon sergeant] were working our way across [the buildings] from left to right, hitting buildings. We both saw movement in a building. I talked to him, he talked to me, we both had him, we were both going to fire at the same time.

"Just as I was about to fire, I saw a Kevlar, a flak and Kevlar, poke his head out the window. [I] got really sick, yelled 'Cease fire! Cease fire!' I felt terrible, I mean, we were just about to engage. We found out where these guys (Marines) were hiding, were hunkered down in this building. Fifteen Marines. I couldn't believe. We almost hit them. No one knew the location, not even their company at that point. Finally identified them, probably the sickest I felt. Literally, the building next to them was full of bad guys that we shot." (I would later interview the infantry platoon sergeant, Staff Sergeant Ismael Sagredo, who was leading the Marines inside the building. Sagredo did not know of what almost happened at his position when the tanks arrived.)

"That fight lasted about two and a half hours. Millions of times I thought… my tank had been disabled, same with my other Marine, by the nature of the fire we were receiving. They hit our tracs, they hit our skirts. My Marines were awesome. You know, nothing that we had done up 'til that point had prepared us for that environment. It was pretty much the basics, back to the basics. You can't really train for that environment."

The tanks marked buildings for Air Force F15 planes, which dropped several 500-pound bombs. As the sun was setting and it was getting dark, they had to figure out how to get the burnt-out Amtrac out of the city. "They wanted me to do it initially, I told them I couldn't at that point. We were still decisively engaged, the sun was setting. I knew I couldn't wait to have a trac come in and pull it out, so I gave the order to have my 3 tank hook up to it, under our cover fire."

His tank backed up to the smoldering Amtrac.

"A small group of grunts from Bravo Company came out and hooked it up to the tank. And with the help of that F15 we were able to break contact and to begin retrograding back to the east. The trac was totally destroyed, the ammo was 'cooking off' the whole time. While this was happening I was surprised no one got injured from that. At that point, we had killed, I'm not sure how many insurgents we had killed, it had to have been a lot."

Despite multiple RPG hits, none of his tanks were seriously damaged. "We ended up saving 15 Marines. They couldn't have done it without us. It was a very happy experience for us, to save those Marines, they were pinned down. That was by far the worst firefight we were engaged in, just the sheer amount of fire against us."

They retrograded out of the city with the infantry leading the way.

The next day, around April 15 or 16, they were actively engaging enemy fighters when a ceasefire went into effect, and his Marines assumed a defensive posture. The two infantry battalions lost momentum due to the ceasefire. Engagements decreased, and the tanks were made part of the QRF a lot of the time. Sometimes enemy fighters attempted to fire RPGs from a range of 500 to 600 meters, but the tanks' thermal sights gave the tankers an advantage.

At the time of this interview Adams' platoon was attached to 2/2, and was ready for a possible five-battalion attack on Fallujah. "I know I've probably missed a million events, but these are my best recollections so far.

"My Marines did an awesome job. I have put in several for Navy Comms [Navy Commendation Medals], and recommended my platoon sergeant for a Bronze Star for that event on April 13."

He said that training was good, but Armor needed to train for MOUT and that the last time Marines fought like this was in Vietnam at Hue City, and the tank now was a lot bigger. "We trained a lot for SASO, to do stuff like pass out water and MREs. I'm not sure when we'll go to SASO."

These Marines were not yet at the halfway point in their seven-month deployment, and ready to take on any new missions given to them. The confidence and pride in doing their jobs was very evident.

Note: In May 2021, Lieutenant Benjamin Adams was now Lieutenant Colonel Adams, and the last commanding officer of the 1st Tank Battalion. He had to oversee the difficult task of de-mobilizing the Tank Battalion at 29 Palms as part of the Marine Corps' restructuring that eliminated Marine tanks. I sent him a copy of this interview and received a very thoughtful thank-you from him as he traveled to his next assignment.

* * *

First Lieutenant Troy M. Sayler

Platoon Commander, 1st Platoon, Charlie Company, 1st Tank Battalion

This hour and a half interview covered Lieutenant Sayler's rescue of a wounded Iraqi man in the middle of a battlefield during a firefight, psychological operations (of a sort) at Camp Bahariyah, and using a main tank gun to take down a minaret that was being used as an insurgent sniper position. He used strawberry milkshake powder from an MRE to mark a wall that his tanks would drive through during one advance. His platoon sergeant, Gunnery Sergeant Nick Popaditch, would lose eyesight in his right eye during combat in early April.

Lieutenant Sayler spent four years as an enlisted Marine from 1992 to 1996, serving on two WESTPAC (Western Pacific) deployments and also going into Somalia. He then left to attend the University of Nebraska (Kearney), graduating in 2000, and spent a year and a half in law school. He reentered the Marine Corps in 2002 via Officer Candidate School, and became a tank officer.

He said that in 2003 he watched the war start on television in his living room at the 29 Palms Marine Corps Base as part of the rear element of Alpha Company, 1st Tank Battalion. "There really wasn't much for me to do there, I PT'd a lot for the first few weeks after I got there." Soon he was placed in charge of tank Marines who were returning from Iraq to 29 Palms for EAS (expiration of active service) or medical issues.

He learned that he was transferring to Charlie Company in November 2003. Captain Skaggs then told him that the company was deploying to Iraq in 2004. "I told him that's why I joined the Marine Corps."

The company completed its training for the deployment in late January, with lots of emphasis on SASO and infantry tactics. They did not expect to be in their tanks when they got to Iraq. Sayler "turned to" with his Marines, ensuring that they got their wills, powers of attorney, etc., done. "Then, on February 28th is when we actually got on the bus. We went from March Air Force Base to Kuwait."

An advance party from the company arrived in Kuwait early to prepare the tanks when they came off of MPF shipping. The tanks began their movement on HETS about ten days before Charlie Company tankers did. Once in Kuwait, the company began its movement into Iraq. "We escorted a very large convoy of Humvees, I want to say it was 120. These vehicles came from storage in caves in Norway."

They moved into Iraq at 0220 on March 21, 2004. The convoy was pretty much without incident, except for one incident north of Skania. They spotted an individual on top of an overpass, and there had been other events where grenades had been dropped off overpasses onto coalition vehicles. A vehicle from a CAAT platoon from 1/2 that was attempting to drive up onto the overpass blew a tire while crossing the median strip, so Lieutenant Sayler sent several of his Marines up onto the overpass to try to cut off the individual there.

"I sent a contact team up there to check it out. In the meantime this individual had gotten into a van, drove off. My platoon was mounted up in four Humvees… I sent my Bravo section on top of the bridge, I sent my Alpha section underneath the bridge to secure the far side, and the top. The Bravo section found what appeared to be a… it actually appeared like a U.S. M18 Smoke Grenade, but it was very, very beat up, but it was on top of the bridge and it appeared that this individual had dropped it." His platoon provided security and then caught up with the convoy after it had passed the overpass. Otherwise the convoy was without incident.

The company pulled into Camp Fallujah, and then made sure that their tanks were ready to go, and that weapons were being properly maintained. Early on they had a mortar attack close to their billeting area.

Around March 26 his platoon was attached to 2/1 at Camp Bahariyah (adjacent to Camp Fallujah). When Sayler got to Camp Bahariyah, his commanding officer, Captain Skaggs, met him at the gate, and told him as soon as he got inside the camp to "coil" his vehicles as his tankers actually had a mission. Sayler went to the 2/1 COC, got a mission and then brought his platoon to the outskirts of Fallujah with 2/1. They were west of the cloverleaf in an overwatch position, and were about 700 meters away from Fox Company 2/1, which was engaged in a firefight that night.

"We were still real hesitant to fire, we had ROEs (Rules of Engagement) drilled into our heads that the tanks were kind of a last resort. We did get fired on. I took, throughout the week we got fired on, I took two RPG rounds within the first 15 minutes. But we just didn't have any clear targets to fire on."

His tanks went back to Bahariyah around the time that the Blackwater Security contractors were killed. "Around April 1, we, the Marine Corps, really wanted the bodies back. The mayor of Fallujah had come to Camp Bahariyah to talk to [Lieutenant] Colonel Olson, the commanding officer of 2/1. We had our tanks parked down there 'cause we had been called to be part of a QRF to go there and get the bodies. Myself and Gunnery Sergeant Popaditch, my platoon sergeant, talked to Major Clearfield, the battalion S3, and he said, 'Yeah, do you think you can park your tanks close when the mayor comes in? It'll be good psychologically.' Gunny Popaditch and I laughed and said, 'We'll go out and park alongside the road.'"

Then Sayler and Popaditch decided to have their Marines download the tanks to "clean" the main gun rounds and machine gun rounds. Colonel Olson pointed these rounds (each main gun round is about 6.7 inches in diameter and 38.7 inches long) out to the mayor, and the mayor said that he did not want the tanks in his city. "It was actually very effective."

On April 5, Fox Company 2/1 called out one of the tank sections. They got engaged in the city and went in. "The Iraqis were trying to push a tractor trailer bed into the road to create a roadblock. My two Bravo section tanks came rollin' around there and got fired on. Gunny Pop, very aggressive, very experienced tank commander, seized the initiative. That initiative allowed Fox Company to get a foothold into the city."

Lieutenant Sayler heard main tank rounds, and he got on the radio to talk with Popaditch to see what was happening. Sayler then went up to the northwest part of the city. He set his tanks in next to the Bravo Section tanks, and within about five minutes was engaged. "I distinctly remember people shootin' at me."

He noticed that the fire wasn't particularly accurate: RPGs were fired around the sides of walls and hit the walls harmlessly. He also saw individuals in black clothing, with black headbands, engaging with RPKs (Soviet-designed 7.62mm machine guns), AKs, and RPGs.

Lieutenant Sayler moved to the map on the wall and showed me the extreme northwest section of Fallujah where he had moved his section. He said there was about 300 meters of "dead" space between him and the city. The thermal sights on the tanks gave them the ability to see enemy shooters attempting to fire on them during darkness.

"Throughout the night we engaged several individuals who attempted to shoot at us. Whenever they tried, they got killed." He said that his wingman saw four or five individuals, all with RPGs, behind a wall, and engaged the wall with a main tank round, destroying the wall and those hiding behind it. "It's just like seein' them in front of you in daylight, through the thermal sights."

Sayler said that his four tanks alone accounted for between five and 30 dead enemy personnel that first night. "Also, my four tanks acted as observers for Spectre (AC-130 H gunship) missions." The Marines used the 105mm howitzer on Spectre to destroy a complex obstacle that the enemy had erected in the city streets. "We also found out that Iraqis would rush out into the street to fire RPGs at our tanks. So… we'd push the tanks out, wait for the Iraqis to come out into the street to shoot at the tanks, and Spectre would take care of them."

Lieutenant Sayler said that in this northwest section of Fallujah, their engagements were at extremely close range, some as close as 20 meters. There were a number of coax (tank machine gun) engagements. The next day, April 7, they pushed down south and Gunny Popaditch was lead tank. He was pursuing another Iraqi when he came around a corner and an RPG strike hit from extremely close range right through the TC's (tank commander's) hatch. The 3 tank looked at it and saw that the top of the tank was on fire.

"Gunny Pop took shrapnel, the loader, Lance Corporal Hernandez, he took a lot of shrapnel through his hands, and the gunner took some shrapnel to his hands. Gunny Pop, from all accounts, was extremely calm. He got down in the tank, he grabbed the gunner's shoulder, called medevac. He was essentially blinded at the time, a piece of shrapnel came in, severed his right optic nerve. From my understanding, his right eye was blinded instantly from the shrapnel. His left eye is still improving. He's back in the States now."

Gunny Popaditch made it back to the area north of Fallujah. He was then medevacked. Staff Sergeant Herrera became the new tank commander, and other tank Marines became the crew for this tank. The tank was still able to maneuver, but the top was messed up. Packs on the tank had been burned, and periscopes were cracked from shrapnel damage. Minor repairs kept the tank in operation.

"The next day my company was working with Echo Company, 2nd Battalion, 1st Marines. Captain Zinnbeck was the commanding officer of Echo Company.

There was a street, which they had been receiving a lot of enemy activity from. The snipers had killed a number of enemy personnel over on that street. The enemy didn't feel too concerned on that street." Lieutenant Sayler pointed out the area of the northwest section of Fallujah on the map.

The Iraqi insurgents were using a building as an assembly area, and the commanding officer of Echo Company wanted to attack the building. He talked to Lieutenant Sayler to begin planning. Occasionally rifle and RPG fire came from the area. Captain Zinnbeck asked about the ability of the tanks to "see" through walls (thermal sight capability). Together they devised a way for the tanks to approach the building through courtyards instead of going down the streets where they would be open to RPG fire. Altogether, three tanks would be involved in the attack, with infantry providing flank security for the tanks.

Zinnbeck and Sayler made a commander's recon on foot, taking fire the whole time. Sayler used strawberry milkshake powder from an MRE (meal ready to eat) to mark a wall with a big X where he wanted his tank driver to go through. When the attack began, he drove his tanks through two walls, then started to "light up" the target building. His .50 cal machine gun engaged the building. Sayler said they got "Real good effect on the target building." On the egress, he got word to pick up the body of a dead Iraqi for intelligence purposes. The grunts put the body on the tank. "It was good for my guys to see the body, he was wearing bandoleers around his mid section, things like that." They fired two more main gun rounds into another building.

Lieutenant Sayler then praised Gunny Popaditch: "He's what every Marine Staff NCO should be like. Former drill instructor. He was on his third tour over here, he was in the Gulf War, OIF1, and this. Actually superb leadership skills. Losing him was very rough, due to his great leadership skills. So when we got to conduct this raid the very next day, with no casualties, that was very good for the morale of the Marines. It was also good to build the armor-infantry relationship."

"Two days after that on April 10, that's when my section got attached to 3/4, and that was the day with the old man." (We had talked about this prior to the interview—Captain Skaggs had told me to be sure to get this story.)

Lieutenant Sayler got a real quick frag (order) to get back to Fallujah to link up with Major Norden, the S3 (operations officer) from 3/4. He went to RCT1 headquarters while the tanks were getting refueled on the camp. He finally met up with Major Norden about 15 minutes before leaving for Fallujah to go into a cordon in the northwest part of the city. He was still writing his overlays within minutes of leaving. The general scheme of maneuver called for two tanks to leapfrog south to support the infantry advance. "We took out a couple, at least one real sniper." Lieutenant Sayler had a good set of notes that he referred to several times during our interview.

"There's an old man walkin' out of a building. He had walked right out in front of a bunch of Marines who had been engaging the enemy. Sure enough, he got shot in the heat of the moment. He was about 200 meters in front of me, and when he first got shot I was like… oh, ya know… I was looking through my binos [binoculars] or my extension sight. Either way I could tell the man was not armed, and I thought, man, that's not good, but these things happen in war."

As soon as the rounds were fired, the man dropped instantly. Lieutenant Sayler could see the man rolling around a little bit, then lay down still. Sayler then saw the man try to get up, and called for a medevac. 3/4 said that they weren't going to send a medevac for the guy. "I called up and said, listen, if you don't get medevac up, I'm gonna go out there and get him myself. 'Cause I'm not gonna watch this, this guy die in front of me." 3/4 gave the okay to do it.

Sayler told his driver to go forward in his tank. They went over the railroad tracks, drove down about 150 meters to the northern edge of the city. "My gunner and I got out. My gunner was the first to reach the old man who was sitting there cross-legged. When I got up I let the gunner deal with the old man."

Lieutenant Sayler helped to place the old man on the front slope of his tank. "When I looked at the man, I could tell he had taken a 7.62 round through his right jaw. It wasn't too bad, but the shock had popped one of his eyes partially out and he was losing blood."

The man slipped down the slope of the tank as it started to move, so they stopped the tank and grabbed the man again, all this while taking occasional fire. Lieutenant Sayler held onto the old man's shirt with one hand, and held his M16 in his other hand and told the driver to back up the tank. Corporal Garcia was holding the man's other shoulder. Once back at the battle position a Humvee from 3/4 immediately picked the man up and took him to the Jordanian Hospital. "That's the story of that," Lieutenant Sayler concluded.

Another enemy tactic was to send women and children across streets with a white flag, and the Marines would not fire. Later in the day the enemy would send military-age men with these groups under white flags.

They went into the city a day or two later with 3/4 going to a building where it had been receiving a lot of fire. "3/4 was very good to work with, 3/4 understood how to use tanks pretty well." Using the grunt phone, the Marine infantry of 3/4 walked the tanks to where they needed the fire put down, and provided security for the rear and flanks of the tanks.

Lieutenant Sayler's tank was the lead tank; it headed west, turned south, went down an alley. He could barely traverse his main gun. "We ended up engaging this building from about 50 feet away, and that's where they had been receiving all this fire." He was trying to weaken the structural integrity of the building with his main gun. His gunner on the coaxial machine gun was "eating away" at the building with his gun. Lieutenant Sayler estimated that he put about 400–500 .50 caliber rounds into the building. "We pretty much destroyed the building, but they were still firing from there. We were getting low on main gun rounds." Later he was told that the enemy in the building had a subterranean means of egress from the building.

His tanks then spent about another week on the northern cordon of Fallujah. His Marines observed a number of Iraqi snipers, and also fired some main gun rounds into the city. He checked his notes and talked about his Bravo Section that was in the northwest sector of the cordon of Fallujah. "They were getting up close and personal on a daily basis." Sayler's section came into Camp Fallujah on April 17 for some quick maintenance.

"On the 14th we killed a sniper with a main gun round." Looking at his notes, he said that some of the enemy snipers were getting better during this time, firing at the Marines from hundreds of meters away.

"The Alpha Section came back to Camp Fallujah where we prepared to attack Al Karmah." The attack came on April 21. 3/4 was to act as a feint on the city. The tanks' mission was to provide attack by fire to draw as many enemy as possible into the south of the town while 2/7 advanced into the city. One night, Lieutenant Wright's tank, which was with Captain Skaggs' section, killed six Iraqis who were setting up IEDs. "The terrain [where Sayler was located] was not tank friendly. There were a lot of palm trees and it was hard to see what was out there." On a short walk at night, he saw prepared positions near the road with no one in them.

The two days there were uneventful for his section.

By that time, all of the tanks needed maintenance, and his Marines needed some rest. His Marines were motivated to get back into the cordon around Fallujah with the other tank sections. Around April 26 Lieutenant Sayler felt that he would be returning to 2/2, but instead was tasked to be a part of the QRF with 2/1. "That was the day Echo Company 2/1 pushed a little bit too far to the east. Essentially they got surrounded by an extremely large Iraqi force." Sayler came up and made radio contact with his Bravo Section, which was already in Fallujah. They were hoping to force the enemy north.

"A lieutenant from Echo Company said that my two-tank section essentially saved the day." He described it as extremely fierce fighting. The enemy fired RPKs and threw grenades. One Marine was killed, and 15 or 16 were wounded during that fight. Echo Company was then able to egress to the north, back to their CP. "That was one of several times we observed the enemy firing RPGs and small-arms fire from the minarets of mosques."

His tanks used the XM 908 (obstacle-reducing round) to take down a minaret near a cemetery that was being used as an enemy firing position. (This XM 908 round was designed to fire into "Dragon's Teeth" obstacles in Korea, and had never been used in combat before according to Sayler.) They found that when they fired this round into a building, there would be a 3- to 4-foot hole in the front wall, but the entire back wall of the building would be blown out: "It's a very, very effective round."

There was a palm grove outside of Fallujah, which had been a "thorn in the side" of 2/1 for some time. The Fox Company CO (commanding officer) talked to Lieutenant Sayler's platoon sergeant, Staff Sergeant Santana, about getting tanks there to take care of it. The palm grove was a hornets' nest of small-arms fire, RPGs and a lot of enemy personnel. The enemy had begun to change their tactics during this time. Instead of firing and running away, they would actually maneuver towards the Marines. "I think that once we were getting more into the Jolan District (of Fallujah) we were running into more of the foreign fighters."

On April 27 Lieutenant Sayler and Staff Sergeant Santana moved their four tanks towards the palm grove. Once past the grove, they began to take a lot of RPG and small-arms fire. The small-arms fire did not concern him, but the RPG fire did. The Euphrates River was to his right, and limited the amount of maneuver possible for the tanks. "The enemy had rigged up an IED along a wall and blown it onto my 4 tank. Didn't really do too much damage to the tank itself, but we found out later that they had done that a couple of other times." The only damage to the tank was a cracked hubcap and some residue on the armor. As they pulled back, they called in some 81mm mortar fire, and set in to try and catch enemy who were fleeing the mortar fire.

Two days later on April 29, he was called to help Golf Company 2/1, and fired rounds into a building suspected of sheltering enemy forces. He said that secondary explosions from the destroyed building confirmed that there were weapons inside.

Lieutenant Sayler was also part of the regimental (RCT1) Quick Reaction Force of tanks, tracs, and Army engineers during General Mattis' ride into the city hall of Fallujah on May 10. He worked up plans to enter the city and coordinate a withdrawal if needed. They were staged at Camp Bahariyah that day in a company coil. The tanks were coiled in a 360 perimeter, with weapons facing outboard. "I got to see General Mattis come in. I got to see the convoy come in. I got to see the Iraqis come in." He had wondered what would happen when the convoy returned from the trip into the city, but the Mattis' ride was uneventful.

Lieutenant Sayler noted that a big factor in MOUT operations was the very limited amount of time to react and make decisions. "You had to be quick and you had to be decisive."

* * *

Sergeant Heriberto Escamilla

Tank Commander, 1st Platoon, Charlie Company, 1st Tank Battalion

A veteran of OIF1, Sergeant Escamilla has seen a lot more close combat action during OIF2. He outlined how he and other tank Marines worked to adapt the gunsights for the main tank gun for close-in combat in urban areas. He also praised the return of the tank-infantry phone that allowed cooperation with supported infantry units. The U.S. Air Force's Spectre gunship also provided welcome support for night operations in the city.

This was the second time I interviewed Sergeant Escamilla. Dead batteries in the voice recorder stopped the first effort a day earlier. But this mistake on my part actually helped him to remember more, and today's interview was much more relaxed and informative. He covered a lot of the details of how the tanks and infantry worked together in Fallujah and this interview lasted nearly 50 minutes.

Sergeant Escamilla was a tank commander with 1st Platoon of Charlie Company Tanks, call sign "Red Three." The Texas native enlisted in the Marine Corps in 1997 and graduated from MCRD San Diego. After training in tanks, he went to 29 Palms in 1998. He then did MEU (Marine Expeditionary Unit) training deployments in Jordan and Kuwait as well as humanitarian efforts in East Timor. This experience helped him "learn how to work with infantry and let them know what our needs are." After about four or five months, OIF1 kicked off and, "I was part of 3rd Platoon." After OIF1, he planned to go to MSG (Marine Security Guard) school, and his paperwork was in process. But he volunteered to return with Charlie Company for OIF2, and hoped to reapply for MSG school when he returned to 29 Palms.

He said that in OIF1, "I believe it was March 28, 2003, interesting because we crossed the LOD (line of departure) for OIF2 exactly the same day, and almost to the hour [in 2004]. Of course last time we were on tanks, this time we're on Humvees."

The night before the attack in 2003, his unit was part of a reaction force, guarding against any possible Iraqi thrust over the 50-mile "no man's land" into Kuwait. They were part of Team Mech, with 14 tanks. At a series of sand berms there, they saw movement using their thermal sights. It turned out to be only dogs. "I heard artillery off to my left, and reported it to higher." He also heard helicopters even though there were not supposed to be helos in the area. When they flew over, he identified Marine Cobras. The Cobras fired three Hellfire missiles into a friendly tank, which was engulfed in fire. About two minutes after the tank was burning, they thought the crew was gone. The CO, Captain Banning, got on the radio, "Really, really calm, and all he said was 'Black, this is Black Six. Just took a Hellfire in the ass. Tank's on fire. Crew's OK. Someone get me another tank,' as calm as could be. After that I had a really good feeling about the vehicle."

During the initial three days of the attack, the only uniformed enemy personnel that Sergeant Escamilla saw was an enemy artillery battery that they caught by surprise. This artillery unit was moving across the front of the tanks, and the Marine tanks engaged them with coaxial machine guns and small arms. He destroyed an enemy tank in combat during the move. The Iraqi tank was about 200 meters away and it took two rounds to kill the tank that was hidden behind a berm.

The Marines engaged these Iraqi T55 tanks with the help of close air support en route to An Nasariyah.

The enemy did not wear uniforms in every city that he encountered. They would sometimes shoot, then drop their weapons, and wave at the Marines. The Marines got to Baghdad when things had calmed down. After about a week they went to a UN compound. The tanks were transported out of Iraq on Army HETS.

The whole tank battalion returned to the USA on the USS *Boxer*. They visited Australia and Hawaii on the way home. "A really nice homecoming. It was really good."

To get ready for OIF2, the company trained to do SASO, with the tanks on standby in Iraq, to help the infantry. It was an intensive three-week course. Even though they were to deploy on Humvees, they prepped the tanks when they arrived in Kuwait. They also prepared the Humvees with ballistic blankets for the floor, Kevlar door panels, etc. "That's how we rode from Kuwait into Iraq. I was a gunner [on a Humvee]." There was a guy on a bridge during the move through Iraq, and the company made sure to clear as many bridges as they could.

At Camp Fallujah, Charlie Tanks' Marines moved into the camp housing; they had air-conditioned rooms, showers, and thought it was heaven. The tanks were already at the camp and the tankers began maintenance on the vehicles. After three days there, they (Red Platoon) were supposed to move to adjacent Camp Bahariyah, but as they entered that camp, they got a frag order and then a warning order to move out to the cloverleaf outside of the city of Fallujah.

"The Army tankers who were leaving told us that the cloverleaf was hell. You stay in one spot for 30 minutes you got RPG'd, the people hated you… so we went there thinking it's gonna be combat from the get-go."

The first night at the cloverleaf the infantry did get engaged, but the tanks did not. There was sporadic fire and a couple of infantry Marines were killed. Tanks were used to push into the outskirts of the city. After about three days out there, the tanks returned to Camp Bahariyah.

On the night of April 3–4, the tanks pushed into the outskirts of Fallujah and stayed until May 7. "We were actually in the city. For the first couple of days without infantry." The tank is designed to operate in open terrain, not in close quarters as it was in Fallujah. They used the .50 cal and M240 machine guns, which were very effective. The tankers had to improvise to use their sights—he showed me sketches of the results of some of this improvisation. Not only was the artwork in his sketchbook very good, a non-tanker like me could easily understand the notes. This information was shared with other tank teams in the company as they improvised ways to use their weapons more effectively at close range, and developed notes on all-around security in the close-in street fighting in Fallujah. I took photos of two of his notebook sketches that show the serious thought that these Marines put into learning and sharing what they've learned on the battlefield.

"We did get engaged. Heavily. RPGs, AK 47s, everything you could think of was comin' at us. We had a Spectre gunship on top lookin' at us, and after a while you actually do get used to it, and you fight back." He said that as the crew fought, they would be talking about all kinds of other things, and other crews reported doing the same.

"What we would do, you'd hear the tanks fire up, the tanks move into the city, and they [enemy fighters] would try to ambush the tanks from the side. As they're comin' towards us, the Spectre gunship's overhead lookin' down with his infrared. He could see the thermals, he could see them approaching us, and say, 'Hey, you got people approaching about this far away from your tanks.' Thanks, traverse over. Wait for them, shoot 'em, well he would shoot 'em, engage them with his 105 and his Gatling gun, his mini gun. It was just a really good team."

I said to Sergeant Escamilla, "In some cases you were just like bait, and they [the gunship] were the fishermen up there."

Sergeant Escamilla agreed, saying, "We knew we were, we knew we were. We were the only ones that could do that, with the heavy armor that we had, the mobility we have, and the communications systems. I think that was a perfect way of using the tank, in front, 'cause usually we send the LAVs [Light Armored Vehicles] or the infantry in front, and I never understood that part. Why, when we had all armor, all the mobility? I'd rather have infantry behind us and have them push up when we think we see something."

When the infantry was all around him, he had to be sure that they were clear before he returned fire. In Fallujah, the tanks and infantry learned to work together in a lot of different situations.

"We were taking RPG fire from a mosque. I'm talking on the radio with the other tank commanders, to see if I can fire into this building, and we have an infantry phone in the back of our tank. I'd never had anyone actually use it. Sergeant Boole, he comes up, and he's pretty nuts, he comes up and says, 'Tanks, tanks, this is Boole.' I didn't even know who he was, I'm sitting there talking to my crew saying who the hell is this guy? He says, 'Tanks, tanks, this is Boole. I'm behind you!'"

Sergeant Escamilla then realized that Sergeant Boole was on the infantry phone. "I say 'Boole, this is tanks,' he says 'Roger, I need to get in this building. There's a wall there. Can you do anything for me?' 'Oh yeah, I can knock down that wall.'" Sergeant Escamilla fired a multipurpose anti-tank round at it. "Boole, he's amazing." Sergeant Boole took his men into the hole just made in the wall by the tank round. "He's the first one to use the grunt phone. That was a good experience working with the infantry."

Later, Escamilla's team took down a mosque with three obstacle-reducing rounds, the new XM 908 rounds. His platoon sergeant was the first one to fire the XM 908. "An amazing round." This stopped the enemy machine gunfire, and the infantry Marines were able to take their wounded out of the area.

While working with 2/1, he was part of a two-tank team when Gunny Popaditch's tank was hit by RPG fire as they were going into a narrowing alley in Fallujah. "I look over, I hear BOOM, I see the top of the tank on fire. I don't see his loader. I'm not sure what he got hit with. I pretty much knew it was an RPG, I just know it came from the right side. And it looked like it came from the inside of a building.

"It shot through the CWS, the commander's weapon station. Gunny Pop was outside. If he was a couple inches to the right it woulda gone right through him… it went from one end to the next and ended up in the loader's station somehow. It shot shrapnel all over the place. and from what I heard the shrapnel came from the back end of the neck, cut across, and ruptured his optical nerve, and I think his eye came out."

The shrapnel hit Lance Corporal Hernandez in the hand. When Escamilla heard Hernandez on the radio, it was chaotic. The packs on the outside of the tank were on fire, but none of the ammo went off. Hernandez's tank moved towards Escamilla's tank, and then went back to the casualty collection point. Shortly after, Escamila took his tank back to the casualty collection point, and the tanks temporarily formed into a three-tank section. "I learned the meaning of three-dimensional warfare really quick."

I asked Sergeant Escamilla to describe the tank taking down the minaret of a mosque with the XM 908 round. They were taking incoming RPG rounds. "Some RPGs travel slower than others," he said, and he could see some of these grenades coming towards them. "Some of the ones that hit, they go so fast. They're the ones you hear go by you, and you feel the heat. I felt heat from an RPG, I said, 'Wow! that must have been pretty close.' It's so fast you don't see it."

He saw two or three RPGs fired from a mosque and reported it up the chain of command. He got permission to fire at the shooter, but didn't have a clear shot at the mosque's minaret where the RPG rounds were coming from. "I couldn't traverse my main guns because of the walls." One of the other tanks knocked down a wall next to a cemetery and gave that tank a clear shot at the minaret of the mosque. "He shot the minaret three times, at the base of the minaret with the XM 908 round and the thing came down. The whole minaret, and it was beautiful. I was cheering, because that was good to see."

Soon after that, he said that he almost shot at a news reporter who was aiming his camera out of a window, but Sergeant Escamilla's gunner told him that it was a friendly. At night, other Marines sometimes took off their helmets for comfort, and this made it difficult for the tankers who were using thermal sights to determine if these Marines were friendlies or not. "When they stood up, because of the body heat, the SAPI show nothing, and that's how I could tell they were friendlies." He passed the word to his lieutenant to tell the grunts to keep their gear on at night to avoid fratricide.

One technique that the tankers developed to do retrograde movements in the city when infantry cover was not available was to move the tanks back-to-back down the streets for a 360-degree measure of security. The minaret takedown was something that had never been done before, either.

Some of the infantry units used tanks as lead and rear guard security elements. If they received fire, the first two tanks in the lead could become a base of fire and the other two tanks in the rear became part of the assault element. The objective was to keep the convoy moving. In the cities they knocked down trees and walls. They also marked targets for the air elements using their small-caliber weapons. On one raid, they knocked down some trees to allow Marine snipers better fields of fire, and once, they knocked down a wall and found a cache of weapons behind it.

Escamilla also noted how enemy fighters have attempted to hook up three RPGs with one trigger mechanism to try and take on the tanks better. They also sent out four-man hunter-killer teams that aimed to take out tanks with RPGs. "We came up against some of those. They would take up different sectors." The teams would wait until the main gun of the tank traversed away from them and another team would fire at the tank from another direction.

"What I saw was guys wearing a tan uniform and a black beret. I knew they weren't anything local." He thought that they might be Chechnyan fighters, but nothing was confirmed.

Both his driver and loader were new to combat, and sometimes he had answers for them and sometimes he did not. In 2003, the enemy didn't seem to want to fight. A year later, the enemy did want to fight. He also described using the M240 machine guns that they brought with them to use on Humvees, and now they mounted them on the tanks in addition to their coaxial .50 caliber machine guns. It gave them another weapons system to respond quickly to the enemy hunter-killer teams.

The 3rd Tank Platoon was sent to help guard the Syrian border area, and hasn't been in the Fallujah area since then. Now Bravo Company tanks were in the Fallujah area, this in an area where the tankers had originally expected to be used in Humvees as convoy escorts.

Sergeant Escamilla was part of the Quick Reaction Force during General Mattis's ride to the Fallujah city hall. The ride was peaceful, and Iraqi forces outside of Fallujah then replaced the Marines. He was hoping this would be successful.

* * *

Sergeant Prince Witty

Tank Commander, Charlie Company, 1st Tank Battalion

A native of Ghana, Sergeant Witty came to the United States in 1996 with his family for a better education. However, he quit college to join the Marine Corps. He was very proud of participating in both OIF1 and OIF2. A tank commander, his story complemented others in his platoon. His tank was one of two as part of the QRF to rescue Marines from 1/5 trapped in Fallujah after the Amtrac they rode in was heavily damaged by RPG fire. He planned to return to college when his enlistment was up: Princeton University as an accounting major.

"I came into the country to go to school. I join the Marine Corps, I don't know why!" He said that he wanted to become a tanker because he liked the big guns. He was in Iraq for OIF1, and helped to secure Saddam's palace in Baghdad. "On the way from Kuwait to Iraq we didn't get involved in any fire until about Basrah. This was my first combat. Scared as hell, at that time I was a tank gunner." Shortly after the fighting ended, the U.S. Army took over the areas and he left Iraq after about only three or four weeks.

For OIF2, he said it had been different because the people were fighting back. When the unit was preparing to come back to Iraq, he said, "We were training to be like grunts [infantry]. We did patrolling with Humvees and stuff, we trained for that for like three months at 29 Palms. They were telling us that no tanks were needed." However, the tanks were brought to Iraq. "We showed up, everyone wants a tank now." Sergeant Witty said that the tanks were split up into two- and three-tank sections to support infantry operations.

"We have lost nobody yet. We've been pretty lucky."

He was attached to 2/1 for about three weeks during the early Fallujah operations, then 2/2 for about two weeks up until the cease fire, and they had just come back from there.

I asked him to describe what his tank section did with 2/1. At first, the tanks were helping with checkpoints outside of Fallujah. Then, "We helped them clear the city and the streets." The infantry would follow the tanks. At night they would go patrolling with the infantry, looking for places that were "hot," and to try to secure the area.

When 1/5 needed help, his two-tank section went to help out, not on a formal attachment. 1/5 had an attached Amtrac blown up by an RPG, and the tanks went in to help tow the Amtrac out of a narrow street in Fallujah.

"The thing was so burned, it couldn't be turned around. There was a body [a Marine] in the trac, and we had to bring it back." The tank was under fire during the retrieval of the Amtrac in the narrow streets of the city. Two Marines were exposed to enemy fire while hooking up the two towing cables to the Amtrac.

"We've been going with the infantry when they go patrolling in the city." He said that the infantry was learning how to use the tanks again to patrol. He said that there had been lots of training to do this before his first deployment to Iraq, but not before the current deployment. "We're trying to teach them how to use us.

"At first it seemed that nobody needed us, then everybody's yelling, 'Tanks!' They need us but they really don't how to use us." But he said that the grunts were getting better at using the tanks properly.

Now that Bravo Company's tanks had arrived, he and his other tankers were running small classes to share what they were learning during the fighting. They were also working to educate the grunts as to how to employ the tanks, and the limitations of the tanks.

"The first war the grunts know how to use us, but we didn't do much with them. In this war, we are doing too much with them, but they really don't know how to use us."

I asked him about the team in his tank. "When I got here, one guy got hurt. We took two RPG rounds, and it blows the periscope. I saw it coming. The round hit the periscope and the glass hit his eyes and shoulder." Sergeant Witty was now working with a new gunner. The rest of the crew was the same as he had last year. "Everybody knows their job, the crew is good."

Sergeant Witty was looking forward to finishing his four-year Marine Corps commitment and going back to college finish his degree in accounting.

"I'll go back, and at least know I did something for the country that give me freedom. So, I glad of that, and I'm proud to be part of the family Marine Corps." He hopes that the loss of life of Marines was not in vain, and that it helps bring freedom to Iraq.

* * *

Corporal Michael J. Fiscella

Tank Gunner, Charlie Company, 1st Tank Battalion

Corporal Michael J. Fiscella is tank gunner, and another excellent, thorough interview subject. He had been keeping a journal during this deployment, and I told him that is why the interview could be so in-depth. Another OIF1 veteran, one of his big achievements during recent combat operations was to destroy a minaret outside of a mosque. Infantry saw someone using the minaret to fire on them. It took three tank main-gun rounds to take it down. He said that it went straight down when the third round hit, and all of the infantry and tankers cheered. He was also involved in a display of loading tank rounds that was designed to intimidate the mayor of Fallujah.

"I went to boot camp almost three years ago, came out and got into tanks." Almost immediately after his initial tank training, he went to Iraq during OIF1. "The first couple of days we had a little bit of combat, then we went on the road to Baghdad. For a couple of weeks we didn't sleep at all. All night, all day, driving up." During that time, he lost a wingman. At a bridge, one of the tanks went around it, and was reported missing during a sandstorm. This tank had fallen into the river, and four crewmen were lost in the tank, leaving only three tanks in the platoon.

"The people in Baghdad totally loved us. It was a totally different atmosphere than it is now in Fallujah. Then, I could go sit on top of the tank in the middle of the street. I didn't have a flak on, I didn't have a Kevlar on. People were surrounding me." He said that people wanted their autographs, were very friendly. Today in Fallujah it was very different.

The tanks then drove back down to Kuwait when things settled down. The pads on many of their tank tracks or treads were worn down by the long road march up to Baghdad. After the tanks were loaded onto the ships in Kuwait, he and the other tankers returned home. "People were waving flags, giving us the thumbs up."

He took leave a few weeks later, and got home in time for his sister's wedding where he wore his dress blues and new set of medals from the war. "I didn't have any post-war syndrome, it was good to be home with family for a while."

When he returned to 29 Palms, he learned he'd be a gunner on the tanks. Around October–November 2003 time, word started to pass that the Marines would be returning to Iraq. The plan was for SASO, and the tankers would be in Humvees. "This time we had months to prepare for the return. We took classes on the culture and what to expect. We got so much information about what was going on." The tankers still prepared their tanks, but did not expect to use them in Iraq.

Charlie Company tanks got to Kuwait in March 2004; the hooches (living quarters trailers) there were air conditioned, and there was a military exchange on the base that the Army had built. The tankers were then told they'd be in their tanks for the first three months in Iraq and then go into SASO. Not many main tank rounds were supplied; mostly machine-gun and coaxial rounds were loaded for the move. In Kuwait, they bore sighted these weapons, got the tanks loaded onto Army HETS, and moved to what is now Camp Fallujah. The tank Marines moved northward in a convoy mounted in Humvees. Corporal Fiscella said that the company arrived at Camp Fallujah and enjoyed the air-conditioned quarters. They also learned from the resident Army units what the conditions were in the immediate area. One valuable bit of info was how to zero the weapons to fire in the close-in conditions of city streets.

"The first couple of days we got tasked to go to the cloverleaf in Fallujah [in tanks]." They were working with 2/1, and then moved their vehicles to Camp Bahariyah.

Corporal Fiscella was also involved in the "tank loading incident" to impress the mayor of Fallujah. He laughed when I asked him about it: "We pulled the tanks up, the mayor was inside the building [at Camp Bahariyah] talkin' with the colonel [Lieutenant Colonel Olson] about what was gonna happen, if they don't go in they were gonna use tanks. So we got the word that we were gonna scare him with loading up rounds. A lot of people don't realize the size of the round that the tank holds. It's about 37 pounds, two and a half to three feet, depending on what the round is. It's a very massive, scary round, especially to people who are used to seeing RPGs, RPKs, AK 47s, small rounds, and you see a main-gun round, it's totally different feeling."

Gunny Popaditch's tank was parked behind Fiscella's.

"We ended up getting six rounds, all MPAT, put 'em on the deck on top of a tarp, and waited for the mayor to come out. At that time we were told to pick up the rounds, walk 'em around the tank. I was the first person to walk with the round. You know, you see six guys pickin' up the rounds, walking around the tank. The mayor got a little bit of an eye-opening."

The Marines then learned that the bodies of the American contractors would be returned. The tankers enjoyed their own little PSY-operation. "We were letting them know we'd use all of our abilities if we need to."

On April 3, the tankers learned that they'd be part of the cordon around the city of Fallujah. Tanks, Amtracs, and infantry would surround the city to trap the insurgents: "We were making like a big loop around the city." When they got into the city, there were not many people inside compared to when they were there before. The cordon was supposed to last ten days.

This was when Gunny Popaditch's tank was hit by an RPG. Lance Corporal Hernandez was hit in the hand with shrapnel and Gunny Pop lost the vision in his right eye. The platoon made necessary adjustments, with Staff Sergeant Herrera as platoon sergeant.

"Pretty much every time we went in [to the city] we were bullet magnets. It was a very close environment. The grunts of 2/1 in some senses didn't know how to work with us."

It took some time to develop a working relationship with them, and the tankers did everything that the grunts asked them to. The tanks knocked down walls and trees for observation. "Each time we went into the city we got shot. I remember one mission we had at night, it was kind of interesting. They used us as a kind of bait." He said that there were helos overhead that were observing enemy moving around the city. The tanks would move into these areas and wait for people to surround them. Air Force AC-130 gunships came in and eliminated the enemy.

There was another area called the Palm Grove that always seemed to have enemy in there. "We'd go into the Palm Grove area and try and clear it out. We'd end up seeing bad guys and shoot them." They were in a two-tank section for this action, and the tanks traveled back-to-back for 360-degree protection. Throughout the interview, Corporal Fiscella made extensive use of notes he had been keeping to review the more significant events that had been happening. He said that traveling through the narrow city streets was difficult for the large tanks.

"It seemed that we were always shooting a weapon at one time." He said that they also used the 240 Golf machine guns that they had brought along for SASO. They put the 240s on the tanks and it turned out that the 240 would be pointed in the same direction as the coax. In his words, having the two weapons was great.

The tankers noticed that the RPG gunners were getting better with their aim. When they would see the main gun traverse toward them, they would hide and wait for a better shot at the tanks.

"We started receiving [incoming sniper fire] from one of the mosques." He could hear that "War Hammer" (Echo Company 2/1) was being shot at from the mosque. "The mosque was directly to our left." This was in the northwest area of the city. "The grunts would always tell us they were receiving sniper fire from the mosque, but when I'd get to the area all that would cease.

"Finally to help them out, Staff Sergeant Santana told me to traverse and shoot. We had the OR round. It's an impact round. It's a very nice round with a steel tip. The cone will crush and it ends up going through a building and then it detonates in the back end.

"I ended up shooting up the mosque. I had to shoot it three times to get it down."

I asked him if this was the mosque or the minaret next to it, and Corporal Fiscella said it was the minaret—the tower. "I hit it three times. The minaret is the most well-built building in the whole of Fallujah."

He said that he didn't know how it stood with the first two hits. He started with hitting the left of the tower and moved to the right. The tower just collapsed on the third hit and the grunts were cheering because this was the source of a lot of shooting at them. I said to Corporal Fiscella that once the enemy makes a sacred place a target, it's now a target, and he responded that he had no regrets as his action saved the lives of Marines.

At night, the minarets in the city would broadcast prayers. Later, enemy would broadcast anti-coalition propaganda. Sometimes the Army PSYOPS (Psychological Operations) soldiers would loudly broadcast American music at night.

He noted that this year things were more serious more of the time than last year's operations. During General Mattis' recent ride into Fallujah, the tanks were outside the city of Fallujah on stand-by as part of a reaction force. "If the convoy got hit, we were going to go in."

Corporal Fiscella added, "I keep a journal. Last war I didn't keep a journal and I wish I had." He said that it has helped him keep track of what he has done and where he is.

CHAPTER THREE

Weapons Company, 1st Battalion, 5th Marine Regiment, Interviews at Camp Abu Ghraib

Tuesday June 15, 2004

I got ready to go to 1/5, and a Corporal Kearney met me at the Main Camp Fallujah chow hall. The ride to Camp Abu Ghraib was about seven minutes. It's about two clicks off the West Gate to Camp Fallujah, but still required an armed convoy. Despite the name, it was NOT the location of the now infamous prison.

At the Camp Fallujah gate all Marines (including me) dismounted the vehicles and charged our weapons, then stayed on the alert while we drove to 1/5's camp.

The battalion's executive officer, Major Jeffrey Chessani, met me and began to gather up the Weapons Company Marines to meet with me. While I waited for them I looked over a small lot next to the battalion CP where they had a sampling of the weapons that they found during their weeks in Fallujah. There were two large recoilless rifles, many 60mm mortars, some 82mm mortars, bunches of rocket tubes, some jury-rigged, that used motorcycle batteries to fire rockets and RPGs. There were also several water pipes on bipods used to fire 122mm rockets. Amazing, the ingenuity of some of the insurgents—if they would only devote their energies to rebuilding the country instead of attacking us!

I briefly met the battalion commander, Lieutenant Colonel Brendan Byrne, and found out that he knew Major Piedmont, so I planned to let John interview him at length before 1/5 returned to CONUS (Continental United States). I did the interviews in a building that the battalion used for its admin and supply sections, in an area that was separated from the other "offices" by plywood walls.

I had seven good interviews, two of the best in the morning. They were very talkative; great descriptions of combat ops in Fallujah, and how one Marine figured out where a sniper was shooting from—they had cardboard over the window and rounds penetrated it and hit the wall. The Marine (Corporal David Silvers) used the laser bore sight from his rifle to figure out the back azimuth and angle of the shot! He then discovered that the sniper was in a mosque's minaret about 900 meters away. He waited until the shooter shot at another target adjacent to their position and saw the muzzle flash. Then his squad coordinated with an Abrams tank to "engage" the minaret with three main-gun rounds which silenced the sniper! Very ingenious, almost like an episode from the TV show *CSI*. Another corporal was very happy that he had gotten to fire an $80,000 Javelin missile to take out a target in a house in Fallujah!

* * *

Sergeant Michael Wayne Rinehart

Squad Leader/Vehicle Commander, Little Wolf, Weapons Company, 1/5

Sergeant Rinehart outlined how his section of the platoon was organized for operations in and around Fallujah. A Weapons Company of an infantry battalion has many vehicles that give it mobility as well as heavy weapons for use by the battalion commander.

"Okay, for 'Little Wolf' we run in [a] six and two package. We have six gun trucks: We have two .50 cal trucks, two TOW [missile] trucks, and two Mark 19 trucks. And then we have two dismount vehicles which contain about 20 dismount Marines, which [are] 81s Platoon-provided dismounts."

"I've been in the Marine Corps for nine years. I served with Weapons Company in 3/1 from '95 to '98. From '99 to 2001 I was an instructor for Weapons and Tactics at SOI, Marine Combat Training Battalion, and then I came over to 1/5, I did OIF1 and now I'm here for OIF2."

He first explained where the term "Little Wolf" came from and why Native American terms were being used within Weapons Company of 1/5: "Each of the units (companies) has an Indian tribe, like Alpha is Apache, Bravo is Blackhawk, Charlie is Cherokee. For Weapons Company the primary call sign for the CO is Wicked Chief. Since he had a chief's title, we went ahead, went with a chief's title for each of the different units [in this company]: Little Wolf, Red Cloud, and Crazy Horse."

For this deployment, Sergeant Rinehart said, "This time around we spent a lot of time focusing on SASO: Stability and Security Operations." In Okinawa and stateside, they did lots of training for this. They planned to work with the Iraqi people to get the economy working and the communities back together. "That was our preparation, and then when we got over here things kinda changed on us a little bit. We ended up moving right into Fallujah."

Before moving into Fallujah, his unit did a lot of mortar and rocket mitigation patrols in the area. The Marines used thermal and visual devices to exploit the weakness of the enemy at night. As long as Marines were in an area, the enemy couldn't employ its mortars and rockets since they would quickly be discovered.

At the beginning of the Fallujah operations in April 2004, he said that they were being used as part of the cordon of the city, working at roadblocks, not letting anybody into or out of the city. When ICDC (Iraqi Civil Defence Corps) personnel came in and relieved them on the outer cordon, Little Wolf went up to help hold the line at Routes Michigan and Violet in the city. Michigan was the main north–south road at the entrance to Fallujah, and Violet was one of the first roads he came across running east to west.

"By the time that Little Wolf got into the area, they had already cleared the primary zones, the main areas there, so Little Wolf started holding the line at Michigan, along with Crazy Horse."

They were tied in there, and were to prevent anyone from crossing Michigan from east to west. They also did back clearing of the area around them to ensure that it was clear of any stragglers and also for any remaining weapons caches. Little Wolf was preparing to move into positions near Violet that Apache had moved out of, but the offensive operations were called off when negotiations began. They held the line at Michigan and Violet for about two and a half weeks. There was some random sniper fire during that time. Rinehart said that they were able to successfully engage some of these shooters: "We hit 'em."

When suppression with M16s didn't work, they fired TOWs and Javelin missiles at some sniper positions on the other side of Michigan. "You take fire from a building for a couple days, you put a Javelin in it, nobody's shooting at you from there anymore, you kinda get the idea he's gone."

When the ceasefire went into effect, all of the Weapons Company platoons from 1/5 returned to Camp Abu Ghraib, and they continued with the mortar and rocket mitigation patrols in the area for a while. These attacks pretty much subsided, and Alpha and Bravo companies went up into Shahabi and al Karmah.

The Weapons Company platoons did presence patrols there. "We always had a patrol out, there was always somebody out, anywhere from four hours to eight hours, depending on what the mission was that night. We tried not to set up a pattern, we'd have a patrol go out at 0800 to 1600, 0800 to 1200, and then there'd be a pause where there were no vehicles out there for maybe an hour or two. And then, another patrol would go out at 1200 to 1600. I think the latest our patrols would go were around 0100, 0200, unless we were doing a raid." He said that raids usually kicked off around 0100.

Weapons Company did several raids. Sergeant Rinehart explained how they were organized. One section would use its trucks to set up an exterior cordon. Then dismounted Marines (from 81s Platoon) would move into the interior cordon. A team of six to eight Marines was set up for interior security. Then a clearing element was sent in.

"First we would clear the building for threat, we'd go through, sort of a low-intensity threat environment. Go through, clear each room. While we're clearing the building, we're also separating the males from the females. We'd bring the males outside, and while we're doing that, our Doc, or Corpsman, he was there, there with the females, providing security."

Then teams of two Marines would go through and clear each room, looking for weapons and caches. HET (Human Exploitation Teams) would question the people.

He estimated that the company had done five or six company raids, and a couple of platoons had done snap raids on targets of opportunity.

I asked him if the 81s Platoon had been operating their mortars. Rinehart said that it seemed as if they might get to fire their mortars in Fallujah, but never did. The mortar tubes got sent out to the rifle companies, and their mortar men used them.

When I asked how the sections got local intel on where to look for trouble spots he said, "Believe it or not, a lot of our information comes from kids, too. They'll point to a house, say, uh, 'Ali Baba', which is 'thieves.' Or we'll come up on a building, and something's just not right about. So a platoon commander sees something." Tips can come from locals, HET, and infantry units.

I had forgotten to ask him about the turnover with the Army when they had first gotten into Iraq. He said that from his perspective, the Army units in this area had done a good job of briefing the Marine platoon commanders and squad leaders on the threat.

At that time, few of the Marines' Humvees were up-armored, but most of the vehicles now had armor that the Marines put on them in Kuwait, like the flat metal siding. They also had armor inside the Humvees, with a piece under the seat, a piece on the back, and a piece on the floor of the vehicles. They recently got armored door kits with the 2-inch-thick bullet-proof glass. Sergeant Rinehart saw the effects of this when he was on a QRF going out to where a Humvee from Red Cloud had gotten hit with an IED made from two 155mm artillery rounds. He said that the vehicle was shredded in the rear, but the four Marines in it escaped with minor injuries.

Asked to compare his experiences in Iraq last year with this year. He said, "Last year, and this year, both, 81s was a provisional rifle platoon. 81s spend a lot of time doing TRAP training—tactical recovery of aircraft and personnel—so we get a lot of time doing ground-mounted stuff. Last year we were focused primarily on mortars since the battalion was moving so fast from Kuwait up to Baghdad. We ended up using more of our artillery and our tank support than we did mortars. Once we got into Baghdad, 81s took on a patrolling role. We went out with different elements, doing kinda what we do now: We did raids."

A difference this year was that they worked a lot with the Counter-Mech Platoon on raid packages. Last year there were several sustained engagements; this year he said it was more intense. The biggest worry for his Marines was the IEDs this year, especially as the insurgents were getting better at emplacing IEDs. Last year (2003) the enemy would fire until they ran out of ammunition and then surrender. The enemy in 2004 shoots and leaves. He felt that there were now more foreign fighters in the mix.

One of his squads was made up entirely of new Marines. In 81s, there was a 50-50 mix of OIF1 vets and new Marines. They blended well this year.

"When I was a lance corporal in 81s, you did mortars. You did a little bit of TRAP training, nobody really focused on it. For these guys to come out of SOI, receiving only a basic 0311 package, and then jumping right into being a provisional rifle platoon for the battalion, executing company-size raids, doing patrols, some foot mobile, some truck mobile, these guys have adapted well."

Sergeant Rinehart said that 95 percent of the 81s Marines would rather be doing what they are now doing than "Messing around with a tube." They enjoy it, getting the training they got prior to arriving here, and now they were in high-paced missions.

* * *

Sergeant Edgar D. Aguilarvaldizon
TOW Vehicle Commander CAAT 1, Weapons Company, 1/5

One of two Marines in the platoon sent to an Arabic-language familiarization course, Sergeant Aguilarvaldizon has enough facility to help with vehicle stops. He continued to practice his Arabic with locals. He was inside the city of Fallujah during much of the heavy enemy action in early to mid-April. Once he became a TOW operator he received in-the-field training with the missile system, and serves as a vehicle commander in CAAT Platoon. In June his vehicle ran over an IED that exploded, injuring several of the Marines in it.

After recruit training, Sergeant Aguilarvaldizon was an admin clerk (MOS 0121). Toward the end of his first enlistment in 2003, he made a lateral move to a new MOS, 0352: TOW gunner. In August (2003) he joined 1/5, preparing to go to Okinawa. There was no time to send him to a formal TOW school. The focus was to train him on the job, and he soon became a TOW vehicle commander. He first shot a TOW missile during a week-long field training operation.

In December 2003, 1/5 left Camp Pendleton for Okinawa. His on-the-job training was helped by other sergeants in the units sharing their experience with him. He served as platoon sergeant, and had to quickly learn how to properly communicate on the radio with the eight vehicles in the platoon.

He was sent back to the States for a month-long Arabic language familiarization course. At the classes, he learned to read and write, then speak some of the language. The battalion sent two Marines from each platoon for this training. Some of this training included familiarization with Arabic culture, in areas such as body language and gestures. The language school graduates then gave classes to their platoons in the basics of Arabic. A lot of this was in informal classes during down time when training on Okinawa.

He has continued to practice with local interpreters, and spoken with local Iraqis at road blocks or vehicle checkpoints (VCPs). He said that sometimes when he did not say the word properly, the local Iraqis would correct his pronunciation. But his main point was that he could be understood by them.

He said it was fast-paced once they left Okinawa. They had a week to pack, and sent excess gear home. They went to Kadena Air Base on Okinawa and then flew into Kuwait. They had their ammo loaded and went to Condition 3. He said that he was kind of nervous, and he had no background in the infantry field. They received briefings on ROEs, and bussed to their base in Kuwait where they spent three weeks. They convoyed up to then-Camp Mercury, now Camp Abu Ghraib. Weapons Company split up into four teams for the convoy. Little Wolf led the head of the convoy. New ROEs were given out.

"As soon as we stepped off, I was nervous again. I didn't know what to expect. I just remember driving off and seeing nothing." It took three days to make the move into Iraq.

Their first missions here were mortar mitigation patrols. They would leave at 1600, 1700 or even 1900 and patrol until about 0300. In his vehicle, three of the four Marines had NVGs (night vision goggles), and the TOW gunner had night sights on his missile launcher, so everyone could see well in the dark. Sergeant Aguilarvaldizon gave lots of credit to the Marines in his platoon with more infantry experience than he had, for helping him through many new situations that he has faced over here.

They did these patrols constantly for about two and a half weeks. Then they got a break, doing PT in the morning, weapons maintenance, and then showers, haircuts, and time to rest.

The mortar mitigation patrols ceased about three days before the move into Fallujah. He and his Marines got briefed on upcoming plans for Fallujah. "We had a company-level one, and then we had a platoon-level one." They stepped off at 0010 on April 3, 2004, and were in position by 0200. Their job at the start was to cordon off MSR Mobile on the southwest side of the city, stopping any traffic from entering or leaving. As the rest of the battalion's forces moved past them into the city, he said that he could hear small arms and explosions. His section then did a convoy back to the FOB to get his platoon commander.

They returned to Fallujah and relieved Red Cloud in its sector. He said it was a "non-sleep" night for him. He and his driver did one-hour sleep rotations the whole night to stay on alert.

In the morning, they got a radio report about a suspicious vehicle in the city, driving off slowly. "They moved off, stopped, looked under their hood, and as soon as we're getting to take off to get 'em, they just took off. We followed them into this house, there were these Arabic people, they didn't know where the vehicle came from, they just were pointing—that the men… left the vehicle." They didn't find anything in the vehicle.

The rest of the platoon joined them and they took up a blocking position. At night they had Marine snipers on rooftops, and took over a garage. They put a 240 Golf machine gun there along with dismounted Marines from 81s Platoon. In the morning of April 8, as Aguilarvaldizon was getting an MRE, there was an airburst from a mortar round over the position. Then another mortar round hit a Marine vehicle outside of the building, setting off the ammo inside of it. Aguilarvaldizon ran to the vehicle with a fire extinguisher, but it was already on fire. The enemy began to fire machine guns at them. The Marines on the rooftop were also being fired on. One Marine got shot in the foot. A Marine chopper came in and fired to suppress enemy fire. He believed that it was a Cobra helo. They then brought the Marines down from the roof.

Later in the day, April 9, they used a ladder from the first building to climb onto another rooftop in another part of the city. Enemy sniper fire continued that day. Bravo Company came through, back-clearing the area. Their CO and radio operator came near, and Aguilarvaldizon screamed at them to move their vehicle because of the sniper fire that they had been taking. He heard a shot pop off and someone screaming for help. It was the lieutenant's radio operator. He was wounded. They did a ground medevac to get the Marine evacuated. The Marine was currently doing well.

During some periods of heavy enemy contact they shot Javelin missiles and AT4s at enemy positions. They moved to a position near Michigan and Violet and stayed there for about 12 days. Contact had died out for them. By this time, 2/2, 2/1 and 3/4 were moving into positions around Fallujah. Possible missions kept changing during this time as Marines planned to go deep into the city.

Once every two weeks Marines in the platoon went back to the FOB where they showered, got internet contact with home, had hot chow, and got resupply.

Finally, on April 29 they moved out of Fallujah. Marines disassembled positions, took down barbed wire, and loaded their gear back onto the vehicles. They rounded up unexploded ordnance, grenades and captured ammo, and set it off with charges to destroy it. He laughed, "You could pretty much say we left with a bang!"

He said it was a relief to be leaving. He said that during the back-clearing operations in Fallujah, Bravo Company had found most of the weapons that were on display in the large lot outside the battalion CP.

Back at Camp Abu Ghraib, they inventoried all their equipment, and the following day resumed the mortar mitigation patrols. Only one time did they spot someone firing rockets, but he said that they couldn't get there to capture the shooters because of canals and obstacles in the area.

Vehicle patrols in this area were quiet until Tuesday June 8, 2004. A Bravo Company patrol was in contact with the enemy. As Little Wolf was driving up the road, a VBIED (vehicle-borne improvised explosive device) exploded, injuring Aguilarvaldizon's turret gunner, as well as the driver and gunner on the rear vehicle.

"We didn't know what was happening. I just told my driver just to stop. He just says, 'It hurts! It hurts!' I told them to bring him down, not knowing if we were gonna take any contact. So once we brought him down, I wanted for him to sit in the vehicle, so I jumped right back up in the gun. We had a Corpsman in our vehicle, so I told him to take him out, and get some cover and concealment, to help him out and aid him. And I had my scout and my driver go out there and cover for him."

The gunner had taken some shrapnel to the back. He said that the round actually made his guts come out through the back. This was an urgent medevac. High-back trucks came and medevacked him to Camp Fallujah. All told, three Marines were injured. One had burns. The Marine with the shrapnel wounds was sent to surgery in Baghdad. All three were currently in stable condition.

Aguilarvaldizon found IEDs during some of the recent mortar mitigation patrols late at night. When they found an IED, the procedure was to call in the find—in his case, his call sign is Little Wolf 8, as there are eight vehicles in the platoon. They cordon off the area and alert the platoon commander, Little Wolf, and wait for EOD (Explosive Ordnance Disposal) to arrive. Sergeant Aguilarvaldizon said that this is where his language skills come in, as he can use his Arabic to tell locals to turn away from the area. The local Iraqis then understand why they were being stopped or diverted from the street. The Marines also blocked traffic when doing raids. Other Marines would ask him to talk to locals and for key phrases.

On a recent raid, they had nine Iraqi individuals targeted, and captured eight of them. They also brought back another five suspicious men. The local FOB only had facilities to hold individuals overnight. For longer stays, the suspects were sent to Camp Fallujah.

On the day of this interview, Marines from 3/1's advance party were beginning to move into the FOB, and the 1/5 Marines were starting to move over to Camp Fallujah. Little Wolf continued the mortar mitigation patrols, and also escorts for battalion needs. They had also escorted the chow runs to Camp Fallujah. He expected to work out of Camp Fallujah until they rotate back to the States. Within a week the whole battalion would be at Camp Fallujah. I told him that the showers and mess hall would be a treat, and the Exchange was nice, too.

Sergeant Aguilarvaldizon said that he has been fortunate, suffering only some bruises during the operations. He felt that he has learned a lot about being an infantry leader, too, in the past six months. His radio reporting skills have gotten better, as well as observation skills. He has developed situational awareness and has learned to speak the language of the 03 (Marine Infantryman). He actually expected more contact than they experienced, although the weeks in Fallujah were fast-paced. Vehicles have had a lot of tire damage, but most have not been seriously harmed. He has also found that his admin skills have enabled him to help many of the Marines in his platoon. This helped keep the morale of his Marines up.

He has been a sergeant for three years, and said that his birthday is November 10, a significant date for any Marine! (The Marine Corps celebrates its founding from November 10, 1775.) He said that when his recruiter told him about this coincidence, he responded that he must have been destined to be in the Marine Corps.

* * *

Corporal David Thomas Silvers
Squad Leader Red Six (Dismounted), Weapons Company, 1/5

Corporal Silvers directed combined arms on several enemy positions. He used an infrared targeting system to direct an Air Force AC-130 gunship onto an insurgent-held building. Later, he used a laser bore sight to determine the origin of an enemy sniper who had been harassing his position. Once the sniper's position in a minaret was confirmed, Marines fired a Javelin missile and tank rounds into the minaret of that mosque.

Corporal Silvers entered boot camp in January 2000, where he was a squad leader and earned a meritorious promotion to Private First Class. At SOI (School of Infantry) he received a Meritorious Mast, and then reported to the Fleet Marine Force (FMF) and went on his first deployment to Okinawa from January to July of 2001 on the gun line for 81mm mortars.

In December 2002, his unit was preparing for a mission to Tajikistan, but the mission went to an Army unit, so his unit prepared for a QRF mission, to serve as a reaction battalion for the western sector of the U.S. For three months he served with an MP unit, working security jobs on a base. He went to Iraq in 2003 as a corporal. He was planning to leave the battalion after that deployment, but decided to remain, and returned with the battalion to Iraq in 2004.

He said that at first, 1/5 was training to renew its MEU (SOC) (Special Operations Capable) qualification and deploy to Okinawa. He went to school to learn how to rig helos for spy and rappel operations. About a month before they were to leave for Okinawa, they learned that they would go to Okinawa, but only for a short time before deploying to Iraq. The SASO training commenced, where the Marines learned how to deal with Iraqis and attempt to rebuild the country. They learned how to work in an urban environment and to deal with crowds of Iraqi civilians.

"When the rest of the battalion left, in December, I was left behind to get the SASO training back in the States, where we did vehicle checkpoints, stuff of this nature. We taught it to [the] battalion, once we got back to Okinawa."

In Okinawa, the battalion ran training. Each company in 1/5 ran a training station. Weapons Company's station was the mounted vehicle patrols, with a heavy guns accent.

"One company would come to us, we would teach that. We would go to another company, say Alpha Company, who taught dismounted patrols, vehicle checkpoints.

We went to their station the next day. And we'd just bounce from station to station, as companies rotated out of each station, do each individual thing. So we got a broader aspect of the entire SASO-type operation."

The battalion got to Kuwait, "Same heat and everything I remember from the last time." Platoons and squads continued the SASO training there. They also did some fire and movement exercises to sharpen these skills. Then for about a week, they outfitted their Humvees with strap-on armor.

Corporal Silvers was part of the frontal dismount security for the convoy into Iraq.

"We were the third or fourth vehicle from the front of the entire battalion, as we pushed up north, and we were the squad that was tasked with clearing bridges. As we convoyed up, there was a threat of people throwing hand grenades, Molotov cocktails, stuff like that, off the bridges onto oncoming convoys. So what we would do, is we'd push maybe four, five hundred meters in front of the convoy. And as we come to bridges and overpasses, sweep 'em, clear out the bridges. We'd just push up the over ramp, move up around, come on down, and get back on the road."

He said it was like a little Slinky-effect, as the vehicles would race ahead, clear the bridges, and the convoy would catch up with them. They did not find any IEDs or threats on their way north.

In Iraq, they pulled into FOB Mercury (Camp Abu Ghraib). The Army units had pretty much pulled out to the MEK (Camp Fallujah) compound.

"Did a couple of Left-seat rides, where they pretty much said, 'Okay, here's your Area of Operations, here's what you're doing.' The next couple, three days, we were the ones doing the operation but the Army guys were riding with us."

The Army left and the Marines took over the area, mainly on mortar mitigation patrols. Silvers said that it had been pretty bad when they first got to the camp, with seven or eight rockets hitting just outside the compound walls in the first few nights. Later on, during some of the sweeps, he saw guys firing rockets, but they were on the other side of canals, which made it difficult to get to the insurgents before they left the firing sites.

Often, the insurgents fired rockets or mortars from built-up civilian areas, which made it difficult to try to respond with artillery fire from Camp Fallujah. The battalion had its Marines spread out on these patrols to make it more difficult for the insurgents to find areas to fire from. Silvers said that there were some nights he saw insurgents getting set up, ready to fire rockets, but when they spotted the Marines, they would take off. This prevented many rockets from being fired at the Marines.

Silvers also said that sometimes during the night, people would shoot up red or white pop-up flares. He wasn't sure if this was some sort of signal plan to alert the insurgents about Marine activity in an area. He said, "We'll be pulling in front of a house, and the house will flicker its lights off like five or six times. It won't be a power surge, because you could tell." He heard reports from other Marines in the battalions about lights flicking on and off at houses. Sometimes it would just be quiet after this. Other times, Marines would see people running from fields, and other times, rockets would get fired. He said that it was weird, having local people saying that they are helping you, when sometimes they are signaling the enemy using their house lights.

Silvers said that things had changed recently. He told me about some ICDC who captured three suspected terrorists, and said that if the Marines had not been there with them, the ICDC would have probably beat the terrorists to a pulp.

Then things happened in Fallujah. Corporal Silvers said that when they heard that they were going to go in and take down a city, he was excited about it. But the first thing he got stuck on was a checkpoint about two clicks outside of the city. For about three days they stopped cars, took no contact, but could hear the shooting going on inside of the city. He wanted to be there in the middle of it. Then after another three days, Red Cloud, another platoon in Weapons Company, was pushing into the city, and Silver's platoon was needed to move up and hold their line. They moved into the position, set up security, and sent Marines onto a rooftop of a building. Some rockets hit in front of their position, but there were no firefights.

Red Cloud continued into the city and started getting shot at. So Silver's four-vehicle section shot right down the main highway into what he called "The Hell's Gate." Red Cloud had three disabled vehicles by this time. "I had to leave two of my guys of a six-man team, on a rooftop, to get snipers that could shoot. I got four guys, out there running around, in the streets."

Silvers himself was running around, telling machine-gun vehicles which way to shoot. Red Cloud was there getting its trucks shot at:

"You could hear this explosion, and you look behind you, and you see a tank main gun just firing down. Pick up your radio, just listen, 'Yeah, that vehicle's gone now!' All right, they're doing their job. And we pull up, we pushed a little bit further, cover their movement out. As we push out, just, people running, and then right behind these people, are other people with weapons, started pointing them back at us. So we just sit there yelling, 'Take them out! Take them out!' And had guys hiding behind things. My SAW gunner got shot in the foot three days later, got taken out of the fight. Him and my designated marksman in my squad, they're laying down prone almost like in the middle of the road. And these two guys come out, with one AK and one RPG. Getting ready to gun 'em up right there in the middle of the street. All I hear is b-d-d-d-d-d-d-ap! I look over my shoulder, my SAW gunner, he's lookin' up, thumbs up. 'All right! Good to go!' Cut 'em in half. I'm like, all right, that's good."

Silvers said that the other two guys in the squad weren't too happy, as they had not been able to shoot the insurgents.

They asked him, "You get some?"

Silvers replied, "Yeah, we did."

"Why didn't you get us off the roof?"

"I tried, just kinda pushed too fast." Silvers added, "To this day, they still give me crap about it."

A few days later they pushed further into the city. Corporal Silvers was at the bottom of the building, a sort of car shop, and he was eating chow. He heard a loud explosion, heard shrapnel landing on top of the building. A mortar round had taken a direct hit on a Humvee in an alleyway. Silvers saw the Humvee on fire, and three of his friends running out of it. Sergeant Ball was bleeding from his head. Quiles was coming over, half in shell shock, and Silvers had him sit down and told some Marines to keep him calm and give him some water. Silvers went up onto the roof to try to see where the mortars had come from. As soon as he got there, they started taking small arms fire from many directions to the north. He said that as soon as he engaged one building, they took fire from another building.

Silvers went back down to the ground, and asked if the Marines had gotten the ammo off the burning Humvee. The Marines there said that they had, and Silvers asked what exactly they had taken out. When he heard the list of items, he said, "'Oh, God!' There was still two cans of .50 cal API (armor piercing), two cans of basic .50 cal, a couple of cans of Mark 19 ammo. And so I told my guys, 'Get away from there!' Told my guys on the roof, push over more. And then right as that's happening, all these secondary explosions, in this truck [Humvee] are going off. I hear that my SAW gunner got shot in the foot. One of the bullets that was shot went through a brick and hit him in the foot, next to his big toe. Clean off!"

Corporal Silvers was still on the ground floor, trying to get cover for all of the Marines there. He had no guys on the roof providing suppressive fire, since he was using these three Marines to move his wounded Marine to cover so that they could bandage him up. He said things were getting hairy quick. The next thing he heard was a Mark 19 round go off. When it went off and hit the wall, he said to himself that he needed to get some cover right away.

He stayed on the radio, and got a hold of Red Five, Sergeant Rinehart. When Rinehart got there, he was able to get the wounded Marine off the roof. The secondary explosions on the Humvee had died down. After they got the wounded Marines medevacked, they then moved to a new position at another building. This new position was known as the Tower, a little concrete shack on top of another building that looked across ASR (Alternate Supply Route) Michigan. "That is where we took the most contact."

Bravo Company was laid out along their left flank. Silvers' squad was helping Bravo by providing some cross fire. Then, "The loudest sound I'll ever hear in my life, is two 240 Golfs, inside an 8 by 12 room, going off at the same time. I think my ears will probably still bleed for the rest of my life!"

Silvers was the senior man up in the Tower, letting Weapons Company know what was going on via radio. In addition to the 240 Golfs, he had a Javelin missile gunner, and several AT4s. Each day when they would take incoming shots, they would determine the origin of the shots, and engage these targets.

"And this one day, we kept getting engaged from this one building. We couldn't do anything. We kept getting engaged, we knew we were getting engaged, see him, and he kept running behind cover."

Silvers asked Sergeant Rinehart if they could put a Javelin into the building, and when he replied yes, Corporal Silvers gave his Javelin gunner the okay to fire an $80,000 missile into the building. They laid down suppressive fires, had the gunner aim and take his shot. It was right on target, and the building burned for about three hours. Silvers was then sure that the insurgents would not be able to go back into that building again.

The next day, they had contact from another building, so they put two AT4s into that building.

About two or three weeks after getting into Fallujah, PSYOPS began. Army PSYOPS personnel came in and broadcast different messages on their loudspeakers. Eventually, the word came down that they were authorized to try to coax the insurgents into fighting.

"So we're sitting out there, it's like 21, 2200 at night, it's dark out, and we hear the PSYOPS guys start playing their Arabic message. And then right after that, you hear AC/DC's *Hell's Bells*! All night long, playing rock and roll."

He said that the insurgents started shooting at them, and because it was nighttime the Marines could see their muzzle flashes and know where they were.

"They fire at us and we get out there and just start mowing things down. And then Spectre, our AC-130 gunship, he came on station, about 23, 2400. And we're sitting out there saying, 'We got engaged from this building right here, this building right here!'

"And he says 'Roger!' After he gets on the radio, 'Got your Pack 2 [an infrared laser night sight, mounted onto an M16 rifle or rifle with a mounting rail] on you?' 'Yes sir.' He's like, 'Light that building up!'

"So I sit there and I put a Pack 2 laser on the building, with a flood on it, and as soon as I did that, the LT (Laser targeting), he hits it with a really powerful IR beam. Spectre can see. He hits it with echo. You hear 'Thunk!' What's that? And then kfuuuoooom! Just the power surround when an AC-130 gunship hits a building."

"Then I hear, 'Is that the right building?' No! No! No! You go two buildings left. And he's like, 'Roger!' And the next thing you know, he puts a barrage, about 15 howitzer rounds into this building. Which, we didn't take any more fire from that building!"

Then Silvers and his squad saw armed men running from the building. The Marines engaged these insurgents as they ran across the street. Then for the next five days, things were quiet in their sector. As Silvers said, "Nobody really wanted to play anymore. Just almost leveled an entire city block in a three-day period of time. It was fun, that's about all I can say, it was fun."

"We had a sniper, shooting at us from a mosque tower [minaret]. Mosque tower probably 950 to 1,000 meters away. And it was high up. We were taking contact from that building the entire time. It was just one sniper, or two snipers, whatever. This guy was good. He got us, he could shoot from that mosque tower, I mean that far away. He put a pattern the size of a man's chest through a window in very quick succession. You just hear, 'Kow! Kow! Kow! Kow!', and 'Psssh! Psssh! Psssh! Psssh!' You just hear the rocks behind your head, blowing off, being shot through the window. And we had it (the window) cardboarded off, there was no silhouette, nothing like that. He was firing through (the cardboard). So finally I got this idea, I'm gonna start marking this guy. So I marked all the holes, couldn't tell exactly where he was coming from at the very beginning. So I said, here's what we're gonna do. Mark these holes, find out what's going on."

"So, one shot went through. It came through the cardboard, hit the back wall. All right. So I mark that one number one, marking number one on the cardboard. We did that four or five times. Then finally I said all right, here's what we're going to do. I got my laser bore, which is a laser, goes outside the barrel of the M16, 240 Golf, or .50 cal. To bore sight means means the optics or sights you have on it, quickly, and without having to actually shoot. Just put it on the end of the barrel, adjust the sights.

"Well, what I did is I took that tactical laser, I stuck the laser bore sight in the wall, and pointed it at that hole. Had the one hole (in the wall), pointed it at the one hole (in the cardboard). I did that and I did the smoke and lasers trick. Where you just take a drag off a cigarette, blow it onto the path of the laser. We follow the path of the laser with our eyeballs and see it goes to that mosque. Next time we took sniper fire, we had our eyeballs directly on that mosque it was coming from. Couldn't see anything.

"I believe it was 3/4. They pulled into the city, on the northeastern side, and we were watching them take sniper fire. So we watched our (mosque) tower, and that gave him away. Him shooting from the side like that. Gave him away. We could see that report, we could see the muzzle smoke and stuff like that.

"That day we put three tank main gun rounds and a Javelin missile into that mosque. Just so we would not take any more sniper fire."

At this point, I told Corporal Silvers that I had talked to the gunner of the tank, and the gunner was real excited about taking the minaret down. So I asked Silvers to describe what it looked like when the tower went down.

Corporal Silvers responded: "Let's just say, I've seen blasts of nuclear missiles, but when he put that first shot into the top, the second shot right in the middle of the tower. When he put that second shot in the middle of the tower, you could just see it. You saw it when it hit, the dust, around it, as the blast carried upwards, which went around, and then right in that hole that was earlier shot, right out, like a big mushroom. I was like, this is great! He's [the sniper] not gonna be there anymore!

"Never got shot from that tower any more. Just huge, massive chunks of this mosque missing." Silvers added that now they didn't have to listen to the loudspeakers from this particular mosque either. He also said that the Marine tanks on the ground were doing spectacular work for them, too. Marines would ask them to knock down walls that were hiding insurgents, and the tanks would take down the walls with a main gun round.

Corporal Silvers said that his squad next pushed further west into Fallujah, into a place that they called "The Hole." The actual hole was a hole about eight inches in diameter in a wall, and through it the Marines could observe people with weapons moving across an alleyway. But this was during the ceasefire and they were unable to engage unless they were fired on. Then, it was really close to when they were pulling out of the city.

"And these guys start putting out roadblocks across the roads. Okay, something's going on. We call it in. These guys have a roadblock going on. There's three guys out there, putting this road block up. And I'm sitting at the hole, looking through, talking on the radio. Hindsight being 20/20, I would have done what I did a little bit differently now."

Silvers had his one M16 with a scope on it. The three insurgents on the roadblock were over 550 meters away, down the alleyway.

"I get cleared to engage. I shoulda put my whole team up, got 'em all on line, and had everybody open up on that alley. But, I didn't. I got kinda greedy. Pulled up, got the perfect lead for 500 meters out. Fire! Aim. Center mass. Didn't calculate for windage. Hit the guy right in the shoulder. The other two guys they take off, running. [I] fire two shots at them as they're running away. We're doing nothing. I see the other guy staying there, he's running back to the right. Fire at him again. He's on the run, I miss him again. So, four shots fired, one hit made."

Silvers said that he felt that he had wasted an opportunity by shooting alone at the roadblock trio. But he was happy with the scope on his rifle, a Leupold.

After the shooting at the roadblock, the ceasefire resumed. An Iraqi force was brought in to take over security for Fallujah. The battalion returned to Camp Fallujah, the companies went back to operations in the area. Weapons Company returned to working out of Camp Abu Ghraib, now conducting mortar mitigation, foot patrols, and raids.

I asked Corporal Silver to talk about his time in Iraq during 2003.

"Last year, I would have to say, was a lot worse living conditions, MREs get old after a month and a half. And, a lot dirtier. But, the fighting wasn't necessarily easier, as it was less restrictive. First time over here, anybody wearing an Iraqi uniform was declared hostile. This war, we're over here, we don't know if the guy across the street crossing his arms with the half-smirk on his face is the bad guy, or the guy sittin' there waving, saying, 'Hello, mister!' is the guy. We don't know who the real bad guy is, you can't tell."

Silvers said that when they actually catch a guy shooting an RPG, he would say that he only shot one round!

In 2003 he was involved in an 18-hour firefight in Baghdad. He said that they rolled into an ambush there; it was like walking into a *Star Wars* movie with all of the tracer rounds. They finally fought their way to the presidential palace and cleared it. They also operated with Special Forces guys. Now in 2004, Silvers said that when they killed enemy, they had to truck the bodies back to camps. In 2003, the Marines would engage and kill the enemy, and keep moving through an area. In 2004 there was now interaction with the people in villages. He said that last year the enemy would shoot and want to fight while this year, the enemy shoots and runs. Another difference was that in 2003, there was NBC (nuclear, biological and chemical) prep, and wearing MOPP (mission-oriented protective posture) gear, "suits and boots," all the way up to Baghdad. This year the Marines simply wore their new desert MARPAT (Marine pattern) camouflage uniforms.

Almost all of his team, except for one Marine, Lance Corporal Johnson, were new to Iraq and combat. Lance Corporal McQueen (married with kids) was now the SAW gunner. Lance Corporal Suggs was evacuated back to the States after having his toe blown off. Lance Corporal Ortega started as a driver and was now an ACOG shooter. Lance Corporal Kingsley came from Alpha Company when they were in Okinawa. Corporal Silvers said that it was a pretty green squad.

Corporal Silvers praised the new ACOG (Advanced Combat Optical Gunsight) that many of the Marines in the division now had for their rifles. I then asked Corporal Silvers to describe his M16A4's sight. "I got here, the scope, the optic system on it, is a Leupold Variex Two. It's a three power by, three to nine power scope. It's just a good scope, it's actually a deer hunting scope, that my grandfather gave to me." His grandfather had willed him the scope and other weaponry when he died a few years ago. There was a note inside the scope's box that said for Corporal Silvers to take the scope with him if he went back to war. Silvers had the scope mounted onto his rifle. "I've gotten some confirms with it." He then pointed out the Pack 2 laser mounted on the rail of the rifle. He also had a private purchased three-point tactical sling on the weapon. He explained how some Marines mounted different accessories on the Rail Interface System of the rifles.

At this point in his tour, he was taking each day as it came. When he hears about contact, he goes to it. He looked forward to returning home when this tour was complete.

* * *

Lance Corporal Angel Quiles

Javelin Gunner & Scout (Wolf 2), Little Wolf, Weapons Company, 1/5

Lance Corporal Quiles said that the Marine Corps has changed him a lot, made him a man. He has learned leadership, enjoyed the comradery, and courage. In OIF1 he was also a driver and Javelin gunner, but never fired the missile in Iraq then.

Lance Corporal Quiles recollected one firefight during OIF1 when the Weapons Company Marines were approaching Saddam's palace. They were taking fire everywhere, shots going by his head, and missiles going everywhere. They were in Humvees. The last Humvee in the column was stopped and they could see someone getting ready to take a shot at them with an RPG.

"They called my vehicle and asked if anybody got a grenade. I had two on me, me being a Marine, I volunteered to go and run across the street while all these shots were flying, and try to blow up this guy on the roof. I run across one block and I cross another block. All of a sudden, all of my guys, they're looking at me like, 'What is this guy doin'?' They spot the enemy on top of the roof. And I throw the grenade, and it blew up right over his head. When it blew up over his head, everbody said that it was good. I ran back, and everything was good. At wartime, you're not a regular person. You have it in your head to do the unexplainable, unexpectable, just anything, 'cause you're at a whole different mindset." He credits the Marine Corps with giving him the courage to do almost anything.

I asked him how many times he had gotten to fire a Javelin missile in OIF2. He answered, "I got to shoot it once, in Fallujah, that was the time I got to shoot it. And it was a thrill, because not many Javelin gunners got to fire. To train, in the training way, it's like a big computer, and it's completely different than the real, actual, when you are about to fire. When you are about to take a shot, the thrill of actually firing, you know, a round, that's like $86,000, it's a big thrill. I got to shoot it, and actually hit, actually destroy my enemy."

Quiles said that the Javelin is a great weapon. It is designed to hit tanks and other armored vehicles by following the heat signature. For his shot in Fallujah, he said, "It was a heat signature where a sniper was shooting at us. And, it picked up the little heat signature. A lot of people wanted to see what a Javelin could do to a house and a person in there. It was a pretty big explosion."

They were in a tower and getting heavy sniper fire. One of the Marines in the tower saw a muzzle flash from the sniper's weapon.

Quiles said, "I brought the [Javelin] crew over there. I sighted in, saw that there was a heat signature. Called it in. And, there was sniper fire there. My lieutenant told me to take the Javelin shot, 'cause we couldn't shoot it with any TOWs because there were too many wires. (The TOW is a wire-guided missile). So I took the shot. There was a person in there and caches that was blown up. I guess I got like two for one!"

He explained that the Javelin locks onto the target, the operator then releases the trigger and the missile goes on its own. He estimated that it was about 200 yards to the house. He said that the Marines around him all got riled up and more motivated now that a sniper was gone. He still had two more missiles that he could get ready to fire.

I then asked him to review events from the time he arrived in Iraq this year. He said that they did a lot of physical training to get used to the heat. The enemy out here was trying to kill the Marines, and Quiles said that the training was "for real." He continued to credit the tough training that the Marine Corps has given him to prepare him and the other Marines in his company for what they face. "I can honestly say that everybody was ready for the fight, and we did real good."

When his section first went into Fallujah (April 2004), they had a blocking position along Route Michigan. He said that he realized that the enemy was right over that line. As they entered deeper into the city, he expected to be doing scouting work. He had a scope on his M16 that he figured he would use to look for snipers. He did not think that he would get the opportunity to fire the Javelin.

On April 8 he was wounded by a mortar round. He was the only one in a Humvee when the round hit the vehicle, and he was pulled out with some minor shrapnel wounds to his wrist. He said that he guessed that God had a blanket over him that day.

Since leaving Fallujah, he and his squad have been on patrols looking for IEDs, and mortar pits, and general presence patrols around Karmah.

Lance Corporal Quiles said that his two tours in Iraq have been completely different.

"Last year it was drive up, destroy the enemy, and take off. We were never in one spot for one time." He said that the longest they spent anywhere in 2003 was about three days. "We'd just keep on destroying the enemy, move north." In 2004 they were staying in areas longer, knowing that there was an enemy out there ready to try to destroy them. He felt more secure last year; this year it seemed that they were fighting more of the time.

He and the Marines he worked with were not relaxing until they get back home to Camp Pendleton. "I still have to have that mindset. The enemy wants us to slip up."

* * *

Sergeant Michael Thomas Vollmer

Section Leader, Crazy Horse, 2nd Counter-Mech Platoon, Weapons Company, 1/5

Sergeant Vollmer joined the Marine Corps in January 1998. After recruit training, he went through Security Forces school, and served two years in Bangor, Washington. He then joined Echo Company, 2/8 at Camp LeJeune, and did a Mediterranean Float with the

24th MEU. He reenlisted October 1, 2001, right after the September 11 attacks. He then transferred to 1/5 in Camp Pendleton, California and began a workup to go to Tajikistan, but that mission was canceled. Plans for the battalion kept changing, and training continued for a possible deployment somewhere during 2002. In early 2003, he learned that they would be going to Iraq.

"Came over here [Iraq] the first time with Charlie Company. I was with Weapons Platoon, machine guns squad leader." After that tour, he returned to the States, then was transferred to Weapons Company. He said that the situation was similar to the changing plans of the year before. No one seemed to know where they would be going, until they returned from Christmas leave, and learned that 1/5 would be going back to Iraq in 2004.

Sergeant Vollmer said that there was not a whole lot of training to prepare for this year's (2004) deployment, as the time was so short. He estimated that at that time about half of the Marines in his company were leaving the unit, either moving on to other units, or leaving the Corps. They were replaced with young Marines just out of SOI. "What training we did have, is little, but we tried to make it work for this new mission, which was Security and Stability Operations."

He said that once they got to Okinawa, they got a lot of quality SASO preparation. They did lots of training on the Marine camp there, practicing road blocks, reacting to IEDs, patrolling, counter-sniper drills, and making sure that everyone in the battalion was cross trained by learning as many weapons as possible. "I know me and one other of the sergeants, we were teaching the 240 Golf medium machine gun to the whole battalion, for that SASO training."

The mindset was that they were not coming to Iraq for war, but to help the people rebuild their country.

Once they arrived in Kuwait, they got all of their big guns, such as the Mark 19s and .50 cals, that they had sent over from Okinawa. They got their ammo and vehicles, and worked some of the ranges. They moved into Iraq in three or four convoys. Weapons Company was split up during the move. The convoys went without incident. They then drove up to Camp Mercury.

"Within the first couple of nights, that's when we got mortared." The Army was still here, and began to take key Marine leaders out to learn the area. When the Marines started patrolling on their own, nothing much happened at first.

"My platoon was the first platoon to get attacked. We were doin' an escort mission, and we were up in Al Karmah, escorting a civil affairs group. Parked outside a police station, we'd been there about 45 minutes, and then some guys ran out from down the street. Shot a couple RPGs at us, and then ran away. Couldn't catch 'em." Volmer said that this broke the ice for those Marines who had not seen combat before.

Then, Fallujah happened. He said that an IED attack hit Charlie Company. Sergeant Vollmer's platoon was sent to block off the southern part of the city. He said that they got mortared for the first couple of days that they were there. No one was injured, but it was nerve-wracking.

They moved into the city, into a screen line in front of the battalion, along Route Michigan, the east–west route through the city. By their last few days in Fallujah, they were focused on the area called Queens in the south of the city. As they prepped for another push into the city, negotiations concluded when an Iraqi general came in with Iraqi troops to take over security for the city.

They left the city and returned to Camp Abu Ghraib to rest and refit. They began to do two patrols a day, and escorts on every third day. "Escorts, sometimes it's a day off, sometimes it's the busiest days." Until recently, these have been section patrols with six or seven vehicles at a time. 1/5's sector was smaller than it had been before Fallujah. "We've been going out. Meeting and greeting the local people. Giving out pencils, talk with the people, see what they say." So the SASO has resumed.

He has been on patrols where he has heard mortars being fired. When mortars are fired, the Marines try to get to these firing positions, but the shooters pack up the weapons onto the backs of cars and leave as soon as they fire. Sergeant Vollmer has not yet caught up with any of these shooters. "Unless you're right there, it's pretty hard to catch them." He said that they have been finding a lot of IEDs lately. But with a smaller area to patrol, the Marines were more alert to changes alongside roads.

He compared 2003 with 2004: "Last year, was just a straight-up push up from Kuwait straight to Iraq, as fast as we can. There's a couple times we outran our Log [Logistics] Train. We didn't have to worry about IEDs, or snipers, really. If someone shot at us from a building, the whole building got destroyed. We were still friendly to the people, and we just pushed straight to Baghdad, fought, and then we came back. The difference between then and now is, now it's not a fight. We're trying to help these people, and we can't just go shooting. If someone shoots at us one time, we can't just go destroy a block."

He said that Fallujah was the closest they came to last year.

To communicate with the people, he and the Marines had "cheat cards" with common phrases in Arabic. He said that the Marines have picked up a couple of key words. They dealt with the children a lot, with simple words. But the communications barrier was still a barrier.

Sergeant Vollmer said that about 50 percent of the Marines in his squad were here last year in 2003. The senior Marines have provided leadership for the newer ones.

* * *

Corporal Tyler Steven Trenda

TOW Gunner, Crazy Horse, 2nd Counter-Mech Platoon, Weapons Company, 1/5

Corporal Trenda enlisted six months after September 11, 2001. After recruit training and SOI, he joined 1/5. Once with 1/5, he did training for the 31st MEU, but expected to go to Iraq. He was with the battalion for OIF1, and stayed in Iraq until May 2003.

"We went back (to the States), had a quick turnaround 'cause we were gonna deploy again. We were supposed to go back out on the 31st MEU." Many of the senior guys left, and new Marines joined the battalion. The plan was to go on leave, return, then go to Okinawa for a seven-month deployment.

When they got back from leave, he learned at a formation that they would be going to Okinawa for a short time and then back to Iraq. They left from Okinawa on his birthday, March 3, 2004, and traveled to Kuwait. Then, "Been doing operations out there (Kuwait), getting ready to leave" for Iraq.

When they got to Iraq, they began to do mortar mitigation patrols, similar to what the Army had been doing. "We'd work different zones, up around Al Karmah, and south of there. Set up OPs, and try and catch the guys that were shooting the rockets and mortars at us. Actually, I thought we did pretty good, it stopped for a while." Insurgents knew that Marines were out there looking for them. They also did two or three raids before Fallujah. They spent about 27 days in Fallujah before returning here.

"One thing we're doing a lot more now is civil affairs stuff, with the people. Making sure their water's good, electricity, kids and the school, we're doing a lot of that stuff. What we were going to do before." They have handed out soccer balls and pencils to the kids.

They have been doing mortar mitigation patrols near Bravo Company's area. Since returning from Fallujah, Corporal Trenda said that they have been busier. They have also been busy getting ready for the Marines from 3/1 to come in to replace them here.

I asked him to go into detail about what he called the middle of the season, when they were in Fallujah. They first were in Blocking Position 7, at a heavy traffic area in the southern part of the city. They didn't let anyone go in or out of the city. Five days later, they went into the city and set up at another blocking position south of Route Michigan. His company had from the cloverleaf all the way to Route Violet. The line companies (infantry) pushed further into the city, while Weapons Company back-cleared their area.

"When we back-cleared, we went through every shop, every house, every car, every thing. Checkin' for weapons, weapons caches, anything, ammo dumps. It was a detailed search."

Corporal Trenda didn't find any weapons himself, but a buddy of his from 81s Platoon did: "He was in someone's house, kinda lookin' at himself in the mirror. And the mirror was like tilted or something, and he kinda moved it and it fell off and behind it was another room just full of rockets, and AKs, everything."

Trenda said that a lot of the weapons sitting outside the COC (a few yards from the building where we were) were items found in Fallujah. Some of the items were homemade RPG and rocket launchers. He said that it is now the job of the Iraqi forces to capture what was still in Fallujah.

Trenda explained how Weapons Company has used the 81mm mortar platoon. They were not using their mortars, but deploying as dismounted Marines.

"We usually use a 'four and two' package. We use two heavy gun trucks and two high backs with the 81s squads in it. When we get contact, we'll establish a base of fire, and the 81s will dismount and maneuver against them."

Last year Weapons Company Marines were all in hard backs and were anti-armor.

"I think it works better, I hope they keep the dismounts." They began this training when they went to Okinawa. It was during this time that the 81s became part of the mobile teams.

There were lot of veterans from OIF1, about half of the Marines in his platoon. He said that this has been good for the newer Marines, and he wished that he had combat veterans with him when he was here last year.

He said that last year was easier in some ways. They knew who the enemy was, and where he was. It was easier to engage targets. Now, "The terrorist guys blend in with everybody else. The only way you can tell if they're bad is when they're actually shooting at you at the moment." Trenda said that he could see a guy ten times, and still not know if this was an insurgent. It's harder to make the decision on whether or not to shoot.

He noted that most of his two and a half years in the Marine Corps have been pretty wild. Usually when Marines return from a deployment they get some down time. "In two and a half years I've done two combat tours! I'm only 22 years old, I've done a lot more than a lot of people my age have done."

He was proud of what the battalion was now doing, and was ready to go home. At this point, they had about ten more days of operations before they returned home.

* * *

Lance Corporal Fue Lo

Vehicle Commander/Driver, Little Wolf, Weapons Company, 1/5

During OIF1, Lo was in the first units to enter Baghdad. At one point, an RPG round zoomed through the open windows of his Humvee without detonating. During the fighting in Fallujah in 2004, his team dismounted their Humvee's 240 Golf machine gun and moved it onto the rooftop of a building to provide cover for other Marines during the fighting.

Lance Corporal Lo enlisted in 2001. After boot camp and SOI he became an 0351—an anti-tank assault man. He joined 1/5 in January, 2002, where he participated in training to prepare for OIF1. After returning to the States, the battalion went to Okinawa and then returned to Iraq for OIF2.

"I think last year [OIF1], it was all one big movement to contact. It was less patrolling, less security patrols. Last year, definitely more enemy contact. More uniformed soldiers we were up against, we knew who we were fighting."

He spent a lot of time as anti-tank support for the infantry companies. He was involved in the fighting in Baghdad last year. "I was told we were in the first unit, the first Marine unit to go in. I'm not sure about that. Went in there [Baghdad] late one night, actually it was early morning. Went in there, got lost, battalion got separated for a few hours." He said that the enemy was firing from buildings, so the Marines just fired back at them. "I saw RPGs, AKs, I believe some heavy machine guns."

He was in a thin-skinned, heavy machine-gun Humvee.

"Going through Baghdad, took one RPG round through the window that went next to my head. Came through the door, and the next thing you know, out the front windshield. It didn't explode. I think they failed to arm it when they launched it, so that pretty much saved the lives in the truck there."

Lo said that most of the training for the current deployment [OIF2] was on Okinawa, mostly involving SASO, geared to avoiding as much damage as possible. When they got to Iraq, they began SASO, along with motorized anti-mortar patrols. This changed when they got ready to go to Fallujah at the beginning of April 2004.

"Initially we were supposed to be part of the outside cordon, allow no one in, no one out. I believe it was Checkpoint 9, that we did, on Route Mobile, next to Miami."

They were there for about three days. He was with the platoon commander's truck (Humvee), and it went down with engine problems, so Lo was assigned as the vehicle scout for another truck. He was then sent inside Fallujah, and for the first week he was on the roof of a building along Route Michigan. The team dismounted a 240 Golf machine gun from one of the trucks and brought it to the rooftop in order to keep the enemy from crossing the road, and to do counter-sniper ops.

Over the next few days, Weapons Company gradually replaced the Marines from Bravo and Alpha companies along Route Michigan. "From what I was told, they were going back to the COC to get mech'd up in the Amtracs to prepare for the offensive. And as they were doing that, we would replace them along the line."

He said that the only action in this sector was an occasional sniper and some mortar fire. "There was one RPG guy, crossed an alleyway, [I] took a few shots, pretty sure I missed." Lo said that this insurgent was about 400 meters away from him, and Lo did not have a scope on his M16 at the time. (He now had a scope on his rifle.)

During the lull before a possible move into Fallujah, he and the Marines he was with continued to improve their defensive positions. He heard that battalion was preparing a target list for any offensive into the city. The farthest he went into the city was along Routes Violet and Michigan.

With about two hours' notice, the company pulled out of the city, and they set a charge to destroy the wire that they had emplaced, went to the COC, and then to the FOB at Camp Abu Ghraib.

After four days at Abu Ghraib, he resumed the mechanized patrols of the areas.

Normal missions were anti-mortar patrols again, escort for other units, and battalion QRF. They worked to prevent indirect fire, mostly mortars, against Bravo Company. Just the day before this interview, Bravo had an urgent casualty, and half of Lo's platoon went for the medevac. The other half of the platoon searched for the RPG shooter near a mosque, but did not find him.

Lance Corporal Lo said that last year was fast-paced, less routine than this year. They saw the enemy in prepared fighting positions. This year they have learned the area well, and have rarely seen the enemy.

I noted that I had seen some of the advance party Marines from 3/1 in the area this morning, and that this had to make Marines like him happy, as it was a sign that they would soon be going home. Lo noted that all around the camp there were signs that said, "Complacency Kills," and that all of the Marines keep on the alert all the time, even those who were getting ready to go home.

He concluded, "Still in a war zone. You want 100 percent aware of what you're doing."

CHAPTER FOUR

Marine Aviation

Travel by Helo

In the spring of 2004, much of the in-country travel in Iraq for my two-man Field History team required coordination at many levels. Ground convoys to those small camps near Camp Fallujah were easily accessible. But the growing IED threat on Iraqi roads and highways made it necessary to fly by helicopter-lift to camps further away. Once I had the lay of the land at Camp Fallujah, I began to plan for trips to bases and camps throughout the Al Anbar province of Iraq.

Even with the best planning efforts, weather and events often caused plans to change. The two main camps used by Marine helicopter squadrons were located at former Iraqi air bases at Camp Al Taqaddum and Camp Al Assad. Marine helicopter squadrons provided lift for personnel and supplies, as well as air-to-ground combat firepower throughout the province.

In the eastern regions of the province, CH-46 Echo helos from Marine squadron HMM 160 based at Camp Al Taqaddum flew low from camp to camp at night, to minimize attacks from insurgents on the ground. They flew without navigation lights, the crews utilizing night vision goggles to see. Marine Super Cobra attack and Huey helos from HMLA 775 escorted the large CH-46s, and also provided close air support to ground units.

Movement west of Al Assad was conducted day and night on the Marine Corps' heavy-lift platform, the CH-53 Echo Super Stallion. These large craft were much less maneuverable than other Marine helos in use, and even with ASE (Air Survivability Equipment) capabilities, were thought to be more vulnerable to ground fire.

My aviation interviews took place in early May 2004 at Camp Al Taqaddum, and at Camp Al Assad in mid-May. I went from meeting with enlisted mechanics, to squadron commanders and planners at the Marine Air Wing level. Topics ranged from information about repairing the helos to harrowing accounts of taking ground fire and landing badly damaged aircraft after combat over Fallujah during Operation *Vigilant Resolve*. Many of these Marines participated in the invasion of Iraq in 2003.

Hoped-for returns to these commands never materialized due to ever-changing demands on our time and the missions of deployed units.

Camp Fallujah, Thursday April 29, 2004

After evening chow, I checked in at the EFCAT tent about the departure times for a planned helo trip to Al Taqaddum: We'd meet at their tent at 2300, then go to MHG area for a ride to the LZ at Camp Fallujah for the lift.

I packed in my room, got some rest on my cot, then dressed around 2215 and walked to the EFCAT tent to meet up with Majors Dukes of EFCAT and John Piedmont. At the MHG building we got onto a small Nissan bus to ride to the LZ.

We waited at the LZ from about 2345 until a big dust and drizzle storm blew in after midnight. An officer from MHG who had arranged for the flight finally took the bus back to his command post and learned that all flights had been canceled for the night. (The next day we learned that our scheduled helo had to land and wait out the storm for a couple of hours near a lake.)

The next evening officers from EFCAT along with Major Piedmont and me assembled at MHG area at 2115. The bus came at about 2150, and took us to the LZ. We put down our packs by a small cement bunker with sand bags around it. This would be our protection should there be any type of incoming fire (mortar or rocket) while we waited for the helos. It was long, restless night. Hours passed and I didn't really sleep because I kept hearing AC-130 planes in the distance that sounded like approaching CH-46s. Every time we heard engines in the sky, we would get our gear ready to move out to the center of the LZ. The area was a black darkness, with just differing shades of black and grey visible. I could make out lines of trees along what looked like walls, and a hard surface road of some sort running across our front. After several false starts, we got used to the idea that we might not be moving soon and I tried to get some rest. It got chilly, so I unpacked my Goretex field jacket, put it on and sat on my pack for a while. I next lay on my back on the sand, using the pack as a pillow. I joked with Major Piedmont and some of the other members of the EFCAT. I was full of anticipation, nervous about what was to come when and if we got a flight.

Saturday May 1, 2004

Our two birds finally arrived at around 0345. They were Marine CH-46 Echos, flying without lights, and they swooped low over a wall and some trees at the end of the LZ as they made their landing. I worried that this approach might be exposing them to enemy ground fire, but weeks later I learned that just outside this wall was another Marine compound adjacent to Camp Fallujah, and our LZ was visually guarded by Marines in watch towers along the walls. Even with earplugs in, the noise was overwhelming, and the sand stung our faces as we picked up our equipment.

The sky was very dark, and the slowing helos were two deep black, long shapes. As they approached the ground, the rotors formed glowing halos from static electricity and dust. The dust and sand stung our exposed skin, but everyone in the zone had goggles of some sort to protect their eyes.

I said my Act of Contrition prayer prior to boarding. Our group quickly walked in a helo "stick" (a group organized for movement) to the chopper, and the crew chief shouted a question to Major Dukes about our destination. These *were* our birds to TQ (Camp Al Taqaddum)! We clambered up the metal ramp, dumped our gear in the center of the cabin, and stumbled to find seats along the sides of the craft. I was about to leave Camp Fallujah for the second time. It was amazing how little had changed on how we boarded and got settled into a helicopter. But I had many questions running through my head. Would this be an uneventful flight? Would there be any ground fire at us as we flew over hostile areas of Al Anbar?

Once airborne, I could see the lights of the city of Fallujah nearby, and also lights of homes and villages that we flew over. We did not fly very high, and cars and yards of homes were very close below us.

I was relieved that the actual helo ride to TQ was only about 20 minutes on this night. At TQ, the helos touched down onto a long concrete runway, then taxied towards a large cement hangar that served as a makeshift passenger terminal. Inside the hangar was well lit. We waited there about 20 minutes for a truck to take us to the billeting area.

HMM (Marine Medium Helicopter Squadron) 160

After sitting in on a meeting at the FSSG (Force Service Support Group) headquarters, Major Piedmont and I walked to the HMM 160 (CH-46E squadron) headquarters building. This building was within sight of the FSSG headquarters, adjacent to a helo runway. The Marines at the helo squadron were ready for us and took us to meet the squadron operations officer, Major Kevin Lee. Piedmont and I split up to separate areas for our interview sessions.

* * *

Major Kevin John Lee

Squadron Operations Officer, HMM 160

This officer had flown for the president of the United States as a pilot for HMX 1. On meeting me, he seemed to know a lot of my background as a high school teacher. It turned out that he had attended the same high school where I was then teaching, and his mother was a library volunteer there! He gave a clear overview of the missions of his squadron in providing transportation support and casualty evacuation for the MEF.

After the usual introductions Major Lee asked me if I was from the Philadelphia area. I said yes, and he then asked if I taught school near Philadelphia. I again replied yes and wondered how this guy could guess this info. The Philly part is easy—my fast-paced accent was a sure giveaway, but my job as a teacher?

Then he asked if I taught at Lansdale Catholic High School. What?

It turns out that Major Lee graduated from Lansdale Catholic in 1986 (a few years before I began teaching history there), and his mother was a volunteer in the school library. When I got my orders in March 2004, she wrote her son and asked that he be nice to "Mr. Kelly" should he meet me when I was in Iraq. What were the odds? We had a good laugh over this. I had a great interview with him, and he set me up with a series of interviews with Marines in the squadron for Sunday.

Major Lee described his early years in the Marine Corps, when he got his commission and his helo pilot wings. He was currently a CH-46 pilot and the operations officer for his squadron. He had served with HMX 1 for four and a half years. This squadron provides helo transportation for the president of the United States. (When the president is on board that aircraft becomes "Marine One.") He served in OIF1 with the 15th MEU as their air officer. He joined HMM 160 for this deployment.

"160 has a very good base of personnel who served in OIF1."

The squadron was organized as sections for current operations. Smaller flight profiles were used for day-to-day operations.

"We came over here separated from aircraft, our equipment. They [the helos] came over on the *Bellatrix*, a DOD [Department of Defense] roll-on, roll-off contract boat. We got our planes [in Kuwait], put them back together, and started training with them.

"The squadron concentrated on NVG (night vision goggles) operations, test firing our .50 cals, and getting our ASE gear working. On arrival in TQ, the squadron pilots flew in the back of Army UH-60s, and the others flew their CH-46s into Baghdad and Fallujah. More squadron training with NVG training continued to get them used to the flight environment in Iraq. The squadron began its mission on the 18th of March.

"A lot of what we did for the first week… was moving folks to different areas of the theater," Major Lee said. This was to get the commanders in a position of better familiarity with the area.

They were taking over missions for two different types of Army units: Transport and also casualty evacuation. He explained the difference between Army medevac and Marine Corps CASEVAC (casualty evacuation). The Marine Corps will go to the man and fight to get him. "The Army will take someone from a level 2 to level 3 facility." The Marines will work to get the wounded Marine in the "Golden Hour" to medical treatment. They run 24-hour CASEVAC operations as well as a lot of combat resupply for the Marines in the AO. This brings supplies to the Marine outposts in the thick of things.

"We thought about how are we gonna service the guys on the ground with crews that are properly rested." They ran 24-hour coverage with six crews and six aircraft. Pilots were on a 14-hour on, 10-hour off schedule. There were day teams and night teams. There was time for dinner and resting, and there's not much else for the crews to do.

"The main threat [to aviation] over here are the man-packed missiles." During flight ops there was often a significant amount of small-arms fire, RPG fire, and some SA (surface-to-air) missile fire at the helos. "We knew that we would encounter this type of threat… most guys encounter some kind of small-arms fire during most flights, along with a significant number of RPGs fired at the aircraft." There was also one documented SA16 missile fired at one of the aircraft in the time here so far. That was defeated by the ASE systems on the aircraft.

Major Lee praised the work done by his maintenance Marines in the harsh Iraqi environment. "We have not had any significant maintenance problems while we are here… The planes are doing great. The Phrogs [nickname for the CH-46 Echos] keep on flying."

The squadron preferred to fly at night. Daytime flights were needed for CASEVAC, but the training concentrated on night flight.

In his opinion, the assault support provided by the CH-46s and CH-53s has been great. The 46 kept on flying in direct support of the Marines on the ground. Before we left the CP, he gave me a time to return the next morning when he would have several Marines in the squadron ready for interviews.

Interview over, we went outside for a picture of the two of us on the flight line; Major Piedmont did the honors with my camera. Major Lee sent a copy of this digital photo to his mother, and it soon wound up on the Lansdale Catholic High School's web site and in the school paper. Major Piedmont and I then walked to the chow hall together.

* * *

Warrant Officer Thomas Ray Smith
Avionics and Ordnance Officer, HMM 160

Warrant Officer Smith served during Operation Desert Storm, *but was deployed to the Philippines. In addition to overseeing the avionics and ordnance for this squadron, he also served on helo flights as an aerial observer and gunner. He spoke highly of the young Marines he supervised who kept the "birds'" weapons and flares operational on a 24-hour basis.*

"Gunner" Smith has been in the Marine Corps for 15½ years. He was a corporal during Operation *Desert Storm*, and served with the unit's current commanding officer (Lieutenant Colonel Coffman), but was deployed to the Philippines during that conflict. One of the big threats to the helos now here were the surface-to-air missiles in the hands of insurgents. The Marine Corps anticipated this and installed ASE on its helos.

Smith was the avionics and ordnance officer in charge for the squadron. He maintains this equipment, and has seen it save one of the aircraft recently.

"Gunner" (the nickname given to Marine warrant officers) Smith also serves on flights as an aerial observer and gunner for the left side of the helo, and assists the crew chief of the bird to prepare for flights. "I can't believe how well we've maintained our weapons systems.

"The majority of my Marines have been in the Marine Corps only three and a half years. In the avionics specifically I got 14 Marines working underneath me and in the ordnance I have seven total. My avionics Marines have been the busiest so far besides the aircrews flying the missions. They're responsible for everything electrical on the aircraft. My ordnance guys are constantly maintaining the rounds and weapons systems, including the guns and flares."

Gunner Smith said that so far the weather and dust haven't been too much of a factor, but he was anticipating that as the weather heated up, it would create challenges for his Marines. "From past experiences out here, the heat really starts to play a major factor [with the radios and electronics systems]. But so far the dust hasn't been too bad.

"With current operations we are on 24-hour operations. We are tasked with having six birds ready to launch at any time, so we really have not been able to get in other training. Right now we are trying to figure out some way of getting each Marine a day off every now and then to relax."

In addition to supervising his Marines, he said, "Since getting here in March, I have been on a flight schedule every day. There was a period of about seven days when I didn't fly a mission, but every [other] day so far I have flown a mission. I just went on a mission this morning where we picked up four Army soldiers injured in a Humvee accident.

"My job as the aerial observer is to assist the crew chief to prep the aircraft for the mission, and make sure the aircraft is ready for flight. Once we're airborne my responsibility is the left hand side of the aircraft, to observe for any ground fire."

His memorable moments have been a couple of CASEVAC missions. One was north of Fallujah where he helped to evacuate a reporter who had received two wounds to the head. "We were able to fly him in to the nearby MEK where he got immediate treatment, before he was sent on to Baghdad, which so far we've heard he survived. From what I understand, he was in a convoy following the commandant's [Marine General Hagee's] visit and the vehicle that he was in missed a turn."

Only twice in the air has Smith had any incidents of receiving fire at the aircraft he was in: Once a Cobra helo that was accompanying his helo was shot at with an RPG round and another time an RPG round narrowly missed his helo.

(Note: RPGs are anti-tank rockets, designed to fire at ground targets, but one practice favored by insurgents here in Iraq was to shoot several RPG rounds into the air at helos and hope for a lucky hit. I would later interview a Cobra pilot whose rotors "thunked" when an RPG round hit them but did not detonate.)

He also said that after years of working with the ASE systems in training situations, you would never really know how they would work in real-world situations. It was rewarding for him to see them work so well here.

Warrant Officer Smith finished by saying, "The biggest thing that amazes me is the way that the Marines have been able to maintain the working hours that they have, maintaining the aircraft to be able to fly 24 hours a day, continuously, non-stop since the beginning of March. We talk about Marines being able to step up, and these kids just keep going and going without any complaints at all. It's just amazing."

* * *

Lieutenant Colonel David William Coffman
Commanding Officer, HMM 160

Coffman said, "Ain't it good to be us," to describe how the Marines in his squadron were prepared to conduct operations since arrival in Iraq in March 2004. He outlined how his Marines prepared the squadron's 12 helos for transit to Iraq, and how they readied them for flight once they arrived in Kuwait prior to flying into Iraq. Their main mission is casualty evacuation, and the squadron had run seven days a week, round-the-clock flight operations since the start of April.

My final interview at HMM 160 was with the commanding officer, Lieutenant Colonel David Coffman. He was commissioned after graduating from college under the ROTC program. A 19-year veteran and CH-46 pilot, he described his duties here in Iraq as "a cheerleader and coach" for his Marines. He said that they are good people who do their jobs, and half of them are OIF1 veterans. He noted, "I am so proud of my Marines and sailors."

On his return from OIF1 in 2003, he began to prepare the squadron for a return to MEU Special Operations training. (He assumed command of HMM 160 in August 2003.) However, when word came to him that the squadron would return to Iraq for OIF2, deployment planning got fast and furious from December into January 2004. His Marines worked to get their 12 aircraft ready to transport overseas by ship. With a 35 percent personnel turnover, additional personnel came from Group,

MAW, and Headquarters Marine Corps. They trained at Indian Springs, Nevada, and then at exercise Desert Talon in Yuma, Arizona.

Lieutenant Colonel Coffman explained the squadron's transportation of its helos to San Diego, California, where they were covered in shrink-wrap plastic to protect them from the elements on the move to Iraq by ship. Some squadron Marines traveled with the "planes" on board the ships, while the majority of the Marines moved into Kuwait on U.S. Air Force transport planes.

The squadron spent two weeks in Kuwait reassembling the helos and getting them ready to fly. Ground equipment moved to Camp Al Taqaddum by overland convoy in March 2004. Once in Iraq, HMM 160 had a one-week turnover with the 82nd Airborne with helo ride-alongs. "They [the Army] did a great job on these ride-alongs.

"During the end of the turnover period, we began to pick up missions to support IMEF. The 19th of March [2004] was the day that Lieutenant General [James] Conway, the MEF CG [commanding general], showed up in theater and we took over the job as primary movers of the MEF CG, the other senior officers, and the FSSG. We moved him to his headquarters in [Camp] Fallujah and we use that date to mark kinda the start point of our support of the MEF for OIF2 missions.

"We then expected to pick up the mission of casualty evacuation as our primary mission as opposed to transporting senior staff. About the 29th or 30th [of March] we were into CASEVAC work. It's been about four weeks plus now that we have been into our current mission [24-hour CASEVAC and on-call missions]."

He described the extensive transition period as a challenge, and was sure that the after-action reports would examine this in detail. Moving a MEF halfway around the world and having a seamless transition with the Army was a challenge. "It was a challenge for the senior leadership to keep the Marines focused on the goal [of taking over full operations in Iraq]."

He said that his preparations enabled him to get his Marines together and say, "Ain't it good to be us!" The meaning was that the Marines had the right training, right equipment, and right attitude for the missions they now faced. He said that he expected that the other Marines in Iraq (his ground counterparts) felt the same way—that they were here to do a job that they were ready to do.

The main mission of his squadron was casualty evacuation, on a 24/7 schedule since the beginning of April 2004. As for planning and equipment, Coffman said, "You never have enough. Take a guess, do the best you can with it." The pace of operations was now wearing on his flyers, and there was some cumulative fatigue. "We have had over 230-something consecutive on-time launches since March 19, and over 100 casualty evacuation missions [with over 200 urgent/priority missions]." He spoke of the "Golden Hour" during a medical evacuation, the critical time to get a wounded Marine to medical care and the role that his squadron plays in making this happen.

"No one, I don't think, including all the way up to the president, from what I've heard, expected business to be this heavy. And like I said, we're not happy with that, but boy, are we proud that we were ready to do it when it happened."

The threat environment continued to be hostile. "There have been some bullet hits from the ground on the birds (helos), but there has been no major damage. Our defensive gear [ASE] works well against man-packed SAs. We understand the threat and honor it, but are not afraid of it."

Some of the helos' .50 caliber guns have hit enemy on the ground. All squadron missions were escorted by Cobra helos from HMLA 775. In the early days of the "surge" (April 2004) they were getting shot at quite frequently. They have seen man-packed shoulder-launched weapons guided by infrared, looking for the engines, unguided RPG rounds, small-arms fire from AK 47s as well as light antiaircraft artillery fire. None of his aircraft had yet been hit by the "big stuff," but they have been hit by small-arms fire. "That's why we're here." The helos do have armor plating and guns to defend themselves, as well as flying with their Cobra escorts.

He said that the CASEVAC mission was bittersweet for his Marines, since they know that their efforts help to save wounded Marines and soldiers by getting them to proper medical care.

Lieutenant Colonel Coffman noted that the heat and dust are not liked by the helos. The aircraft can carry less gas, and the casualty evacuations cannot carry as big a load. He was also concerned about the wear and tear on his Marines, and he and his staff worked constantly to ensure that their Marines' quarters have working air conditioning, access to television, and rest. They also ensured that the Marines get hot chow regularly.

"I am so proud of my Marines and sailors. We have one hundred percent mission accomplishment, the Marines have met their goals. You're not going to beat us!"

Lieutenant Colonel Coffman in conclusion: "I am thankful, I feel like the luckiest guy on earth. I have no doubt that we are the envy of all Marine aviation. We are here in place, doing everything that we've worked on doing and trained to do."

* * *

Al Assad, Sunday May 16, 2004

During my two weeks back at Camp Fallujah after the visit to Al Taqaddum, I visited many of the commands working out of this camp and interviewed scores of Marines, sailors, and one Army soldier. I also made plans to travel to Camp Al Assad to conduct interviews with Marines in the helicopter squadrons there. My point of contact was a member of the "Fusion" team, Major Casey Travers. He made the arrangements for Major Piedmont and me on where we'd stay, and which units we'd meet. I worked on my end to get the travel requests processed for the flight there.

Today I got a message from Major Travers that he had relayed our historical interview info via SIPRNET to the commands up there, and asked what our travel plans were. I returned the email thanking him for his help (especially when he included the outline I had attached to the email explaining our work), and said that we would finalize things today once MHG had verified our flight times. He notified me that at least three commands were interested in field history interviews.

I packed up my gear and went to MHG building at 2100 for a flight to Al Assad. At the LZ several helos landed and took off for other destinations. Each time a helo came in, the LZ would spring to life as the large dark shapes swooped in and blasted us with sand. Then it would return to complete silence and darkness when each bird lifted off. I alternated between standing and laying down on the sand, using my pack as a pillow. Our birds finally arrived around 0120 on Monday morning and then made stops in TQ and Hurricane Point (at Ramadi) before getting in to Al Assad at about 0220 on Monday morning.

Once the helo landed at Al Assad, Major Piedmont and I packed our gear and ourselves onto a small bus on the flight line that then drove about a half mile to a temporary office building used as a transportation center. This area was fully lit up with large lights outside the building, something that we were not used to seeing at Camp Fallujah at night. Major Travers met us at the transportation office, and after checking us in, drove us in a pickup truck to our temporary quarters in "Tin City"—a nice four-man room with air conditioning. These aluminum trailers had small rooms with a door and a window. The window of our trailer was blocked out for light, and each room had two sets of bunk beds and two large wall lockers. We stacked our gear next to each bunk, unrolled our sleeping bags onto real mattresses, and got ready for sleep. The showers and head trailers were about 50 meters away from our trailer. With all of the outdoor lights, it was relatively easy to find our way around. These living quarters were a few miles away from the airstrip on this huge former Iraqi Air Force base.

* * *

Colonel Mant Campbell Hawkins II
III MAW Battle Captain

There had been an initial decision not to bring Marine fixed-wing aircraft for OIF2. Harrier jets were in high demand in the Fleet. Given what was perceived to be the threat at the time, it seemed that Harriers would not be required. Colonel Hawkins felt that 12 hours into Fallujah, we needed them. Visits by General Hagee, Commandant of the Marine Corps, helped to make the need for the Harriers known.

As for casualties, Colonel Hawkins said, "We've had more casualties here in three months than in all of OIF1." He later showed me the Wall that had photos of all the Marines wounded and killed during current operations.

Colonel Hawkins graduated from The Citadel in 1980 and then entered the Marine Corps. He was one of the "Hornet Babies," as he joined the first Hornet jet squadron in the Corps, and was now the oldest one left on active duty. He served as a Top Gun instructor at Miramar Naval Air Station, and did a variety of deployments. He graduated from the Marine Command and Staff course with a Master's degree, and later graduated from the Air War College at Maxwell Air Force Base. He was involved in workup for the MEF work up to Iraqi Freedom 1 under General Hagee. General Amos pulled Colonel Hawkins from the command of MAG (Marine Air Group) 41 at Fort Worth, Texas to help set up operations at Al Assad.

As the battle captain for the 3rd Marine Air Wing (III MAW), Colonel Hawkins' main job was to run the wing for General Amos. "He basically has given me the steering wheel, accelerator, the brakes on his wing, which is a heady responsibility for an 06 [a Marine Colonel] to assume," he said, adding that his main responsibility was to get the right airplanes to the right place at the right time. The AO was a 9,000-square-mile area, from Baghdad out to the western border with Syria. He pointed out the whole area on a large map of Iraq on the wall. He named many of the small outposts where the Marines have forces (I would soon have visited almost every one of them).

The MAW flew helicopters out of Al Assad and Al Taqaddum to get critically wounded Marines (level 3 care) to medical facilities in Baghdad. "We've got a camp here at Taqaddum [pointing at the map] on the edge of the lake, that we forward base a lot of our helicopters to support the Ramadi-Fallujah fight. It's saved a bunch of time getting into what we call CASH (CSH—a U.S. Army Combat Support Hospital) South." He showed where all of the care facilities in the area were located, and noted that Taqaddum is a level 2 medical facility.

He spoke at length about the "Golden Hour". There were a number of the level 2 care facilities in this region of Iraq, but some were an hour away from the helos. Also, many times the helo evacuation areas were "hot," meaning that they were taking or were close to taking enemy fire, both direct and indirect. Sometimes Marines had to be moved by ground transport to a safer LZ, and sometimes the helos would land, but then get pinned down due to hostile fire.

"The CG's two primary focuses have been CASEVAC and medevac. The difference is CASEVAC is a Marine Corps airplane with a Navy Corpsman in it versus a medevac. We have an Army helicopter squadron here that's a medical/surgical squadron, and they have level 2 care on their helicopters. So when a medevac H-60 lands, level 2 has landed at the point of injury, or the point of pick-up. That's a big plus that the Army has stayed here to do that, and we've got helicopters strategically placed around the AO so that if we can, we try and get them to them as quick as possible."

Colonel Hawkins noted that the second thing on General Amos' priority list was close air support to whoever needed it. "It might be a CSS [combat service support] convoy, it might be the division, it might be a MEF convoy, it might be troops in contact." Fixed-wing support would come in from the Combined Air Operations Center (CAOC) in Qatar to support troops in contact. The key word to get this support is "TIC" (troops in contact). The Marines have adapted this term to get the support from the CAOC.

Food, water, gas, and oil must get to the areas where they have to go. The wing worked to ensure that the convoys could move and the lines of communications stayed open. In the early April time frame, units needed to have their five days of supply (DOS), as the ground supply lines were being hit hard.

The wing also worked to help detect and destroy the ever-changing IED threat on the ground. Colonel Hawkins noted that sometimes the insurgents did simple things like throwing a pair of boots over a power line to mark where an ambush would take place, or tie engineer tape around a telephone pole to mark IEDs or ambush sites.

"We take special care to keep track of every enemy incident, each IED, VBIED, every small arms fire, missile fires, indirect fire, unguided rockets, every single thing, we try to take special care to track that." This helped to determine when and where the bad guys were out. He added, "I think you'll be surprised at how predictable the times are, which is why we convoy and try to fly, go where [and when] they aren't."

The wing coordinated with the Direct Air Support Center (DASC), located at division headquarters under General Mattis at Camp Blue Diamond (Camp Ar Ramadi). More coordination was required to move aircraft in the eastern sector of his AO. The threat levels have been labeled black, red, yellow and green for planning purposes. Green zones are relatively safe from ground fire at aircraft. Going into a black zone requires the CG's approval. Colonel Hawkins can approve movement in areas listed as red or less dangerous. He said that at times there have been 15 to 18 flights a day into the black zone to get critically injured Marines treatment in Baghdad. Common sense was also a factor in addition to these matrixes.

On this base there were artillery Marines from 2/11, who also worked with the 7th Marines (RCT7). Colonel Hawkins then showed me on the map where the 7th Marines (under Colonel Craig Tucker) operated in the western regions of the Sunni Triangle. The 7th Marines did a sweep to clear an area where helos were taking fire from the ground.

"It's all classic guerilla insurgency. What you'll find a touch different is a foundation of religion." He said that it's hard to describe the enemy well. They are former (Saddam) regime members, some Baathist Party members, sometimes not the same folks. There are *mujahideen*, who he said could be described as Syrians, some Jordanians, Saudis, Chechnyans, Yemenis, and a lot of Iraqis. Also, smugglers, gangsters, bad guys who are just entrepreneurs who trade in drugs, weapons, and people-transporting to make money. Sometimes they come together to fight and sometimes they argue over who will control an area.

Hawkins said that the insurgents were fighting a "maneuver" war against us. They were smaller, lighter, and chose when to attack.

"They're very good at intelligence. They're very good at keeping track of what we're doing, watching what we're doing, and looking at it from their standpoint, what's the best time to pick us apart."

He said that flight ops were 24/7, and there were some zones that his helos would fly to any time of day, and other areas they won't fly to at certain times. There have been a lot of joint (U.S.) assets to support the MAW. His normal day starts about 0730 and goes until around midnight. During the Fallujah ops he would formally turn over his responsibility to Jeff Marshall, but he would stay involved in current operations. He said it was a lot like being on a ship—always working. It's 12 on, 12 off, seven days a week. It's only been within the past three weeks that he has had time to do any physical training to help clear his mind. There is a gym right next to the MAW building.

I asked what he expected when preparing for this deployment. General Amos told him there was nothing he could do to prepare for this, but Colonel Hawkins did meet with staff officers to learn what he could. He has also done some reading on radical Islam. He said that a book, *The Other Side of the Mountain,* has helped him to prepare mentally for the deployment.

There has been a lot of Marine Corps Reserve participation with his group. One of these reserve officers was the air boss at Al Qaim. "I've got [SMCR] guys on the Iraqi Survey Group, who are out looking for chemical or biological weapons."

There had been an initial decision not to bring Marine fixed-wing aircraft for OIF2. Harrier jets were in high demand in the Fleet. Given what was perceived to be the threat at the time, it seemed that Harriers would not be required. Colonel Hawkins felt that 12 hours into Fallujah, we needed them. Visits by General Hagee, Commandant of the Marine Corps, helped to make the need for the Harriers known.

As for casualties, Colonel Hawkins said, "We've had more casualties here in three months than in all of OIF1." He later showed me the Wall that shows photos all of the Marines wounded and killed during current operations.

"I had never been rocketed before." In training Colonel Hawkins had seen rounds hit away from him, or artillery going overhead. "A 122mm rocket hitting close is a significant event." They dig a big hole. It is harassing fire, since the launchers are crudely made. One example was of a PVC pipe cut in half and a rocket laid on it and aimed at the camp. The Marine who was killed by a 122mm rocket was out near the Exchange, and another rocket hit about 25 meters from a basketball court nearby. Most times the rockets have been fired from the north, on the other side of a river. He said this was a classic insurgent tactic, firing from the other side of a river to make it tougher to pursue them. After this, helos have been used to scout the areas and the rocket attacks had not happened in a while.

He said that on this camp, Marines currently travel and work without helmets or flak jackets during daylight hours. At night, both were required for personal protection. Indirect fire was still hard to track in a timely fashion. By the time the bad guys pop out a few mortar rounds, then they were in a pickup truck and on their way.

* * *

Colonel Gerald Allen Yingling, Jr.
Chief of Staff, III MAW

The Marine Air Wing chief of staff described the challenges of bringing all the elements needed for the current aviation deployment. Some helos and equipment arrived on both Navy and MPS shipping; personnel arrived by aircraft. Not all parts and backup arrived at the same time, and there were challenges moving everything to bases via air and ground throughout Al Anbar province. Only recently was the decision made to deploy fixed-wing Harrier jets to support operations.

At about 0945 I went to the office of Colonel Yingling for a scheduled 1000 start. To break the ice on meeting the colonel, I asked if he was any relation to the Yuengling family of beer fame in Pennsylvania. He said that he was distantly related, but not to the money end of it. And the spelling of his name was slightly different, too. He goes by Gerry, and as a helo pilot, his call sign is "Panda."

He noted that his flying days were over now that he was the MAW chief of staff. He took over as chief of staff when General Amos took command of the wing in 2002, and in August of that year began planning. "We were immediately involved in preparations for a possible war in Iraq." There was a long period of preparation by the MEF. "In late October, it looked like we were actually going to war in Iraq." During OIF1, the Marine Air Wing had the southern portion of Iraq to deal with. At the end of major combat operations in 2003, he thought that Phase IV, security and stability operations, would begin in Iraq. The wing staff continued with this work until October 2003. "We had had the areas around Halah and Al Kut… and northern Babel province." The British then assumed responsibility for this area.

By late 2003, however, it looked like an insurrection was growing in Iraq. He discussed the introduction of the foreign fighters into the current operations in Iraq, and how the U.S. leadership decided to rotate forces into the country and plan for a much longer deployment of forces into the area. There was a lot of discussion about the size of the Marine force that would redeploy. The decision was finally made that the Marines would deploy into western Iraq in Al Anbar province to relieve U.S. Army units. In January 2004 the Marine Corps began pre-deployment site surveys, and started flowing forces in (to Iraq) in February. "Around March 16/17 is when we actually assumed the authority here from the Army, three weeks ahead of the planned turnover."

There was a little bit of a problem for aviation. Colonel Yingling continued, "As our aircraft were arriving we were immediately expected to be able to support all of the flight ops of the division. The only problem is when the aircraft come in, not all of the parts and pack-ups that are coming in off the ships arrive at the same time." "Black-bottom" (MPS) and "grey-bottom" (Navy) shipping brought in much of this aviation equipment and it arrived at different times. It then had to be convoyed up to the various bases in Al Anbar. "We had to be very careful on the amount of flight operations we were expected to be able to support. That caused a little time differential with the Army before we could actually make the swap-out.

"We had good turnover with the Army." Early in the planning stages the wing decided to bring in just helos; the Harrier jets would be left home until there was a decision that they were needed. "It's now the 18th of May and we've been here since March, and the decision was made about two weeks ago that we'd bring Harriers in. We have 20 of them [Harrier jets] arriving today, that have just come in from the East Coast and the West Coast.

"We knew that we would be providing CASEVAC, we knew that we would be having three Forward Operating Bases plus one airfield." He described the outlying FOBs in the west and south of Al Anbar, and a small base at Taqaddum. The wing would also provide convoy escort due to the high threat of IED ambushes. Also, the CH-46s and CH-53s would move troops and cargo. "Because of the lack of ASE, and the high heat signature and man pad threat on the [CH-]53s, we primarily operate them from Taqaddum to the west, and north and south from there and we use the [CH-]46s to the east."

The missions have stayed pretty much as anticipated. The Harriers would be bringing in a Litening Pod (an advanced targeting system) and the ability to do downlinks to provide the pictures to ground units.

I asked about the role of the U.S. Air Force support.

"We have liaison officers… down in Qatar, and they actually do our inroads with the CFACC (Combined Forces Air Coalition Command)." So the wing has the ability to pull in fixed-wing aircraft, as well as aircraft from aircraft carriers. Requests can be immediate or preplanned. "The support from the Air Force is excellent as shown by some of the fights we've had in Fallujah and Ramadi."

Asked about the use of the unmanned aerial platforms, he responded that just about every type of asset is available for the MAW, and detailed discussion was not possible in an unclassified interview such as this.

Most of the current MAW staff was new for this deployment, although many had experience at the squadron level from last year. The experience at the lower levels has proven valuable for planning at the MAW level. Many have been "on the ground" fighting the war in 2003, and bring this experience with them. "We're very fortunate with the staff.

"During OIF1, as we moved into Iraq, there was a requirement for us to forward base. We moved one of the Air Groups, MAG 16, from the ship up into Jubail. MAG 39 and portions of MAG 16 moved up." Colonel Yingling estimated that there were about 19 FARPs (Forward arming and refueling points) as they moved up into Tikrit. He said that the biggest difference this time is that we're well entrenched inside Iraq, and "things are a little bit more predictable." There are a lot of planned missions and the majority of aviation forces are based at Al Assad and Al Taqaddum. Yugoslavs built the Al Assad base back in the 1980s and some of the aviation maintenance facilities were very good. "We call it Iraqi nice, but the facilities are actually nice."

"The pilots aren't flying the long, long hours that they did last year." The transient times were now much shorter to get where the aviation assets needed to be. Missions in 2003 might have three to four hours of transient time, along with refueling. "We're probably flying, maybe 90 to 150 hours a day, and we have a lot less assets here than we did the last time [OIF1]. The answer is that we are not flying more than we did last time."

The Harriers were coming in today (May 18, 2004) with an East Coast squadron "minus" (10 jets) and a West Coast squadron "minus" (10 jets). A normal Harrier squadron consists of 16 jets. There were about ten C-5 aircraft coming in with the gear. "We have to build a high power turn-up ramp here at Al Assad, which is a requirement for the installation of guns." He didn't expect to have the Harriers operating for about seven to ten days. "We plan to use the Harriers to augment the convoy escort." Harriers can also be launched from strip alert at Al Assad and provide close air support much more quickly than the helos. They can also operate at high altitude undetected and see ambushes and IED sites.

Colonel Yingling guessed that the Marine Corps would be in Iraq for three to five years. When III MAW leaves in March of 2005, II MEF will come in along with II MAW. All four Marine wings were needed to source the assets for Iraq operations. Squadrons would rotate out, like-elements replacing the units here. By March 2005 the headquarters would be back in CONUS. "It's gonna be a long evolution for the Marine Corps."

All of the airframes were planned to stay in place here. ASE gear has protected many of the craft. A Cobra helo was hit by an SA16 missile over Fallujah, but was able to land with the crew. If the other aircraft hold up after about a year, they will be looked at to see if they can remain in Iraq.

In conclusion, Colonel Yingling said, "I guess I've been extremely fortunate, this has been a tremendous job, being the chief of staff and being able to go to war twice with this Air Wing. The Air Wing is operating very effectively. The Marine forces on the ground, I'm extremely proud of the way the division and MEF have operated, FSSG. The challenges the Marine Corps faced, people are gonna scratch their heads, never in the history of the Marine Corps have they operated this far inland, for this extended amount of time. If somebody woulda told me a year ago, when I was sitting in Kuwait and we were doing OIF1 that I would, on the 18th of May 2004, be sitting in an Iraqi Air Force base, 140 miles to the west of Baghdad, I would have thought that they were crazy. We have many challenges ahead."

He hoped that the government of Iraq would emerge from this and eliminate the foreign fighters. He hoped for a stable Iraq that would be a cornerstone for stability in the Middle East.

* * *

Colonel Jon G. Miclot
Commanding Officer, MACG 38 (Marine Air Control Group)

Colonel Miclot took command of the group just the day before this interview, and his emphasis was mostly on his recent time as G3 (Operations) at III MAW. A very dynamic interviewee, he used his PowerPoint slides from his G3 days to outline what the wing has been doing in OIF2.

Colonel Miclot began by saying, "I'm gonna go through a brief here on OIF1, the build up to OIF2, and what I see right now." He had his PowerPoint slides on a laptop computer screen that made it easy to follow, but difficult to take notes as I tried to keep up. He discussed leaving Iraq after OIF1, then returning in November of 2003 to check out Camp Al Assad. In OIF1 he said that speed and maneuver were key elements. It was challenging to keep moving the supplies (which included ammo, food, fuel, and water), to the rapidly moving 1st Marine Division. The distances of hundreds of kilometers were much longer than those which Marines have usually dealt with. The AO was 103,000 square kilometers! A lot of open desert, along with urban areas.

With regard to OIF2, Colonel Miclot discussed force determination, as the Marines were to replace Army divisions in Iraq with smaller Marine units. The 1st Marine Division would be replacing the Army 82nd Airborne Division and all of its attachments for the next 13 months. This originally meant six Marine battalions, but currently this was augmented by an Army BCT (Brigade Combat Team) of three battalions. A graphic showed how large the 82nd Airborne's AO had been, with only a few major MSRs (Main Supply Routes) and several key cities, as well as the Euphrates River.

The ACE (Air Combat Element) at this time had about 120 aircraft in Iraq, primarily helicopters, with about 5,500 aviation Marines. "As of yesterday the Harriers began to show up. Up until then the Marine fixed wing portion was a bunch of C-130s." The Harriers were bringing a surveillance package with them. The threat has changed since the planning began last fall.

The Army had 70 aircraft (helos) that could shoot. The Marines brought about 54. In medium lift helos, the Marines brought 36 CH-46s, while the Army had 41 of their H-60s for lift. In heavy lift, the Marines brought a squadron and a half of CH-53 Echos, and six C-130s. Colonel Miclot outlined the type of Marine aviation elements here. Generally the helos flew at night and worked to escort convoys with Cobras and Hueys when possible.

At this time they were attempting to get up a radio relay balloon ("Aerostat") here at Al Assad to provide better communication between aviation elements. There were times of day when the enemy was not as active, and much movement by Marines and Army units was done then. But Colonel Miclot noted, "They're not dumb and they'll figure it out." Air Survivability Equipment has been installed on their aircraft, and he estimated that this gear so far has saved at least seven aircraft. "It's well worth the cost and time we put into it." The ASE upgrades were now complete for the rotor wing, and the C-130s would be getting the protection soon.

The MAW constructed an aviation map of Iraq, using the color codes green, yellow, red, and black, based on the historic weapons threats found in each area. The green areas were relatively safe, with little fire directed at aircraft. The threat level proceeded up to black, which were areas that have been hotbeds of antiaircraft fire.

Colonel Miclot also discussed the "Golden Hour", that amount of time critical in getting a wounded Marine or soldier from the field to medical care. A CH-46 can cover 110 nautical miles in that time, and the placement of aviation facilities throughout Iraq had been templated to attempt to bring all supported Marine ground units within the Golden Hour range for the helos. He pointed out the air detachment facilities on the large wall map. From Al Assad it takes about 70 minutes to get to the Syrian border. Al Assad is a huge base and many large commercial aircraft can come in to bring in supplies and parts. It was an ideal base to support the aviation operations throughout the country with its two mile-long runways and large buildings at the main side area. In addition to the MAW units, Marines from the 7th Marines and CSSB (Combat Service Support Battalion) 7 were based at Al Assad.

He then described the bases, starting with Camp Al Taqaddum (TQ). KC-130s can land there and it is only 15 miles from Fallujah, within easy range of the Cobras and CH-46s. The Pioneer Drone surveillance aircraft fly from TQ. Out near the Syrian border they took over a train station (Camp Al Qaim) and have stationed two Cobras and one Huey there. CH-46s and CH-53s provide some of the resupply to the small camp. The camp is only about 15 miles from the town of Al Qaim. The infantry battalion 3/7 operated out of this camp.

Korean Village is a small camp in the west of Iraq near the Jordanian border. I had heard this camp's name, and wondered why it was called Korean Village. Colonel Miclot explained that Korean laborers who were brought in to work on the railroads had built this small outpost. He said it was a desolate outpost, and when I later visited there, I would have to agree.

Down south near the Saudi border is Mudayasis. "There's not much goin' on down there. We only have two medevac planes [helos] down there. We can stage down there. Other forces have come through and used our fuel." He said that the Marines love it down there. The Marines there live in bunker areas that are air conditioned, and there was a provisional infantry company from 3/11 (an artillery battalion) working as security. They work with the locals, the ICDC and border police and the Marines run things at the small-unit level.

A big challenge for helo operations included the dust, and enemy firing from cars, date palm groves, and so on. His Marines also got involved in locating and destroying IEDs that threaten their ground supply convoys.

Colonel Miclot said that currently the deployment was for seven months. There was some talk at higher levels that the tours might be lengthened to a year. His view was that the seven-month deployment keeps the Marines focused. So far, the commandant of the Marine Corps has argued to keep the tours at seven months.

His new job with the MAW is CO of MACG 38. "This is the brains of the wing," he began. It involved command and control, interface with the division, an Air Control squadron, Communications squadron, his LAAD (Low Altitude Air Defense) battalion that augments ground security, and a Pioneer squadron from Cherry Point, among others. He already knew many of the people that he now commanded.

* * *

HMLA 167, Thursday May 20, 2004

I met with Marines from both the CH-53 and Cobra/Huey squadrons: Five interviews at HMH 465 (CH-53 Echo Super Stallion helos) in the morning and five at HMLA 167 in the afternoon. Included here are several of the more significant interviews.

167's Marines' experiences dealt mostly with actions in and around the Fallujah fights during the spring of 2004. I spent the second part of the day at this Cobra Attack Helicopter Squadron. These "slick" aircraft (no wheels, only landing skids) each hold only a pilot and copilot and provide escort for both helos and ground forces. They have also provided ground support fire.

Master Sergeant Gregory Scott Staggs
Squadron Maintenance Chief, HMLA 167

As maintenance chief, Staggs' main duties were to ensure that the squadron's helicopters were ready to fly, and also quickly repaired when hit by fire from the ground, and that his enlisted Marines got proper rest whenever possible. He ensured that aviation Marines at remote camps were rotated back to Al Assad for rest, and also spent time flying missions to help supervise enlisted Marine crewmen. His most harrowing flight was near Fallujah when the Huey he was in began to get hit by rifle and machine gunfire from the ground.

The squadron's maintenance chief, Master Sergeant Staggs, enlisted in 1982, and did four unit deployments to Okinawa in his first nine years. He next was assigned to HMX 1, the unit that provides helicopters for the president of the United States. In his last year and a half there, he went all over the world in support of the president. Since 1995 he has been with HMLA 167 in a variety of billets. He served as squadron career planner for three years during this spell.

To help prepare the squadron for this deployment to Iraq, some squadron personnel went through Exercise Eagle Talon while the helos were prepped for movement. The Marines also did ground training in things such as convoy operations and tactics. Staggs left with many of the squadron Marines and flew via commercial planes to Kuwait, arriving there February 13. The majority of the squadron went to Udari, Kuwait, to wait for military C-130 transport up to Al Assad. The remaining aircrews waited for the helos to arrive by ship to prep them for flight. It took the crews only 24 hours to get all 27 aircraft ready for flight and off the ships on 21 February. These aircraft flew 550 miles into Al Assad without any mechanical problems.

Master Sergeant Staggs said that the Army units here at Al Assad were helpful in getting the Marines settled in. It saved a lot of time in learning about the electrical systems, and the layout of things on the base. "We had to go through some growing pains with our computers and electronics." The lines on base were 220, versus the 110 lines in the U.S. Items needed electrical converters to work properly.

"We were full up 'round here within a few days."

As squadron maintenance chief, he managed his personnel, deciding who goes when, where, and why in a department that has eight to ten divisions. Al Assad was the squadron's main "hub" with two smaller FOBs at Al Qaim and Korean Village. He made sure to rotate the maintenance crews and aircrews in and out of these small bases to ensure that there was the proper manning out there. The Marines had been working 12-on 12-off for three months at this point, and Master Sergeant Staggs kept tabs on the mental health of his Marines. He tried to see that Marines got an occasional day off from work, have unit cookouts, and also ensured that Marines stayed in touch with the home folks by calling regularly.

"It seems that every time I turn around I'm making a roster for something. But it's a job I wouldn't trade for any other. I guess for me, it's the pinnacle of my Marine Corps career. I never thought I'd be in this position, and every day it's just something new."

He does fly on occasion in order to help train some of the younger Marines on the crews. "In three months many of the younger Marines have received over a year's worth of experience... they're eager to fly more." He also noted with pride that none of the ground convoys escorted by squadron helos have been attacked. "And we have found some IEDs that were laid, and we were able... to have EOD go out and blow 'em in place."

"One time, when we couldn't get radio comm with a convoy, I had to land on the side of the road, run out to the road, stop the convoy, give them the frequency we were on so we could talk to 'em."

Another time when there were comm problems with a convoy, there was no place to land. The convoy was traveling about 40 miles per hour, the helos were moving at about 60, 80 knots above them. "I emptied out a water bottle. Got my pen out, found a piece of cardboard, wrote down our frequency on it, crammed it in the water bottle. Just flew by them, pointed to the water bottle, then threw it at 'em. They stopped, ran out, picked it up, looked at it, punched in the frequency, and we started talking to them." Since then, he said that there haven't been any comm problems with the convoys.

When things heated up down in Fallujah in early April, "We got tasked to support the squadron down at TQ [Al Taqaddum] for Fallujah." Forty-three maintenance Marines and seven aircraft were sent: Five Cobras and two Hueys, on about April 2. "Within two days of that, we had aircraft coming back with bullet holes in [them], aircraft hit with RPGs, and things like that." His Marines would have the birds come in, shut them down, inspect them, fix them, rearm and get them back on the flight schedule.

Staggs continued: "The worst incident we had was we had a Huey shot up. Took quite a few rounds. My Airframes Division worked on that aircraft for about 16 hours straight, repairing it. Within the next day, it was up for test flight, took it around, aircraft was good to go, and in less than 24 hours that aircraft was launching back out on a mission."

As for his experiences of flying in and around Fallujah around that time, Master Sergeant Staggs said, "Initial launch, very scary. Not knowin' what to expect, just seeing Triple A, small arms tracers just aimed direct at you or off in the distance. Explosions off in the distance, buildings blowing up... pretty scary."

He did most of his flying at night. "Flying in, you would see firefights. You'd hear it on the radio, then all of a sudden you'd see a firefight start up about a click from you. And you'd see a couple of tracer rounds going one way, and then you'd see a wall of fire comin' back. Just return fire [from Marines there]. You'd see that for a little while, then it'd go quiet. You'd see explosions all around. You'd see Triple A just sprang up in the air every once in a while. And you're sittin' there on [NVG] goggles, and you're like, well, I'm on goggles, they can't see me. And for the first three nights I really thought that." He was convinced that since the enemy didn't have goggles, they couldn't see the helos.

The next night, they were supporting a unit at a little town north of Camp Fallujah. "We flew ahead like we normally do on our escort mission. And we saw some barriers and dirt pushed up on the road. We stopped the convoy and said, you know, something's not right."

It was an industrial area. The ground convoy was getting impatient about the stop, but the helo Marines felt that it was a trap and pushed a little further north.

"As we pushed past this circle, we were flyin' along, I was on the left side of the aircraft, with the mini gun, and next thing I see, I see flashes just stringin' past me. I just turned and just open up on the gattle [M134 mini gun], returning direct fire right to where those tracers were comin' at us. I didn't have time to say we're takin' fire, the only thing I could do to protect the aircraft and us, is open up. Thank God I had a mini gun. That weapon puts out about 50 rounds a second, so it's got a bark and a mean bite. My pilot, he heard me open up, he's like, 'Top's firin', but he's firin' in the wrong direction.' Didn't realize that those were tracers comin' at us. It was an anti-aircraft gun. They were leadin' us." The pilot then broke off to the right while Master Sergeant Staggs kept his gun on the enemy until they stopped firing on him. The helo flew low, and then informed the ground unit of what had happened.

The pilot plotted a grid to mark the area. After another pass in the helo, all hell broke loose again from their six o'clock (behind the aircraft).

"We're takin' Triple A, we opened up again, bank. I hit my deflection on my gun, so I had to quit firin'. My crew chief on the right side, Staff Sergeant Casalzo opens up with the .50 cal until he lost deflection. And at that time we were banking. My Dash 2, [a] Cobra, was coverin' our six [area behind the helo], he's about to come in on the Triple A and he saw a white plume, a flash and a plume, and they thought they'd launched RPGs at us. And that was the second one [engagement that night]."

Staggs then backed up and remembered that earlier that night an RPG had exploded behind the tail rotor of his aircraft. "It almost felt like it lifted us and threw us forward a little bit. That got our attention. What the hell's that?"

"As Dash 2 saw the plume, it was ready to dive in but realized that the missile was coming at him. He [Dash 2] banked, launched chaff and flares, and the missile exploded, damaging some of the oil lines on his gearbox, and destroyed the avionics. The pilot saw flashes in the cockpit, then everything went dead. The engines were still on line, but the gauges showed zero pressure. The pilot flew the Cobra to Camp Fallujah, about 5 miles south of the encounter. He landed safely inside the compound." Master Sergeant Staggs' Huey then went to Camp Fallujah and stayed with the damaged helo until daylight.

On another mission, helos were launched out when a sniper stopped a convoy. The helos fired at the suspected building, and then M1 tanks came and finished off the building.

He said that in talks with veterans of last year's operations, he learned that then the helos were "weapons free," meaning that they could shoot at anything suspicious. Now, the helos had to wait for an enemy to shoot at them in order to return fire. (This was as of May 2004.) "You always wonder, is this the flight I'm going to go down?" Crews often take a 240 Golf machine gun along in case a helo goes down, since the .50 cal is too big to lug around and the mini gun needs the helo's electronic power to operate.

Master Sergeant Staggs said that everyone in the squadron works hard to get returning helos ready to get into the air again. "It just makes you proud." He said it was almost like a pit crew at a NASCAR race, with everyone teaming together to keep the birds up and running. "It happens so quickly and professionally. Everybody knows their job and they do it methodically."

About two weeks earlier, he was with a convoy escort near the town of Hit. He saw a man walking his two little girls to school. This made Master Sergeant Staggs proud of the job that the Marines were doing to try and make life normal for the Iraqi people.

* * *

Captain Samuel Lee Meyer

Cobra Pilot & Aviation Safety Officer, HMLA 167

During 2003, Meyer flew many hours at night, often on 8- to 12-hour missions. He did not expect to return to combat in Iraq a year later. During his current missions, he felt that he was helping to save the lives of Marines on the ground engaged in combat. His closest call came when the rotor of his Cobra helicopter hit an RPG round that failed to detonate. Another RPG exploded near his helo, but he was able to safely land the damaged bird on base.

Captain Meyer graduated from North Carolina State University at Raleigh, NC in 1997. Commissioned as a second lieutenant, he went to Flight School after the Infantry Officer Course. He has been in the squadron a little over three years.

Meyer was sent from HMLA 167 to augment HMLA 269 in OIF1, so this was now his second tour in Iraq. For OIF1, he deployed on board ship, and was part of a raid on Safwan Hill on March 20, 2003. "I flew at night, I was a night fighter. We participated in battles up in Baghdad, went to Nasariyah towards the end." Later he flew up to Tikrit. They were forward deployed from the ship. "We left in May, and returned home in June 23, 2003."

He said that the fighting was unlike anything he had seen before. "You shot every piece of ordnance you had to support the Marine on the ground. Intense fighting at times." He said it was a lot of hours of flying at night, often 8- to 12-hour missions every night. He also flew at Basrah. "Flying at night with oil fires, and 300-foot ceilings and winds gusting up to 25 knots is by far the most challenging conditions I've ever flown in."

Captain Meyer said that after years of training to do this, it was not the glorious and glamorous action he expected when he finally got to do it, "Your first job is to ensure that 18-year-old Marine gets home to see his family and you hope that by doing that you're going to allow yourself to go home and see your family."

"It was an eye-opening experience for me." Captain Meyer added that it was a rewarding feeling when a Marine looks him in the eye and tells him that his close air support saved that Marine's life.

When major combat ended in OIF1, the Marines planned to pull out of Iraq quickly. All of MAG 29 from the U.S. East Coast moved out quickly and returned home. They were home in less than six months after they left the United States. "I wanted to see my family," said Meyer.

On his return to CONUS, he returned to HMLA 167, his "home" unit. Now on this deployment there were augments to the squadron from HMLA 269.

I asked him about his feelings about returning to Iraq this year. He replied, "Sir, I never in my wildest dreams ever thought I'd be coming back here. I thought it was done, because the Marine Corps fights the wars, the Army, they hold the ground. They're the big occupying force. I've been told this is the biggest occupation by the Marine Corps since World War II."

In late fall 2003, the squadron started to hear rumors about returning to Iraq. He knew that a return would be different. "The sexiness, or the glamour of war, for most people who had been in, was gone. And they were like, 'Hey, someone else can go have their turn, 'cause this is no joke.'" The squadron said that those who had just deployed for six months had to go again, and the response by many was, 'okay,' this was their job.

For OIF2, he said that to say there was not a knot in his stomach would have been a lie. He had seen the Army helos get shot down on TV. He said that things were quiet at Al Assad when they first got here, and rotations with the outlying FOBs had been established.

On April 1 things began to change with Operation *Vigilant Resolve*. Captain Meyer was told to pack his gear and be ready to go to Taqaddum to support operations in Fallujah. "We got our in-brief that night, next morning I was a day section leader, with my CO, who has been my XO, as my Dash 2 Huey pilot."

They went out and immediately a FAC (forward air controller) came up and called that he was being engaged on the west side of the city. "We came up by the bridges that the people (American contractors) were hung from. We came in, and tanks were firing their main guns into the city, marking targets. There's nothing better than an Abrams M1A1 main gun tank round for a mark. It was really neat to see this, and to feel it as you watch it happen, because you have a front-row seat. But you also realize that you are providing close air support with your rotary wing asset. And, while it's nice to watch, it's almost surreal."

"The FAC says, 'That's my target, you're cleared hot.' You know, I strafe my target with a bunch of 20mm from my gun. And you'd see people run out, and you know, all right, these are bad guys. Now they're gonna stop bein' bad after you take care of them. So, I never had any problem with that, because I don't look at it as killin' people, I look at it as protectin' my Marines."

He finally ended up working on the eastern part of the city, making a couple of runs over some targets. Captain Meyer said that at times the FACs were "hanging the helos up" a while, and he was looking and seeing a lot of fire coming up at the helos. Then a FAC called "troops in contact."

"So we came in over an area of the city we had flown over before to avoid being shot at. And as soon as we came over the city, it immediately erupted. My copilot called, they're people immediately underneath us." They were driving right into the Marines. "I guess three RPGs came up, and one of 'em hit me in the main rotor." Meyer didn't know what it was at first, but said that it pushed his aircraft almost to the end of controllable limits. "I looked at the gauges, we were okay, we were still flyin'."

I asked about being hit. He said that later he discovered that the RPG round came up, hit the rotor blade, and the rotor blade cut the RPG round in half without detonation as its fuse did not go off then. There was an explosion above the rotor blade that pushed Captain Meyer's helo forward and down. He called his Dash 2. They were operating with a Reserve Unit, 775, and they heard what had happened. Two Cobras from the north came in to suppress the threat and were also shot up with small-arms fire from the ground.

This was all in the first day at Fallujah! "I never thought I'd be doin' this again. I remember rolling into the attack, looking down, thinking, 'Okay, I didn't think we were ever gonna have to do this again,' and now here we are in an urban combat environment. And in some ways, more intense fighting than I saw in the first war." Last year he destroyed many targets of opportunity, but didn't get shot at as much as this year.

Captain Meyer then returned to base, thinking that he only had a few more feet to get the helo down onto the runway. The crash fire rescue team was ready, but he landed without a problem. "I walked into our ready room, and they told me, 'Hey, we don't have enough copilots now. We need a night medevac mission, and we need you to be the copilot.'" He replied, "All right." He went from almost dying to going right out to another mission. Fortunately, the mission was canceled. Operations like this continued for almost two weeks in early April. He recalled this was the first time he was close enough to actually see the man who was operating the weapon shooting at aircraft in his section. "That is up close and personal."

His personal response to all of this combat is that it's been a job:

"There is no glory, there is no high fives, there is no look how great I am. There is just, I do my job. I wanna do it so nobody gets hurt. And so I can go home. My goal, here, is not to get a 50-hour flight month, which is a lot of flight hours. It is to survive. And it is to go home and see my family, it's to be able to look at myself in the mirror at the end of the day and say I did my job well. Really, you can take every medal… I am just a simple man who did my job."

He also realized that now men like him are a part of history. He has experienced things that he never expected. "At the end of the day, someone will say that guy did his job." What gets him excited is when a mission will save the lives of Marines on the ground.

He hoped that this interview would help to tell the story of the Marines here, not any personal recognition for himself. A very mature, thoughtful, and complete half-hour with this young officer came to a close. This was one of the best interviews to date.

* * *

Sergeant John Jeremy Belcher
Helicopter Crew Chief (UH1N), HMLA 167

During his deployment, Sergeant Belcher worked at camps and FOBs throughout Al Anbar. In flights aboard Hueys over Fallujah, he manned a .50 caliber machine gun, and fired at ground targets as they targeted his chopper and the "Dash 2" chopper. He described an RPG round that came up and hit the rotor of that Cobra helo, and the sights of seeing incoming anti-aircraft fire at the helos.

Sergeant Belcher was a helicopter crew chief and mechanic for the UH-1N ("Huey"), and a mechanic for the AH-1W ("SuperCobra"). He enlisted in the summer of 2000, and after recruit training went to Pensacola, Florida to train to become an aircrew member. At Camp Pendleton he received specialized mechanic training. He reported to HMLA 167, which had done an air show in his town when he was in high school. He also received WTI (weapons tactics instructor) training. In 2002 he "chopped" to HMM 264 and did a Mediterranean deployment, and helped fly supplies into Iraq during OIF1. He also served in operations off Liberia. In December 2003 he left HMM 264 and rejoined HMLA 167.

During his current deployment, he has been at four different Forward Operating Bases in Iraq, moving about every two weeks: Al Assad, Taqaddum, Korean Village near Ar Rutbah, and Camp Fallujah.

"Highlights, I'd probably have to say Fallujah. All the other FOBs, for me, it was relatively quiet. Very little gunfire, very, very little conflict. Obviously, we'd go out to Hit, [also] near the Syrian border, we had a little bit of trouble out there." He said that there were individuals firing at the helos from the other side of the Syrian border. The pilots had to make decisions there about how and when to engage this type of fire.

"Fallujah, completely different story. That was my highlight out here so far. I spent just a little over two weeks in Fallujah, I was just back from another FOB, was here [Al Assad] for two days, just about long enough to get laundry done. While in Fallujah I had an AO [aerial observer] with me. I used him as my GAU-17 gunner, and I worked the .50 cal." He said that, "We all talk about our training, but when there's individuals actually shooting back at you, instead of you just shooting at a stationary target, you get a couple things running through your mind."

The ROEs (Rules of Engagement) at that time in Fallujah were that the choppers were not to fire unless fired on. Sergeant Belcher said that most of the people in Fallujah had some kind of weapon, be it an AK 47 or an RPG7 launcher. "I can definitely say in Fallujah the hardest part engaging anything there was so many civilians. You'd be on one street and you'd be doing CAS [close air support] for tanks or ground troops. So you'd be shooting down this street at enemies and on the next street over there'd be kids outside playing kickball, somebody walking their dog. It was almost unbelievable.

"We did take rounds periodically, roughly every two or three days." Rounds hit the elevators, the blades, and the chin bubble of one helo. "I took a round directly underneath me, about four inches, to our bottom fuel cell sump plate." Another round entered the helo and penetrated the fuel cell.

"Our Dash 2 took an RPG hit. I can now tell you about it, without a doubt, if we were being fired at with SAMs, RPGs, Triple A's. The small-arms fire we normally took was from AKs, most of that sounds like bubble wrap popping. Everything else has its distinct whistle, its own distinct hum. The first couple times you get shot at it takes a little getting used to, it's a little unnerving. But after that you know exactly what's happening. I flew mostly during the days, I flew very little at night. I don't know if it was advantageous or it was working against me. During the daytime you can hardly ever see where the shots are being fired from."

He noted that the enemy was very intelligent, and that after two days of operations they understood how the Marines were maneuvering. They wouldn't shoot at the helos until the helos turned for a break. The Huey helicopters have 360-degree coverage with their weapons, but when turning, they cannot fire directly underneath them, which makes them vulnerable. The Cobras also have some limitations when maneuvering. The enemy watched and tried to fire at the aircraft during these exposed times.

I asked Sergeant Belcher to detail the incident when his Dash 2 was hit. It happened when the Marines on the ground were advancing into the city from a railroad line outside of the city. The helos were called in to provide close air support because "The ground guys were pinned down." The helos began firing the mini gun on the left side first, then the .50 cal, at enemy in the open. Then the helos began to receive fire from a mosque. He had his reservations about firing at a mosque, but decided that it had to be done. "These guys are firing at us, and they had our guys pinned down. The 'snake,' the Cobra, came in behind us and they began to fire 20 mike mike [mm] at the troops in the open. As we were firing, two RPGs came up and basically bisected the Cobra and Huey. It came up on the right side, right in between us, and as soon as that happened our ASE systems fired off chaff and flare, and we broke to disengage." He said that he could see a smoke plume and the Cobra being hit near the main rotor. "We got lucky. The RPG 7 didn't actually explode. It just caused cosmetic damage." The helos then flew back to Camp Fallujah.

"I counted as good days where I didn't have to shoot at anyone and nobody shot at us." However, one day on a CAS mission, the individuals on the street in Fallujah ran off the street as the helos approached. The helos then went outside of the city and they saw what looked like dust on the ground. The crew realized that it was anti-aircraft fire (AAA) shooting towards them.

He also mentioned the mortar fire received on the base. Some "farmers" were seen in a field, and later it was determined that this was the origin of the mortar fire. Sergeant Belcher's lesson from this was to treat everyone with suspicion.

"Fallujah got mortared unbelievably. You could set your clock almost to the mortars. We had some [younger] guys come up [to Fallujah]. I was like, 'Hey, you're just in time for the morning mortaring. It's 8:45 now, they usually mortar between 8:30 and 9:15.' Sure enough, five minutes later, mortars are hittin' us." He said it also happened at 0300 every day.

He said that they found eight AAA pieces about a week ago, about 11 miles from an FOB where he was working. "We destroyed them with rockets and .50 caliber machine gun so they couldn't be used later." He was hoping that things would stay calm, as they have been for the past few weeks.

He expressed hope that the Iraqis would decide what democracy is, and settle things down in the country.

CHAPTER FIVE

Infantry—2nd Battalion, 2nd Marine Regiment

Camp Fallujah, Wednesday April 22, 2004

I attended both the MEF and then the RCT1 briefings today. At the MEF briefing, MEF commander Lieutenant General James Conway expressed dissatisfaction at what the negotiations in Fallujah have produced. The Fallujah authorities assured the coalition negotiators that they would rid the town of rebels and weapons. Today at the briefing we saw the results of this weapons "clean out": On the briefing screen was a photo of the back of a small pickup truck with a few RPG rounds, some mortar rounds, and a few rusty rifles! This from a town of 200,000 residents! General Conway indicated that unless things improved there, our forces were likely to go "kinetic," a way of saying that the MEF would resume offensive operations.

I had been reading the U.S. news media on the internet, and watching occasional news broadcasts here on the TV in the mess hall, and the way that they report current events in Fallujah. They claim that the Marine offensive was "stopped." It makes it sound as if the enemy fighters held off the Marine offensive. What they do not say is that the MEF stopped offensive operations to allow the local Iraqi authorities and leaders to negotiate with the insurgents there. Marines who I have talked with in my short time here were all confident that they could have taken the entire town in a few more days at the rate they were fighting earlier this month. They were frustrated with the delay, but seemed to understand the need to allow the political process to take its course.

At 0810, RCT1's brief began. The regiment's S3 (operations officer), Lieutenant Colonel Austin Renforth ("Sparky"), presided due to the absence of Colonel Toolan. At the conclusion of the brief, Major Piedmont and I met with Major Christopher Dixon, the executive officer of 2/2, to ride to their area of the camp. Major Piedmont had spoken with Major Dixon a few days earlier about our desire to conduct oral history interviews with the Marines in his battalion.

One of the battalion drivers took us in a Humvee to the area of Camp Fallujah then occupied by 2/2, about 2 miles from the center of the camp. Several Marines there manned a .50 caliber machine gun at a guard post a short distance away from the gate in the wall. At the gate itself there were other Marines on guard, all fully armed. The headquarters for 2/2 was in a rectangular cement block building near the southwestern part of Camp Fallujah. Inside the building, any windows of rooms used as offices were covered in cardboard and tape, or painted black to prevent light from leaking out at night. Furnishings were sparse—cots, wooden benches, wood crates, and field desks.

* * *

Major Christopher Dixon
Executive Officer, 2nd Battalion, 2nd Marine Regiment (2/2)

I sat down with Major Dixon in the small room that served as his office and sleeping quarters. I used a cot as my chair, while Major Dixon sat by his desk with a map of Fallujah behind him. In the next hour he created a thorough picture of what 2/2 had done in its short two months in Iraq so far. In the next two days I would learn a great deal about the major events that 2/2 has been involved with: Patrolling near Mahmudiyah, VCP shootings, a mortar attack on a bridge defense, a Quick Reaction Force responding to a large ambush in Lutafiyah, and a sweep through that village.

"I began my military career after graduating from the Virginia Military Institute in 1991, and accepted a commission in the Marine Corps," Dixon began. He served on active duty until 1998, then went into the Marine Corps Reserves for a few years. He was a DEA agent until he rejoined the active Marine Corps. He commanded a variety of Marine security missions, finally serving in Afghanistan in 2003. He then joined 2/2 as the executive officer at Camp LeJeune, North Carolina.

2/2 is normally a part of the 2nd Marine Division, but was sent to join the 1st Marine Division for OIF2. The division needed the manpower, and 2/2 was not due to deploy overseas for another year and a half, so it was an available unit. The battalion flew into Kuwait in March 2004, and then traveled on a 12-hour convoy from Udari, Kuwait, to Al Mahmudiyah, Iraq. Mahmudiyah is about 20 clicks (20,000 meters or roughly 12 miles) south of Baghdad. The battalion was there to relieve a unit of the Army's 82nd Airborne Division, the 3rd of the 505th, also called "Three Panther." The transition began with left-right shadow patrols with the Army to familiarize his Marines with the area. Typically, on the early patrols, the Army unit would run its patrols, and the Marine unit would be along to observe and get an idea of what goes on. Eventually, the Marine units run the patrols, and the Army units ride along to observe and see how well the Marine unit has learned the area. "It's more of a tribal area," said Dixon, "As opposed to an area where the religious factions are more important."

A big issue in March was the upcoming Arbaeen Festival where Shiite pilgrims travel south through this area to visit the shrine in Karbala of the martyred Muslim leader and grandson of Mohammed, Husayn ibn Ali, who was slain shortly after the death of Mohammed himself. "We were told to expect a flow of up to three million religious pilgrims through this area during the festival."

The battalion assigned its companies to different villages in this region, Golf Company to Usafiyah, Fox Company to Lutafiyah, and Easy Company to Rasheed. (See page 105 for more about referring to Echo Company as "Easy" Company.) Many of the Marines from the 81mm platoon formed the nucleus of a Combined Action Platoon that worked with Iraqis in the local ICDC. 2/2 began working with local authorities.

"To date we've had 50 Marines wounded and one Marine, Sergeant Michael Speer, killed in action. Some of the wounds were caused by IEDs that were detonated by various means, including wired ignition, doorbells, wireless ignition, cell phones, etc.," said Dixon.

Initially the Rules of Engagement here required that Marines wait until someone showed clear hostile intent, but in recent operations when the Mahdi Militia made its presence clear, Marines were authorized to shoot at these militiamen in their uniforms that consisted of black clothing and a green headband.

Bridges on the MSRs (Main Supply Routes) across rivers and ravines became targets for the insurgents, and among the areas that 2/2 had to guard to ensure a flow of coalition supplies. One important bridge was the Jurfa As Sukr, the "Saddam Bridge." I would soon learn of several mortar attacks on 2/2 companies guarding bridges when I interviewed the Marines in its rifle companies.

The 1st Armored Division took over control of 2/2's AO at 0900 on April 21, 2004, so the Marine battalion was at this time preparing to move into a section of Fallujah within days, taking over an area currently occupied by the Marines of 1/5.

Major Dixon was a history major at VMI, and has carefully kept records of his battalion's actions here. He referred to the Marine Corps experience with insurgencies and the use of its *Small Wars Manual*, originally published in the 1930s, to help train for current operations.

I ended my part of the interview, and Major Piedmont conducted an interview with Major Dixon to learn of what he had done last year in Afghanistan.

As soon as we were done with Major Dixon's interviews, he walked us across a gravel and sand area in the blazing sun to the tents that sheltered the men of 2/2, and introduced us to several company-level officers there. I started interviews at Fox Company while Major Piedmont went over to Golf Company.

* * *

Captain Timothy Bairstow

Commanding Officer, Fox Company, 2/2

In the two months here to date, Captain Bairstow's infantry company has seen lots of action in and around the Fallujah area. During the turnover with U.S. Army units, things were fairly quiet, but soon picked up with many IED detonations and firefights against local insurgents. His Marines had also endured incoming mortar rounds, and one of his Marines was killed in action. At the time of the interview, he was preparing his company for operations inside Fallujah.

A prior enlisted Marine starting in 1988, Captain Bairstow went from private to sergeant before being commissioned in 1995, and served on several deployments with 1/2 as a rifle platoon commander and executive officer. He served in the Mediterranean, Africa, and South America. He was tall and lean, without any regional accent. His captain's bars were the newly authorized black color—up until current operations Marine officers had always worn the shiny metal officers' rank insignia, either silver or gold, on their uniforms in garrison and in the field. Those shiny insignia flashed in the sunlight, pointing out at a distance where the officer in a unit was located, not something that anyone wanted in combat. The new insignia were welcomed by Marine officers in Iraq, and I was also wearing my set of black lieutenant colonel insignia. We sat down at one end of a large locally produced tent with a plywood floor. At the other end of the tent, one of the platoons in the company was conducting briefings about current operations, but the tent was large enough that I could conduct my interviews in relative quiet.

Captain Bairstow first outlined the training his company did to prepare for urban combat prior to the deployment. Once the company arrived in Kuwait, they held some live fire training while waiting for the convoy into Iraq. They spent three days doing this specialized training. "The distance and amount of vehicles were something we had not encountered before," he noted. The convoy would stretch out to about 2 miles in length. There were mechanical problems during the convoy just inside the Iraq border. They traveled to FOB St. Michael, later known as FOB Mahmudiyah, to meet up with the Army units there.

Captain Bairstow described the turnover with the Army, starting with the Left-seat, Right-seat rides. The soldiers commanded the patrols and the Marines rode along. In the second week the Marines rode in command of the patrols and the Army rode along. "It was a pretty benign environment," he said. "They [the Army units] could ride around with small four-vehicle patrols without a lot of combat power. A big concern at that time was disbursing money to local authorities and leaders, and trying to ensure that the money was being spent properly on reconstruction projects.

"At the same time, we had Marine patrols going out day and night to show that we were concerned with local security." There was one incident when a "daisy-chained" (several explosive devices linked together) IED hit one of his convoys. "Fortunately, only two Marines were slightly wounded thanks in large part to wearing their body armor and the strapped-on armor of their vehicles. The protective goggles are the reason that they can still see now."

He described how he deployed the platoons of his company in and around Lutafiyah. Marines at an oil storage facility received mortar fire over the course of several nights, and the company sent out patrols to areas where the enemy could possibly set up mortars, and succeeded in moving them further away from the Marines' position.

He outlined night fighting in and around Lutafiyah, where one Marine was wounded and one (Sergeant Michael R. Speer) killed with a shot to the head.

On April 11, Captain Bairstow went on an unannounced visit with the town council to express the company's displeasure with the attacks and number of enemy in the area. That day, a sizable enemy force ambushed an Army convoy on Highway 8 moving from south to north. Marines did not know that this convoy was coming into the area. Fox Company started to clear from south to north to the enemy's position and help the Army convoy get out of the ambush. A QRF from 2/2 came into area and went through the ambush area in Humvees and 7-ton trucks. Captain Bairstow then drove his small force through the zone on Highway 8, also without getting hit.

Another QRF from 2/2, consisting of a rifle company and a platoon from Fox, went towards Captain Bairstow's force. He had rotary wing (helicopters) air on station to support an attack to clear Lutafiyah from south to north. However, the enemy cleared the town, and townspeople later reported that the enemy fighters were members of Al Sadr's army, in black uniforms with black and green headbands. According to a local Iraqi gas station owner in the town, these fighters were not locals, did not care what happened to the town or its people, and took what they needed from the locals. These fighters were also manning their own checkpoints when coalition forces were not around, stopping locals to seize weapons and money. This local businessman described these fighters as being from other parts of Iraq and some Syrians. Captain Bairstow wanted to go into the town and clear it out of these forces, but the battalion's priority was protecting three of the bridges along MSR Tampa.

On April 12, he, his executive officer, and his weapons platoon commander were wounded by mortar fire at one of these bridges as they were bringing out more Marines.

"Both I and the Special Forces units with me called in air strikes to destroy vehicles that were fleeing after this attack," Bairstow said. "Over the next three or four days we received sporadic mortar fire, that was sometimes accurate. I think that we were up against a trained force, something we had not expected during our workup to deploy here.

"The enemy did prove very adaptive while we were on the bridges." The fighting began with small-arms fire one day, the next day they used 57mm rockets, and by the third day they were using 82mm mortars. "We wanted to go to Lutafiyah and finish up this business, but we received orders to come here to Fallujah." His Marines wanted to go into Lutafiyah, but he said they were now ready to get into the fight in Fallujah.

Captain Bairstow arranged for me to meet with several of his platoon leaders, who then set up interviews with their Marines. This would become the general pattern I followed on my visits to Marine units throughout Al Anbar province. Asking unit commanders or the operations officers of units was almost always a very effective way of getting a good sampling of what their units had done, not to mention that I was following the proper chain of command! HD (History Division) had not sent me with a quota of certain officers or units to interview. It was up to me and Major Piedmont to use our judgment as to whom we met with, and where we would travel.

* * *

Lieutenant Brandon McDaniel

Platoon Commander, 1st Platoon, Fox Company, 2/2

A young officer on his first deployment, his Marines were heavily involved in actions in and around the village of Lutafiyah, anything from mortar attacks and security patrols, to full-scale firefights with enemy fighters.

Lieutenant Brandon McDaniel attended OCS between junior and senior years of college and was commissioned on college graduation. 2/2 was his first unit and this was his first deployment after completing his officer training at Quantico, Virginia.

McDaniel said that the platoon did lots of SASO training to prepare to deploy. He described the movement from Kuwait to Iraq. Shortly after arrival in Iraq, his platoon spent ten days straight at Lutafiyah in contact with the enemy. "Anything from mortar rounds during the day and night to pretty big firefights." He had set up a patrol base at the oil refinery between Mahmudiyah and Lutafiyah, and sent out squad-size patrols on counter-ambush and IED search missions. He put an observation post on an oil tank there, but the enemy suppressed this with an RPK gun during the night.

"On April 9, I sent out a squad-sized patrol, led by Corporal Soto, to conduct 'Snap' vehicle checks." The patrol squad encountered a counterfeit IED: A dead dog with wires visible underneath it. They called for EOD support. He then received fire from a small town nearby. That led into a ten-minute firefight in the town.

The company commander called for CAAT White, which came and provided his platoon with supporting fire from its Humvee-mounted .50 caliber machine guns.

Staff Sergeant Reichert was about a click away from this ambush, supporting Corporal Soto's patrol with a sniper rifle. The CAAT team moved the squad out of the town.

Lieutenant McDaniel then discovered that one of the CAAT vehicles had been left in the town. He mounted some Marines from his platoon to reenter the town. "We received lots of fire as we went back to the town." Several Marines in his platoon were wounded during the fighting that day, the most serious were CASEVAC'd by vehicle back to FOB St. Michael (St. Mike).

"The company later ordered us to participate in a company sweep through this town. We decided to search a house in a palm grove, and next to us, 2nd Platoon searched the house and found three men along with a Russian sniper rifle. My platoon formed a cordon around the house, and Corporal Soto was wounded through the elbow. He was evacuated by a helicopter."

Later, "We were ordered to guard Bridge 10 on Route Tampa. We were on our way there and stopped to get ammo from 2nd Platoon that was on Bridge 9. I parked my vehicles near the bridge, and then the bridge began to receive about three or four mortar rounds right on the bridge. Lieutenant Triviso (Weapons Platoon), Lieutenant Trainor and Captain Bairstow were wounded. Captain Bairstow ordered the company to form on line and we suppressed the mortar fire with our 240 Golfs [machine guns]."

He and his Marines had done all of this during their first month in country.

"My Marines did very well under fire and did exactly what they were supposed to do. It's amazing to see these 18-year-old kids react under fire. They do things you'd never think, you never expect them to and they handle it a whole lot better that you'd expect them to handle. I think the training we received has been right on the money, it's prepared us for what we're doing," said McDaniel.

The last thing he noted, "The main point I want to get across is that the way these Marines act under pressure is very admirable, it's just amazing to see them under fire."

It had gotten hot and noisy inside the tent, so for the next several interviews I moved a cot and folding chair outside, where there was a strong breeze moving the hot air.

* * *

Lieutenant Anthony Triviso

Weapons Platoon Commander, Fox Company, 2/2

Lieutenant Anthony Triviso had wanted to enlist in the Marines when he graduated from high school, but his dad convinced him to apply to the U.S. Naval Academy. After graduating from the Academy, and completion of the Basic School at Quantico, he was assigned to 2/2. Much of his training when he joined the battalion was preparing for possible missions in Liberia and Afghanistan, missions that did not take place. He remarked that the SASO training in the States prepared his Marines well for the situation when it first arrived in Iraq in early March. Triviso said, "At first, the SASO training seemed to work." While his platoon manned a vehicle checkpoint on a bridge, he received shrapnel wounds to the back of his legs that put him out of action for a short time.

During the season for the pilgrimage to Karbala (the Arbaeen Festival), Lieutenant Triviso ran a checkpoint on a road about 20 clicks (20,000 meters, or about 12 miles) away from the rest of the company. He ran a VCP (Vehicle Checkpoint), and IED patrols in the area. On one of these patrols, his platoon was hit with a daisy-chained IED consisting of five 155mm artillery shells. "We only had minor injuries that time," he said. "Three of our five vehicles were damaged, but armor on these Humvees prevented greater injuries."

His platoon was providing security on Bridge 9 when it was hit by mortar fire. After some of the rounds hit, Triviso saw the XO and the CO, and they said to him, "Hey, Tree [his nickname], you got blood all over the back of your leg!" "I couldn't move my leg. I looked and saw an M19 [40mm grenade launcher] on a vehicle and yelled for it to engage the enemy." The company got on line to fire at the enemy. Triviso had his own 60mm mortar section and his 240 Golf machine guns to fire in the direction of the enemy.

He yelled, "1st Platoon, get up here on the fuckin' berm and get into the fight." He asked observers if they could see any civilians in the area. "Negative." There were no civilians, and friendly helos fired their 20mm rounds towards the enemy. "Then the helos moved off and fixed wing dropped 500-pound bombs, and we all cheered."

Enemy fighters were seen fleeing the area in vehicles. Lieutenant Triviso was medevacked for treatment of the shrapnel wounds in his leg, but returned to his platoon the next day. He said that as of today the leg was still a little stiff, but he was not leaving his platoon. "Every one of the officers in this company feels the same way."

On April 9 a Marine rifle company and two STA platoons relieved his unit. They then moved here to Camp Fallujah, awaiting possible action in Fallujah.

* * *

Second Lieutenant Brandon Stibb

2nd Platoon Commander, Echo Company, 2/2

Things were quiet for Stibbs and his Marines when they first arrived here, but at the end of March a convoy he was on was hit with a daisy-chained IED. That began several "pretty intense" weeks of fighting near Fallujah. Several times his Marines faced challenges with limited communications gear within his platoon. He was on his first deployment.

Second Lieutenant Brandon Stibb had the robust build of a college rugby player, a little over six feet tall. He graduated from the University of Wisconsin in 2002, then attended The Basic School and Infantry Officer Training at Quantico prior to reporting in to 2/2. He briefly discussed training with the unit and preparation to move to Iraq. On arrival, he said that things in Iraq were fairly quiet and they began the turnover with U.S. Army units. He said that on March 31 things heated up when a convoy he was on was hit with a daisy-chained IED ambush. His men escaped this with very few injuries. He described the limitations of travel over the limited number of usable roads in the area between Lutafiyah and Mahmudiyah. The enemy hit them on a canal road, and one of the vehicles was rolled over, but no Marines were seriously injured. "The convoy training paid off," he said.

"We got some intel that there were some individuals in north Lutafiyah who were responsible for the recent IED attacks, so I was made part of a search mission there. We found nothing there except for one individual who had some video game controllers that were gutted out, which had been known to be used for IED detonation. So we went into a cordon of the area and in the first four houses we found nothin'.

"Where we found our big find that day was near Canal Road, just south of where we had searched. There we found lots of weapons, homemade grenades, etc., a big find.

"For Arbaeen, we were assigned to protect Muslim pilgrims from any attacks as they traveled south."

By April 7, he had received mortar attacks and small-arms fire, with only minor injuries to his Marines. April 9, 1st Platoon was at an oil depot. Lieutenant McDaniel's platoon was taking small-arms fire there, and Lieutenant Stibb's platoon along with the CAAT Blue detachment was sent to come to the aid of 1st Platoon. "I was placed between 2nd and 3rd Platoon. A big problem was that we had only three small ICOM radios [Motorola radios] for communication within the platoon. The problem with these was that they are commercially available, unsecured radios [used mainly for communication in garrison]."

When he and his Marines got near the area, it was hard to tell where the fire was coming from. Fire was coming heavily down the Canal Road, and he got a report that a Marine "was down." He finally learned that Corporal (Sergeant) Speer had been hit in the head and was dead. Lieutenant Stibb got across the road thanks to one of his fire teams that unloaded with a SAW and everything that they had.

"When there, I saw, Corporal [Sergeant] Speer was down, he was done. I was talking with Captain Bairstow and battalion and told them what had happened [to Corporal Speer]."

Stibb and his men then went on a search of a nearby building, and in one building found a sniper rifle with about 30 to 40 rounds and four men in the house, who all said that they had no idea how the rifle got there! He detained all four and brought them in for questioning. He said that one of them did provide some valuable intel.

(Stibb did not go into detail.) They then continued a search of nearby houses, and stopped the search about 2000. It was getting dark.

More mortar fire began again after dark. By this time, he and his men were more educated on where the rounds were coming from. They then moved to the FOB by vehicles, and had a day without a mission, a day off.

The following day, his platoon went on counter-mortar patrols. "The enemy are pretty bad shots with the mortars."

He described his version of the protection of the bridges along with Weapons Platoon. He explained that the enemy was targeting bridges in the area, figuring that by destroying many of the bridges in the area, they would funnel coalition convoys onto the remaining bridge on Route Jackson. "Smart move on their part, makes sense."

Bridge Company finally got there with lots of weapons, which was good as he only had two of his squads with him (along with part of Weapons Platoon and Lieutenant Triviso). During one of the mortar attacks, several of the officers of the company received mortar shrapnel on this bridge. A three-day mission lasted for five days, but, "We're Marines and we're there until the job's done."

"A pretty intense few weeks, but it's what I trained to do for 11 months [at Quantico].

"I know that Sergeant Speer would want us to do the mission, not moan over his body. He took care of his squad and himself and it hurts to have him gone."

The short time here at Camp Fallujah was being used for a little training and a lot of rest for his men.

By this time it was mid-afternoon on a hot day, and Major Piedmont had also finished up a series of interviews with Marines from another rifle company in 2/2. Both of us needed time to review the material that we had gathered, write up summaries, and ensure that the valuable information we recorded today was saved. I now had almost three hours of recordings to pack up. I thanked 2/2's executive officer, Major Dixon, and made tentative plans to return and continue the interviews at the soonest time possible. After evening chow I began to summarize these interviews and store all of the photos into my laptop computer, but I found that I was making a lot of mistakes because I was so tired mentally and couldn't concentrate. I still had a lot of sound and photo and files to store when I called it a night. This reinforced what Colonel Nick Reynolds had said to me back in Washington, DC back in March, about pacing when doing this work. Even though I was really just beginning, I could see the need to stay properly rested to maintain a focus when getting and summarizing interviews with these Marines.

Friday April 23, 2004

At today's MEF brief, things seem to be intensifying in and around Fallujah. General Conway did not preside at the brief; instead, his chief of staff, Colonel John

Coleman, ran the show. There was supposed to be a big meeting Saturday here at Camp Fallujah. Details were not discussed at the brief, but my guess was that it involved either a political solution for the fighting in Fallujah, or military action if negotiations failed to achieve the desired results.

After the brief this morning, Major Piedmont and I hitched a ride out to 2/2 with Major Dixon again to continue our interviews there. At the tent area, we split up, John went to meet with Marines from Golf Company and I went to "Easy" Company.

A word about use of the World War II designation of "Easy." Even when I was a new lieutenant in the 1970s, the Marine Corps had used the current phonetic alphabet designator "Echo" when using the letter E over the radio, or referring to one of the rifle companies in a battalion. So why was this unit called "Easy" Company? It turns out that Echo Company, 2/2, had a World War II veteran of Iwo Jima speak as a guest at their Marine Corps Mess Night two years ago. This vet had watched the company in training for a few days, and was highly impressed at the espirit de corps of these Marines. He said something to the effect that "Despite what the Marine Corps calls you fellows, you are still 'Easy Company' to me." So the company took on this honorific title after the battalion commander said that they would henceforth be known as "Easy" Company.

* * *

Sergeant Judd Anthony Word

1st Squad Leader, 1st Platoon, "Easy" Company, 2/2

A veteran of FAST training (Fleet Anti-Terrorism Security Team), Sergeant Word had seen a lot of action here. After the March turnover with the Army, he led his squad during a Vehicle Checkpoint (VCP) incident where they had to shoot at a vehicle that ignored the VCP and raced towards them. On Easter Sunday, 1st Platoon was called as a QRF for a ten-vehicle Army convoy carrying Bradley Fighting Vehicles that was being ambushed. After they pushed through the ambush area, they entered buildings in the area where they found enemy ammo and cell phones.

A tall, lanky, easy-going redhead, Sergeant Ward had extended his original enlistment by five months so that he could make this deployment to Iraq. He was involved in OIF1 in 2003 with Non-Combatant Evacuation Operations (NEO) in the Mediterranean on the USS *LaSalle*. He also attended an urban sniper course that only lasted two weeks, but he felt that it was great training for conditions in urban fighting that he has seen so far.

Sergeant Word outlined the current deployment to Iraq. His platoon flew on C-130s from Kuwait into Baghdad and then traveled overland to Mahmudiyah. He also described how the Marines took over operations from Army units in that area, and his first patrols there. His first contact with the enemy was on a "snap" VCP after other platoons had received mortar fire near Tampa.

"We searched a couple cars, traffic was routine on the road, and… a sixth car was comin' down the road, he was about 300 meters down the road and he just floored it. It was a blue car with two passengers. It had two passengers, and we had an ambush set up down the road. We went ahead and engaged the blue car. We had two enemy KIA and no friendlies hurt. In the car we found an RPG sight with night vision capabilities and a map of [Route] Tampa and the surrounding area."

His second major contact was when an Army convoy was hit near Lutafiyah (the April 11 fight), and there was a report that some U.S. soldiers were still there with their vehicles. "We were on a battalion QRF and we were, it was on Easter Sunday. The report was that a convoy hit near Lutafiyah with a couple vehicles down and a couple personnel down inside the vehicles." As 1st Platoon rushed to the area of the attack, it encountered RPG, small-arms, and mortar fire from rooftops and inside of buildings. "We pushed forward to where the 18-wheelers were. There were about ten 18-wheelers, each with two Bradleys [U.S. Army Bradley Fighting Vehicles] on them.

"While were searching an abandoned building we found linked ammo and cell phones." They began receiving small-arms fire from other buildings. His squad was on the extreme left flank of the battalion at Lutafiyah. His platoon covered the roads outside of the town to prevent enemy from leaving the town. "We pushed down the road in Hummers while the rest of the battalion searched the town.

"About a week ago, we learned that we'd be moving to this location [Camp Fallujah]." Sergeant Word felt that his training in FAST platoons helps him to better train and lead his men.

* * *

Lance Corporal David Graham Braun

Second Fire Team Leader, 1st Squad, 3rd Platoon, "Easy" Company, 2/2

Lance Corporal Braun's first few weeks in Iraq have been intense. To date his squad shot at a car that was attempting to run a vehicle checkpoint, and fought in Lutafiyah to help rescue an Army convoy that was ambushed there.

Braun enlisted in November 2001, and joined 2/2 at the end of May 2002. "Our workup for this deployment involved a lot of MOUT and SASO training." Graham stands a little over six feet tall, with a nice set of tattoos on both forearms. He carried his M16A4 with a new scope (ACOG with 4-power magnification) and an assault sling.

"I think the date was April 8, we were searching buildings [near Lutafiyah], we heard what sounded like mortar fire. We narrowed it down to about three houses where we thought the mortar fire was coming from." They didn't find anything there, but the area seemed suspicious and local people were following them at a distance.

He, along with other squads, was involved in firing on the vehicle that ran a VCP that had been set up. "We were told to 'light 'em up.' We found a mortar/RPG site with night vision capabilities."

He described the fight in Lutafiyah: "Half of our platoon was on QRF for the fight in Lutafiyah." They got the report of the vehicles that were hit in the town. "On the way down to the town we got word about the Army convoy that had been hit. On our way there we saw a big cloud of smoke in the town. There must have been about 12 vehicles that had been hit."

On their way to the hit convoy, they encountered a truck full of people, every one of them with weapons. These people started shooting at the Marines' own 7-ton truck, so the Marines engaged the enemy with fire. "It reminded me of *Black Hawk Down* as we went into the town to get to a gas station there. You could see rounds hittin' the dirt near us." They then got on top of a building for overwatch. People on a nearby building were firing at the Marines. The Marines fired at them with small arms, .50 cals and 40mm grenade rounds. His men then engaged a man walking along the street with some type of weapon—later discovered to be an RPG launcher. "The time of this firefight all told was about four to five hours.

"I've gotta say, it's the biggest rush I've ever had in my life being involved in a firefight. I mean you always wonder when you watch all the war movies who's gonna freeze up. When you're actually involved in the firefight it's scary because when you're involved in 'no-shit' combat, it's just kill or be killed, it's a rush."

My appreciation of these young Marines was quickly growing as I continued to conduct these interviews. Their confidence in themselves, the men they led, and their leaders was impressive.

* * *

Second Lieutenant Ilario G. Pantano

Platoon Commander, 3rd Platoon, "Easy" Company, 2/2

I finally sat down with the platoon commander of 3rd Platoon, "Easy" Company, who had been introducing me to his Marines all morning: Second Lieutenant Ilario G. Pantano. He seemed older and more mature than most second lieutenants. Turns out, he had originally enlisted in the Marine Corps in 1989. After completing his initial obligation, he thought that the big threats in the world had dissolved so he went to college and then became a banker in his native city of New York.

"I was going to a business meeting in New York on the morning of September 11. I was on 28th Street and 5th Avenue watching the Towers burning. I formerly had worked in 4 World Trade Center as a commodity broker. I lost a number of friends in the financial sector as well as in the firefighting sector. That day I knew I had to come back [into the Marine Corps]. I felt compelled back to service, I knew the war had opened up a new front."

He obtained an age waiver, and was commissioned as a Marine officer after completing Officer Candidate School in March of 2003. He finished IOC (Infantry Officer Course) at Quantico in December 2003, and joined 2/2 in January, 2004. So technically even though he was a "boot" or new lieutenant with his first platoon command, he was older, mature, and had several years of prior enlisted experience. He only had a couple of months to work with his platoon to prepare for this deployment.

"We had experts from all areas speak to us to prepare for cultural sensitivity in Iraq." According to Pantano, the Marine Corps spent a lot of money to prepare for SASO. These Marines took over for the 82nd Airborne in the area near Mahmudiyah, south of Baghdad.

His platoon was on the battalion QRF that responded to the large vehicle ambush in the town of Lutafiyah on Easter Sunday. "We found an ambush of Army vehicles that was five clicks [a click on the map is 1,000 meters] long." They made a linkup with a platoon of Fox Company, then searched to find the flank of the enemy position on the ambush.

"We assaulted to where the ambush started at the end of the kill zone. We assaulted through, took some positions, found satellite phones [Thorias] set to activate IEDs, linked machine gun ammo. We took positions to repel enemy attacks."

On one side they received enemy fire, and there were large oil containment tanks to their rear, some on fire and ready to "cook off." An Army QRF element with about five vehicles, led by an Army colonel from the 132nd, arrived. They (the Army QRF) fired their .50 cals and M19s to suppress the enemy fire. The enemy was using some dump trucks for cover. Pantano's platoon also used rooftops to fire at the enemy. This lasted about 40 minutes.

Next his platoon moved out in the battalion sweep of the town of Lutafiyah, finding many AK 47s and many military-age males in houses. They found that very few women or children were in the homes.

"Easy" Company next took on the bridge defense mission around April 17 to 19. The company responded to enemy mortar fire with mortar fire of its own. This cut down on the enemy mortar attacks. The Army assumed the mission of bridge security and "Easy" Company moved to Camp Fallujah.

Pantano's opinion was that they had prepared to spend some time in the area of Lutafiyah cultivating better relations with the local people, but now they have been moved to the area near Fallujah for possible actions there.

* * *

Major Brian Warren Neil
S3 (Operations) Officer, 2nd Battalion, 2nd Marine Regiment (2/2)

As operations officer for the battalion, Neil worked with the commanding officer to plan all activities for the Marines. On April 15, 2004, they were ordered to move from Mahmudiyah, south of Baghdad, to Camp Fallujah to participate in operations here. During this time they were ordered to search the village of Karmah, and withdrew from the fighting in Fallujah. Missions have constantly changed. Their current disposition south of Fallujah has allowed them to begin some of the civil affairs reconstruction that they had planned to do.

Major Neil enlisted in the Marine Corps Reserves in 1988, and served about five years as a Reservist, with a year of that on active duty during Operation *Desert Storm*. In 1993 he graduated from CCNY, John Jay College, and was commissioned as a second lieutenant via the Platoon Leader Course in May that year. He then served in a variety of infantry and intelligence billets. He joined 2/2 in 2001 after he finished AWS (Amphibious Warfare School). His first billet with the battalion was as a rifle company commander with Fox Company. He has been the battalion S3 (operations officer) since June 2003.

I asked Major Neil to concentrate on events since the beginning of April in Fallujah, and was rewarded with almost an hour of detailed information from the officer who develops the big picture for the battalion commander.

"The battalion received orders to displace from Camp Mahmudiyah, south of Baghdad, to Camp Fallujah around the 15th of April." Their advance party then went to Camp Fallujah, and the battalion began convoy movement to Camp Fallujah on April 20. The rifle companies came in at different times over the next three days. On April 23, they received orders to commence combat operations at the town of Karmah, about 10 kilometers from here. Elements of RCT7 (Task Force 2/7) had already attacked into Karmah, and were in possession of the town.

"What we were fragged to do was conduct a relief in place and continue offensive operations in Karmah." They conducted the actual relief at 1800 on April 25. "The task organization for this was Fox Company (reinforced), three CAAT platoons, and the battalion COC as well as some snipers and a PSYOPS detachment."

Major Neil said that the town of Karmah was relatively empty. He estimated that only about 30 percent of the population was still there. 2/2 continued a detailed search of the town that TF 2/7 had begun. "We assumed all of their battle positions that isolated key points into the city, and we conducted a detailed search of the town." They found several weapons and ammunition caches both in the town and outside its limits. "We had two sniper positions up on MSR Michigan and ASR Chicago, right at the junction, which was several kilometers north of the city of

Karmah." On April 24–25, Marine snipers interdicted two different rocket/mortar launch points of origin. They neutralized a vehicle, and took a few detainees as well.

On April 26, Weapons Company, 1st LAR (Light Armored Reconnaissance) Battalion, relieved 2/2, and 2/2 returned to Camp Fallujah. While this was ongoing, Golf Company was assigned to 2/1 on the northwest portion of Fallujah in the Saqlawiyah area, and Echo Company (reinforced) was Op Con (Operational Control) to 1/5 in the southern portion of Fallujah at a place called Traffic Control Point 7, right on the Fallujah dam and bridge over the Euphrates River. Once 2/2 returned to Camp Fallujah, these two companies reported back to the battalion.

On April 27, "Easy" Company conducted a combat patrol and became engaged in firefights, sustaining nine casualties while uncovering enemy strong points on the southern edge of Fallujah. (The southwest portion of Fallujah was named "Brooklyn" and the southeast portion "Queens" by RCT1).

The southernmost control line in Fallujah had been named Phase Line April. This is where several of the enemy strong points had been located. Battalion positions received some small-arms and 60mm mortar fire from these positions. 2/2's headquarters was located in a large building about a kilometer south of the Phase Line.

On April 28, Fox Company moved north along Phase Line Henry. As they passed TCP 8 around 1300, they started receiving fire. Since the battalion had not yet received orders to commence offensive operations, Fox Company extracted themselves under fire, with the help of tanks and some AAVs from TF 1/5. 2/2 then began to engage the enemy with its snipers from the sniper platoon, also two teams of snipers from 3/24, and 81mm mortars.

"On the southern edge of Queens we identified six targets, and we called in several sections of aircraft [primarily U.S. Air Force F-16s in the CAP—Combat Air Patrol—Stack over Fallujah] that supported us, and we ended up destroying six buildings that contained enemy fighters, that were positively identified and we were receiving fire from."

He said that about 15 to 16 GBU 12s (guided bomb units) were dropped and a GBU 31, JDAM, were dropped by the aircraft to accomplish this. This continued for about three hours that afternoon. Tanks also engaged targets. He referred to his extensive notes to outline a complete breakdown of the task organization of 2/2 that day. By about 1630 that afternoon, the enemy fire began to drop off in the Queens area, but then things picked up in the southern end of Brooklyn.

The fighting in Brooklyn was similar to the earlier fighting that day. "Easy" Company was involved here. Then things quieted down along the whole southern area of Fallujah. "During the day, we sustained two wounded in action. One, Lance Corporal Meister, was shot through the arm, there was another casualty, I don't remember his name, so the total wounded was about 11 wounded in action." He said that it was hard to estimate enemy dead. It could have been in the neighborhood of 30 to 40 enemy fighters.

That night, 2/2 issued a frag order to "Easy" Company to attack an enemy strong point, and the attack took place at 0400 on April 29. This attack was to destroy the remnants of the enemy strong point on Phase Line April, and to check for enemy equipment and anything of intelligence that they could gain. "Easy" Company attacked, and received some sporadic fire from other positions. They cleared the position, and determined that there were some rubble obstacles constructed in the city. Then 2/2 received notice that offensive operations would be ceasing, and that when negotiations had concluded, they would conduct a relief in place with an Iraqi security force (to be called the "Fallujah Brigade") that would replace them outside of Fallujah. There was then no enemy activity in Fallujah, and RCT1 assigned 2/2 a new AO south of Fallujah.

During a leader's reconnaissance of this new battalion sector, late on April 29, the TAC (Tactical) COC was hit by an IED. "We conducted an immediate action drill, cleared the area." The battalion's assistant ops chief, Staff Sergeant Slaughter, wounded one insurgent and another enemy fighter was captured. The wounded insurgent was dropped off at Abu Ghraib prison for medical treatment.

On April 30 the battalion was to move to its new area (Zadon) from TCP 8. This move began at about 1700 at a heavy equipment compound. Major Neil then explained how the individual rifle companies and attachments were deployed that evening into the morning of May 1.

This new battalion AO, Zadon, was southeast of Camp Fallujah, and very rural. The mission at this time was to conduct offensive operations in the zone. "This area was largely untouched." He said that different tribes had varying degrees of influence, and the area had been largely untouched by coalition forces since the invasion last year. "Our job was to get in there, engage the population through civil affairs, our intelligence affairs, and begin offensive operations." Each of the companies started to conduct security patrols and have the civil affairs detachments begin to assess needs in the areas. The civil affairs Marines were out every day, meeting with tribal leaders, clan leaders, and local government officials, to establish what was in need of repairs and what other civil affairs projects needed to be started (such as farming equipment, water treatment, irrigation, etc.). Currently 15 projects were under way.

"We were there about three days and Camp Zadon received indirect fire, mortar and rocket attacks at about 1500 in the afternoon." Gunnery Sergeant Roger Baum of the Human Intelligence Attachment was killed during this rocket attack. A point of origin for the mortar attacks was determined, and 2/2 engaged this position with a section of F-16s with six GBU 12 bombs. "That really set the stage for insurgent activity in that area."

The enemy fire was accurate, and there was also activity in "Easy" Company's zone. After May 4, the battalion aggressively sent out counter-ambush and counter-mortar patrols. It was a combination of motorized patrols and foot patrols. They managed to capture six enemy who were piling weapons into a weapons cache. "We were able to obtain a good amount of intelligence from these captured enemy that pointed to a fairly complex network that was in the Zadon area." From May 7 to 11, the patrols continued, and then the IEDs began to pop up more often. "Easy" Company was IED'd for the first time on May 8.

2/2 then planned a battalion (minus) cordon and search, using Golf and "Easy" Companies, the CAAT platoon, and the 81mm mortar platoon, to take down five targets. "We conducted this battalion cordon and search at 0300 on the 12th." It took about 14 hours and several weapons caches were uncovered, with about a dozen suspects captured. Two of those captured were on a list of persons of interest. "From the 12th until the 23rd [today], we've uncovered about 28 weapons caches in the immediate vicinity of Benchmark 55." This morning another cache had been found. He noted that a couple of these sites had been re-used after 2/2 had uncovered them. CAAT White found a sizable bunker system and weapons at a cement plant nearby, and later the area was booby-trapped in case the Marines would return.

Major Neil said, "Recent intelligence has indicated that this was a known staging area for forces loyal to Saddam Hussein, and this is where they would keep their weapons and ammunition for storage." It's in the middle of a rural area, and has easy-to-identify terrain. He added that most, about 75–80 percent, of the weapons caches found are over a year old. Some of the buried equipment was degraded by not being buried properly. 2/2 has found chemical protective gear, IED components, as well as SA7 surface-to-air missiles, small-arms ammo, and anti-aircraft weapons.

He discussed an anti-coalition "bunch" in the Farhan area. On civil affairs operations, units from 2/2 asked to search an area, and found a large weapons cache in a palm grove, and six individuals from a family there were detained by the HET detachment. Fox Company continued aggressive patrolling and civil affairs operations.

As the end of May approached, Major Neil said that 2/2 had disrupted some of the small insurgencies in this immediate area. IED activity had been fairly light. The civil affairs section was signing contracts, and several mosques, schools, and water projects were under way. He said that about 16 more projects were planned. The difficulty was finding quality contractors in this rural area and getting the work under way. Also, there were no Iraqi police or ICDC forces in the area for security and police protection. "We are developing a plan to have an ICDC unit work in the area." By the end of June, 2/2 hoped to recruit and train a local ICDC platoon for Zadon, and to have an ICDC company of about 120 individuals trained by September.

Major Neil noted that the battalion had gotten back from Iraq last year, and then quickly got ready to redeploy this February. He said it was a young battalion. The SASO training prepared them for a relief in place with the U.S. Army units, and that work began before things went bad in Fallujah. In a short time, 2/2 went into a high intensity of combat operations. "Now that Fallujah's concluded, we've started to ratchet back to security, stability operations." He felt that the Marines need to mentor the local Iraqi security forces. The battalion has developed into a cohesive unit, capable of a whole range of operations.

* * *

Lieutenant Edward Minnich Trainor
Executive Officer, Fox Company, 2/2

Trainor described working with support from Marine tanks and aviation during firefights in the southeast section of Fallujah. After many weeks of combat operations in and around Fallujah, as Projects Officer, Trainor was able to begin working with local leaders to rebuild the area's infrastructure. He explained the process to have local leaders propose work, contractors bid for contracts, and how the process unfolds once approval is given. Combat and patrolling continued at the same time.

Lieutenant Trainor graduated from Penn State in 2000 and received his commission via NROTC. He began TBS in June 2000 and then attended the Infantry Officer Course in January 2001. He next reported to 2/2, and has been a member of the battalion for his entire career so far. He served as a rifle platoon commander, then Weapons Platoon commander, then became the battalion S3 Alpha (assistant to the operations officer) in June 2003. He became company executive officer for Fox Company in October 2003.

"When we departed the U.S., I left as part of the advance party. I departed on the first of March, where the company departed on the third of March. We flew into Camp Udari, which is in Kuwait. There I linked up with the rest of my company when they arrived." He went with the advance party and flew into Mahmudiyah, Iraq on March 12. Fox Company operated there from its arrival until April 20 when it convoyed to Fallujah.

When he arrived in Mahmudiyah, he began the turnover with the Third of the Fifth Army battalion there. During this time, he went on the "ride-alongs," to learn the AO, including the dangers and the friendly situation. "On my first convoy, my convoy was IED'd, with an explosive device, injuring one soldier, and he was sent home. Later that afternoon we were fortunate, I got to go out again, and I engaged an Iraqi who was trying to detonate an IED. So I got a little bit of redemption." I asked him what he meant by engaged, if that meant firing his weapon, and he said that is exactly what he meant. "At that time I was carrying an Army M4."

The company arrived safely at Mahmudiyah on March 15 and began SASO, to go out and meet the local population, learn what the Iraqi citizens needed, help them to become used to a free Iraq, as well as to learn about the anti-Iraqi forces (AIF) who were operating in the area.

"This went very well for about two weeks. We were preparing for a big operation known as *Arbaeen.* Arbaeen is the Shiite holiday where they do a long walk from Baghdad, south to Karbala. That route happened to go directly through our AO. Therefore, it was very important for us to provide safety for the Shiia Iraqis as they moved through our AO."

However, this was at the time that Muqtada al Sadr started to make trouble with his army, and a lot of firefights broke out. Fox Company had three platoons at separate patrol bases: South of Mahmudiyah near Lutafiyah; a patrol base north of Lutafiyah; and the third patrol base on the Jafa Sakr Bridge which is about 15 clicks (kilometers) west of Lutafiyah. Lieutenant Trainor stayed in Mahmudiyah to provide logistical support to the patrol bases, while the company commander (Captain Bairstow) went out to the patrol bases. As Arbaeen began, Lieutenant Trainor went with the battalion commander to the Jafa Sakr Bridge. He brought the FAC to assist in calling for air support.

"That night and every night after that we were mortared. One night in particular, that was on the 8th of April, we were mortared with a 15-round barrage directly on our CP. As that barrage occurred, we had a squad-size element in an ambush, ready to take out that mortar element. When the squad-size element moved to go to the mortar positions of the enemy, they were immediately cut down by RPK fire and RPG fire. The CP… clearing out of the way from the mortar barrage, was immediately trying to provide support for that squad that was now cut off from the rest of the platoon. As we were trying to provide support, the rest of the platoon was attacked from the west by a platoon-size element of anti-Iraqi forces. When we were attacked from the west, it was heavy RPK fire, AK 47 fire, RPGs, and a few mortars still firing from the position to our north."

They couldn't support the cutoff squad while the platoon was being attacked by this platoon-size element of the enemy. In order to do that, "We called close air support, with the forward air controller, call sign 'Rookie.' He effectively called on a hunter-killer team, which consists of one Cobra and one Huey gunship. We rolled the Huey gunship and the Cobra into the enemy position and destroyed the enemy. Simultaneously we were suppressing the enemy from our own positions. Fortunately, no Marines were injured during that attack. As soon as the close air strike hit the AIF attacking us from the west, the [enemy] position to the north that was suppressing our squad broke contact and ran." The company couldn't confirm enemy killed, but he said that it was an intense 90-minute fight.

The day after this fight, Lieutenant Trainor was returning to FOB Mahmudiyah and the battalion S3 grabbed him and told him that the remainder of Fox Company was in a fight at the patrol base north of Lutafiyah.

"I jumped aboard immediately with the battalion TAC. When I got into the vehicle, I was in the vehicle with the battalion commander and the battalion sergeant major." The sergeant major told Lieutenant Trainor that one Marine had been killed in action, and two other Marines had been shot. When he arrived at the patrol base, he helped carry the killed and wounded Marines onto a medevac helo that had been called in. By the time Trainor and the battalion commander arrived at the north patrol base, the fighting had died down.

On April 11 an Army convoy was moving north through their AO along Route 8, also known as Route Jackson. The Marines did not have any warning that this convoy was moving north. Simultaneously, Captain Bairstow had received orders to go to Lutafiyah to talk with the sheiks there about the recent fighting. As Captain Bairstow and a platoon were moving south to the town, they saw the Army convoy moving north and getting attacked by a large ambush force that destroyed vehicles and was "Laying havoc against that Army convoy." This convoy broke contact and moved immediately north to FOB Mahmudiyah.

Captain Bairstow and his security platoon began to fire into the ambush, and were then decisively engaged in a firefight. "Quickly a battalion QRF was launched with a company-minus size element to go support Captain Bairstow in the firefight." Once this force linked up with Captain Bairstow, they moved through the ambush.

While this was going on, Major Dixon (battalion XO) was running the battalion operations back in the rear, and Lieutenant Trainor was back with the remainder of Fox Company. "A call came to the battalion that a bridge, known as Bridge 9, along Route Tampa, had nearly been destroyed, and that Second Battalion, Second Marines [2/2] was responsible for securing that bridge at all costs." At about 2300 on April 11, Lieutenant Trainor was given the mission to take 60 Marines with him and secure the bridge. He prepared his Marines and left at 0300 on April 12 to secure the bridge. Captain Bairstow along with the remainder of the company linked up with him on the afternoon of the 12th.

Captain Bairstow and Lieutenant Trainor were meeting on the bridge discussing the security of that structure when a mortar barrage hit the bridge. "One round landed approximately 10 meters from our position, wounding both the company commander and myself." Despite minor wounds, they decided to stay in the area of the bridge. Marines in the area commenced a firefight towards the area that appeared to be the point of origin of the mortar rounds. They received some AK 47 return fire from the area. The Marines swept through this area, did not find the weapons or personnel there, but they did see a vehicle pull away from an area behind it. The getaway vehicle was a blue pickup truck with several men in it, according to an Apache helicopter that was flying overhead. Once it was determined that these were the individuals fleeing from the mortar strike, "We called in an air strike and put a Mark 82 bomb on the vehicle. That vehicle was destroyed."

For the next five days they held the bridge, and received either mortar or rocket fire every day. On April 16, "Easy" Company relieved them and they were able to go to FOB Mahmudiyah for rest and refit. Fox Company also had a memorial service for the Marine who had died the week before. Next they received orders to move to Camp Fallujah and began to pack up the company.

The conditions at Camp Fallujah were austere compared to those at FOB Mahmudiyah. At Mahmudiyah, they had enjoyed air-conditioned tents, a chow hall, an internet cafe, and a gym. At their section of Fallujah, the tents were falling down, and chow was trucked in Vat cans from the main chow hall. For the next week, Fox Company Marines improved their living quarters, and awaited orders to participate in operations at Fallujah. The rest of 2/2 arrived there on April 23. "We knew that we were eventually gonna be ready to push out and hopefully support the Marines that had been fighting fiercely in Fallujah."

On April 28 the mission came and Fox Company, followed by the battalion TAC (Tactical Operations Center), moved to about two clicks south of Fallujah, just east of the Euphrates River. The battalion set up its COC and Fox Company established a blocking position about 600 meters north of the COC. Any potential enemy attack would have to go through Fox Company before getting to the battalion COC. "We could see the city from where we were at."

Captain Bairstow with some of his platoon commanders and one rifle platoon for security went towards Fallujah to conduct a leaders' recon.

"As soon as he [Bairstow] left friendly lines, probably the heaviest firing I've seen was directed right at the leaders' reconnaissance element. They were immediately, decisively engaged. The platoon commanders got out of the vehicles and led the platoon into covered and concealed positions to where they could first, survive. And number two, return fire and try and destroy the AIF that was shooting at them."

Lieutenant Trainor was with the rest of the company. A few stray shots came his way. He wanted to support the leaders' recon element, but only with direct fire weapons, as it was hard to see where all of the Marines were hidden.

"At my position we were taking heavy fire, from one building in particular, it was approximately 500 meters to my north. It was a machine-gun nest, inside of a house, firing out of a window… they suppressed us pretty good. Co-located with that machine-gun nest was a sniper. Unfortunately, we found out the hard way there was a sniper. I had my mortar section leader come to me to discuss the grid on that house, how quickly he could get fires put on that house. As he was talking to me, he was shot directly through his right bicep, by the sniper position. When he went down, immediately medical assistance was provided. Fortunately, we were right next to the battalion COC, so I had a couple Marines carry him over to the COC, where they immediately sent him to the Bravo Surgical Unit here at Camp Fallujah. He was taken care of."

I asked if the Marine survived, and Lieutenant Trainor said that he had, with the shot through his arm being his only wound.

Lieutenant Trainor and his men were effectively pinned down; the target was too far away to effectively engage with small-arms fire, and he was too cautious to put 60mm mortar fire on the building because he didn't know exactly where friendlies were, and his mortar section leader had just gone down. He felt that it had to be a precision shot on that building. Snipers on top of the battalion COC couldn't see anything, so they couldn't do anything until the leaders' recon had pulled back.

"The leaders' recon element called in four air strikes onto positions to their north to enable them to break contact and pull back to our position. When they pull back to our position, I now have no friendlies in front of me, but we were still taking fire from the machine-gun nest. I talk to my company commander, told him where the machine-gun nest was, and asked him if I could use one of the tanks that was attached to the battalion. He immediately gave me the tank, and since I knew where the position was, I went ahead and talked the tank into a firing position. I walked behind the tank, talking to him on his intercom phone, which is directly behind the tank. Walking behind him, a couple of rounds [were] plinging off the tank, I was able to walk him into a good firing position."

To mark the target building, Lieutenant Trainor had some of his Marines open up with tracer rounds on the house. "As soon as they opened up on the house, the tank destroyed the building. The main gun destroyed that building, [then we] received [a] report that there was another building approximately 300 meters to the west of that building, where there was some enemy activity. So we destroyed that building as well with the tank main gun. As soon as the tank main gun went off, everything was quiet. There were no more rounds coming from the enemy, and there were some reports of white flags being seen from the town of Fallujah."

The enemy was no longer willing to fight after the tank fired its main gun.

After this, the company moved north to a blocking position 400 meters north of the battalion COC and there was no more enemy fire for the next three days. On 30 April, Fox Company along with 2/2 was ordered to move about 12 clicks south of Fallujah and resume security and stability operations in and around this AO. This put space between 2/2 and what Lieutenant Trainor referred to as the FPA (Fallujah Protective Authority), to allow them to work on area security. He said that there was some hesitation on the part of some of his platoon commanders about this, but it seems that this was a good move, as the Iraqis who have come in seemed to be doing the job. Trainor said, "We were no longer getting shot at."

For the next two weeks they conducted SASO, and were now working out of Camp Fallujah on the same type of operations with very few incidents. There was one patrol that was rocketed when they were out on a patrol base, but no one was injured.

I asked Trainor if his company had found any of the weapons caches that I read about on the MEF briefings. "About three days ago we found a weapons cache located behind a target house, that was given to us by our S2. In that weapons cache we found RPGs, some rounds—60 mike mike rounds, 82 mike mike rounds, obviously AK 47 rounds, RPK rounds. Most notably we found DVDs that were terrorist training videos, and they were put out by Osama bin Laden, with his face all over the front. After watching some of these terrorist training videos, you could see the major theme was from Osama bin Laden, since his face was on every training picture that was taken and put on that DVD."

For the first time in my interviews, I was talking with someone who was also directly involved in civil affairs projects. Lieutenant Trainor was the projects officer for his company, and was responsible for helping the Iraqis to build better facilities for their children, working with schools. "Each contract is given to me by either the sheik or an engineer who wants work to be done on their school. This is easy to do because we go to all the schools and speak to the headmaster and see what kind of work needs to be done. The [local Iraqi] engineers within two or three days will present me a proposal of what they would like to do to their schools." The proposal outlines what they want to do to the schools, how much it will cost and what the finished product will look like. Lieutenant Trainor then takes the proposal along with two other proposals to the battalion CAG (Civil Affairs Group) officer, Major DeVito, and they discuss which proposal they will send to Regiment. If Regiment approves, Trainor tells the engineers. If not, he tells the engineers the reasons and outlines the things that need to be changed.

Once Regiment approves and gives him the funding, Lieutenant Trainor sits down with the engineers and goes over the details of the contract with them. When he signs the contract, he needs to know where the laborers will come from, and 95 percent of the time, the contractor/engineer is from the town anyway. Most of the workers are usually from the local area. When there is no local contractor available, outside contractors from Baghdad or Fallujah are brought in, with the understanding that they bring in some local laborers. This also pumps in some money to the local economy. Once the headmaster, sheik, and local contractor agree to all of the terms, dates are set to accomplish certain things. "We pay one third of the cost to the contractor on contract signing day. Once one third of his work is complete, I come investigate again, make sure that everything is working well, as long as everything is working well, I tell him to continue working, he follows along with his proposal. I inspect again at the two-thirds point, and at the two-thirds point is when I pay him another third of his total cost. Finally, at the two-thirds point when I pay him, I also establish a time when I'm gonna come inspect the school for final inspection." On the final inspection day, Lieutenant Trainor pays the remainder of the money and they have a ribbon-cutting ceremony and turn the school over to the headmaster and the sheik of the town.

He outlined the exact type of repairs that are being done at schools: There are three areas: First, the basic structure, such as repairing walls and fences; second, the plumbing which includes water tanks for the bathrooms and cleaning; third is electricity, where fans and electric lights are installed. After that there are cosmetics, such as soccer fields, basketball courts, and plants to make the building look better on ribbon-cutting day.

Each company within the battalion has the same civil affairs activities ongoing in their AOs. "Each company has a projects officer in their company that works directly with the CAG, and then works directly in their zone with the sheiks and headmasters." Fox Company currently had projects with two different schools. One school (Al Rasafi) was approved for a $130,000 project with the contract meeting scheduled for tomorrow, and a school project at Arabiyah School had been submitted for $145,000. Lieutenant Trainor expected regimental approval for this in a day or two. He was also looking at four other projects, including a mosque, another school, an irrigation system, and another school that has been recommended by CAG but that he has not yet inspected.

Lieutenant Trainor concluded by commenting, "We've been through enough as a company to know that we can operate under combat situations. And we're prepared to do that if it goes back to it. None of us want that to happen. Currently the civil and support operations in our zone are motivational. We get times when we can go out and play soccer with the children. The Marines love that. Marines love seeing the Iraqis enjoying what we're doing out there. And that's what we foresee over the next three months."

* * *

First Lieutenant Walker Clark Koury
Platoon Commander, 3rd Platoon, Fox Company, 2/2

Fresh from his own officer training at Quantico, Koury began to train a platoon made up of mostly new Marines in November 2003. His veteran NCOs helped to take the platoon through its workup for the deployment. His platoon was part of Fox Company's reaction force that helped to rescue an ambushed Army transport vehicle convoy. During a company leaders' recon outside southern Fallujah, he and the others came under heavy enemy fire. He was able to work with a forward air controller to have Air Force F-16 jets drop heavy ordnance on enemy positions, and later had his machine gunners mark targets for Marine tanks to hit.

Lieutenant Koury went to Colgate University in New York, entered the PLC (Platoon Leader Course) program and received his commission in May 2002. He attended TBS starting in fall 2002. He was still in training at Quantico, and said that when the Iraq war began, he and his classmates there watched it on TV, and the big joke was that they had missed the war. "None of us even thought that we would get the chance to go here." After Infantry Officer Course in 2003, he reported to 2/2 at

Camp LeJeune. He was the only lieutenant platoon commander then, as 2/2 had just gotten back from Iraq and many company officers had orders elsewhere.

It was uncertain what 2/2 would do next, until about mid-November 2003 when they got word that they would be going to Iraq. "At this point I basically got an entirely new platoon from SOI (School of Infantry, the post-recruit training for new Marines). I kept about nine Marines who had been here before, and about six NCOs." So he and the NCOs began intense training with the platoon. Emphasis was on SASO. This included lots of urban patrolling and meeting with locals. They deployed on March 2, 2003. I interrupted at this point, to ask if 2/2, an East Coast unit, had done any training with the West Coast units before the deploying. Lieutenant Koury replied, "Yes, sir, they flew us out to March Air Force Base in February. It was absolutely great training because it's a deserted housing complex from a military base [there]. The 1st MEF actually puts on scenarios there, [in] which platoons go out there for a three-hour exercise, 24/7." The units go through the town for the training. He said that it helped his platoon and Fox Company in developing its command and control procedures.

Lieutenant Koury then resumed his description of the initial deployment into Iraq. They went to Camp Udari in Kuwait, and received training from the British Royal Marines on how to do urban patrolling and search for weapons, the Winthrop Method, that he said they had developed in Northern Ireland. "We've had quite a bit of success so far using this technique." He said that the training from the Royal Marines has been invaluable thus far.

"We convoyed up to the town of Mahmudiyah on, I want to say, the 14th of March, and began operations there. And as soon as we got there, we basically saw that it was what we trained for." It was fairly quiet, with a few IEDs, and stayed quiet until the first week in April. He described the events then as a national uprising between Sunnis and Shias in Iraq. This is when everything they had trained for changed. "We immediately went into conventional operations."

He said that it was difficult for some of the younger Marines to gear up for this, since they had not had a lot of training for direct firefights, calling for mortars, reacting to incoming mortars, etc. He relied heavily on his experienced NCOs. The squad leaders had been in Iraq last year, and they really helped to transition the Marines into combat operations. During the day, the platoon was continuing with SASO, but at night, the FOB was receiving mortar fire, and fire from small arms.

On the night of April 9, his platoon was patrolling the town of Lutafiyah, and was holding the police station there to prevent it from being overrun. When they got the word about a large firefight taking place, they returned to the FOB, got what vehicles they could and got to the firefight too late to help, as the shooting had died down.

After the first week in April, a priority was guarding main supply routes. MSR 5, also called Route Tampa (and Iraqi Route 8) was the route that 3rd Platoon had to guard. When IEDs destroyed bridges on some of the MSRs, supply convoys would have to re-route through smaller towns in an area. "On April 11, an Army convoy was diverted off a main MSR through the town of Lutafiyah, because of a bridge that had gotten blown. I don't know if anyone in the Army had checked beforehand to run through our sector at Lutafiyah, because right off the bat, we would've told them, it is NOT some place you want to take a huge convoy. The convoy was destroyed by quite an advanced ambush. They destroyed about four or five vehicles. They destroyed APCs (Armored Personnel Carriers), fuel carriers. My platoon ended up reacting to the ambush. We rolled south along [he thought] MSR Jackson. As soon as we started rolling down that we started taking a large volume of small-arms fire from the entire city of Lutafiyah. Everyone who owned an AK came out of their house, and, uh, came on the rooftops and started shooting up our trucks. You could hear bullets bouncing off the side of the trucks. We returned fire and I eventually linked up with my CO down in Lutafiyah and my platoon ended up clearing up the majority of the southern section of Lutafiyah. My platoon took over the police station, because it was obvious to us the police knew about this, because they made no effort to stop it."

His platoon took the station, and took the weapons from the police. The Marines went through the city, but did not find any weapons. But it was his opinion that the entire town knew what was going on.

During the next week, 3rd Platoon was guarding a bridge about 10 clicks west of Mahmudiyah, and there Lieutenant Koury had to ensure that his new Marines learned how to dig proper fighting positions, machine-gun positions and make fire plan sketches of the defenses. Fortunately, his own training at Quantico had prepared him for this. Round the clock, he always had a patrol out in the area. Once, they received mortar fire, but the active patrolling prevented a repeat of this.

They next were sent to the town of Karmah for a week, where, he said, the locals were very friendly. They worked in a Firm Base and got along well with the locals.

On April 28, the entire battalion (2/2) loaded up and moved to the southern portion of the cordon around Fallujah. "I guess, the mood of the Marines was really good, because we had finally gotten to, 'Who's the enemy, he's in the town, and it's old school. We're gonna bring in tanks, planes, and we're gonna kill 'em.' Morale was really good, because it's no more of this hiding around. A lot of the Marines knew they were gonna be part of history." This was shaping up to be a really big battle. "If you came into the Marine Corps to do something, this is it."

They staged about two clicks outside of Fallujah, and Captain Bairstow told the platoon commanders that they would be going on a commanders' recon up north towards the city. Lieutenant Koury left his platoon sergeant in charge of the platoon to go with the company commander, Captain Bairstow. He was in one of five Humvees going north towards the outskirts of Fallujah, About 800 meters up the road, this convoy started taking enemy fire. "We were about five to six hundred meters from Fallujah, and immediately, this small arms started opening up." They pulled the convoy off the road near some houses. The Marines dismounted the vehicles, took cover behind the buildings, and started returning fire. Along with the CO and platoon commanders was about a squad and a half of Marines from one of the rifle companies as security. "There was the crack of bullets over our head, and it became very difficult to move."

Lieutenant Koury opened up the door of his Humvee, using the titanium-armored door as protection, while he ensured that the Marines from the vehicle got out. He started returning fire. "I started hearing this pinging noise, and I look round. The doors of my Humvee are getting holes punched in them. I mean, they were firing, what had to have been armor-piercing rounds, 'cause these doors, if you look on the front, you can see where rounds had just bounced right off. And at this point, we knew we were up against a serious enemy. He was either firing a very high-velocity round, or armor piercing. It was going right through the doors."

Realizing this, he got down low. The Marines started setting up sectors of fire. He grabbed the nearest corporal there and took about six Marines to clear a house and use it as a base of fire. A machine gun they had immediately went down, and he stripped a 240 Golf machine gun from one of the vehicles. The gunner got the gun out, and they moved to a fighting position inside of a house.

Because this was a company recon of leaders, this was not a full platoon out there, and radio comm was difficult between everyone. They realized that they were basically stuck there because of the volume of fire they were receiving, but there were Marine tanks nearby. "This was a pretty nice sight to see, when you're pinned down, look back, and see a pair of tanks rolling up to your position."

The tanks, off to their left, started engaging targets in Fallujah. A FAC, Captain Anderson (call sign "Rookie"), came up to Koury and asked him which buildings were shooting at them. A sergeant had told Lieutenant Koury where some of the fire originated from, it was next to a mosque. "The FAC called in, I think, a pair of F-16s. They dropped some 500-pound bombs, and immediately, the [gun]fire began to stop!"

By this point, they had tanks, air, and ground fire. He said that this is something that a Marine lieutenant always envisions, having combined arms to give him overwhelming firepower in a fight. "This was combined arms to a 'T'. We had guys on the ground spotting, we had tracs come up for help, we were calling in our 81s. Snipers were behind us on a building suppressing for us. Air was coming in, tanks were coming in. It was just like what we did at 29 Palms [Marine Combined Arms Training Exercises]." Lieutenant Koury said it was an extremely hot day, and he was exhausted by the end of it. He said that he was exhausted an hour into the firefight. When he would run from one house to another, the one thing he remembers was the exhaustion.

When he got back to the company area, he discovered that it was also under fire. His platoon sergeant told him that they had been taking fire from an area in the east of Fallujah. His platoon was deployed in skirmisher positions, and there was a well-placed enemy machine gun position firing at them. Someone had the idea that they still had the tanks with them, so they rolled the tank and its main gun up. "It was great, 'cause I actually got to act like John Wayne. I used the phone in back [of the tank]. If they didn't have the grunt phone, we couldn't have done it. The grunt phone literally, by itself, took out the thing [machine gun], because the tanker couldn't exactly tell… I was able to talk him onto the building, using the grunt phone.

"I used the grunt phone because I had to tell the tank commander the position of my platoon, so that he didn't run over my platoon, or fire on them. So the XO [Lieutenant Trainor] says 'Okay, I'll organize the tank, you go get your platoon.' We actually used a 240 Golf to mark the target. And as soon as the tanker saw it, just put a round right through the building. The funniest thing, as soon as they did that, I don't know if they're all insurgents, something like 10 people come out, all waving white flags from the position right ahead of us! They start walking towards our position." That ended any small-arms fire from that sector of Fallujah after that afternoon.

His platoon then dug in as the very right flank of the battalion's battle position. They dug in all night, ending with what he described as "textbook" fighting positions. "It was a good thing, because that night they hit us with a 120 rocket, or it was something big. I've had a lot of mortars shot at me, and this was the biggest thing ever shot at me." It landed only about 30 meters outside of their position, but no one was hurt.

Then the word came down that the Marines would be pulling out of Fallujah due to a political agreement. "There was an agreement that an Iraqi Fallujah protection army was gonna take over and we would pull out, move southwest into the countryside." The platoon did this, and found a nice house that they rented from a local civilian to build a new Firm Base. He said that the people here were actually very friendly.

Over the past three or so weeks in the local countryside, he said that there have been no firefights, but that they have been finding "tons" of weapons. He noted that the insurgents have a network of people observing for them. "We've never spotted a guy emplacing an IED, we've never caught a guy transporting weapons. They always have lookouts."

It's easy for people in civilian clothes to blend in. The first day they were there he was driving around in a Humvee with a CAAT team and the team got lost. They cut through a farmer's field to get back to a road. "And lo and behold, right in front of us there was this guy walking across a field, and he had an armful of RPK machine guns. Because, they apparently just watch the roads and know when our vehicles are coming down the roads. And this guy looked at me and, there's a gunnery sergeant up front and I was in back. And we just come within eye contact, we couldn't believe what we were finding. And he just dropped his RPK and started running off."

He and the gunny took off in chase with their pistols drawn. They caught him, and when they started looking around the field, it looked like he had an arsenal buried there in his yard. "This was the first time we actually caught somebody putting something [weapons] in." The problem would usually be that when a weapons cache was found, no one could be held accountable and prosecuted for this.

The area has been peaceful. They have gotten in good with the tribal leaders, and the local people have acted nicely towards the Marines. In his opinion, when the local sheik likes the Marines, he can keep the area safer. Also, he said that his Navy Corpsman is probably one of the best assets he can bring with him on a patrol because of the medical knowledge he has. "We had a [Iraqi] kid who was gonna die from an ear infection because nobody knew how to clean it out or understand what it was. My Corpsman just had some antiseptic and some antibiotics and gave it to the kid. Within a week, the kid was totally fine." The Corpsman can also clean up cuts and infections of locals. He said that his Corpsman has had the most work of anyone in his platoon.

"There's no greater teacher than combat." Koury said that his training prior to getting here was an excellent preparation. He only wished that he had been able to take the platoon to a CAX (combined arms exercise) before deploying. But the NCOs have the experience to lead the Marines. It has been a much more NCO-intensive operation than he anticipated.

Many of his peers from Quantico have been deployed to Iraq. He ran into a lieutenant buddy of his out on a bridge. He said it's like a TBS reunion when he gets into the main chow hall at night. He looked back on this time last year when he was a lieutenant still in training. He never thought that he would be here as part of the largest battle of the war so far. "I know I haven't missed out on anything, sir."

He lost one Marine in his platoon two nights ago. They were pursuing a mortar attack, and a Marine got hit by a truck on a road and was killed.

Lieutenant Koury was still officially a second lieutenant. His promotion would be effective the day after this interview, May 24!

* * *

Staff Sergeant Thomas L. Reynolds III

Platoon Sergeant, 3rd Platoon, Fox Company, 2/2

During a nighttime leaders' conference on a bridge, incoming mortar rounds began to explode around Reynolds and the other company leaders. He was unharmed. Security and stability operations never really ended, but he was part of the relief team that rescued an ambushed Army vehicle transport convoy, and also part of the fighting south of Fallujah.

His Marines have found many enemy weapons caches in areas they have occupied, often freshly cleaned and ready to use. Most of his Marines are new to the Corps and to combat, but have responded well to everything asked of them.

Staff Sergeant Reynolds entered the Marine Corps in March 1994. Before joining 2/2 in January 2004 he was a recruiter. He described the training since then, which involved satellite patrolling, and quick reaction drills with weapons to familiarize the new Marines with their weapons. He estimated that 75 percent of the Marines in his platoon were new, in combat for the first time. All of his NCOs served in OIF1 in Iraq.

When the platoon arrived in Iraq near Mahmudiyah, it began SASO. He noted, "The threat that we were facing at the time was like no other threat anybody's, I will say, that I never expected." He noted that SASO never really ended, but around the Arbaeen festival, they were at an old ice factory and received mortar fire, RPK fire and small-arms fire. It started getting to be a daily occurrence. Before this there was anticipation and excitement. He said that many Marines wanted to know what it was like to face combat. He was part of the Quick Reaction Force that came to the aid of the Army convoy that was hit in Lutafiyah. "We went down to the Temple Jackson intersection. We ran through a gauntlet, getting there, sir. I'd say anywhere from a three-click gauntlet, takin' fire from both sides of the road. And, it was pretty consistent fire, all the way down to the Temple Jackson intersection." From there, they started clearing through southern Lutafiyah, but did not capture anyone who was a threat.

About a week prior to that incident, the platoon got called to consolidate with the rest of Fox Company in a palm grove area in Lutafiyah. They started going house to house in the city for a short time.

He apologized for not getting the dates right on the events, but recounted most of the significant events for me. Fox Company had gone to secure a bridge. The platoon commanders, platoon sergeants, and the company gunny were there. "Me and Lieutenant Koury started walking back. He had to relieve himself. It was a good thing. A mortar round [then] landed right there in the middle of the bridge. It wounded our company commander [Captain Bairstow], our executive officer, our weapons platoon commander, it also injured a gunnery sergeant, and the first sergeant also got hurt in that." Had he and Lieutenant Koury not left moments before, they most likely would also have at least been wounded from the mortar fire.

I asked if the company knew where the rounds originated, or took any action, as I had an idea of this from other interviews with members of Fox Company. "Yes, sir, we started receiving small-arms fire from the east side of [Route] Tampa. And 3rd Platoon was on line, closer to the bridge, returning fire. We also had an Army unit that was out there with us, and we were all returning fire. Then 3rd Platoon pretty much started sweeping through the area, swept through a field, went to the houses and swept through the houses, with no luck, sir." Reynolds continued,

"Some of these individuals are pretty good, farmers by day." He did not see any blood trails in that area.

"We found some caches, sir, some weapons caches, large caches. [We] found an RPK machine gun, RPG rounds, explosives, we found grenades, mortar rounds, an IED itself that was waitin' to be set. Numerous, numerous, numerous things we found." I asked where the caches were found. "Actually sir, it was in the area of Mesra, we had done a raid in that area, and we ended up searching a palm grove area right next to his [a farmer's] house." That was one of the areas where he and his Marines found the weapons and ammo.

His Marines also found Iraqis with more weapons than needed for self-defense. (At this time, Marines would not confiscate a lone AK 47 from an Iraqi's home.)

After the beginning of April 2004, his company was sent to take part in cordoning off the outer portion of Fallujah. When the leaders' recon got engaged there, his platoon started receiving sniper fire—including small arms and machine gunfire from about 600 meters away. Staff Sergeant Reynolds and the executive officer, Lieutenant Trainor, were back in this area. Whenever Marines would pop their heads up, "There would be pops of smoke right in front of them," from enemy shooters. It was hard to pinpoint the origin of this fire.

When one of the Marines was wounded in the arm, Staff Sergeant Reynolds went to him and cut off his sleeve in order to start first aid. A Navy Corpsman showed up and took over. While the Corpsman was working on the Marine, a sniper shot off a branch overhead that fell on the Corpsman.

The Marines had to be careful where they moved due to the sniper fire, but had their 240 Golfs "rockin' and rollin'." Marine air support came in close, and the enemy fire died down somewhat.

Once the leaders' recon element returned, Staff Sergeant Reynolds and a fire team from 1st Platoon went up and started marking a target with SAW rounds and M16 tracer rounds. "Once we got the thumbs up, we got off two rounds [tank rounds] at two different buildings." This ended the main action that afternoon in that sector.

That night they received indirect fire, some rockets and some mortars, at this position. One night a rocket landed right outside their position.

Then they began to conduct counter rocket and counter mortar patrols. They found more RPG rounds, and an RPG launcher. "All of these weapons were freshly lubed. No rust on them. They were clean, nice, they smelled good. They smelled like they had been cleaned inside, so they were well-maintained. They weren't buried, or anything.'

Staff Sergeant Reynolds then jumped back to events in Karmah, before the events in Fallujah. He was not working off a set of notes during our interview, but was trying to recall the most significant events in his time here. He again apologized, but I told him that the order of events was not important, just his ability to recollect and share them.

3rd Platoon was at Karmah for about five days, without significant action. They cleared houses of excess weapons, met with locals, did handshaking, "I enjoyed that place. It was pretty nice."

I asked if there was any handshaking and meeting people taking place now: "Oh, yes sir, definitely. Every time we go out, we stop. We wave to kids, we pass out soccer balls, toys, give 'em candy. We go up and shake everybody's hand. Anybody that'll accept our handshake, we'll give it to."

He said that the current area the company was working in had much more friendly people. He was hopeful that the schools and irrigation projects would help these people out. This area is mostly rural, with smaller houses for the most part. There are also a few substantial houses.

One of the Marines in his platoon was killed by a truck during a patrol. The patrol was seeking the origin of some rocket attacks and to try and catch the individuals involved. The Marine was out on the road as part of the security effort when a truck hit him.

Staff Sergeant Reynolds remarked on the attitude that he works to preserve in his platoon. He wants them to be ready to be aggressive when necessary, but to work with the locals to keep the peace.

As for how his young Marines have responded to the various levels of operations here: "Couldn't ask for better. Couldn't do it. Everybody says the Marine Corps has changed. Throughout time these guys are professionals. It's all they are. They know their job, and they learn as they go. And they're great. I couldn't ask for a better platoon. They're awesome."

As the interview ended, the Fox Company CO, Captain Bairstow, met me and asked if I would join him for lunch. We went to the mess hall area for 2/2, where Marines served up hot chow from Vat cans sent from the main mess hall on Camp Fallujah. It was the same fare as that in the main hall for the most part, which usually had a choice of two meat servings, along with vegetables and dessert of some sort. Canned sodas, bottled water and coffee were available, too. I had interviewed Captain Bairstow in April, and during lunch asked if I could update that interview today. He agreed, and when we finished chow, we found a cool room in the company CP building and sat down for his second interview.

* * *

Captain Timothy Michael Bairstow
Commanding Officer, Fox Company, 2/2

This was my second interview with Captain Bairstow—the first was on April 22. During the interim, Fox Company had been continually in action. It was just over a month since I met Captain Bairstow and first interviewed him. A lot has happened with Fox

Company in these 30-plus days. He described the "air show" that took place during the leaders' recon of Fallujah as they destroyed enemy fighters there using combined arms. After April, the company occupied a schoolhouse in the town of Karmah for several weeks. They ran security and counter-IED patrols, and searched homes in the area for contraband weapons and ammunition. After leaving the city, he located a building to use as a Firm Base for the company. His Marines have greatly matured in their two months here.

Towards the end of April, 2/2 was sent north to Karmah to relieve two battalions: One infantry and one LAR, from RCT7. Captain Bairstow accompanied the commander of 2/2 to this area. Bairstow said that there was some anticipation that 2/2 did not have the assets to take over the role that the RCT7 battalions had as part of the clearing of Al Karmah. However, they learned that the mission would not be as extensive for 2/2 as it had been for the prior battalions. "RCT7 had essentially cleared most of the town with the exception of five sectors of the town [Al Karmah]. We established a cordon as best we could, and started to systematically clear the remaining sectors of the town." He said that the formal relief-in-place niceties did not take place. RCT7 units left and 2/2 moved in.

Fox Company found a suitable Firm Base within the first 40 minutes of entering the town. They occupied it shortly before nightfall. It was an abandoned schoolhouse three stories high, with a walled perimeter. "It had great observation over about a third of the town and most of the approaches to the Firm Base itself. Tactically, it was ideal." They found some weapons inside of the school building. Searches of households mostly turned up one AK 47 per house. However, they also found houses with excessive ammo, medical supplies, and evidence that large numbers of people (about 40 to 50) had been sleeping in the houses. "The people slowly started to filter back in [to the town] as we began the cordon." Captain Bairstow said that when Fox Company first entered the town, it was a complete ghost town, with stores left open, unlocked, food on ovens in some homes. Everyone had left in a huge hurry when they heard the armored vehicles and helicopters moving for RCT7's attack.

Once the smaller units from 2/2 arrived, local Iraqis began to return to the town. "Surprisingly, we didn't get that poor of a reception from the local townspeople as we thought we would." Within three days, every building in the town was searched. The only enemy contacts during this time were a few rounds of indirect fire. He said that some Marines got jumpy when they heard explosions, not knowing at the time that EOD was nearby disposing of captured munitions.

They left Al Karmah and returned to Camp Fallujah. Golf Company remained detached from the battalion. Fox Company and the rest of 2/2 joined the Cordon of Fallujah on April 28. Captain Bairstow referred to a map of Fallujah while describing the movement of his company. Fox Company occupied an approach to the area of Fallujah named Queens by the Marines. There, he organized his leaders' reconnaissance in Humvees, with his platoon commanders, and two squads of

Marines. His plan was to advance to some HESCO barriers, and look for some suitable buildings closer to Fallujah for a defensive position. It turned out that these barriers were north of a line that was being used by insurgents inside the city as a "trigger" line, where they would fire on approaching Marines.

They soon started receiving RPK fire from the southern portion of Fallujah. "In my head, it's 'Oh, here we go again!'" He had his Humvees park in defilade positions and start returning fire with their small arms. "Luckily, we had brought the FAC with us, so we called back to get some air support. Meantime, looking to support us with 81s [mortars], but they had to fire a little bit deep [into the city] because of our close proximity to the enemy on the southern edge of Fallujah." The battalion's scout-snipers were also supporting the leaders' recon element. Tanks had just been sent to support both Golf and Fox Companies, so he began coordination with two tanks that were sent to him. Captain Bairstow said it took only about 10 minutes to get the tanks into the fight, and they began to hit the enemy positions with their heavy machine guns and tank main guns. The battalion S3 also pushed some AAVs that had arrived to Fox Company. "Those guys were furious." He said that the AAVs used their firepower to suppress the enemy fire, and some of the enemy fire was RPGs. However, he said that one RPG against an AAV didn't do much.

He wanted to move his vehicles away from the southern part of Fallujah to make use of close air support. Communication between the Humvees, AAVs, and tanks was difficult, but he finally coordinated with all units that a red star cluster would be the signal to move back. Some enemy rounds hit some of the vehicles, but all vehicles remained in operation. "None of the Marines had a scratch comin' out of that portion of the fight."

Captain Bairstow got his Marines in the Humvees back to the HESCO barriers, then counted in the AAVs, and also got the two tanks back south of the barriers. Then, "The FAC called in four air strikes with Mark 82s, and then handed the air fight back over to the battalion air officer, who was up at the same position as the snipers were." The aircraft then dropped more ordnance. Later on, he got back some video footage taken by the pilots of the damage they had done. "I had a greater appreciation for why the 'Fujahideen' agreed to setting up the Fallujah Brigade." He said that no matter what kind of bunker buildings the enemy had set up, they ceased to exist after air strikes.

While this was going on, a sniper had pinned down the rest of his company (described by Staff Sergeant Reynolds and Lieutenant Trainor). His XO, Lieutenant Trainor, called and said that he had identified a sniper firing on his position, and Captain Bairstow at first thought that this was the sniper in front of the leaders' recon. It was a different sniper and it limited the movement of Fox Company. He let battalion know, and it was suggested that Fox Company do a deliberate attack against the position. Then, Lieutenant Trainor heard a noise in the background, and remembered that the two tanks were still with the company. Trainor suggested, "Sir, why don't we just take the two tanks and put some main gun rounds up there?" Captain Bairstow agreed with the XO, and told him to do this. After two main gun rounds were fired at the position, the XO told him, "Sir, the sniper's gone." This made the assault unnecessary. The sniper had injured one Marine, who at the time of the interview was now back in the States. The rest of the night was uneventful.

The next day they watched an "air show" of attacks on Fallujah that went well into the night. A large enemy rocket hit about 40 meters in front of one of the company's positions. "Of all the sounds I've heard in Iraq, the sound of that rocket was probably the most unnerving. RPG, RPK, AK 47 really hasn't bothered me much, but the rocket really gets under everyone's nerves." That one rocket was the closest contact that they had the rest of the time that they were there.

In about another two days, at the end of April, they got word that they would pull out of Fallujah. "There was not much happiness about this." Captain Bairstow said that as commander, he was relieved that he would not have to lead his company in what he felt would be a costly assault on Fallujah. "But like every other member of the chain of command, and I think this went all the way up to CG, we were incensed at the fact that we finally had the enemy pinned at the place where he had chosen to mass. Now, we were just gonna let him slip out, and fight us with the same old ways he had. That was a tough one to explain to the Marines. Even I didn't understand it at the time, but there were people who had insights that we didn't, who were involved in the negotiations, understood why the Iraqis were motivated to allow the Fallujah Brigade." He was amazed that things have been relatively quiet in Fallujah since then.

The company left and went to find a new Firm Base. The battalion spread out, and Fox Company's northern boundary was very close to his old position southeast of Fallujah. He was between MSR Mobile and the Euphrates River. He looked for a suitable building for the Firm Base in this area. A school that would fit the bill was in use, and he looked for another building. He then realized that he would have to settle on a building soon. He went to a house that was under construction, and offered the wife of the owner $1,000 rent and a guarantee of passage back into Fallujah. This large house became the Firm Base for Fox Company. His Marines began to improve defenses there. He had a squad of engineers under a Sergeant Escobel. The engineers found an Iraqi bulldozer, hotwired it, repaired it, and used it to construct barriers around the Firm Base. For the next ten days, Fox Company conducted mounted and dismounted patrols. "What really shocks me is that this place is the friendliest place I've been to in Iraq. I was not expecting that right outside Fallujah. Most of these people are very simple farmers." Captain Bairstow said that it was hard not to have a conversation with locals without being invited into the home for tea or a meal. He added that this has been a refreshing change.

Across the Euphrates River, there were reports that two men were digging there. There were suspicions that they were implanting an IED. Fox Company coordinated with an Army unit (1st Brigade Combat Team) that had responsibility for that AO across the river. He sent a rifle squad to engage this enemy. Captain Bairstow said, "This was the first time, as a commander, I knew I was giving an order for somebody to kill someone, which seems pretty basic. But up until now, [it was] someone trying to engage us, or someone trying to shoot us." A patrol from 1st Recon went out there the next day, but found no trace of bodies.

Bairstow said that the rest of the time there was mostly spent in being nice to locals, and trying to get civil affairs projects started. Some Marines violated policy by buying things from the locals, but this helped create better feelings. The owner of the Firm Base house was very friendly.

Captain Bairstow said that while Fox Company was at this Firm Base, he was concerned because it was so close to a road, and he feared a possible VBIED. The Firm Base was returned to the owner, and now foot patrols leave from Camp Fallujah. Since taking over this zone, only one indirect fire mission has happened. He feels that his company's patrols may have something to do with this. They also check on Fallujah Brigade checkpoints outside the city.

Fox Company also handles some of the claims for reparations for damages caused during the fighting in Fallujah. One humorous reparations event happened when a local family received $10,000 to repair a refrigerated truck damaged by small arms fire. The day after the payment was made, the same family came in with another damaged refrigerator truck. On closer inspection, Captain Bairstow noticed that the truck had been recently painted. It turns out that it was the same truck that was already compensated for! He said that this tribe was then cut off from any further reparations claims.

Captain Bairstow then noted a death in his company here. It came when a patrol went out on a counter-mortar patrol attempted to cross MSR Mobile. That Marine (Lance Corporal Andrew J. Zabierek) was struck and killed instantly by an 18-wheeler (truck) in the dark. The company conducted memorial services this morning.

He said that one of his current missions is to capture an enemy PSYOPS vehicle, allegedly a Mercedes Benz car with a loudspeaker system used to threaten local Iraqis from working with coalition forces. "We came pretty close to capturing him last night." Fox Company sends a platoon into an area during the day, and once in a while the enemy will send this vehicle into that area to threaten the locals. So Fox Company has been following up its open daylight visits with covert, dismounted patrols at night. "Last night as a patrol came walkin' up, they heard squealing tires, taking off." They came close to the vehicle, but could not stop or capture it.

He saw one of the terrorist training videos that his Marines captured along with a cache that also included 17 RPGs, six rounds of 82mm mortars, and several thousand machine gun rounds. He also described the accidental cache discovery when one of his platoons caught an Iraqi carrying weapons in the open. This would be used as a case for the new Iraqi authorities.

He enjoys the relative security for his Marines on Camp Fallujah. The tents his Marines are using still do not have operational air conditioning, and get up over 110 degrees in the daytime. He said that the Fallujah fight seemed kind of fun—largely because there were no deaths for his Marines then. There was a lot of fighting, and they put a pretty good hurt on the enemy. The adrenaline level was high. He recalled being with his company Corpsman and hearing a round "crack" over their heads, and then laughing about it.

He said that his Marines have matured and aged rapidly in the first two months here. "Now, they know all the right things to do, and more or less unhesitatingly." The death of Lance Corporal Zabierik hit his Marines hard. While we spoke, Captain Bairstow said that Lieutenant Trainor was out this afternoon trying to finalize several contracts to improve schools and irrigation systems that will spend almost a quarter of a million dollars. He noted that the Iraqi tribal system has sometimes made it difficult to get projects approved. Local leaders often want "their guy" to get the contract, even if he does not have the qualifications. Sometimes a qualified contractor from outside the area can get the contract if he ensures that he will hire local workers. I ended by telling Captain Bairstow I hoped that I would be able to meet with him when he would be present at the completion of one of the successful local projects.

* * *

Corporal Michael Edward Cazzola

Team Leader, 1st Squad, 3rd Platoon, Fox Company, 2/2

Since his platoon arrived in Iraq, he has been near the receiving end of mortar and rocket attacks at many areas near Fallujah. During the company leaders' recon of Fallujah, he was involved in the two-hour firefight with enemy fighters inside of buildings in the town.

This motivated young Marine went to Parris Island in December 2000, spending his first Christmas and New Year's away from home there, and graduated in March 2001. After graduation from SOI, he went to 2/2, and has been in the battalion since. He has enjoyed his time with the battalion. His first deployment was with the 24th MEU, and he had the experience of lots of training before going to Kosovo for peacekeeping operations. The MEU then went to Djibouti, Africa for what was supposed to be a training exercise, but Fox Company was detached to secure an airfield there. On the trip back home, they stopped in Bahrain for a brief shore liberty, then made a stop in the UAE (United Arab Emirates) for training on shore.

Corporal Cazzola was detached from the company to serve with Combat Cargo on the USS *Nassau*. He worked in the well deck to help chain down vehicles for transit, and then went onto the flight deck, where he helped to load and unload supplies and weapons onto aircraft. The battalion was extended after this seven-and-a-half-month deployment to remain overseas for OIF1. He remained on the ship while the 24th MEU went ashore to augment operations in Kuwait and Iraq. Finally, the MEU headed home on Memorial Day weekend in 2003. Personnel went home on leave.

After leave, Corporal Cazzola was sent to Squad Leaders School, and on return to Fox Company, he met up with a "bunch of new Marines." The company soon learned that it, along with the rest of the battalion, would be returning to Iraq. "We left March 2, 2004 to return to Iraq… since we been here, it's been crazy. Words can't explain it."

During the changeover with the Army, it was very quiet in Iraq. "Towards the end of March, that's when it started. We had a platoon on a night vehicle patrol, an IED went off. Exploded, one of the vehicles, one of my best friends in it. Flipped over, in a canal, and he was trapped under water for a minute. The guy got out. He's okay." Cazzola continued: "Another one of my buddies was blown off. He was the gunner on the Humvee. They thought he had broken ribs, he was medevacked, but he's back here with us. I would say he was gone about three weeks."

Two days later, a big weapons cache was found. This was right before the Shiite festival started in April. "They found RPGs, RPKs, det cord, everything." This was near Mahmudiyah, at a place that these Marines called Saddam's Garden.

That day the company moved out to Lutafiyah for a week of field operations to act as security for the Arbaeen festival "parade." "We set up in a salt factory as our Firm Base for the week. We're gonna send out patrols, all that. The first night, we got the Firm Base set up, and me and my squad leader were looking at the map, plotting where to go on patrol and just, BOOM! BOOM! BOOM! We started getting mortared." The three mortar rounds hit near the building. The next night, about 13 mortar rounds hit right outside their position, but no one got killed. However, a friend of his, Corporal Went, had his ankle shattered by a mortar round while he was walking back into the FOB. He was now back in the U.S. Another corporal, Showalter, got some shrapnel to his shoulder, but was now fine.

The next morning Fox Company sent out patrols, and asked the locals if they knew anything about the mortar fire. Cazzola said, "They just said they hear noises. They're not really giving us too much information. I don't know if they don't know, or just scared, probably more than likely they're scared."

The next night the company sent out an ambush to the south side near where they had been hitting the Marines, and the enemy attacked from the north. "It was probably the weakest attack while we were there." The enemy fired only about three poorly aimed mortar shots that night. Then the next day the enemy fired a few mortar rounds during the daytime, something that they had not done before. They fired at a Marine foot patrol. Corporal Cazzola did not give dates for the events; he worked from his memory.

He lost one of his best friends during the week at Lutafiyah. Sergeant Michael R. Speer of 2nd platoon was shot in the head in there on April 9. He paused after mentioning the name, then gathered his thoughts and continued.

"Then we started clearing houses [at Lutafiyah]. We set out inner-cordon, outer-cordon, search the houses. We do that until night time, we get ready to pull out of there." The next stop for his platoon was to go to Camp Fallujah to help with the operations at Fallujah. They went with the battalion to Al Karmah, and had peaceful patrols there without taking fire.

After a brief stopover in Camp Fallujah, he said the plan was to join in the cordon of Fallujah, be in the defense for two days, and then switch into the offense, "take it by storm." 2/2 went up to relieve 1/5 outside the city. Then, "The leaders' recon goes out, 'cause they want to get a little closer… as soon as they leave, they must have gone, I don't know, maybe 300 meters up the road, they get ambushed. RPGs, we heard it, and we had no idea what was goin' on, from the left of us, all we heard was gunfire and a coupla explosions." He continued, "All of a sudden, gunfire's comin' over our heads. They had us pinned down for a while." He said it was the start of about a two-hour firefight, and that his guys unloaded on the city whenever they spotted a target. Some of the enemy fighters had sandbags in windows and knew what they were doing. When the main fighting died down, in the evening there was an enemy shooter firing at them from a nearby house. That was when the tanks came on the scene. The tanks had helped with the leaders' recon fight that afternoon, and now helped out his platoon. His Marines opened up fire on the house to mark it for the tanks. "We basically blew up the house where we thought the sniper was at."

He also described getting attacked by something big, perhaps a 120mm rocket. "All you can hear is just a squealing noise, and it gets louder and louder, and it went right over this berm where the second squad of my platoon were in position. I was like oop, it's gonna be a long night." But that was the only noise that night. The night after this, he again heard the squealing noise, and said that the round hit about 50 feet from him. He thought he was a goner.

Then came the word that the Marines were being pulled out of Fallujah. Fox Company moved about 10 miles to the south and operated out of what he described as a mansion. Things were quiet in that area.

Three nights before this interview, he was on a patrol crossing a road. He said that usually local drivers would stop when given the signal. That was the night that a Marine was hit by a vehicle and instantly killed. The memorial service was held this morning.

I finally asked him about the young Marines he has been leading. "They hold their own. They're Marines. I couldn't imagine if that was me in that position, comin' right out of boot camp, tellin' me I was goin' right to a combat zone." He said that he was pretty well trained by his first deployment. "They're gonna be some experienced one-year lance corporals when we get back to the United States."

* * *

Private First Class Richard Eric Speir

Rifleman, 1st Squad, 3rd Platoon, Fox Company 2/2

I next met with one of the (about to be) one-year lance corporals that Corporal Cazzola had described, Private First Class Richard Speir. This young Marine reported to Recruit Training on June 16 2003, then completed SOI, and joined Fox Company, 2/2. Almost immediately the battalion was preparing to deploy to Iraq. This young redhead looked just like the students I had been teaching earlier this year. My notes of this interview describe it as unvarnished and open.

He said that boot camp was a good experience for him. "I got to Fox Company in November of 2003, and the day I got there they told me, 'Don't unpack your bags too much, we're goin' to Iraq in March.'" Part of the training was two weeks at March Air Force Base. He said that it was pretty quiet here in Iraq when they first arrived at Mahmudiyah. "We started patrols outside the Firm Base. Nothin' too much really happened. And then they had a holiday in early March, Arbaeen." He and the Marines in the platoon were told to expect about 100,000 people to be walking down the highway to Karbala for this festival. He was told Iraqis had not been able to do this for 20 years or so.

His platoon set up in the salt factory in Lutafiyah. "Within two or three hours of gettin' there, they started mortarin' us. I don't really know how many there was. That was pretty close, pretty scary experience." He really didn't know what was going on until someone said that they were being mortared. The next night about ten to 15 mortars hit, and one Marine was wounded and sent home; another had minor wounds and was still out here.

He remembered on one patrol walking through a streetlight, and within about ten minutes, "They started dropping mortars on our patrol. And then we just ran all the way up to the intersection to try and cut 'em off. 'Cause what they would do was pull up in a car, jump off and shoot off a few mortars, and then jump back in and leave. So we ran up there and try and catch 'em." They didn't get there in time, as it was about a 1,000-meter run to that area where they thought that the mortars were coming from.

On another day he was on top of a truck with a 240 Golf, acting as security, when 1st Platoon got hit and Sergeant Speer was killed. PFC Speir rode in this truck that went with 2nd Platoon into Lutafiyah. He said the town was like a ghost town that day. He stayed on the truck with his gun, and was looking at some buildings. "They [enemy fighters] started shooting some RPGs and machine guns off the buildings at us. Then, I shot off somewheres about 75 to 100 rounds at them. Then the CAAT platoon and everybody else started shooting at them also." After this firefight, the Marines searched the town, finding some weapons.

He also was on a force that went to Lutafiyah when the Army convoy got hit in the town. "We swept through the city." No Marines were seriously wounded that day.

After about a week at Camp Fallujah, they went to Al Karmah. "They told us that Al Karmah was supposed to be the next Hue City. When we got there, the people greeted us, wavin' and smilin', the ones that were still there. We did patrols out of an abandoned school that we used for a Firm Base for about a week."

When they left Karmah, they stopped in Camp Fallujah for a day, then went to Fallujah itself to take part in actions there. When the leaders' recon got hit, "We start takin' rounds. I remember I was right up on the berm, right up where they were shootin', I was firing rounds where I saw muzzle flashes comin'." He estimated that the enemy was about 600 meters away, and the shooting went on about two hours. Then jets came in and two tanks shot up some buildings. He saw some people come up with white flags. "They had all they wanted after that."

He said that on one occasion, an incoming round or rocket hit within 40 meters of where he was.

When the company moved to a large house south of Fallujah, some Marines slept in the rooms, and some outside. During that time, one platoon at a time would return to Camp Fallujah to get showered and some hot chow. The remainder of the company did patrols out of the house/FOB. The Marines talked with local people there. Since returning to Camp Fallujah, they have been running patrols out of the camp.

The other night on a foot patrol, when the platoon was crossing a highway, "I had just gotten across the highway and there was a truck comin'. One of my best friends [Lance Corporal Zabierek] was behind me, he was my roommate back at Camp LeJeune. He was comin' across, and, uh, I know the truck saw him. I believe it was an 18-wheeler, I know it saw him 'cause it beeped its horn way back." PFC Speir estimated that this truck was coming at 60 to 70 miles per hour. "They said my friend went to run back, get out of the way of the truck, but with all the gear, we had packs on this time, water and stuff. The truck never slowed down. He never tried to hit the brakes, never tried to move out of the way. I don't know if it was intentional or what, but he got hit. From what the Corpsman said I don't think he even knew the truck hit him. And we had his memorial service this morning. Pretty rough day." PFC Speir said this has been the worst part of being here so far. "Hopefully, we won't lose anybody else."

I asked him when he actually graduated from high school last year. It was May 25. Three weeks later he was at Recruit Training. Since joining the Marine Corps last June, he has only had a short period of leave after Christmas.

The area where his platoon is working in now has been quiet. He said that the people are friendly, and he has been given tea and locally made bread. "A lot of the time we'll take toys and school supplies to give to the children, and they enjoy that." At night, the Marines patrol to ensure security.

CHAPTER SIX

Infantry—2nd Battalion, 1st Marine Regiment

Camp Bahariyah, Friday May 28, 2004

I got up at 0430 today, and got ready to meet up with the ride to 2/1 at 0500 this morning. 2/1 was based out of Camp Bahariyah, about one or two clicks off Camp Fallujah, but due to security constraints, "You can't get there from here" on foot. Everyone must ride in an armored convoy. Major Piedmont and I met with Captain Amend, the S4 (logistics) officer for 2/1, and rode with their chow convoy to the battalion CP.

It was early and no one was available to interview yet, but this was our only time to get there. John and I found a place to rest up and then at about 0730, a Marine brought in plates of hot chow, for the good major and me.

We attended the battalion morning briefing, run by the executive officer, Major B. McGowan, and he introduced us to the officers and NCOs present. From there, Major Piedmont and I went off to meet with Marines who fought at Fallujah in April, and were now running security and anti-mortar patrols near Saqlawiyah, a village north of Fallujah. I started with the Fox commanding officer, Captain Kyle M. Stoddard, an affable, talkative officer. His was a dynamic interview, with a great overview of events here starting with arrival right into the details of the heaviest fighting in the Northwest section of Fallujah.

This interview gave a ground commander's eye view of the fighting and how Marines at all levels were prepared for the fight by their training. I spent the day listening to the stories told by a variety of Marines with 2/1, ending with an evening interview with the battalion commander, Lieutenant Colonel Gregg Olson.

* * *

Captain Kyle Marvin Stoddard

Commanding Officer, Fox Company, 2/1

Fox Company was one of the first infantry units to enter Fallujah near the end of March 2004, shortly after the handover with the Army. His first encounter with enemy fire occurred during a meeting at the Fallujah Provisional Authority Center inside the city when insurgents began to fire mortar and small arms rounds. As things heated up in early March, he suffered the first death of one of his Marines. He and his Marines fought through ambushes, and during night operations fired a wide variety of weapons at the flashes from enemy gunfire.

Captain Stoddard started his career as an enlisted Marine in the Reserves, joining after graduation from Florida Tech. After a year with the Reserves, he put in a package for the Officer Program and then went onto active duty. He joined 2/1 in May 2003. He and his Marines arrived in Iraq in March 2004, and started the "Left-seat, Right-seat" turnover patrols with the Army units that were preparing to leave.

"Within the first month of us being here, we went to an FPAC [Fallujah Provisional Authority Council] meeting with the Fallujah Council in Fallujah there, and I was bird-dogging [following] the [Army] company commander. And I broke off with one of his platoons, and we were there about four hours. That's when they got hit the first time with the mortar fire and the small arms fire that came from the roofs. We sustained roughly about 19 injuries that day, five from the Marine Corps, 14 from the Army."

One of his squad leaders was injured that night. It woke Stoddard up for the amount of blood that he'd see later on. Prior to this, the Army had not had casualties of that number since they had arrived here. He heard an explosion on the roof of this building as he approached it. He felt that the Army may have gotten complacent.

"About a week after this, the 1st Marine Division of the Marine Corps took over from the 82nd Airborne of the Army. The next day a Marine Corps truck driver was killed on the cloverleaf just outside the city. On March 26, Echo Company 2/1 was sent to secure the northeast sector of the city, and my company made its entrance to the city."

They were looking for insurgents who had observation on the two main routes outside of the city, Route Michigan, which runs east and west through Fallujah, and Route Mobile which runs north and south just to the east of that city.

"So we went in, and about ten minutes of going into the city, we started receiving small arms fire." The Marines did cordon and knocks about 400 to 1,000 meters into the city, starting at 0430 that morning.

"We did a mission with Task Force 221." They searched five homes for "high value targets" suspected to be in them. The days kept getting worse and worse. "You could just feel the tension in the air." One evening they were receiving mortar fire, and saw an individual on a cell phone who they suspected of calling in the mortar fire on their positions. Both Fox and Echo Companies got involved in firefights when the XO gave the word to pull out of the city. "Then on my left flank, where I had two platoons, I had one of my Marines get killed. They were hit with RPGs, and RPK fire from two different locations, the south and the west." It was an L-shaped ambush. He said that there were many short engagements like this where insurgents would expend a magazine of ammo and then get out of the area.

On March 29 his company occupied the cloverleaf east of the city. He had traffic control points at each point of the cloverleaf. At one of the TCPs, an insurgent ran the checkpoint while others engaged the Marines with a short firefight. "We were also getting harassing RPG and mortar fire there." A couple of days later the Blackwater Security killings happened.

Finally, his company was tasked on April 5 with setting up two blocking positions (BP 3 and BP 4) in the northwest section of Fallujah, known as the Jolan District. When he went on a leaders' recon, some local Iraqis were waving off him and the other Marines, trying to warn them of danger. "We had two Iraqi women kind of like wave us off and two Iraqi males. I was like, oh, here we go. I had a CAAT section with me, I had three or four CAAT vehicles with me, the CAAT leader and the battalion gunner." As they drove around, all the civilian vehicles in the area cleared out. The tension grew. Several locals signaled them to move away.

That night, the Marines went back and began to set up bunkers and barriers. He had combat engineers and Navy Sea Bees join him. A convoy of about 60 vehicles came into the area. They then rolled into their new positions at about two in the morning. The engineers were getting ready to set up their HESCO barriers. Captain Stoddard walked over to the map on his wall to show me exactly where this activity was taking place. As he was speaking to some of the engineers, he saw a red-star signal cluster shoot into the air. Then he saw this "red star cluster" land near him and explode. It was not a signal rocket. It was an RPG round! Several other RPG rounds hit around their position.

His observers could not see enemy, but could see flashes from where they were firing. The most serious firing came within the first five minutes of this attack. He estimated about 60 RPGs or mortars were fired. Another Marine was killed by small arms fire that night as he was running to take cover. Once the other Marines got to cover, the enemy fire was not accurate, the enemy were hoping to get off a lucky shot when they sprayed the area with gunfire. To respond, the Marines had their M16s, .50 cals, Mark 19s and 240 Golfs engaging the enemy. "The flashes were everywhere."

That same night a Spectre gunship came on station, and it was the first time he worked with it. Captain Stoddard said, "Spectre's the AC-130 gunship. That was probably the best piece of gear I've worked with. They were flying overhead and they said, 'We see roughly 60 to 70 people right to your front. We can't see if they have weapons, but they are gathering.'"

Up until this time, the ROEs were still restrictive, and he hesitated to fire on this suspected enemy. The curfew had not gone into effect yet, either. Captain Stoddard had his CAAT vehicles pull back to lure the insurgents to start firing at them. He told Spectre that when they got engaged by the guys behind the buildings, to shoot at them from the gunship. When the CAAT vehicles moved, within 30 seconds the insurgents began to shoot. Then Spectre immediately began to fire and report on new sighting of enemy fighters. Captain Stoddard gave the okay to shoot at these new fighters.

Within a few days, Captain Stoddard got word to move into the outskirts of the city, the first few rows of buildings. He described Fallujah as a "hornets' nest." "They had booby traps and obstacles set up." He said that when tanks showed up, it made all the difference in the world for his Marines. The coaxial guns on the tanks were very effective in suppressing enemy fire. "The Iraqis were afraid of the tanks." He added that close air support also helped his Marines. He said that the Air Force support was from very high altitudes, and had lots of restrictions on the proximity of friendly forces, and was not as responsive as Marine fixed-wing close air. The Marine Hueys and Cobras provided great close air support.

"It was very surreal. We killed these guys continuously." He said that every day two or three insurgents would come out and try to shoot at a tank, and the tanks would kill them with their coaxial guns.

When the peace negotiations started during their second week at Fallujah, fighting slowed down. By the third week of being there, insurgents were sniping at more and more of his Marines. He felt that the insurgents wanted to lure the Marines back into the town again.

When the Fox Company Marines would approach the town, they knew that the Air Force's "Slayer" (AC-130 H Spectre's code name) was overhead ready to provide massive fire support for them.

Captain Stoddard observed six insurgents carrying ammunition and weapons into a mosque. They left the mosque soon after this with more weapons and equipment. "We were able to film it, videotape it, while they were fighting us from the mosque. We were able to achieve all of our goals." A couple of days later, they found a weapons cache, and then were sent to Saqlawiyah.

In Saqlawiyah, the local officials told them that there were no insurgents in the area. Fox Company occupied a home and ran patrols into the area. The IP (Iraqi Police) and ICDC did not want them there. Many of the fighters in Fallujah had come into the town to get medical attention. "We were rocketed once, and mortared twice, no effects."

On May 13 they hit an IED on the way to a meeting with town officials. The IED's hole was packed with C4 and various artillery rounds. Stoddard was traveling in the fourth vehicle that day, and heard a loud sound in front of him. He saw a blue plume of smoke. "I'm like, oh, boy." The IED was a pretty direct hit, but was on an angle. One of his Marines was killed instantly, and his first sergeant was hit on his left side, crushing his face. Part of his jaw was missing, and his cheekbone was crushed. "It was a wake-up call." White phosphorus also wounded one of the

Marines. His Marines realized the importance of doing thorough IED patrols. In the last three days before today they have found multiple IEDs in the area.

Captain Stoddard said that the SASO training was valuable. His Marines learned convoy operations and how to deal with civilians in an area. "It got us used to doing what we're doing now." Even when the IED hit, his Marines reacted with practiced skill. Medical aid was provided, Marines established security. SASO training also got them in the mindset for urban operations and combat. He believed that his Marines have probably killed about 200 insurgents in their short time here.

During the fighting at Fallujah he was visited by the Marine Corps commandant, General Michael Hagee, and the MEF commander, General James Conway. Captain Stoddard described the visit, and how civilians walked about the town seemingly unconcerned with the possibility of being wounded or killed.

He described how some of the insurgents have assembled the IEDs in stages: One group would dig a hole, another would emplace the IED, and another group would install the trigger mechanism. It was a constant effort by the Marines to look for and prevent these devices from being emplaced.

Stoddard said that adrenalin kept him going during the fighting in Fallujah. He was busy calling in fire and coordinating the fighting of his platoons. He has had three Marines killed and 20 casualties to date. "It has made the company tighter." One Marine who was wounded in the head returned to the company to fight the same day that he had stitches removed. "This was a big morale booster for the other Marines in the company. A tough kid."

* * *

Lieutenant Joshua B. Jamison
2nd Platoon Commander, Fox Company, 2/1

Lieutenant Joshua B. Jamison, USMC, USNA Class of 2002, was leading his first rifle platoon. A young man with a clear outline of the fighting his platoon did in Fallujah including the use of tanks, close air support operations, and marking targets for aviation with M19 guns, he showed a mature understanding of the reason for the decision by higher-ups to withdraw from Fallujah.

Jamison began TBS at Quantico in June 2002, attended the Infantry Officer Course, then reported to 2/1 in June 2003. He took over his platoon in August of 2003, when they had returned from leave after participating in OIF1. "A lot of the veteran NCOs and junior Marines stayed with the platoon to give it the leadership it needed." At that time, he thought that he had missed out on the chance to participate in combat.

The platoon did lots of live-fire training before learning that they would return to Iraq for OIF2. They then went through extensive SASO training. "We were well-prepared for coming over." He said that the SASO worked well in a lot of the little villages he's been to. They were ready for SASO and understood the culture, but were also ready to switch into combat operations when needed.

Their convoy into Iraq from Kuwait was uneventful. At Camp Fallujah, he and his Marines did the Left-seat, Right-seat turnover with the Army units here. Then came the first time that he was on the receiving end of hostile fire: "I was here for three days, and we went into the FPAC in the middle of town [Fallujah] on a ride-along, along with the Army unit. That's where we, I took my first contact. I'd never been fired on. We got hit by mortars and small arms fire." He said it was strange for him, as he was there on a leaders' recon, without his platoon.

After this his platoon did several counter-mortar patrols, one of them 36 hours in duration, and all were uneventful. "The first day we went into Fallujah in a combat sense was on March 26th. We did some satellite patrols in the northeast section of the town." He said that he and his platoon were green during these first patrols, and did not meet the type of enemy action that they later encountered in April. They did slow-paced patrolling with some light casualties.

On April 4, a few days after the civilian contractors were killed and displayed, his Marines were upset, as they were only a few clicks away from the bridge area. Planning ensued for entering Fallujah again. His platoon re-entered the northwest sector and set up checkpoints. "We rolled in and took a couple of RPG shots, and fired back at where they came from." Lieutenant Jamison said that later he learned that this was a way for enemy fighters to give advance warning to fellow fighters inside the city that the Marines were entering the city. "They definitely had a defense in depth set up for us, and they thought we'd be rolling into town in force that night."

A couple of hours later his platoon positions received several RPG shots. Spectre (the AC-130 gunship) was in the air and suppressed the enemy. That was the first time they received an effective attack from the enemy. He was proud of how his Marines responded.

On April 6, his platoon was about 500 meters outside of Fallujah, and the CO wanted him to send a patrol into the town. He was told to use Humvees, but did not feel comfortable using the vehicles. "I chose not to take Humvees, just one dismounted squad." This patrol made it about one block into the city, with large numbers of angry city residents. Then they entered a danger area, the squad leader was leading his Marines across, and one Marine (Lance Corporal Brad Simmons) was shot in the head. Two tanks came to provide protection for the medevac. Lieutenant Jamison pushed in with a squad to provide protection for the tanks. The enemy had ambushes set up in the city, with RPGs down alleyways, and obstacles that he believed were mined. "A lot of points we were being fired at from all directions. We were just hidin' in rubble piles."

He said that a lot of the enemy fire was directed at the tanks, not his Marines. He heard lots of small arms "pings" on the tanks. Realizing that he was in full-out combat was a surreal moment for him. By about 1700 that afternoon, he found two houses to occupy for the evening. He did not want to pull out of the fight, nor did his Marines. He wanted to keep engaging the enemy, and perhaps be a strategic foothold in the city. No one slept in the buildings that night.

"It turned out to be a perfect place." He could keep in contact with the company back outside the city near the train trestle, in a secure site there. He did not use a map survey, it was just a decision made on the moment. There were about two dozen children in the basements of the buildings, and the Marines fed them for two days until they could be safely evacuated.

Lieutenant Jamison said that on the platoon level, it was a coming of age. They actually saw enemy die there. During the stay, he routinely had mortar fire called in, along with a Mark 19 gunner to shoot targets in the area. They would mark targets for fixed-wing air support. During the next five days, he called in several 500-pound bombs from fixed-wing aircraft on targets. At the end of this time, his platoon was moved to another area in that part of the city, and they occupied five buildings.

"They called a ceasefire. We were still getting fired on and still shooting at people." He was still receiving mortar and RPG fire. While the negotiations were taking place at the higher levels, his Marines kept engaging the enemy when fired upon. His NCOs worked to keep his Marines alert. His Marines wanted to keep pushing forward into the city.

In the middle of the ceasefire, on April 24, his platoon could see enemy fighters loading weapons at a mosque. His CO gave the okay to send some of his Marines to set in near this mosque and watch for weapons movement. They spent 22 hours there. One morning they saw one enemy with a flak jacket and a rifle in the street. Jamison did not allow his Marines to shoot at that time. Later that day they saw five or six armed enemy enter the mosque, and his Marines shot them as they left the building. Combat cameramen were there and recorded the weapons on the dead enemy in the mosque courtyard. They searched the bodies and removed the grenades, ammo and weapons they were carrying.

His Marines received praise for their actions, but felt that they were just doing their job. When word came to pull out of the city, they pulled down their defenses to allow Iraqi forces to come into the city. He told his Marines that there had to be an Iraqi solution to the problem of the insurgency, rather than level the city. "You're going to have to have Iraqis there to solve an Iraqi problem."

None of his wounded Marines had been killed to that date. Even Lance Corporal Simmons who was shot in the head had returned to the platoon! I asked about that wound, and Lieutenant Jamison said that the surgeon told him that the round had entered the back of the head, and exited the front of the skull! It only took that Marine two weeks to return to combat duty.

Since then, Jamison's platoon has been involved in patrols in Saqlawiyah. When they were riding on the road, an IED exploded and killed one machine gunner and a staff NCO. The vehicle was destroyed. This was supposed to be a friendly area, and here was an IED exploding. It was frustrating, too, since there was no one to shoot at. He said that his Marines were coping with this pretty well. This was the low point for the platoon.

Since then they've been doing route-clearing operations, sending squads north of Saqlawiyah. The entire company was performing these operations, rotating.platoons to do the work there.

Lieutenant Jamison was not with the platoon last year during the invasion of Iraq. His experienced Marines said that the fighting this year was much more intense that what they experienced last year (2003). This kind of urban fighting has not been seen since the Vietnam era.

Jamison said that he has appreciated the opportunity to serve as a rifle platoon commander in Iraq. His Marines were responsible for killing 11 enemy fighters, and he was able to call in tanks, mortars, and close air support. He has had the full range of close-in combat experiences, sending out patrols, coordinating combat operations on his own in the city of Fallujah. "It's been a great experience."

To summarize, he said that he was blessed to "fall in" on a great platoon with seasoned NCOs. He felt that his guys could handle almost anything. Also, from his experience in Fallujah, he saw women and children leave the city before the fighting began in earnest. The people who were shot at were enemy fighters. He had "eyes on" those his Marines were fighting. They were bad people the Marines were fighting in Fallujah.

* * *

Sergeant Todd Lewis Luginbuhl

Squad Leader, 2nd Platoon, Fox Company, 2/1

Sergeant Luginbuhl led his squad in a wide variety of combat operations during April in Fallujah. He has had the opportunity to see the full range of supporting arms available to Marine infantry units, with the added support from Air Force AC-130 gunships and fixed wing aircraft. Even with this available support, he said that the M203 grenade launcher has been a key weapon due to its instant response time. Since withdrawal from Fallujah, his squad has been working in route security patrols.

Squad leader Sergeant Todd Luginbuhl entered the Marine Corps in 1996, serving with 3/5. He left the Corps in October 2000, and returned in January 2002, joining Fox Company, 2/1. He came back in as a lance corporal, and has worked his way up to sergeant again.

In OIF1, he was a squad leader during the invasion, working along with British forces. He said that last year (2003) was much more low key. Fox Company was part of a MEU that was trailing the major RCTs invading Iraq. They left Iraq on April 21, 2003 and rejoined their ships in Bahrain to continue a deployment on float. He returned to the U.S. in July 2003.

Sergeant Luginbuhl said that the platoon did a lot of organized MOUT training on its own. Most of the Marines in the platoon were veterans of last year. Fox Company went on a combined arms exercise in December 2003. "We came over March 1 or 2, we were in Kuwait. By the 16th we were in Iraq. About the 26th we began combat operations."

I asked him to describe the turnover of the Army units that were here then. He said it was mostly officers and platoon sergeants going out with their Army counterparts. "When we first got here we were getting mortared a lot, from outside the city, from north and south so we knew the first missions were gonna be patrols to discover the mortar men."

He said that the Army was not in the city of Fallujah long enough to see what kind of enemy they had on their hands. Once the civilian contractors were killed, the mission became more clear to him. He said that when the platoon went into the city, within five minutes they were hit by two RPGs. Soon a larger enemy force hit the platoon and he mentioned the Spectre gunship suppressing the enemy fire. That night he was close to an intersection in the northwest section of the city, near a bridge by the railroad tracks. For the next two days, it was normal combat operations—controlling civilians in the area.

His 2nd squad leader (Corporal Madrigal) took a nine-man patrol on a short one-block deep and one-block wide patrol into Fallujah. During the return, the enemy triggered an ambush. One of his Marines was shot through the head with an AK 47 round. The wounded Marine was extracted by three or four CAAT vehicles, and tanks covered the evacuation of all the wounded. The two Abrams M1 tanks had arrived that morning (April 6). They aimed the big guns right down the street of the city. He referred to a large photomap on the wall of the CP when explaining this.

A firefight ensued between the tanks and enemy shooters in the city. 3rd Squad went on top of a building to get an overwatch position. The rooftop security was pulled off the buildings as the enemy continued shooting with small arms, RPK and RPG fire. Sergeant Luginbuhl went onto the top of one building and determined that there was a very large number of enemy in the area. They went as far as one platoon and two tanks could go into the city. "Then we figured out that there were more enemy there than we could deal with." There was the possibility of being surrounded, so he had his platoon "bound back" out of the city, with the tanks providing cover for the move. He talked with his lieutenant (Jamison) about what to do next, and they decided to clear out two buildings. These buildings gave good observation to nearby areas. He estimated that the firefight that night lasted about an hour. It died down a little when they reached the buildings.

They used the tanks as bait for the enemy, and the Spectre gunships would site in on enemy approaching the tanks and engage them with their weapons systems. At that time the enemy would never attack after midnight. The thermal sights on the tanks also allowed his Marines to know where enemy was in the area.

The Marine helos—Cobras and Hueys—gave lots of good intel on locations of gathering enemy. The Air Force also provided support with 500-pound bombs from its jets, but Sergeant Luginbuhl said that it took too long to get these bombs dropped due to the many levels of coordination required. Mortars also took a while to fire while waiting for coordination and approval. "Our best weapons systems were the M203 grenade launcher, the ACOG-scoped M16, and the Mark 19 40mm grenade launcher. It was our instant-on mortar, it was quick and effective."

During the fight, Lieutenant Jamison coordinated and the squad leaders fought the fight. "It worked flawless." The lieutenant keyed in on the big guns and Sergeant Luginbuhl led his squads.

On April 9 they moved towards a mosque where an individual was observed with weapons. They marked the mosque with smoke grenades from the M203s, and then Hellfire missiles (air-to-surface missiles fired from a helo) were shot at the buildings south of the mosque. In the area of the dome of the mosque there was a small weapons cache.

On the return to friendly lines, the tanks provided covering fire. At an intersection they began to take heavy fire from the east. "Four of us were caught in the actual kill zone." They were too far from the origin of the fire to assault on to the source of the ambush, so they moved out of the kill zone.

On April 11, the day before Easter, they were outside Fallujah, oriented towards the south. "They were blind firing at us." He heard rounds coming at them at around 0800 that morning. From then on, the enemy would maneuver and take pot shots, but not mount any real attacks. The platoon moved to a schoolhouse where it stayed until April 28, about 500 meters east of the city. For the first few days they would receive sporadic fire before noon.

On about April 14 Sergeant Luginbuhl took a patrol out, with Spectre overhead watching for enemy. The next day the enemy sniper fired a couple of rounds. A Marine threw a grenade onto a nearby building, then the sniper ran away, but the Marines could not hit him with their gunfire. Closer to April 28, Luginbuhl again took out a nighttime patrol down a road nearby. They kept a mosque under observation during the day. Later in the day they observed six individuals enter a mosque and come out with weapons. His Marines engaged them by fire.

Their next Area of Operations was near Saqlawiyah on the Euphrates River up in the north. There was a lot of ground to cover with not a lot of manpower. He felt that the insurgents had a lot of help in the area, and it was more difficult to uncover weapons caches. "We took a couple of rocket shots from across the way, but nothing damaging."

Sergeant Gilbert Guadalupe Alcantar, Assistant Section Leader, Alpha Company, 3rd Amphibious Tractor Battalion.

Captain Michael Dale Skaggs, Commanding Officer, Charlie Company, 1st Tank Battalion.

Lieutenant Benjamin Scott Adams, Platoon Commander, 2nd Platoon, Charlie Company, 1st Tank Battalion.

First Lieutenant Troy M. Sayler, Platoon Commander, 1st Platoon, Charlie Company, 1st Tank Battalion.

Sergeant Heriberto Escamilla, Tank Commander, 1st Platoon, Charlie Company, 1st Tank Battalion.

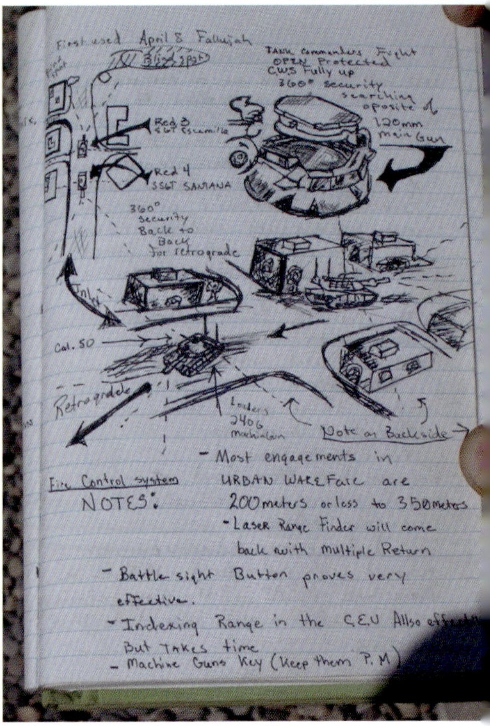

(Above and bottom) Two tank employment sketches Sergeant Escamilla. (Author's personal photo)

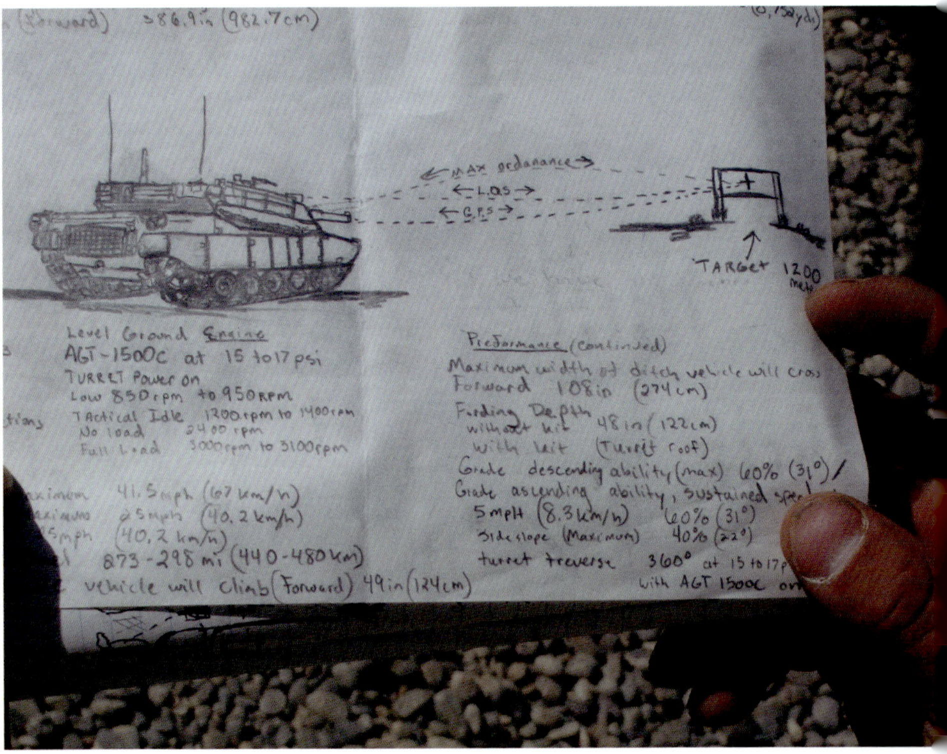

rgeant Prince Witty, Tank Commander, Charlie
ompany, 1st Tank Battalion.

Corporal Michael J. Fiscella, Tank Gunner, Charlie Company, 1st Tank Battalion.

rgeant Michael Wayne Rinehart, Squad Leader/
hicle Commander, Little Wolf, Weapons
mpany, 1/5.

Sergeant Edgar D. Aguilarvaldison, TOW Vehicle Commander, CAAT 1, Weapons Company, 1/5.

Corporal David Thomas Silvers, Squad Leader Red Six (Dismounted), Weapons Company, 1/5.

Corporal Thomas Silvers with M16 and rifle scope

Lance Corporal Angel Quiles, Javelin Gunner & Scout, Wolf 2, Little Wolf, Weapons Company, 1/5.

Sergeant Michael Thomas Vollmer, Section Lead Crazy Horse, 2nd Counter-Mech Platoon, Weapc Company, 1/5.

Corporal Tyler Steven Trenda, TOW Gunner, Crazy Horse, 2nd Counter-Mech Platoon, Weapons Company, 1/5.

Lance Corporal Fue Lo, Vehicle Commander/ Driver, Little Wolf, Weapons Company, 1/5.

Crew chief inside the cabin of a Marine CH-53 E during travel to western Iraq. (Author's personal photo)

Major Kevin John Lee, Squadron Operations Offic
HMM 160.

Warrant Officer Thomas Ray Smith, Avionics a
Ordnance Officer, HMM 160.

Lieutenant Colonel David William Coffma
Commanding Officer, HMM 160.

Colonel Mant Campbell Hawkins III MAW Battle Captain.

Colonel Gerald Allen Yingling, Jr., Chief of Staff, III MAW.

Colonel Jon G. Miclot, Commanding Officer, MACG 3

Master Sergeant Gregory Scott Staggs, Squadr
Maintenance Chief, HMLA 167.

Captain Samuel Lee Meyer, Cobra Pilot & Aviation Saf
Officer, HMLA 167.

ergeant John Jeremy Belcher, Helicopter Crew Chief (UH-1N), HMLA 167.

H-46 and Cobra helos launch for daytime rescue mission at Camp Al Taqaddum, Iraq. (Author's personal photo)

Major Christopher Dixon, Executive Officer, 2nd Battalion, 2nd Marine Regiment, 2/2.

Captain Timothy Bairstow, Commanding Officer, Fox Company, 2/2.

Lieutenant Brandon McDaniel, 1st Platoon Commander, Fox Company, 2/2.

Lieutenant Anthony Triviso, Weapons Platoon Commander, Fox Company, 2/2.

econd Lieutenant Brandon Stibb, 2nd Platoon ommander, Fox Company, 2/2.

Sergeant Judd Anthony Word, 1st Squad Leader, 1st Platoon, "Easy" Company, 2/2.

Second Lieutenant Ilario G. Pantano, 3rd Platoo
Commander, "Easy" Company, 2/2.

Major Brian Warren Neil, S3 (Operations) Officer, 2n
Battalion, 2nd Marine Regiment, 2/2.

Lieutenant Edward Minnich Trainor, Executive Office
Fox Company, 2/2.

ieutenant Walker Clark Koury, 3rd Platoon Commander,
ox Company, 2/2.

taff Sergeant Thomas L. Reynolds III, Platoon Sergeant,
rd Platoon, Fox Company, 2/2.

Corporal Michael Edward Cazzola, Team Leader, 1st Squad, 3rd Platoon, Fox Company, 2/2.

Private First Class Richard Eric Speir, Rifleman, 1st Squa
3rd Platoon, Fox Company, 2/2.

Captain Kyle Marvin Stoddard, Commanding Office
Fox Company, 2/1.

Lieutenant Joshua B. Jamison, 2nd Platoon Commande
Fox Company, 2/1.

Sergeant Todd Lewis Luginbuhl, Squad Leader, 2nd Platoon, Fox Company, 2/1.

ergeant Kevin S. Keeley, 3rd Squad Leader, 2nd latoon, Fox Company, 2/1.

taff Sergeant Jason M. Velez, Section Leader, CAAT latoon, 2/1.

Sergeant Jeffrey S. Duarte, Squad Leader, CAAT Platoon, 2/1.

Lieutenant Colonel Gregg P. Olson, Commanding Officer, 2nd Battalion, 1st Marine Regiment, 2/1.

Major Brian McGowan, USMC, conducts 2/1's morning briefing for company commanders and staff at Camp Bahariyah, Iraq, on May 28, 2004. (Author's personal photo)

Guard tower at Bravo 1/5 camp outside of Shahabi, Iraq. June 2004. (Author's personal photo)

First Sergeant Scott Aldan Van De Ven, First Sergeant, Bravo Company, 1/5.

Corporal Ernie Moreno, Squad Leader, 2nd Squad, 3rd Platoon, Bravo Company, 1/5.

Lance Corporal Delphine Philberto Velarde, SAW Gunne
3rd Squad, 3rd Platoon, Bravo Company, 1/5.

Lieutenant Stephen Gallagher Lewis, 1st Platoo
Commander, Bravo Company, 1/5.

Corporal Jason Charles Howell, Squad Leader, 1st Platoo
Bravo Company, 1/5.

Captain Jason Eugene Smith, Bravo Company Commander, 1/5.

ance Corporal Anthony Francis Ewers, Radio Operator, nd Platoon, Bravo Company, 1/5.

Staff Sergeant Ismael Sagredo, 2nd Platoon Sergeant, Bravo Company, 1/5.

Corporal Jason Picard, 3rd Squad Leader, 2nd Platoon, Bravo Company, 1/5.

Sergeant Ronnie Garcia, Squad Leader, 2nd Platoon, Bravo Company, 1/5.

AAV destroyed by RPG attack being loaded onto an equipment trailer at Camp Fallujah. (Author's personal photo)

Captured weapons displayed outside of 1/5's command post. (Author's personal photo)

Civil Affairs convoy debrief at Camp Fallujah after an early April morning visit to the Jordanian hospital outside of Fallujah. (Author's personal photo)

Field History Team 2004: Major John Piedmont, USMC, Lieutenant Colonel David Kelly, USMC, at Camp Taqaddum. (Author's personal photo)

Field Historian Major Piedmont, USMC, conducts field history interview at Camp Bahariyah. (Autho personal photo)

igh Five: Corporal Jay Picard, USMC, greets a young resident of Shahabi during a presence patrol, July 2004.)fficial Marine Corps photo)

eutenant Stephen Lewis, 1st Platoon, Bravo Company 1/5, reviews his squad leader's plan for a nighttime patrol Shahabi, Iraq. (Author's personal photo)

Lance Corporal David Graham Braun, Fi Team Leader, 1st Squad, 3rd Platoon, "Eas Company, 2/2. (Official Marine Corps photo b Lt Col David Kelly USMC)

Author Lieutenant Colonel David Kelly, USMC, in a work area at Camp Fallujah. (Author's personal photo)

Back at Camp Bahariyah, the company was now doing route security and route clearing. They were working in the area between Saqlawiyah north to the Thar Thar Bridge. "One platoon will stay out about 48 hours, with another squad with another platoon."

They stand OP (observation post) and send out a fire team out to do patrols in the area. At night, he'd set out his teams, sending out three teams of four or so Marines to observe. Sergeant Luginbuhl said that it was difficult to differentiate friendly Iraqis from insurgents. "Who's the good guy and who's the bad guy," is tough to decide. He said it was easier during the Fallujah operations.

I asked him to compare operations here this year and last year. "It was easier last year, we were in the MEU that had little support compared to everyone else." They rode in trucks, not armored vehicles and were more of the rear security. There was more time to train before the invasion last year.

He said that it helped to have veterans from last year's training to be in the platoon this year.

* * *

Sergeant Kevin S. Keeley

3rd Squad Leader, 2nd Platoon, Fox Company, 2/1

Sergeant Kevin S. Keeley received a meritorious battlefield promotion to sergeant for how he led his squad at Fallujah. In early April, Fox Company used a four-tank section to gradually move into the northern section of the city. After careful observation on a mosque, his squad attacked six armed insurgents spotted leaving the building.

He joined the Marine Corps on September 24, 2001. "I decided that rather than going to college right away, I'd rather serve my country." After boot camp, he trained as a machine gunner and served in OIF1 from January through April in 2003. He became a squad leader prior to his return for OIF2.

The company flew into Kuwait and continued training there before moving to Iraq by ground convoy. They took over from the 82nd Airborne near Fallujah.

After some minor skirmishing, the platoon began its month-long operations in the northwest part of Fallujah. "We were to cordon off the outskirts of the city, and trap the insurgents in the city." The Marines established cordons, and no one was going into or out of Fallujah.

At a bridge in that area, they set up a TCP and began receiving RPG and small arms fire. "Nothing accurate or persistent." In another day or two, Fox Company began sending patrols down into the city. The 2nd Squad from his platoon got into an ambush, and made it back to friendly lines. One of the Marines was wounded behind the ear and was medevacked.

"We gained a foothold in the first block south of the bridge." Four tanks were attached to the platoon. Over the next few days using squad patrols, the platoon gradually pushed forward into Fallujah a block or two at a time. He pointed out this area on a large map on the wall. (A video camera would have been an ideal piece of gear to have to capture this portion of the interview, since he did not reference grid coordinates.) For about two weeks the platoon kept close observation on this part of Fallujah, including a mosque that was being used by insurgents to store weapons. "We'd take fire from that mosque every day." This continued until the ceasefire took place.

I asked him about what he did that earned him a meritorious promotion to sergeant. "I was promoted for leading that ambush on that mosque… we had direct observation on these six personnel."

The insurgents went into the mosque, then they rolled back out about 20 minutes later, and that's when Sergeant Keeley's squad initiated the ambush. "We had photographs of them operating out of that mosque. They had weapons and several hand grenades."

When the Fallujah ceasefire went into effect, the ICDC were supposed to take over the blocking positions that the Marines had set up. "We got rolled back up to Saqlawiyah." His Marines continued to patrol the area and spoke with Iraqi security forces there.

His squad had just gotten in from a four-day rotation and had found a 155mm round IED hidden along a road. They were now enjoying a few days' rest here at Camp Bahariyah.

The battalion commander was supposed to be meeting with the mayor of Saqlawiyah, and the convoy was hit en route to the city by an IED. Keeley lost (wounded) a machine gunner from his squad. The main focus of his platoon now was searching for IEDs.

When I asked him if he had final thoughts, he paused for a few moments and then responded, "Yeah, a comment, actually. The way we handled it should have been done a long time ago. We went in there and took care of the job. We went in there and got the job done." The Army had told them not to go into the city for more than a half hour. "It seemed that the Army was kinda beatin' around the bush."

He was obviously proud of the way his Marines had responded to the hostile conditions in Fallujah, and to their continued focus on current operations.

After noontime chow at the 2/1 chow tent (prepared at Camp Fallujah and sent over in VAT cans), I went to the CP and met with Sergeant Duarte of CAAT Platoon, Weapons Company for afternoon interviews. He drove me across the camp in an armored Humvee with a Marine manning the .50 caliber machine gun in the gun turret. There was never a time over here that I felt that any movement anywhere was routine. Marines were always alert and "on duty."

At a hard-sided bungalow-type building I first met all of the CAAT platoon members who I would interview and briefed them as a group on what I was there to do. This saved time as I didn't have to repeat myself prior to each interview.

* * *

Staff Sergeant Jason M. Velez

Section Leader, CAAT Platoon, 2/1

Staff Sergeant Velez' Combined Anti-Armor Team section was used in general support for 2/1. During fighting in northern Fallujah, he found that using the Mark 19 grenade launchers provided an excellent way to mark targets for helos firing TOW and Hellfire missiles.

Velez has been in the Marine Corps for 12 years, starting as a Dragon gunner. He was with 3/5, and later served as a weapons instructor at Camp Pendleton. He then served on recruiting duty before joining 2/1. He gave a good explanation of organization of his section, and what they did during the Fallujah fighting.

Staff Sergeant Velez was on a deployment with the 15th MEU when OIF1 took place. He landed in Kuwait in February 2003, and was in Iraq during the ground war starting in March. He described 2/1's role. "We had a small piece of the pie. Our job as part of 15th MEU was to secure the southern part of Iraq." Most of the operations in Al Nasariyah were in humanitarian operations.

He explained that CAAT stood for Combined Anti-Armor Team. "CAAT is pretty dynamic." It's made up of heavy machine guns and TOWs mounted on Humvees. They currently had about 16 vehicles: Eight TOWs and eight heavy machine guns. They provide the anti-armor capability and the heavy firepower for the battalion.

"So, we're used on screening missions for the ground troops for the line companies, we're used in overwatch positions, used for route reconnaissance, for reconnaissance searches and extractions. So you name it, it's just kinda a bag full of tricks for CAAT."

During OIF1 his section was tasked with security for reconnaissance units with the 15th MEU. They worked to secure the Al Fawh peninsula. He said that fighting was intense for the first 48 hours, then it seemed that the Iraqi forces just didn't want to fight. Mostly the Marines were involved in stability operations. After a month in Iraq, they returned to the ships.

He described OIF1 as just a "blink of an eye," from the invasion to the return to the ship. Staff Sergeant Velez said that when he was leaving Iraq in 2003, he hoped that he would not have to return.

Once he learned that his unit would be returning to Iraq, he knew that it was in the most dangerous area of Iraq. The plan was that once they got rid of the insurgents, they would then provide humanitarian aid to the Iraqi people. The training prepared them for the security and stability operations.

"We got here, and we relieved the 82nd Airborne, I believe the five o' fifth of the 82nd Airborne. And right off the bat, we figured our mission was a little bit different than theirs. We kinda piggy-backed for a couple of weeks." They went out on patrols with the Army units, the "Left-seat, Right-seat" turnover for about two weeks. "Once they left, that's when 2/1 went into the city for a 24-hour period to let the insurgents know that the Marines are on the ground now, it's gonna be a whole different ball game."

Sections from CAAT Platoon were attached out into the three infantry companies of the battalion, and Staff Sergeant Velez's section was held in general support of the battalion. That first day into the city, they received some small arms and RPG fire. The Marines wanted to make it clear that they would go into the city. "I think that set the tone." After the first 24-hour period, they continued with counter-mortar and counter-IED patrols outside the city of Fallujah.

After the killing of the American contractors in the city opened the way for Operation *Vigilant Resolve*, operations to cordon off the city began. "I can honestly say, and I think that every Marine that was here last year for OIF1, that those first five days, from April 5 to the 10th, we saw more action than we did in the entire war in OIF1. It was intense." He said that so far his platoon has had a "halo" around it in April. There had been no Marines killed despite being hit with small arms fire, IEDs and ambushes of different types. Staff Sergeant Velez's section was working along Route Mobile south of Fallujah to ensure that no enemy fighters entered or left the city.

Their first firefight came after receiving sporadic mortar fire on their CP. One of his squad leaders, Sergeant Duarte, discovered the origin of the mortar fire, and the section went and found the mortar men setting up and got into a firefight with them.

His TOW gunners got engaged during another fight. Tanks that were enveloping an objective as part of the attack got stuck, and needed a wrecker to get them out of the area. The tanks were receiving both small arms fire and RPG fire. The CAAT section was called in as a Quick Reaction Force as security for the tanks. They were receiving some RPG fire from a building only about 50 meters from them.

"Our section rolled up, and they [the insurgents] started engaging our vehicles as well, and one of our TOW gunners launched a TOW missile into the building, and pretty much took care of that problem with a TOW missile."

The Mark 19s were also used as the "weapon of choice." The grenades, their velocity, the casualty radius, made them effective in Fallujah. Also, "About two weeks ago we were tasked with securing the train station north of the city." During a 45-minute firefight, Sergeant Duarte called in Huey and Cobra helicopters. He used the Mark 19 grenades to mark targets for the TOW missiles and Hellfire missiles fired from the helos at the buildings in this northern part of Fallujah.

Once the cessation of the attack in Fallujah took place, his section did a lot of escorting for their battalion commander (Lieutenant Colonel Gregg Olson) and officers in the battalion. During General Mattis' ride into Fallujah, Velez's section was on standby near the city.

For the past week or so, they were on counter-IED patrols with Golf Company. "This is what we are currently doing." I asked how the patrols are organized and how his CAAT section is used. He responded that it depended on how the company commander wanted to use the section. "As CAAT section leader, I advise the company commander how to best use this asset."

On some dismounted patrols, a CAAT vehicle will cover the rear of the patrol, other times vehicles will remain in a rear area as a QRF, called into action when needed. Currently Golf Company was covering Route Mobile, insuring that IEDs were not being emplaced. There were OPs in addition to the patrols.

Most of his Humvees currently had only factory armor, and were not yet fully up-armored. Only three of the Humvees in the platoon have been up-armored. He's seen vehicles that have been up-armored that have received only minimal damage from IED explosions. He knows that the Marine Corps was working on this issue. "We've been lucky to date."

As the interview wound down, I asked how his Marines were doing. Staff Sergeant Velez said, "The Marines are talking that it's the halfway point to getting home. They know that the pack can't come off until they get the word to go home."

They were frustrated when they were not allowed to finish the job in Fallujah in April 2004. Since the ceasefire, his platoon has not fired a shot. "The morale is high, they know that they did the right thing here, they performed… amazingly." He had a few veterans in his platoon, but also a large number of new Marines. They came out here and had shots fired at them, and performed "magnificently."

Finally, Staff Sergeant Velez remarked that, "At times it can get frustrating. It's hot as hell and it can be frustrating running these patrols. This is something that needs to be done. I think when it's all said and done, in a few years, I believe that Iraq will be a democratic country. I think our kids and grandkids will be able to read history books.

"And we'll be able to tell them that at one time it wasn't that way. And we basically, we're one of the first steps in making a difference. I reiterate that to my Marines. And I tell them that what they did here, they basically wrote another history of the Marine Corps. It's something they should be proud of and I'm proud of as well."

* * *

Sergeant Jeffrey S. Duarte

Squad Leader, CAAT Platoon, 2/1

Sergeant Duarte was meritoriously promoted by Division Commander General James Mattis for actions (controlling air and his CAAT section's weapons) during the April 2004 fight near the train station in northwest Fallujah. In addition to providing screening and heavy weapons support for 2/1, his vehicles were also used for medevac missions.

Duarte enlisted in March 2001, and joined the FMF in September 2001, shortly before the September 11 attacks. 2/1 returned from a deployment around that time. Then he began to train with the battalion as it got ready for another deployment in January 2003. The Float (Marines' nickname for the forward deployment of a Marine Expeditionary Unit on Navy amphibious shipping) went from San Diego to Kuwait. After landing in Kuwait, he participated in the invasion of Iraq in March 2003. About 500 meters on the other side of the border, the CAAT platoon received intense artillery fire. They secured Uhm Kasr, and then went on to Al Nasariyah. By the end of May 2003 they were pulled back, and did a Float back to the States with liberty ports including Australia and Hawaii en route.

He did the Corporal Course then took 30 days' leave. Returning from leave, he attended the Squad Leader Course for eight weeks, and rejoined the battalion in December 2003. After Christmas leave he began training the new Marines who had joined the platoon.

"And, we left for Kuwait March 1st for OIF2. When we got here we thought it was gonna be a lot different than OIF1." However, he noted that during the changeover with the Army that they hadn't been doing a lot of the work that the Marines were doing at the end of Nasariyah. "They [the Army units] really never went into the city, except for FPAC meetings, Fallujah city council meetings." Sergeant Duarte went into the city to see how the Army conducted the meeting. During this meeting, they took a mortar attack from insurgents. A good number of soldiers and Marines were clustered there and got injured. Sergeant Duarte's and other vehicles rushed the injured back to the medical facilities at MEK (Camp Fallujah). He said that this helped the Marines to get into the correct mindset.

"Then that's about the time that the civilians got murdered in Fallujah." His vehicle and another CAAT vehicle were the ones that later actually brought the burned bodies to Camp Fallujah. "We were just on general support and we had just finished taking someone to the MEK anyway, we got back to the FOB here, and some civilians had brought in, actually on the TOW [missile] truck, two vehicles and the four bodies in the back of a truck. They had wrapped them and everything, but the bodies had been so badly burnt that they were real small." The doctors from the BAS (Battalion Aid Station) put the remains into body bags, and the bodies were transported to the BAS area.

The big offensive on Fallujah started around that time. At first, it was just 2nd Battalion, 1st Marines (2/1) moving to the city. "My squad of vehicles was usually used as a screening force, but on the outskirts of the city. Basically for overwatch and support by fire." They moved in about 0200 and went about a block into the city. By noon of the first day, his vehicle joined up with about seven other vehicles to patrol areas that they had cleared, and to be ready as a QRF for any units that needed them. They ran several medevac missions during this time. "My vehicle has a .50 caliber machine gun, we also have two TOW vehicles, one with a 240 Golf [7.62mm machine gun] and one with a SAW [Squad Automatic Weapon], and also two Mark 19 [automatic grenade launcher] vehicles." This gave them a lot of firepower to support the infantry units. "Found a few IEDs while we were doing that." In a few days, 2/1 was pulled back to the outskirts of Fallujah.

A couple of days later they got word that they'd be going back to Fallujah, and his vehicles were attached to the battalion for general support. "Ended up setting up on Route Mobile for a couple of days." On the third day there, they were sitting on a TCP when they started to receive mortar fire. Sergeant Duarte took his two vehicles towards an area where he thought the mortars were being fired from. As they moved to this area, they drove into an ambush. They returned fire with their .50 cal and 240 Golf, and called for reinforcements. More reinforcements in the form of three CAAT vehicles arrived, and also some ground Marines from 81 mortars. The enemy quickly left, but also left behind a good-size cache of weapons including mortars, rifles, and cell phones. They took one of the insurgents' vehicles and loaded it up with the weapons. This fighting took place about a click east of the city. When they arrived at Camp Fallujah, it coincided with the arrival of Marine Commandant General Michael Hagee there.

Sergeant Duarte's next major action came when another CAAT section got hit in an ambush on what the Marines called "Ambush Alley," and he went to help them out. Then the ceasefire in Fallujah began.

A big action took place at the train station north of Fallujah. His section was called to the area and received fire from insurgents. He called in two sections of Cobra helos to get "eyes on" the enemy. His section ran out of ammo during this fighting. "At the end of it we had destroyed the whole section of houses near the train station." He said that there were many secondary explosions in the homes that they fired on, showing that weapons and ammo were stored in them. Duarte said there were five Marine battalions at the city at this time.

"That's when the battalion put in for me to get combat meritorious promoted [to sergeant] for controlling air and controlling my section in several instances."

The 1st Marine Division commander, General James Mattis, meritoriously promoted then-Corporal Duarte to his current rank of sergeant. A couple of days later the Marines started pulling people out of the city. Since then, his vehicles have been involved in running counter-mortar patrols, and security for infantry units.

Having a core of experienced Marines has helped the new Marines to react to the evolving situations. He also said that during the invasion in 2003 the Rules of Engagement were simpler for his unit. This year there were changing Rules of Engagement. The firefights were more involved, and the rates of casualties higher.

He reflected on the value of the training done back home to prepare for the fighting here. "If you fall back on your training, everything will be just fine."

Sergeant Duarte drove me back to dinner at the mess tent, where I ate with him and the corporal who was our .50 cal gunner. Next he drove me back to the CP where I waited for the evening battalion brief run by the XO.

* * *

Lieutenant Colonel Gregg P. Olson

Commanding Officer, 2nd Battalion, 1st Marine Regiment (2/1)

Lieutenant Colonel Olson gave a great overview of fighting the battalion in and around Fallujah in 2004, from the initial meeting with U.S. Army forces that had been here up to the current operations which had the battalion keeping the Main Supply Routes (MSRs) open. He discussed how units used the Air Force AC-130 Spectre ("Slayer") gunships effectively at night to destroy enemy targets in Fallujah, and a technique using the tanks to draw enemy fighters into the streets and then calling on the gunships to destroy them. He also described how Fox Company got photos of enemy fighters using a mosque in their zone to fire on Marines. This was very important in preventing criticism of damage to mosques, since there was now proof that the enemy in the city was using them as military positions.

Battalion Commander Lieutenant Colonel Gregg Olson finished the day with an interview of almost an hour. The groundwork for this interview had actually been laid last year in 2003, when Field Historian Major Ted McKeldon of History and Museums interviewed him.

I began the interview by getting some background on Lieutenant Colonel Olson and his battalion's deployment.

He said, "I took command when the battalion came back from MEU (SOC) deployment in July, 2003. The battalion came back on the 12th of July, on the 17th of July we held the change of command. I relieved Lieutenant Colonel Al Ingersol and he went off to school. Sergeant Major Carter and I put the battalion on post-deployment leave, and [we] started reorganizing for a new workup cycle."

At that time he assumed that he would be preparing for a MEU (SOC) deployment that was scheduled to depart in June 2004 as the ground combat element (GCE) of the 11th MEU.

"As it turns out, instead of going to the MEU, we wound up going to the regiment. And that decision was made in the fall of 2003, based in large part on personnel figures, where we were in our life-cycle as a battalion, and... what it would have taken to staff another battalion to go to OIF2, rotation number one."

He has about 980 Marines, including reinforcements, in his battalion. In early November 2003, while at CAX in 29 Palms, California with the 1st Marine Regiment, he learned of the decision to deploy 2/1 to Iraq.

"Before the Christmas holidays I was pretty sure that we were going to Iraq, and we started structuring our post-Christmas training for that. Pre-Christmas the big target was CAX, post-Christmas the big target was get ready for Iraq, stability and security ops training."

The 1st Marine Division had established training to prepare for the deployment to Iraq. This included familiarizing with Iraqi culture, and SASO training at the March Air Force base facility. "Prior to that we had some gates to hit: Convoy lane training, cordon and knock lane training, cordon and search lane training."

2/1 trained at this from January to March 2004, and began deploying at the end of February, sending a small advance party to Kuwait.

"I got off the plane the first of March after leaving Southern California. Walked right off that plane, met Colonel Toolan [commanding officer of RCT1] at the bottom of the ramp, he said 'I got a deal for you. I can get you to Fallujah tonight! Who do you want to take with you?' I said, 'Well, I'll take a [S]2 rep, I'll take my headquarters commandant rep, and I'll take my S3 officer, and we'll go link up with the 1-505 Parachute Regiment and start turnover and ride-alongs.' It was an opportunity that just seemed too good to pass up."

Lieutenant Colonel Olson took a truck on the runway to get to a departing C-130, flew to Al Taqaddum, ended up getting on a convoy to the MEK, and went to Camp Bahariyah. The 1-505 Regiment (U.S. Army) was about a month away from leaving Iraq, and was meeting with officials in Fallujah, doing cordon and knocks, and cordon and searches.

"They had done a pretty good job of rounding up former regime elements, but they still had the international terrorist network kind of guys, the Islamist-extremists kind of guys, some remaining FRE [Former Regime Element] guys. They [1-505] had a pretty good target deck developed."

The 1-505 worked with U.S. Army Special Forces units in the area. Lieutenant Colonel Olson went on several missions to develop a feel for the area, including counter-mortar and counter-rocket patrols, security patrols on MSRs, basically getting the "lay of the land" in the Fallujah area.

"I had an opportunity to go to two city council meetings with them, a couple of their security meetings where they meet with the chief of police, the heads of the ICDC battalions. The first city council meeting I attended was in fact attacked by insurgents. And then the next city council meeting that we attended with our advance party, our leaders' recon, was also attacked. That was the one on the 18th of March when we had a number of guys wounded. And unfortunately, one Iraqi civilian, a young kid, an entrepreneurial boy named Omar, was also killed by the terrorists that day. That was a watershed event, because here they had shown their propensity to attack coalition forces, symbols of authority, without regard for civilians in broad daylight."

Olson and his staff spent the month of March at Camp Bahariyah getting ready for the arrival of the battalion. He described the turnover with the Army on the Left-seat, Right-seat patrols: "The first couple or three days, the Army was in charge, had control, had the 'dot' for the mission, our guys would ride along in the right seat as observers." They did the counter-mortar and counter-rocket patrols, and some cordon and knock missions. The second part of the turnover, the Marines were in charge of the missions with the soldiers riding along to observe and critique. They then "surged" the patrols against mortar and rocket positions, because the base camps in the area were getting pounded by mortars and rockets.

There was a turnover ceremony from the Army units in the area to the Marine Division on March 24 and the counter-mortar and -rocket patrols saturated the area to ensure that the ceremony would not be disrupted by insurgent fire. "That was our first big battalion operation."

"The next big event was Quick Reaction Force for a U.S. Special Operations Force mission. And as it turns out, on my way out of the city that night, they got hit by an RPG and small arms ambush. During which about 30 RPGs were fired at 'em. It also hit an IED on the way out of the city, and there were a couple of Special Operations Force guys who were wounded. They went to set up a site to CASEVAC their wounded guys, and we QRF'd that. So in our first mission with them, we actually ended up participating with 'em, and solidified a relationship that continues to this day that is really solid.

"They make their toys available to us. We use their AC-130, we use some of their ISR [intelligence, surveillance, reconnaissance] assets, we've used their snipers, and they have provided us access to their intel. It's been the relationship that the Memorandum of Agreement, Special Operations Command and the Marine Corps were looking for two years ago, when we said we need to get closer. Well, we're pretty darn close now. I've got Special Operations guys in my COC. Not every day, but frequently. Same thing with the U.S. Army Special Forces guys, the Green Beret guys. They also provide intel, provide us an idea of what their operations are turning up. We provide them our intel, we share with them. It makes for better product and situational awareness for all hands. "

On March 26, a Humvee from a Marine Wing Support Group, part of an ACE CSS convoy, got disoriented and went into Fallujah. That Humvee got attacked and some Marines were killed; the vehicle was burned and stripped of a machine gun.

"It was a daytime attack, very brazen, right there in downtown Fallujah." 2/1 was given permission to determine who the shooters were, to show the Marines' resolve that actions like this would not be allowed to take place. Rifle companies would enter the city at the end of March. "The mission evolved from just showing your resolve to making sure [that] the Fallujahns understood we'd do something about it."

Lieutenant Colonel Olson set up cordon and knock in a row of houses where shooters had been seen at the end of March. They also had a list of targeted cell leaders to capture. His Marines wanted to let the inhabitants know not to be afraid. As the operation began, the Marines began receiving RPG and small arms fire. On a map, Lieutenant Colonel Olson showed how two of his rifle companies were entering the city from south to north, through the Askari neighborhood, and went up through the city. At that time a third rifle company was south of the river working more routine security and stability operations there.

"As we saw that this fight in Fallujah was gonna turn from a coupla cordon and knock into a day long, it ended up being some 13 hours on the ground in the city, with platoon-size firefights firing regularly. We recalled portions of that rifle company and brought 'em up to make sure we had an infantry reserve close by."

A portion of a 1/5 CAAT platoon reinforced the initial actions. "Echo and Fox Companies went into the city, started a portion of what we expected them to do which was platoon and squad-size satellite patrolling, and found themselves in platoon and squad-size firefights."

"We didn't use any supporting arms that day. We didn't end up firing anything larger than a 40 millimeter grenade launcher. Uh, did fire some coax [machine gun] from the tanks at one time when they moved down."

They had made a conscious decision not to stay in the city that night, so the inhabitants would see that the Marines were not too bellicose. The battalion drew back and overwatched the town that night from positions along the highway. "They shot some mortars from the city, they shot some RPGs, they probably fired 30 or 40 RPGs that night. But that was just a precursor of things to come. I mean, 30 or 40 RPGs by the first day of April was pretty routine."

He continued, "It did give us an indication that the Iraqis were gonna move to where we were, and that they would come and fight ya. They weren't particularly good at it, but of course it's a complex battlefield." There were guys firing RPGs who would then dart into a private home, making it difficult for the Marines to decide who the shooters were when they entered these houses. "To our credit, the Marines did real well about who they shot and who they didn't. We had the optical gunsight-scoped rifles basically in every fire team, and there was a lot of well-aimed shots taken, and there wasn't a lot of supporting arms used."

The battalion sat on its cordon at the eastern part of the city to show the Iraqis that the Marines could stay there and wouldn't be deterred. Some negotiations happened with the city council and the mayor, and it was agreed that the Marines would pull back to their bases, and man some checkpoints along with Iraqi forces to put a joint face on security for the city of Fallujah.

On March 31 that changed with the killing and mutilation of the four American contractors in Fallujah, where the local police allegedly sat by and did nothing. "And that prompted a response on a grander scale. It prompted the initial cordoning of the city by two battalions, and then as it became apparent that there was gonna be a fight, bringing on two more battalions."

Initially 2/1 was responsible for the north and eastern part of the city, and a peninsula that controlled two bridges. Lieutenant Colonel Olson pointed out the areas on a wall map. "Some of the initial challenges with the cordoning of the city [were] that we weren't allowing anything out. But there were Iraqi security forces, police, city council members, there were a lot of folks who had to come out of the city to conduct official business. For instance, the cops, some of whom didn't live in the town, go off shift, and then what do you tell 'em? 'Sorry you can't go home?' So the cordon, it wasn't porous, but it wasn't airtight."

He said that the city council members and mayor came out and tried to negotiate the cordon away, but he remarked that, "It wasn't gonna happen. It wasn't gonna happen until they gave up the foreigners that we knew were in the city who were partially responsible for the actions, until they gave up the attackers, until we got the bodies back. I worked with a police chief. And on the night of the attack we actually got the two vehicles and three of the remains back. That negotiation took place here, and we kinda gave 'em an ultimatum. Said, 'Look, things are gonna get bad for Fallujah, unless you get us the remains back.' When they couldn't get us all the remains and they couldn't get us the attackers, it was a couple days later when we actually were successful. The police chief came and saw me in a one-to-one meeting, explained to me how embarrassed and upset he was, and I said the best thing you can do is get the fourth set of remains back. And that afternoon he was able to produce the fourth set of remains." These remains were brought to Camp Bahariyah and sent on to Camp Fallujah where mortuary affairs was located.

Olson said that because no attackers or cooperation were produced, the cordon stayed in place and deteriorated for the Marines watching the city. "We started to get mortared, we started to get rocketed, we started to have small arms engagements, we started to have RPG engagements. And before too long, we found ourselves deciding, making a conscious decision to begin offensive operations, to reduce the ACF [anti-coalition forces], AIF presence in the city. And we were given an order to attack, to seize a foothold, in the Jolan neighborhood up on the northwest corner of the town."

By that time, additional combat power in the form of three battalions, 1/5, 2/2, and 3/4, had come to tighten the cordon. 3/4 came in from RCT7 out in the western part of Al Anbar province. 2/1 gave up the cloverleaf east of Fallujah to 1/5, and gave up the northeast corner of the city to 3/4, and concentrated its efforts on the northwest corner of Fallujah.

"We made our initial penetration with one company, and followed it through with another company. Fox Company had the lead, they were the first ones in to the city proper. We followed their lead around with the forward command post, pushed in on the morning of the second day with Echo Company, and by the end of the middle of the second day had two companies up in the city."

"Fox's first night on the railroad trestle was pretty eventful. It was our first opportunity to use the AC-130 to reduce the bad guys who were clearly moving against us. In one instance the AC-130 reported, 'Armed men, movin' up, gettin' on line behind a wall.' Then we saw the RPG volley come out from behind a wall, and that's when we cleared Slayer [the AC-130] 'hot to engage the target.' And we just freakin' smoked 'em. So we develop this great night detection technique of the FACs working with the AC-130 to get visibility on what was going on the battlefield, and we'd send the tanks, pretty well armored and pretty much impervious to anything the enemy could throw at them. Send the tanks down to stir up trouble at one of the roadblocks. The bad guys'd come at the tanks and try and get their IO (Information Operations, or shaping of information) victory of killing one of these impervium-armored M1A1s. Tanks'd light 'em up with coax, pull back, as they [bad guys] came flooding out in the void created, we'd bring in the AC-130 and just wipe 'em out. And that worked repeated numbers of times. It worked actually really well."

Use of supporting arms fire escalated to the use of both rotary wing (Marine helicopters) and fixed wing (U.S. Air Force jets) assets. Primarily precision-aimed munitions were used. Artillery was not used, and 81mm fires were used minimally; many were marking missions.

With the two-company foothold, Lieutenant Colonel Olson displaced his battalion's main command post to an apartment complex that had been cleared by ICDC forces from the 36th Battalion, which was primarily made up of Kurds.

"They made sure there were no bad guy Iraqis on our flanks or rear, and then we in fact ended movin' our command post into the apartment complex. That apartment complex has just had a half a million dollar contract let for renovations, not 'cause it was war damaged, but because it was in need of renovations." For the roughly month or so that the battalion occupied the buildings, the residents received payments from the Marines.

With this foothold, every day it was a combination of snipers, small arms, moving of formations against each other, and urban patrols, in a battalion security area about 400 to 1,000 meters deep into the city. Olson used a combination of small arms fires and patrols to control the area.

"Snipers just did a phenomenal job." He said that they killed bad guys by the dozen, and that when negotiations began, one of the requests by the bad guys was for the Marines to pull the snipers out. "Between the snipers and the ACOG-armed riflemen, we shot a lot of guys with single shots." He described some incidents where Marines would put a hat on a stick, or roll a tire into the street to draw the bad guys' gunfire, and Marines would observe to see the shooters "turkey neck" out of hiding, and then shoot them.

Lieutenant Colonel Olson said there were several significant platoon-size engagements, including a big fight while crossing a cemetery. There were a lot of friendly casualties that day. For about three weeks it was "push and pull," and the ROEs did not change, there was never a question of use of force when enemy was bringing the fight to the Marines. When the ceasefire negotiations began, his Marines were more discriminating in how they engaged the enemy.

Various types of vehicles were used throughout the fighting, from jury-rigged to fully armored Humvees, tanks, and AAVs. His battalion used the AAVs as "battle taxis" to move Marines to the city, but he did not use them inside the town to fight. The two rifle companies in the town had forward air controllers, and the company south of the river found itself engaged in a variety of fights. "They did a whole lot with not a whole lot of combat power." This company was actually made up of two rifle platoons and attachments from the CAAT platoon. "The success story over there was the offensive mindset by Captain Stevenson and his two lieutenants really kept the enemy from getting any kind of initiative."

He interrupted the interview briefly to let the sergeant major of the battalion know that he would be going out to TCP 1 at about 2100 tonight.

"That's kind of the Readers' Digest condensed version, I don't know if there is anything else you kinda want to hone in on?"

I asked what has happened since the battalion was ordered to pull back from Fallujah.

He responded that Saqlawiyah, a small town north of Fallujah, has been their focus of effort. It's rural, it's tribal, it's agrarian, and offers a lot of opportunity to operate with the Iraqi security forces, including police and ICDC. Lieutenant Colonel Olson also noted that he could now do some small-scale CMO (Civil-Military Operations) with his money (about half a million dollars), such as school rehabs, irrigation, and get farm experts and electricity guys to help build up the infrastructure in this area.

His focus was now in keeping the MSRs open and free of IEDs, keeping an eye on Saqlawiyah and helping the Iraqi security forces develop. This was more in line with what he originally expected to be doing here in Iraq.

Lieutenant Colonel Olson again praised the training that his battalion received to prepare for this deployment. The combined arms exercise in California helped the Marines learn how to do communication and resupply over long distances, how to do supporting arms coordination, and how to make changes in task organization. These are all things that they have done here. Secondly, the week of scenario-based lane training at March Air Force Base with live-action role players helped to develop squad leader skills. "It was very true to life in many ways… interactive in many ways."

I asked Major Piedmont, who was observing the interview, if he had any questions for Lieutenant Colonel Olson. Piedmont asked if there was a single thing that kept Olson awake, or really caused him worry during the operations in Fallujah.

"In the very early going we had some issues with ammunition supply. We came up here with an expectation of, some of the resources would follow. And, there were some days when I wish I had some more .50 cal link, or wish I had more Mark 19 ammo, or wish I had more of certain DODEX [Department of Defense intelligence system information system extension]. We never ran out of bullets and had to go to bayonets, but there was a couple of days where we had to get emergency resupplies of stuff. That was the only thing that I can honestly say."

He also said that positionally, he was pretty happy with the displacement of his companies. The positions in town were mutually supporting, and he kept the offensive mindset, and when Slayer came on station in the evenings, it enabled him to relax somewhat knowing the supporting arms capability overhead that the plane brought. "The bad guys didn't play when he was on station." Also, he said that the bad guys got tired and didn't often fight between about midnight and dawn.

Piedmont's final question was about actually being in command of a battalion in combat after a career preparing for it.

"What surprised me was, how much like training a lot of it was. The same issues of battle space management, the same issues of observe-report, synthesizing information, turning it back around, all those same issues, it surprised me how… I was happy to know how well-trained my Marines were, from PFCs to lieutenant colonels." He noted that he didn't like taking casualties. That truly concerned him when he saw his badly wounded Marines at the BAS. "We've had eight Marines killed, and almost 90 combat-wounded." Many of the wounded have remained with the battalion.

He said that some of the Marines who do "knuckle-headed" things in peacetime are the ones who respond in real combat situations. And the Marines who were the best Marines at Camp Pendleton have turned out to be the best Marines here. "I was really happy to see how well the Marines have done." The tour of the battalion was only half done, summer was coming on and he felt that the complexion of the fight may change, especially as the move to restoration of Iraqi sovereignty approached. "I know the Marines are ready to work with the Iraqis."

He felt that the results of the battle of Fallujah would be written about a year from now. (Note: The later November 2004 battle for Fallujah would turn out to be the decisive fight that year.)

Fallujah has traditionally been a dangerous place throughout history. "But I do think the actions of four Marine infantry battalions broke the back of an insurgency that was trying to get itself organized." He noted that the insurgents came to the negotiating table first and, "They don't negotiate when they are in a position of strength."

As we ended the session, Lieutenant Colonel Olson said that he was available to tie up any loose ends: "I'm here 'til October."

I finished up around 2100, and then waited a short time for a three-vehicle convoy from 2/1 to take us back to Camp Fallujah.

CHAPTER SEVEN

Infantry—Bravo Company, 1/5

Camp Shahabi, Thursday June 10, 2004

When I checked SIPRNET today I learned that Major Piedmont and I would spend the day and night with 1/5 at three of their Firm Bases. I'd interview Bravo Company and Weapons Company Marines, and Major Piedmont would do Alpha Company and Charlie Company. I hoped to be back at Camp Fallujah in time on Saturday to interview RCT1's commanding officer Colonel John Toolan as I had arranged earlier.

Friday June 11, 2004

Here is the interview schedule that I worked up with the S3A officer of 1/5: Today at 0700: Both field historians leave Camp Fallujah. Me to Bravo 1/5's Firm Base, Piedmont to Alpha 1/5's Firm Base.

For June 12—Finish Bravo interviews, leave for Camp Abu Ghraib to interview Marines at Weapons Company and H&S Company, 1/5. On return to Camp Fallujah interview Rear Admiral Kubit, USN. Major Piedmont leaves Alpha Company Firm base for Charlie Company 1/5 interviews.

By now Major Piedmont and I were adept at making travel arrangements. Also, we were better at maximizing our time with outlying units.

After morning chow, I packed up gear for an overnight stay with 1/5 Marines. Marines from 1/5 picked up Major Piedmont and me at 0700. It was an impressive little convoy of seven armored Humvees. Some had gun mounts, all had armored floors and doors. The trip to Bravo Company's area took only about 20 minutes. We went out of the Camp Fallujah north gate, onto a main highway, and then right (north) again. It was a security-conscious ride. When we first got to the gate as we left Camp Fallujah, we dismounted and charged our M16s, then kept them at the ready the whole ride. Even though the roads around here were patrolled constantly, we were all on the alert for any IEDs or ambush sites. Fortunately, it was a quiet ride. I got out at the Bravo Company camp, and Major Piedmont remained with the convoy to go on to the Alpha Company camp.

The camp for Bravo Company 1/5 was inside an "Oil for Food" camp—a large warehouse area adjacent to the village of Shahabi. The camp was very rudimentary—the Marines slept in one of the warehouses that had sand-filled HESCO barriers throughout to compartmentalize any incoming mortar rounds. A cinderblock or cement wall surrounded the camp, and there was a guard tower on the corner of the wall adjacent to the village. The head facilities consisted of two large round pits, and one plywood shack with four seats and burn barrels under them. No running water—but lots of bottled water was available.

The company commander, Captain Jason E. Smith, was not aware that I was en route (I had made the liaison with the battalion XO, Major Chessani), but in about ten minutes the company first sergeant, First Sergeant Van De Ven, had a bunch of Marines for me to start interviewing, beginning with him. I listened and took notes for seven hours straight, and as this was the rifle company that had the platoon involved in the Amtrac loss on April 13 in Fallujah, I could start to piece together several events since I had already interviewed many of the Amtrackers and tankers who were involved in the vehicle loss and rescue of 2nd Platoon, Bravo Company 1/5. One interview (with Lance Corporal Velarde) was just about ended when I heard four or five incoming mortar rounds explode very close to the warehouse I was using as my work space. It sounded like they were just outside of the rear doors!

* * *

First Sergeant Scott Aldan Van De Ven

Company First Sergeant, Bravo Company, 1/5

When Bravo Company first arrived in Iraq, the Marines were assigned to camp guard at Camp Abu Ghraib while the rest of the battalion went out on patrols in the areas around Fallujah. This soon changed in the beginning of April as the MEF began to cordon off Fallujah in preparation for offensive actions. Even after firefights on April 5, the Marines were restricted by the Rules of Engagement in effect. The biggest event would be the events surrounding the AAV ambush where one of the company's squads along with a platoon commander were surrounded by enemy fighters. He vividly described facing the death of his Marines, and his frustration at the Marines not being allowed to bring the fight in Fallujah to a quick completion.

While First Sergeant Van De Ven had his Marines rounded up for my interviews, he sat down with me for his own interview. Another very informative interview that lasted about an hour and a quarter. The "Top" had a great memory of recent events.

Van De Ven enlisted in the Corps in 1987, and joined his first operational unit in 1988. He served with VMFA 323 (a Marine fighter attack squadron) during

Operation *Desert Storm*, and then served on the drill field at San Diego from '92 to '94. He returned to VMFA 323 and did two WestPac tours on the USS *Constellation*. He was assistant Marine officer instructor at the University of Michigan's NROTC detachment from '98 to 2001. He was detaching from there on September 11, 2001 to head back to California. He served as an aviation ordnance man on the USS *Constellation* for OIF1. After selection for promotion to first sergeant, he was frocked (allowed to wear his new rank insignia before being formally promoted) and joined Bravo Company in August 2003.

In 2003, 1/5 was part of the 31st MEU, and was training to go to Okinawa. "We found out on December 1st that we were gonna go to Iraq. Captain Smith called me, cell phone, said he had a meeting. He was in Louisiana, we were on pre-deployment leave, and he'd like me to take it. We knew that it meant we were going to go to Iraq. He didn't say anything. I went to the meeting, found out we were headed to Iraq. Went to Okinawa, participated in SASO training, very much like the division did back in March, but it was our own generated training."

On March 5, Bravo Company flew from Okinawa to Kuwait. They participated in what the Marines called Task Force Gypsy, where they moved vehicles from Kuwait up into Iraq. On March 22, 2004, Bravo Company joined 1/5 at Camp Abu Ghraib (previously called Camp Mercury by the U.S. Army). He noted that this was not the same camp as the now-infamous prison camp with the same name.

He said, "We had camp guard, we basically were thrust into camp guard. A lot of Marines were disappointed about that 'cause now they were going to be stuck. Other companies were forming patrols, throughout the east of Fallujah, north of Al Karmah, and Al Shahabi, so they [Bravo Marines] were kinda depressed."

After the killing of the American contractors in Fallujah, it seemed that they might be getting involved there. The company began to stage on 4 April, and by early morning on April 5 had staged southeast of Fallujah.

"Our role, we were gonna be the main effort for the battalion, battalion objective number one, which was gonna be the soda factory. We thought we were gonna be going the morning of the fifth, as it was my understanding that the other companies could not get to the traffic control points on time on the western side."

First Sergeant Van De Ven said that they could hear Charlie Company 1/5 engaged on the cloverleaf east of Fallujah.

Bravo Company got word that it was to step off towards its objective at 2300 on April 5. "About 2000, 2nd Platoon went out with a recon with our scout snipers. They rolled into the soda factory. Outside the soda factory, picked a location. We didn't know if there [were] occupants, we didn't know if there was any resistance. Captain Smith decided instead of moving down in our Humvees that we'd actually walk down and leave our Humvees where they were staged. We had four 7-tons [trucks] and the rest were Humvees. This way instead of going down the road and being seen and heard, walking in is always better."

They stepped off at 2300, and at 0100 their SAW gunners fired into the factory. They (2nd Platoon, Bravo Company) breached a concrete wall and detained seven individuals and their weapons. These Iraqis worked in the factory. 4th Platoon (Weapons Platoon was being used as a fourth rifle platoon, he explained) went north of the factory. The only shot fired was by a Marine who killed an attacking dog. The company continued to move west without incident to Phase Line Orange in an industrial area. They spotted some locals looking at them, but no shots were fired. Some of the Marines did engage a vehicle that had individuals who pointed AKs at them. One lance corporal fired his 240 Golf at the vehicle and disabled it.

By now it was about 0400 on April 6. When they reached Phase Line Orange, Captain Smith gave the order to put all of the company onto the roofs of buildings there. "We had one portable ladder, [and] a couple other ladders, and put everybody on the roofs." They oriented toward the west and north, and went to 50 percent alert. It was a cold early morning. The first sergeant heard Muslim morning prayers in the city, then he and the company radio operator grabbed a short nap of about 40 minutes.

When they woke, Captain Smith took a short nap for about 30 minutes. They then put a vehicle checkpoint out under Corporal Dawson of 1st Platoon. Once the sun was up, some vehicles drove by at about 0830, checking out the Marines' positions. Bravo took some incoming shots from the north. Corporal Dawson's squad began firing.

"It was real loud. It was one of the first times we had a squad engaging," said Van De Ven. "Instinctively, there were squads that already punched out, through their platoon commanders, they were already heading across Michigan." Now the entire company was moving. They headed towards a large mosque in the area. Corporal Dawson's squad went into the mosque and found some small arms and ammunition inside.

Van De Ven went with Captain Smith and they determined that the mosque had been cleared. The company was now on Phase Line Violet, although they didn't know it was a control measure at the time. Captain Smith went into an apartment building there and let the inhabitants know that they had to leave the building. He apologized to them for the inconvenience, but told them that they would be compensated for the evacuation. Captain Smith asked them to tell where the insurgents were located, but no one claimed to know anything. As the company was moving back to Phase Line Orange, they took RPG and "pop shot" small arms fire. They also took gunfire from what they thought was an ICDC building. It was actually an electrical plant. This building had sand bags on its roof. The Marines were still in their SASO mode, not firing without seeing where they were being shot from.

They figured that they were sitting ducks in this position, so they broke into an old auto shop and set up a command post. Captain Smith was on the radio there, and there was traffic about a KIA and a WIA in the company. Van De Ven would later find out that it was an enemy KIA, and the WIA was Lance Corporal Cargyle, who had been shot. At about sunset, two RPGs were fired, and landed on top of where 2nd Platoon was planning to set in a defensive position. First Lieutenant Joshua Palmer of 3rd Platoon suggested that he take his platoon west of the position onto a higher building to provide better cover for the next morning. The battalion commander (Lieutenant Colonel Brennan T. Byrne) visited the company CP around this time.

Still on April 7, the company was taking accurate sniper fire from unknown shooters from the vicinity of Phase Line Violet. "Violet is the mosque, the big, gigantic mosque, north of Michigan." The company was taking mortar fire, RPG fire, and small arms fire. From the sound of the fire, the shooters were probably about 700 meters away. Despite this, the Marines still were looking for hostile intent from those shooting at them.

On April 8, things were busy again. A platoon was unloading its packs from vehicles when a mortar round dropped and hit Corporal Rodriguez in the back, dropping him. (Rodriguez was at the time of the interview still at Camp Abu Ghraib, and still had some nerve damage in his back.)

Van De Ven said that the enemy fire seemed to be coordinated and accurate, with RPGs and small arms fire. When the Marines spotted an enemy sniper to the west of them, 2nd and 3rd Platoons took off and headed west, into an alleyway that Bravo Company called "Shit Head Alley." 3rd Platoon faced north, Weapons Platoon faced west, and 2nd Platoon went south. Van De Ven was in the company COC. Captain Smith went to the battalion CP.

Van De Ven went in a Humvee to run a medevac to get Staff Sergeant Harrell and Lance Corporal Amati, both wounded. He said that there was blood all over, and both Marines were going into shock. He got them to the cloverleaf outside of Fallujah. Van De Ven got slightly choked up at this point as he recounted the end of this medevac run: "I'm takin' Harrell off, and… Harrell's tryin' to breathe. I'm yellin' at him, I'm tellin' him, that uh… he, he's got a wife and kids and needs to fuckin' fight this. And, he blinks at me. He's got a hole in his neck, a real small hole in his neck. And I think he's gonna make it."

Van De Ven again paused to gather himself before continuing.

"I think he's gonna make it because he blinks at me. So, we put him down, I think Amati's gonna die because Amati bled so much, there's a ton of blood. I know they're still fightin', I don't know at this point, the CO and the gunny are all up. Yellin' at everybody, 'Get back in the vehicles!' They're engaging, we have no medevac. I didn't know that, so we rip back down there. We get back, and… the CO now, is stoked." Captain Smith wanted to find out who had shot his Marines.

The first sergeant took Smith to the area where they picked up the wounded, and they headed towards Shit Head Alley. En route, they heard firing, but knew that it wasn't real close to them because the crackling noises of gunfire were not passing near them. He and Captain Smith charged into a house where they saw Lieutenant Chris Ayres. The lieutenant was directing the Marines there. Van De Ven asked one of the squad leaders, Sergeant Peres, about Lieutenant Joshua Palmer. Peres had earlier been with Staff Sergeant William H. Harrell. Peres shook his head left and right, very calmly. Van De Ven said, "So I know right now, somethin's not good. I walk into the house, and Lieutenant Palmer had been drug right where he had been shot. Lieutenant Palmer had also been killed. Captain Smith at that moment had been pullin' off a blanket from Lieutenant Palmer's head. He had been shot in the neck."

Marines searched this house and found an insurgent with a suicide belt of C4 explosive strapped on him. There were two other males in the house, but they had no weapons with them. These males had burn marks on their hands from firing RPGs, but the Marine who captured them did not shoot them.

"At this point, you can imagine, we just medevacked two Marines. It's our first serious, no kiddin', these Marines might die, medevac. We medevacked Cargyle on the 6th, the morning of the 8th we medevacked Rodriguez." Lieutenant Ayres went in to blow up an insurgent with a hand grenade. The grenade went off prematurely, and Van De Ven ran after Smith, who was fine. Van De Ven said, "It was some loud, loud, stuff."

Bravo Company was now spread out pretty thin along Shit Head Alley; they had tanks in support of them, but Captain Smith said the company was too thin. He wanted to retrograde back to the Firm Base on Violet and figure out the situation there. He recognized that they could not keep on chasing after insurgents who fired on them, as they would continue to run into a gauntlet if they did. They moved back to the Firm Base at about 1500 or 1600, still taking sporadic fire. Several of their Marines had been medevacked out.

Then on April 9, they were on Phase Line Violet. They were taking fire from the mosque to the north.

"I'm on the roof, talkin' to the Marines, see what's goin' on, machine gunners… and, I see a rifle come out of the minaret. Had I not seen that, I might not have believed it. I've got one of the machine gunners [I have an] M16, since we've come in to Fallujah on the 5th. He [the machine gunner] was carrying a 240 Golf. I engage, they engage, almost a company, the battalion comes through, they engage. We eventually later go into the mosque to see what we could find. Too late, hit and run tactics."

April 10 was quiet, and they took fire again on the 11th. "Captain Smith had convinced the battalion commander, who convinced his superiors that we need to put some elements to the west. We're just sitting ducks sittin' here on the corner of Michigan and Violet and we need to break it up a little bit."

The company set out LPs (listening posts) and OPs (observation posts). The XO took 3rd Platoon out west. They then planned to move south. They wound up in Shit Head Alley again, and First Sergeant Van De Ven observed from a rooftop.

He was on an ICOM radio and could hear what sounded like a medevac. He went off the rooftop down into the company CP and learned that Captain Smith was calling for a medevac, so he and Gunnery Sergeant Hill got into a Humvee and some Marines rode in another Humvee providing security for the medevac. They got to Shit Head Alley, and insurgents were firing on them from a water tower. They then got to where (PFC George D.) Torres and another Marine named Pangelini were waiting to be medevacked. Torres had blood running down all over his face. When Torres was placed in the back of the Humvee, Van De Ven could see Torres covered in blood from the knees down.

Van De Ven was still trying to figure out where the fire was coming from. There was a gun mount on the Humvee that was not locked down, and when he turned the vehicle, the mount hit him. It scared the hell out of him. He then raced the vehicle to the cloverleaf east of Fallujah. He could now see the injuries to the two Marines. Pangelini could talk. He had two small wounds from an IED. Torres had a head wound, but Van De Ven couldn't tell how bad it was. "He doesn't look like he's real bad. He's breathin', I could see him breathing. They put the tube down, gagging. We go back to the CP, Marines are pretty upset."

Later that evening, Captain Smith got word that both Torres and Pangelini were in surgery and were stable. "We just go about our business." He later learned that Torres was a real spark plug in his platoon. At a meeting, Captain Smith learned that Torres died. "That one, it caught everyone off guard. To this day, you say someone's stable, I don't even give a crap, 'cause they don't mean it." Pangelini was medevacked to Germany and he was currently stable.

On April 12–13, Bravo Company moved elements west. Staff Sergeant Mosley led a coordinated attack on an ICDC building that was held by insurgents.

"They fire a straight volley of 203 fire, AT fire, SMAWs. It's almost like the old times where 'Archers up!' They fire: 'AT4s up!' 203s fill the gap, SMAWs are aiming in, 203s get done. There's some insurgents inside, this type of building."

The first sergeant said that every evening during this time in April the AC-130 gunships were firing, but Bravo Company never had any direct involvement with this fire support. However, he noted, "It was a good sound!"

On the morning of the 13th, 2nd Platoon needed a resupply. Van De Ven went with 3rd Platoon and some reporters in a Humvee. Insurgents were firing on the Humvee bringing resupply to 2nd Platoon. Amtracs had just been attached to the company, and the plan was to roll two Amtracs west, one to an alleyway where the Marines felt insurgents were forming up, and another to the north of that area. This way the Marines could better close in on the area. Each Amtrac had about a squad of Bravo Company Marines.

Soon after one of the tracs left, Van De Ven heard a BOOM and knew that the trac was engaging the enemy. He said that in the CP, "I hear, 'Medevac! Medevac! Medevac!' The north trac comes rollin' back, and just makes it to the alleyway in

Michigan. It's burnin'. People jump out, there's a Marine there, I could see our Corpsman, Doc Gage, jumpin' up and down. And the tracker took an RPG, it just peeled his left knee wide open. [This was Sergeant Gilbert Alcantar, Alpha Company, 3rd Amtrac Battalion, who I interviewed at Camp Fallujah.] We put him in, right back to the cloverleaf, talkin' to him the whole time."

Van De Ven and the rest of the medevac then returned to the company CP, and Captain Smith had gone with the battalion S4 officer. The XO told him that they had a "down trac." He continued, "So, we jump in two vehicles and we're headed for Shit Head Alley."

As he headed there, it became clear to him that the vehicle was not anywhere near Shit Head Alley, that it wasn't where the Marines thought it was. Instead, the trac was southwest of their position. His was the lead vehicle on medevac, heading south on Violet and taking small arms fire along the way. He turned west (a right turn) and then saw insurgents firing from their north. The insurgents were firing in a westerly direction at another of Bravo Company's squads. He said, "We fire at those clowns, uh, I think we dropped two of them. Then we take two RPGs. Thank God, the one that went by us, dud. I continue to duck. When we hit the deck, it [the second RPG] went off. Our vehicle sustained, definitely, some injuries."

They then got back into the Humvees and continued on into the city. Two more times they took fire en route. The SAWs were useful weapons at firing at the enemy hidden inside of buildings. His Marines on the medevac were now almost out of small arms ammo, and the SAW gunners were out. Some of the Marines with him were Marines who were on the first Amtrac that had been hit earlier, and had stayed with the first sergeant to return to the company. When he got back to the company CP, the battalion QRF had formed up there.

This QRF had tanks, Red Cloud (a CAAT element), and First Sergeant Van De Ven's little medevac Humvee group. The QRF went west on Violet. When it stopped, Captain Smith dismounted and continued on foot. Van De Ven did not see him again until they came to a mosque (the mosque that later had fire called on it). Here they were facing east, trying to go south. There was RPK fire coming down the alleyway, and Captain Smith was standing in the alleyway, firing and trying to get someone to go down the alleyway.

"Red Cloud comes, .50 cal fire, he backs out as Captain Smith's directing the tanks up there. The tanks, now, don't want to go down the alleyway. Which I gotta be honest with ya, sir, as a 9999 former aviation ordinance man, they got a lot of armor, we're there with no armor, I don't know why the tanks aren't firin'. Don't know why they're not goin' down there. Captain Smith is down the alleyway, yellin' at the tanks. Takin', I mean I'm seein' rocks around Captain Smith, poppin' up. He yells at them. Somewhere, I guess, he's firing M16, he realizes, get some form of cover. So he moves now. The tanks come along, and he follows along with the tanks."

Smith told the other Marines to follow and they then ran into a courtyard, while taking small arms fire. Someone had just taken off from the courtyard, and the eight Marines there snagged three RPGs and RPKs left there. They put them in the back of the vehicle and continued to press south.

They reached the main road there, Phase Line Yellow. Van De Ven was now with Captain Smith. They saw a sergeant yelling at a young Marine having trouble breathing, that he's not going to pass out. He described it as a typical Marine Corps moment. "Rounds going off, sergeant yellin', 'Get the fuck up, you're not gonna pass out!'"

Van De Ven said that Captain Smith then broke into a courtyard, and the first sergeant had no idea what Smith was doing.

"He doesn't know that our Marines are in that house. They do a Mexican standoff, you know, where they're lookin' at each other. Old style: 'Don't shoot! Don't shoot!' Captain Smith, first man in. The Marines said they'd never been happier to see him. I don't know if they weren't happy to see him before, but they were happy to see him then! You know, that they don't shoot each other."

"We get there, hook up with Staff Sergeant Sagredo, find out that Lieutenant Ayres has been hit with an RPG. [I] go inside the house, the house looks like something from a *Kill Bill* scene, or an old Western. Got all kinds of holes in it. I break out my flashlight to see Lieutenant Ayres, aaaaand, next thing, one of the Marines, 'Turn that off! Turn that off! Turn that off!' A grenade had been thrown in the kitchen where they were at, and had exploded and broke the gas line. Which was a propane gas line.

"Lance Corporal McCarver has been put in for a Silver Star, for his actions, along with Staff Sergeant Sagredo, for staying with the trac, pulling Lieutenant Ayres out of the trac under heavy small arms fire. RGP fire. This is before we got there."

Van De Ven then backed up a little to describe what had happened to these Marines before the elements of the QRF got there. He had assembled the details from statements of the Marines needed to submit combat awards.

"Staff Sergeant Sagredo had stayed with the trac as they [the Bravo Company Marines] dismounted from the trac. Garcia, then Corporal Garcia, come over to the sergeant, Sergeant Ronnie Garcia from Texas. He busts through a courtyard, unknowing, it's the house clear now. They were in a hasty defense. [He] directs all the Marines, puts the Marines on a roof, comes runnin' back out. This time, Staff Sergeant Sagredo and McCarver are pullin' Lieutenant Ayres into safety, gettin' him in this courtyard. Getting small arms fire."

The trac driver had also been heavily wounded. "He was dead, and the trac was burning. Corporal Kolm. And Garcia, knowing this Marine's left in the vehicle, knowing you don't leave Marines behind, knowing that this trac is burned up, so they know he's not alive. They run out there and try to remove his body from the trac. They can't. Kevin T. Kolm, from New York, I find out later. Romero, Corporal

Romero, and then-Corporal Ronnie Garcia, pull them back. So by then, Garcia's done some amazing things. Meanwhile, McCarver's inside, helping the doctor [Corpsman], Petty Officer Viegas, he's got burns to his face. And his hands. And shrapnel in his right leg, who won't leave Lieutenant Ayers' side."

The Marines who saw Ayres saw him breathing, but he was ghost-white and cold.

Van De Ven then picked up the story again where he entered the house. "Right away I realize, we have a medevac. I walk in this room, I step in, I'm not steppin' in water. I know that's his blood. I'm, 'Oh, my God.' This is our patrol. Somethin' mixed with some water they were tryin' to get him to drink. But you knew, this is not good. Pupils, just wrecked. Just huge peepholes, not gonna make it. So I come out, I tell Captain, 'Sir, we gotta evacuate a Marine now.' Says all right. So he directs one of the vehicles to come up. Vehicle comes up. They carry Lieutenant Ayres out. Viegas, somebody tries to take [Sergio] Viegas' edge [of the blanket holding Lieutenant Ayres] cause they had run into some shrubs. And he is protecting like a mother, he's like, 'I got it!'" On the medevac, Viegas held an IV that gave Lieutenant Ayres a blood-clotting agent.

They were still taking small arms fire at the house and Captain Smith said that they weren't going anywhere. He said that they would stay there, and either drag the Amtrac with that Marine out of there or they're staying until the trac moves. Smith said, "The trac is not staying here with that Marine in it."

Lieutenant Garver of the QRF said that he would stay. Captain Smith began to try and coordinate air support. They talked some air support on station, and ran some gun strafes. Another trac tried to pull the damaged trac without results. Finally a tank hooked up to the trac and dragged it out of the city. (I also interviewed this tank commander—Lieutenant Benjamin Adams—earlier.) It was now after sunset and the bad guys had gone. So finally they walked out and back to their Firm Base.

On April 14, battalion directed Bravo Company to pull back to east of Violet. They stayed in an enormous defensive position in Fallujah from then until April 29. Word kept changing, but they finally mounted the tracs and went back to Al Karmah to a schoolhouse there. They stayed there for four or five days and began conducting patrols. They took incoming rockets at about 0600 on May 5. The rockets overshot the school. On May 11 they started to take mortar fire, and this continued for the next several days. Van de Ven said that aside from the mortar attacks, this was a pretty quiet area. An IED wounded PFC Dunn with shrapnel to his face and he was medevacked.

The company began to send Marines back to the rear for a couple of days at a time to rest and clean up. Bravo Company then left the school house at Al Karmah and went to its current location, the Oil for Food camp at Shahabi. He said that the Marines were disappointed about this, because it looked like the mortar men had run them out of town. But politically, he felt that a schoolhouse may not have been a good place for the Marines to be.

"The first night here [Shahabi], on the 15th, we take small arms fire on that tower [he pointed to the tower that was visible about 50 meters from the warehouse we where we were], and RPG fire and mortar attack. And basically every day since then we've been mortared, or some form of attack."

While on patrols in this area, some Bravo Company Marines found individuals who denied firing weapons, but had gunpowder residue on their hands when checked here at the camp. The chemical test kit used by the Marines will indicate a recent use of firearms.

Here at the camp, Bravo Company had a platoon on guard, a platoon on patrol, and a platoon at a police station that they have stood up in town. When the camp was mortared on May 22, a patrol was out in the area, and moved so fast towards the origin of the shots that they came upon a group of individuals setting up an ambush. These men were running away, but had left their weapons. The Marines did not use deadly force, but captured the insurgents and brought them in for interrogation. The camp was not mortared from May 24 until June 5. Van De Ven was on the phone talking with Gunny Hill about some gear issues when a mortar landed around 5 meters from him!

On June 8, a car bomb went off outside of a police station. First Sergeant Van De Ven wanted me to talk to Corporal Moreno, who was currently on a patrol. He also said that there had not been a significant mortar attack since June 8. (That would change during one of my interviews here later today!)

I then asked about the near-term plans for Bravo Company. They had begun an effort to work with and train the local ICDC. He said that 3/1 would be taking over for 1/5 later this month, June 17–30. That would coincide with the return of sovereignty to the Iraqi government.

"We should be done operating outta here, back at Camp Fallujah, on about the 30th, followed by two weeks in July at the MEK. Then we'll be flying out, heading to Kuwait and to home." Home would be the States. The battalion has given a "be-prepared" to return to Iraq in March 2005. If they return, that would be the third trip to Iraq for some of the Marines of Bravo Company.

Van De Van expressed some frustration that the Marines were not allowed to take Fallujah in April. "We coulda crushed Fallujah." The Marines who fell will never come back. He noted that he was only 35 years old, but had high praise for his young Marines: "These kids, I'm only 35 years old, I act like I'm an old man, but I'm not. These 18, 19, 20-year-olds, are singing songs when they're fillin' sandbags, taking the fourth roof of an apartment building that they're in that they've had two hours of sleep. On watch the night before. Young people that are getting shot at that don't hesitate, they want to run the direction of. One young PFC asked the general [Mattis] if he could go with him through Fallujah, 'cause he's been there. The final thought is, it's a privilege to be a part of these Marines' lives, some of their greatness. What we do, no matter if we're burning, if they're burning diesel toilets or chasin' bad guys, they seem to find the best of it. Makes bein' a Marine that special thing that only us Marines, I think, understand. I'm just honored to be a part of this."

Throughout the whole interview, he kept mentally lining up his Marines who had played significant parts in the events he described. As soon as this interview was over, he began to send these Marines to my workspace in the warehouse to start meeting them and recording their stories.

* * *

Corporal Ernie Moreno

Squad Leader, 2nd Squad, 3rd Platoon, Bravo Company, 1/5

A veteran of the invasion of Iraq in 2003, Moreno vividly described the actions of his Marine squad during some of the heaviest fighting in April. One of the actions involved his Marines greedily finishing ice cream cones while on the run into action. While working on room searches with his platoon commander Lieutenant Joshua Palmer, Palmer was shot and killed by an insurgent hidden in a room. Moreno was one of the key leaders when the AAV his squad was riding in was disabled by multiple RPG rockets. He broke into a building to use as a temporary Firm Base while surrounded by enemy fighters. When the battalion QRF arrived, his Marines were basically out of ammunition.

This articulate young leader gave a very thorough interview. For almost two hours he recounted the events that he and his Marines participated in since arrival in Iraq a few months prior. His memory was clear and his descriptions of the events vivid.

Corporal Moreno started boot camp in August 2001, and joined his first FMF unit in January 2002. The unit had just returned from a deployment then, and immediately started seven months of intense training. They went to Bridgeport, and to CAX at 29 Palms. He said, "Every field op we had was two-week field ops, come back for the weekend, and then go back out for another two weeks." There was lots of movement, hiking, MOUT training, everything that could prepare anyone for combat.

After that workup, around Christmas of 2002 they were told that they were getting ready to go to Okinawa. During his leave, a friend who did not take leave called him on New Year's Eve and told him that the battalion was going to go to Iraq. After return from leave, gear that had been packed up for the move to Okinawa had to be unpacked as they awaited orders for Iraq. In early March 2003 they headed out for OIF1.

OIF1 Moreno said that last year (2003) they went right through Iraq.

"Started with the Ramallah Oil Fields, the Army calculated that to be at least nine days, fighting in the oil fields. It was one night, and then two days just guarding EPWs (enemy prisoners of war). From there, we continued to push, we got contact from the Saddam Canal area. It was supposed to be an ambush, commander said, 'Nope, we're turning in, we're attacking.' Turned to attack, was about [a] one-hour-long fight. Captured some EPWs, took the canal, and we slept there for the night. We continued to push. Finally we got to Saddam City. Saddam City was, people there actually liked us. I mean, we're expecting a big fight in Saddam City, 'cause that's where the Baath Party headquarters was. We got there, and just hundreds and hundreds of people outside, cheering for us, or just throwing confetti at us. Offerin' us cigarettes, and that was the first time we were actually like, 'Wow, you know, these people they want us here, they care, we're doin' the right thing here.' You know, made us feel good."

The battalion pushed into Baghdad and took one of the palaces there, he thought the name was the Al Nasariyah Palace. "That night goin' through Baghdad, we called it RPG Alley, 'cause it was zero one, zero two in the morning, everyone was dead tired, and we just heard the first loud explosion. An RPG. And we had over 100 RPGs just shot at us that night. We're inside tracs, and if you're standing up inside the tracs, you can just see hundreds of the *Fedayeen*, just runnin' between buildings, back and forth, on rooftops shootin' at us. All of us was opening fire, the tracs got lost 'cause every turn we'd go they'd be settin' there waitin' for us, we had to keep turning." Once they got to the palace, they remained there until it was time to move back down to Kuwait.

Once back home in 2003, everyone thought that was the end of their time in Iraq, and began to "spin up" to go to Okinawa. They did get to Okinawa in mid-December 2003 and learned that they were no longer going to be part of the MEU, but would go back to Iraq. They began to train for security and stability operations, searching vehicles and houses, and learning how to deal with Iraqi civilians. On arrival in Iraq, they had to run convoy security for the tank battalion and Amtrac units that were moving north into the country. They also had to deliver a bunch of Humvees. This convoy went without incident.

They arrived at FOB St. Mère Église (Camp Fallujah) and then went right over to Camp Mercury. Corporal Moreno said that on this drive, a lot of the Marines were using flashlights to find gear in the darkness and move into buildings. There was too much light, and insurgent mortar men picked up on this and sighted in on the Marines' camp. "It was real dark outside, and people were like, 'Shit, we're being mortared!'" There was some confusion, and some of the new Marines were scared, as it was the first time they had taken any type of incoming fire. The veterans of OIF1 told them to just calm down.

The Army showed the Marines around the area as the Marines were taking over. They warned that the area around Al Karmah was dangerous. Battalion and Bravo Company were getting a feel for the area and set out security patrols around the camp. In those first days here, these patrols found caches with mortar rounds, 155 rounds, and containers filled with anti-aircraft and machine gun ammo. When EOD was called in, it sometimes took weeks for them to get out and destroy these supplies because they were so busy all over the entire region doing it.

The company then prepared to move up to Al Karmah, and learned what sort of signs to look for when searching for IEDs, or if civilians were on the city streets or not. At Al Karmah, 3rd Platoon sent out satellite patrols of individual squads to maximize coverage of its area. This made it harder for insurgents to know where the Marines were and how they would react to any hostilities.

"Soon as we pull up, what they told us would happen was happening. People start closing up shops, all the kids got let out from school early. Called it in, to let them [Battalion] know, hey, they're closing up… by that time the two squads were inside the city, patrolling. Every kid we saw, we called the kids over, and we came loaded with candy, bags and bags of candy. We started givin' out candy to the kids, givin' em pencils. By that time, kids'd start swarming us. And when you have the kids around you, it's safe, 'cause no one's gonna try to do anything with all the kids around."

Corporal Moreno said that this was new for the people in the town, since the Army had never done anything like this before, talking with the kids, being friendly, giving out pencils and candy. The Marines wore their new digital camouflage uniforms, garnish on their Kevlar helmets, and were on foot. They also gave out pamphlets that outlined some of the reconstruction plans for restoring electricity and water systems.

When the patrols were over, the Marines returned to Camp Mercury and reported the day's events to the battalion S2 officer. It was a peaceful, quick day for them.

He noted that his company had not had time to set battle sights for the rifles since arrival in Iraq. As April approached, it seemed to him that Battalion and Regiment were planning something big. Their Al Karmah patrols stopped.

The plan for Fallujah was laid out for the companies in 2/1. By April 4, Bravo Company 1/5 was packed, loaded, and ready to move towards Fallujah. On April 5 they moved towards an open area near the cloverleaf east of the city. They set out vehicle checkpoints and stopped vehicles in the area. Moreno said he could see the tracer shots and heard explosions from the fighting when Charlie Company went in to take the cloverleaf, but Bravo had to stand tight where they were. They were only about one click from it.

On April 6, three of Bravo's platoons (1st, 2nd, and Weapons) went foot mobile into the south of Fallujah. They went on foot in order to make the move with as little noise as possible. 3rd Platoon stayed behind with the company vehicles. Their objective was a soda factory, and it was quiet when they got there, so 3rd Platoon moved up with the vehicles.

They then patrolled this part of the town, which was largely industrial: Auto body shops, brake shops, etc. Moreno said it was kind of like a horror movie set, all dark, with dirty shops and oil-covered dogs barking at them. When Weapons Platoon arrived, they drove back to the area of the soda factory, and were attacked with an RPG, taking the first casualty in the company there. Bravo Company stayed south of Route Michigan, as another Marine unit had responsibility north of the road. They patrolled the area until about 0400, and went up onto rooftops to let the insurgents know that the Marines had already taken some ground.

After sunrise, 3rd Platoon was told to prepare for another patrol. They went down to the streets and walked around. People on the other side of Michigan noticed the presence of the Marines and started to pack up and leave the city. By the end of the patrol, many of the Bravo Marines had been awake 48 hours without sleeping. They returned to the rooftops, got chow and water, and laid down to rest for a bit.

Moreno said, "I started falling asleep myself, just, when you get to that point, where you're about to go into that deep sleep, we hear a, kinda like a BOOM! And you hear somethin' whiz by you: 'SSSSSSSSSS.' And it missed our building and the building behind, just hit that building and just exploded. And we started takin' AK fire, and right away all the Marines jumped up and, you know, our first instinct was—got up, put all our stuff on, Camelbak's probably the most gear that we had off. And we ran down, downstairs. Weapons Platoon stayed up and they were already engaging from on top of the rooftops."

3rd Platoon crossed Route Michigan, with directions from Weapons Platoon. They received fire from a rooftop, engaged the guy shooting, and got him. They then ran down a narrow alleyway, realizing that there was no place to hide there.

"As we were reaching an intersection, we see a man just pop the corner with an RPG already on his shoulder. He fired the RPG. The Marines just kinda looked at each other, like, 'Okay, what are we supposed to do? There's nowhere to hide."

Moreno said that everything was now in slow motion. He could see the head of the RPG coming at him and his Marines. The Marines pretty much made themselves part of the wall. He said that then the RPG suddenly dove into the ground and exploded about 25 meters in front of them at a pile of trash. "We got right back up and started running down the alleyway to where we saw the guy. Turn the corner, saw the guy just run into a house."

Almost immediately this guy was on the rooftop, shooting at them with an AK. The Marines got the guy with a 203 shot. Then they resumed the patrol, searching houses and asking people if they knew where the bad guys were. He said that many of the women and children in these houses were terrified at the appearance of the Marines, but Moreno and his men tried to calm them down and let them know that they meant them no harm.

They searched an ice cream factory, and when they got ready to leave, the workers offered them ice cream. Once their Corpsman took an ice cream cone, the Marines accepted the workers' hospitality.

"As we were walking out, we received some more fire. And, here we are, really have no water, haven't really ate, and we had ice cream cones. We don't wanna let go of our ice cream cones, so, like, we stick the ice cream cones in our mouth. We're just kinda holdin' them in our mouth as we're opening fire back. And we're running down the alleyways, take big ol' bites outta the ice cream cones, set there, chew it."

They kept moving ahead, looking for enemy, while finishing the cones! He said that not one of the Marines let go of the cones. I laughed and remarked, "I'm just seeing the movie of this in the future!" He said that it was comical relief for the situation they were in. The company commander radioed them to move back.

On the way, they saw what looked like a bunch of ammo crates stacked on top of some rooftops. They radioed this into Captain Smith, and he told them to check it out and then return to the Firm Base. Another squad had an axe that they used to break into a house, and found a steel grate they used as a ladder to get onto the rooftops. The crates were empty. They were now near Route Violet.

They got back to the company Firm Base, got water and chow from the company Gunny. They then went back onto the rooftops. A single shot started a barrage of enemy fire at them. They went off the roof and into the streets. Moreno said that at just about every alley they received RPG fire. He gave a vivid description of what it's like to be on the receiving end of an RPG shot:

"An RPG flew by, hit one of the other buildings next to the building we were. Once again, we're running across Michigan, chasing after these bad guys. This time when we're chasin' after the guy, pretty much every alleyway we turned into we were takin' RPG shot. I mean, when you see an RPG coming at you, it's like in the movies. You figure in the movies, you have like that in slow motion. I don't know if your body just goes into a survival mode or something, that puts everything in slow motion. You can react better, and analyze the situation a lot more, but you can see an RPG, the tip of the RPG flying towards you. It's like you're in a third person perspective, you see your actual self just running out of the way, and rocket flying past your shoulder, exploding in the back. It's pretty crazy how everything happens."

One of the RPGs hit an electrical transformer, another hit a water tank that then leaked onto the street.

Moreno's squad had a quiet day on April 7, then moved out on April 8 into an area of Fallujah that had small work trenches for car repairs. They were told to watch out for any insurgents running from fights north of them. Around noon, they took possession of an electrical station. That night it was quiet, and Marines took shifts to get sleep on the rooftops. They slept on mattresses and blankets. The next morning, Lieutenant Palmer, their platoon commander, started spreading the squads out on the rooftops. The squad was told to search the area for weapons. They discovered an Iraqi family in a building, and confiscated an AK 47 and ammo there. The family's children spoke some English. The Marines warned the family to leave the area for their own safety because things might be getting dangerous. Several Iraqi families packed up and left the area. The squad reported back to Lieutenant Palmer.

As the squad was getting ready to take up positions, many of the Marines went to make head calls. Moreno said that he then heard a loud explosion. He got to one of the squad radios, replaced dead batteries, and heard a lot of chatter from the other squads. Word was that someone was hit, most likely by a mortar. On one of the radios, Corporal Lee told Moreno that someone had shrapnel wounds from the mortar round. It was his squad leader, Corporal Rodriguez, who was hit while helping to unload the squad's packs at what was going to be a temporary rest area in the city. Before the medevac Humvee took Rodgriguez, he handed Moreno his camera and asked him to take a picture. He assured Moreno that he was fine. Moreno said that Rodriguez told him, "Oh, by the way, you have the squad," and that was how Corporal Moreno became squad leader.

Now back on the rooftops, the Marines started receiving sporadic pop shots. They could not see any muzzle flashes, but could hear rounds passing nearby. Moreno and his squad tried to figure out the origin of the shots. One of his Marines stood up, and drew the fire of the enemy shooters. Moreno had two SAW gunners with him, and one of his team leaders had 203 gunners with him. They all fired toward the enemy and temporarily suppressed the fire. When they notified Captain Smith, he ordered all of the Marines off the rooftops.

Lieutenant Joshua M. Palmer let them know that they now had a frag order to help Weapons and 2nd Platoon who had a sniper holed up. Lieutenant Palmer took off to lead the squad-and-a-half with him. Other parts of the platoon were with the company CP element and the battalion CP. As they approached the target area, they saw the other Marines staggered along the walls of an alleyway. Soon they saw a wounded Marine near a wall with other Marines around him. It was Staff Sergeant William H. Harrell of Weapons Platoon, shot in the neck. "He was layin' there, he was still alive, pretty much gasping for air. He was white, real white." Moreno said that at that time he thought that the staff sergeant was probably not going to make it. Moreno set up security for the medevac that was on its way.

Lieutenant Palmer linked up with Lieutenant Christopher Ayres to coordinate and plan what to do next. Shortly after this, Lance Corporal Mike Amati was next to a wall, when sniper rounds went through the wall, wounding him in the leg, and also hit his magazines, causing some of the rounds to explode in his magazines and giving him shrapnel wounds. Moreno said that a round may have exploded before it entered the magazine, as there was a hole the size of a 50-cent piece in the magazine. "We dragged him into safety, next to Staff Sergeant Harrell." They also returned fire in the direction that it had come from.

Next, Lieutenant Palmer led the way, with Moreno right behind him, followed by other Marines. "We run out, down the street, to the alleyway, we make a left turn. And, we're comin' up to the house where the snipers were. Kinda stacked up, outside the wall, of the house real quick, 'cause it was a concrete wall, couldn't see inside the yard."

Moreno could not recall exactly who was there with them. Lieutenant Palmer told him to throw a grenade inside the yard to make sure that it was clear. "[I] get a grenade, throw it over the fence, thing goes off, go in through the entrance to the yard, and there's doorway in the middle, a window on the left side and a window on the right side."

They carefully got to the house, stacked on the sides of the doorway, then threw another grenade into the house and entered quickly. They cleared a living room area, then went into a kitchen that was clear. There was a doorway that was partly opened, and they did not go into the room. He described the continual clearance of the house, and how they yelled to a squad on the other side of the house to let them know where they were. Lieutenant Joshua Palmer was working in tandem with Corporal Moreno in their part of the house.

At another doorway, Moreno said, "I was going to be the man running in the doorway first, so I was stacked in front of the door. And, Lieutenant asked me if I had a grenade. I was like, 'Yes I do sir.' He's like, 'I'll throw the grenade, soon's the grenade goes off, you'll be the first one in.' He's like, 'I'll follow.' I was like, 'Roger that, sir!' I handed him the grenade, [he preps the grenade]. As he goes around me to throw the grenade in, I guess he exposed himself just enough [for] the sniper to see. Sniper opened up with I believe it was like three rounds, that he shot through the door." Moreno felt that the shots were fired just before the grenade went off.

"All I saw was Lieutenant was like, ready to let go of the grenade, when he got hit, I guess he let go of the grenade, the grenade still flew, made it inside the room, and from there, Lieutenant just kinda flinched back, jumped back and kinda did an about face. He fell face first into the ground. Grenade goes off, and I'm yelling into the next room, 'Lieutenant got hit! Lieutenant got hit!'"

Then one of Moreno's SAW gunners came into the room. At the doorway, he opened up with his SAW. Next came Lance Corporal Fiero, who Moreno ordered to drag Lieutenant Palmer away from the doorway into the hallway. A Corpsman began to work on the wounded officer.

Staff Sergeant Mosley, Corporal Gonzales and PFC Torres arrived, and planned to enter into the room. As they got ready to enter, Gonzales yelled and asked if anyone had a grenade. Torres looked at him and told him that Gonzales had one on his vest, so Gonzales laughed and grabbed his own grenade. Gonzales threw the grenade into the room, it went off, and Mosley got ready to go in. Mosley saw movement, went to fire his weapon, but it jammed. Moreno moved him out of the way and entered the room with Gonzales. The room was smoky from the grenade explosions. They saw two doorways on the left side of them, and a staircase. Corporal Gonzales saw a body in the prone position, behind an RPK. The insurgent was dead.

Then, Moreno said, "Right after that, a grenade just comes out from behind that corner. Corporal Gonzales was just pushin' to see in. I don't know if he said anything, I didn't hear anything. But I kinda, 'You saw something first!', and then I kinda saw it as it hit the ground." Gonzales was kneeling to get ready to change his magazine. Before either of them could get out of the room, the grenade went off. Corporal Moreno then pointed to a pallet near where we were sitting to give me an idea of the distance. It was not more than 25 feet away.

Moreno said that once again, everything was in slow motion again: "You could see the brightness from the explosion, you could see the sparks comin' out from the grenade. And, I dunno, we all just kinda went deaf pretty much, for a little bit. And as soon as the grenade goes off, Corporal Gonzales flies back, and pretty much lands in front of my feet. He has both his hands covered over his eyes, and he's kickin' back and forth, saying, 'I'm hit! I'm hit! I'm hit!' I'm over here, I was pissed off, that's already two Marines in the same house. And I was mad, and at the same time I really couldn't see what was going on 'cause debris flew into my eyes and everything went blurry. And my eyes were kinda burning a little bit. You could still see, but not that good. I reached down, I grabbed him from the back of the flak jacket, and I just turned around and I just ran outside the room, and back into the room where PFC Torres was."

Moreno yelled to Gonzales to move his hands, and Gonzales replied, "I can't see, I'm burning, I'm burning!" Moreno didn't see any blood on him, and figured that Gonzales just had debris in his eyes like he did. He took out his canteen, and poured water on Gonzales' eyes, and Gonzales wiped the water off his eyes and said, "Okay, I'm good, I'm good!" Gonzales then jumped back up, and he and Moreno stacked once more at the door to the room.

Moreno continued, "He looks at me and he's like, 'You ready?' I'm ready. And, bam! once more, running inside this room."

Moreno was on the left side by the door, and Gonzales was on the right side where the dead enemy body was. "We come in, this time the dead body is laying on its back, the weapon's no longer there, the weapon was moved back and there was another door that led to the back of the house. That door was open, and the weapon was laid in that doorway, still facing in the direction where we're coming from. Maybe the second guy that was there was planning on hitting us again."

By this time there were more Marines in the building, and this other insurgent had left the building. The Marines did capture two snipers in the area that day, but Moreno wasn't sure if either was the one from this building.

Back inside the building, they checked the body, and said that the dead man looked like he was part of some organization. He was shaven, well groomed, had good boots, a khaki uniform, a brand new LBDU (load-bearing utility) vest with magazine pouches filled with AK rounds right across the front, an AK, a pineapple grenade and some other type of grenade. They removed the ammo, and then found that throughout the house there was ammo staged near windows. The insurgents could run from window to window and had ammo waiting for them throughout the house.

Not all of the rooms in this house had been cleared yet, and Marines were standing next to one of the doors to an unsearched room. "A male swung the door open, and the Marine kinda aimed his weapon up, and the guy got scared and ran back inside the room. The door got closed."

The Marines were getting ready to go inside this room, and, "The door opens up, we raise our weapons (to prepare to fire), and a whole family comes outta that door. I'd say about three women come out, I dunno, I'd say about eight, nine children: about five little girls, four little boys. The women had two little infants, holding them in their hands. And two males were coming out. I don't know if they were males of the household or the snipers. By this time, the Marines were jumpy, as they [the civilians] came out. The Marines are screaming at them, 'Get down!'"

The Marines separated the men from the others, searched them, flexi-cuffed them, and laid them against the wall. The women and children were screaming the whole time.

Then two Marines got ready to go search that other room in the building. The door was flapping open. Corporal Moreno said, "I was looking inside this doorway, I see this little girl, you know. And right as they were getting ready to throw a grenade, I was like, 'No! No! No! No! Stop! Stop! Stop! Stop!', and they stop and look at me."

He told the Marines that he saw a little girl inside the room. "I have a little girl myself, and it reminded me of my little daughter. I'd say I was a little terrified, just the thought of the little girl, you know. To me, that little girl was my daughter, just the thought of me seeing my little girl getting blown up kind of freaked me out. I told them to stop, and the mom, little girl's mom, I guess, saw what was going on and she was freaking out. She called the girl out, and the girl ran out. At the same time, the Marines are just yelling, and the little girl gets scared and runs back inside the room. I yell at them, 'Just go inside the room!' I'm pretty sure there's nothin' in there."

The Marines went in, ready in case something happened, and they got the little girl out and walked her to her mom. Then they cleared the room out, it was empty. One of the other rooms was cleared.

2nd Platoon somehow got on the roof, and cleared the building from the roof down. Having that whole family in the building added to the chaos. They kept the family inside, and translators came and the two men were taken outside. 2nd Platoon caught another guy, one of whom was indeed a sniper.

The Marines felt that the lieutenant (Palmer) was already dead from his wounds. They didn't know the status of Lance Corporal Amati or Staff Sergeant Harrell. After they exited the building, they began to take sniper fire again from the southwest. By this time, tanks were en route to them. The squad got word that sniper fire was coming from a mosque. They jumped a fence around this mosque, then hit a locked door with some 203 rounds.

"Corporal Gonzales shoots a 203 behind one of those little pillars outside the mosque. Shoots a 203, and as soon as the 203 leaves the breach, there's a team of four Marines with the XO running towards the door, and they see the 203 round just penetrate the door and go straight through."

They pulled back and waited until another 203 round went through the door again. Then they knocked the door down. Inside the mosque, they found an AK with a few loaded magazines. Then they searched the mosque and the little tower. Soon they were again receiving small arms fire. The CO told them to take cover and wait for the tanks.

When the tanks learned which building was the origin of the shooting, they got clearance to open fire on it with the main guns. The tank fired one round, and the small arms fire died down for a short while, then started up again.

Captain Smith told the Marines to move to the second floor of buildings. A second tank round was fired, with results like the first shot—small arms fire soon resumed.

Captain Smith calmly ordered the tanks to fire one more shot. The third shot ended enemy firing out of that building. Corporal Moreno said that they received some intel that some of the snipers were Syrian, and some were Syrian-trained.

Back at the CP, they learned that Lieutenant Palmer was already dead, Lance Corporal Amati was critical, but still alive, as was Staff Sergeant Harrell. Harrell died a short time later. Corporal Rodgriguez was getting shrapnel taken out, but was supposed to be fully recovered in a short time. In just one day, four Marines from the company had been taken out of the fight, and three of these were from 3rd Platoon. Corporal Moreno said that the Marines had a range of emotions. Some were mad, some were shocked. "Reality started to sink in a lot more." That day was the first time since they were over here that someone had gotten hit. Lieutenant Penado, who had been company executive officer, was now assigned to take over as 3rd Platoon commander. He had led 3rd Platoon last year in OIF1.

Moreno and the other Marines from his platoon set up security at the apartment building, and Marines were able to get some sleep in shifts. A curfew at 1900 was set for the town. The PSYOPS teams announced the curfew over their public address speaker system. Things were usually quiet after the curfew, but one day, Moreno said, "One of my SAW gunners looked at me, was like, 'I saw a little kid, and he was probably no more than 14 years old, with an RPK,' and I was like, well, why didn't you shoot him?"

The SAW gunner said that the kid had just popped around the corner for only a moment. "So we called the snipers, the snipers saw him, and the sniper just sat there kinda waiting, and once more, the kid came out, round the corner. The sniper took the shot, and he [the kid] dropped to the ground, and [the] RPK was laying there, pretty much in the middle of the road, on the bipods. The sniper pretty much knew, 'Yep, we can have a lot more people trying to come out and pick up that weapon.'"

The snipers kept the area under observation. "And surely enough, here comes another guy peekin' out the corner, running out to try to grab this RPK. Sniper took the shot, put him down, and right after he took the shot, about three or four guys [insurgents] turn the corner and start shootin' in our general direction. They don't know where we're at, they're just kinda sprayin'."

Not wanting to have the Marine sniper compromised, he moved out of the way, and Moreno picked out the site with his ACOG on his M 16. "I went, I took the shot, and I saw the guy come, he's like roll over. I don't think I got him, though." Moreno said that he then saw the RPK slowly move into the alleyway. He thought that the insurgents may have snagged it with string or a piece of rope to recover it.

Movement continued for the next couple of days. He wasn't sure of the days when things happened at this point. The platoon was tasked with taking some buildings west of Route Michigan. The first building his squad came to was empty of occupants, and combat engineers blasted open the door with C4 and the Marines cleared the rooms up to the rooftops. They then set in on the roof. Eventually some random "pop shots" were heard, and some rounds could be heard whizzing by them. Lance Corporal Marco from Weapons Platoon came up with his ACOG on his weapon and scanned the area to try to find the origin of the shots. Then a shot hit the step Marco was standing on. Marco was okay, and from then on, Moreno said that they started receiving more accurate sniper shots, pinning them on the roof. When Marines poked their heads over the walls of the roof, they would draw fire. Moreno said he got mad, and took the ACOG sight and scanned the area himself to see where the shooter or shooters were. He called in to platoon CP that he was pinned on the roof, but was not in immediate danger. He then got word to hold tight there for the time being, and if they needed to move, to pop a smoke grenade to screen themselves, or wait until nightfall.

Corporal Moreno wasn't sure of the day that the one Amtrac was hit, but described what he saw. "We could see the smoke from the downed trac, and could hear all the traffic going through the radio. And we could hear Blackhawk Main, asking Marines that were by the trac, asking them what their exact location was, what the Grid was, how they got there. 'Cause they're trying to get the medevac to them." The medevac [actually the QRF with Captain Smith] got lost trying to find them. The Marines on the roof could see the smoke from the vehicle, and hear the radio traffic, but couldn't help out.

On the radio, Moreno could hear the medevac group trying to find the trac, which was in a part of town that they had not gone into before. He could hear Staff Sergeant Sagredo (who was waiting for the medevac in a building near the burning trac) on the radio, and said that he stayed calm throughout. Sagredo reported that they were pinned inside a building, and they were running low on ammo. On the radio net, Moreno heard that the battalion QRF was on the way, and two birds [helos] were coming on station, lighting up enemy buildings with their main cannons. He said that what he was hearing reminded him of the movie, *Black Hawk Down*. Only in this case, the Marines all got out.

Soon, the company got word to pull back and tie in better with the rest of the battalion. They went into a textile factory, set up observation posts and bunkers, and cleaned up the area. Then began the two-week pause in offensive operations during negotiations. These were two quiet weeks. They then pulled out of Fallujah to Camp Mercury. They took up positions at a school house in Al Karmah, and received random small arms fire during their stay there.

On leaving Al Karmah, Bravo Company set up positions in its current location, the Oil for Food camp next to Shahabi. They took mortar fire each night for the first few nights here. They sent counter-mortar patrols out at night to look for the shooters. IED attacks began to pick up again. The Marines also sent out lots of patrols to let the locals know of their presence and to discourage IEDs.

A couple of weeks before today's interview, a React team saw an enemy mortar team packing up its weapons after shooting, and pursued them in Humvees. They finally captured the four insurgents. Inside their vehicle was a machine gun, AKs, lots of AK ammo, and an ambush set up for the React team near a junkyard. The insurgents had ammo staged throughout the junkyard to hit the team when it came looking for the mortar teams, but that day the Marine team had gotten out to them faster than expected.

Moreno said that a couple of days ago a police station in Al Karmah was attacked by insurgents. A videotape was found on a rooftop of the planned attack. (They did not get the cameraman.) He said, "Everybody's getting worn out, everybody's ready to go home." They expected to be sent home sometime in July. But he said that Marines were always looking for a good fight!

There was also another firefight when they were on patrol with some ICDC. It was near two bridges, and they began to take mortar and small arms fire. They managed to keep the ICDC troops with them, and some of the Marines compared the fight with watching a movie. By this time in the tour, when they heard shots fired, it was second nature to them as to what everyone had to do.

Moreno had this to say about the "fog of war": "A lot of people ask us, like, about the confusion sometimes, the fog of war thing. Yeah, it's there, communication wise, the units not knowin' where they're at. But as far as your squad, individually, everybody knows what they're doing, everybody knows where they're going to pretty much, by each other's body language. And we can pretty much just look at each other and, know, all right, we got people here, we gotta do this. All right, we could give each other a nod and this either means 'hold here' or 'run into this house' or 'run to that building'. We just worked with each other so long that you just pick up on facial expressions, body expressions, everything just flows so quickly and [you] don't have to say a word. Your men already know where they're goin', hold here, watch the rear, cover that house. It's pretty cool how it just works." He compared it to sports when someone goes up for a pass and the receiver just happens to be there at the precise moment he needs to be.

His squad had a total of nine individuals, including the Navy Corpsman, and six of these Marines were new to combat. The Corpsman had served in a hospital for his first year in the Navy, and volunteered to come out with an infantry unit. Corporal Moreno said that he worked hard to get the new Marines to work as a squad. He did not plan to reenlist, but knew that he would miss a lot of the camaraderie of working with other Marines.

He said that the scary part of fighting in Fallujah was going inside of a building for the first time and not knowing what was inside. He also said that going on a nighttime patrol was not a good feeling. Once in Al Karmah, they began to do squad-size patrols. He did not start out here as a squad leader, and has had to learn how to prepare map overlays, routes, patrol orders, and so on. He was up all night preparing his first squad patrol order and asked his platoon sergeant for help.

"Me and my squad going out to patrol for the first time, without my platoon commander being there, [without] my platoon sergeant being there, telling us what to do, kinda guiding us. Pretty much us alone out there, and the city, not knowing what's going to happen."

He said that at first it took a long time to get everything done, now he can do it in less than an hour. Now, when visiting officers come to the company, the platoon commander often sends them out with Corporal Moreno's squad. He takes his leadership responsibility seriously, and felt that people back home don't realize all of this.

"I'm glad that I've seen the things I've seen. Makes you appreciate the things you have back home."

* * *

Lance Corporal Delphine Philberto Velarde

1st Team SAW Gunner, 3rd Squad, 3rd Platoon, Bravo Company, 1/5

Velarde saw a lot of action in the streets and buildings of Fallujah during combat operations there. Early on he realized that this was the real thing when one of the Marines in his platoon was wounded outside of the city. Velarde was one of the Marines who escorted Lieutenant Palmer's body back to Camp Fallujah after a house-clearing operation. A civilian photographer took a photo of him that wound up on the cover of TIME *magazine. This was a good long interview of an hour and 18 minutes with a surprise ending.*

Velarde joined the Marine Corps in September 2002, and completed recruit training in December that year. He then attended the School of Infantry, and was sent to Kuwait as a "direct shipment" to catch up with 1/5. He did guard at Camp Commando, and security on convoys up to the Iraqi border. He then joined the unit as they were leaving Iraq. He admitted that he was "busted" in rank back then. He served 60 days on a battalion NJP (non-judicial punishment).

On return from Iraq in 2003, the battalion was getting ready to deploy as the 31st MEU. But on return from leave, Velarde learned that the battalion would first go to Okinawa, get its gear, then return to Iraq. He said that when he talked to his mother with the news, she flipped out, but his dad, who was prior service (U.S. Army), dealt with the news better.

The battalion left for Okinawa in December 2003, got new desert camouflage uniforms there, received classes on dealing with IEDs and lessons that the U.S. Army had learned in Iraq. They also got training in SASO. They did practice patrolling in urban environments. During one of these days when his company was not training, he was videotaping another company training. The Marines enjoyed liberty opportunities in Okinawa and they became close there.

He was promoted back to Lance Corporal on March 1, 2004, and the battalion was back in Kuwait on March 5. After about a week and a half, they left for Iraq, escorting some trucks on convoys. Sometime during this convoy, he got the nickname Dolphin from the Marines in his platoon.

"Once we got here [Camp Mercury/Abu Ghraib], we took over camp guard first. Bravo Company was in charge of camp guard." Charlie Company was over at the prison, and Weapons Company was getting their vehicles ready. "We found quite a few things around the camp that the Army didn't find, that we didn't have reports of."

Velarde said that one day his squad found some unexploded ordnance (UXO) and then found more right away. While they were waiting for EOD teams, they saw some guys with donkey carts nearby. The Marines stopped them, and these men had wire in the carts that they said they had found and were going to sell for scrap. However, Velarde said that this is exactly the type of wire used in some IEDs.

"I will never forget the night we moved up to the house in Fallujah. I will never forget that night. It was the coldest night in my life!"

He said that the squad was in a 7-ton truck, and he was in the turret of the truck. They set up 360-degree security. The next morning, they set up VCPs to find out what the civilian vehicles were doing in the area. The platoon started to be tasked with different missions, with squads sent to different areas. His squad was tasked to serve with the company CP group for security.

The plan called for Charlie Company to secure the Fallujah cloverleaf, then they would move into the city. Then a message came over the battalion TAC radio net that an IED had gone off near the cloverleaf. Three Marines were hit. One of the wounded was a buddy of Corporal Velarde's from SOI, Lance Corporal Ramos. Velarde said that is when it really hit that this was serious business. The company commander had two SAW gunners and a 203 gunner as security. They moved to a complex known as the soda factory. A SMAW shot blasted a hole in a wall.

With Weapons Company leading, the company swept through the soda factory and then got on line to sweep the area. Velarde said that the CO (Captain Jason Smith) wanted all of the company's Marines on roofs before sunrise. They also set up the company CP in a small mechanic's shop.

While checking out an unfinished building in the area, small arms fire started coming from a mosque in the area. The Marines searched the mosque without finding anything.

Velarde described having an RPG flying over his head. He said that there was an Iraqi man trying to tell them about the shot, and he was standing in the center of the road. The shot went over the heads of Velarde and the other Marines, and exploded near the man, wounding him with shrapnel. Later, they were taking fire from down Route Michigan, and were trying to get Marines back across the street. They fired suppressing fire to allow the Marines to get back. He said that the ACOG sights on the rifles worked wonders in the fighting in the city. Marines who had "eyes on" the enemy with their ACOGs were taking out enemy snipers. They also kept watch that enemy fighters were not taking up fighting positions.

Velarde said that at this time frame, early April 2004, many RPGs that were fired at Marines did not explode. He was attached back to his platoon for a day, and when he got to the top of a building, snipers began to fire at the building. He remarked to Lieutenant Palmer, "Just another day in paradise, sir!" Palmer laughed, and responded, "Yeah, just another day in paradise." Those were the last words that he exchanged with the lieutenant.

On about April 7 or 8, the company commander, Captain Jason Smith, came to him and the other Marines at the company CP and told them to mount up. Velarde said, "We thought contact was happening over in our lines. We run straight over to the building, where we find Lance Corporal Amati, found shot, a guy in the 2nd Squad. Took one in the hip."

During the clearing of a house, his platoon commander, Lieutenant Joshua Palmer, was hit under his arm, missing his flak jacket and killing him almost immediately. Velarde went on the escort with Lieutenant Palmer's body and two enemy prisoners of war out to the cloverleaf.

On about April 11, his squad was called up and the XO told them that they had to move forward. The platoon broke up to do satellite patrolling, a technique learned from the British. Velarde moved with Lance Corporal Torres. They heard an RPK fire at them, and they returned fire. Torres ran across the alleyway and was hit by gunfire. As Velarde started to move to Torres, another lance corporal was hit by gunfire. Torres was face down. Under cover fire, Velarde ran across the alley, then held Torres in his arms. Torres had a head shot wound and had a faint pulse. His face was covered in blood, and Velarde told him that a medevac was on its way. Velarde pulled Torres' Kevlar off his head and tried to bandage his head. The Corpsman on the medevac immediately began to assess the wounded Marines.

Velarde decided to go with the medevac. Torres was still breathing. They "hauled balls" to get back to the cloverleaf. Velarde said that Torres was a fighter. Once at the cloverleaf, they handed Torres over to medical personnel, and Velarde grabbed an M16 and returned to the city.

Back in the city, the Marines in the squad learned that there were RPG ambushes set up on almost every corner of every block in the area they faced. Later that night, they moved forward to what they named "Hotel Fallujah," an apartment complex. They stayed for the next four days.

Once, when Velarde went back to the CP for a resupply run, the first sergeant grabbed him and said, "Yeah, that's him!" He took Corporal Velarde over to his computer and brought up a picture onto the screen. It was Velarde and another Marine from 3rd Platoon on the cover of *TIME* magazine! The April 19, 2004 issue.

"I remember when the picture was taken, too. When the first contact was taken on Violet, battalion commander made the decision to bring in two M1s [tanks], 'cause we'd taken heavy fire, and just bring 'em in, show 'em, hey, we're not movin' from here." He said that all of the leaders were very calm when this was happening. He remembered the photographer going out into the middle of the street, and Velarde yelling to him that he might get shot out there.

Shortly after this, his platoon was moving in two Amtracs into what he called the "Wasps' Nest, the Beehive." It was in the west part of Fallujah, on the south side of Michigan, going towards a canal. Lots of elements were moving into the city, and 1st Squad's communication went down when they moved about 500 meters away. Velarde said that many of the team leaders in his company had their own personal Uniden radios that the first sergeant had gotten for them. Listening on these radios, the rest of the platoon could hear 1st Platoon moving into one ambush after another. "We were trying to figure out where they were at, you know." The squad was giving reports of where they were. Velarde said that Marines could see where the M1s (Abrams tanks) were moving into the city.

They soon heard that Lieutenant Palmer was hit, and an Amtracker was badly burned.

Velarde remembers Corporal Torres saying to him early during the time in Fallujah: "Hollywood's got nothing on this. They'll never be able to reenact any of this." Things happened so fast, and decisions had to be made in instants.

As negotiations began, the Marines held onto areas they had taken, and offensive operations into the city ceased. When Velarde got to the rear, he called home and spoke with his cousin, who had seen his picture on the cover of *TIME* magazine. His cousin also told him that he was on the front page of *USA TODAY*.

Back home, local reporters came and talked to his parents and visited his former high school. He also called his fiancé who also had seen the *TIME* cover. She was not happy to find out that he was in the middle of some of the big fighting in Iraq. He assured her that he was fine.

Around April 30, they learned that they would be moved back to Camp Abu Ghraib, and then to Al Karmah.

Currently, the Marines in the company were busy keeping a presence in areas near Shahabi. They patrolled, gave candy to kids in the area, and looked for IED emplacements. They were trying to keep friendly relations with the local Iraqis, but still stayed alert.

There have been some nice incidents, one when they were patrolling and stopped to talk with a family and some of the Marines started kicking around a soccer ball with some of the children. The family shared cooked vegetables. "One thing we gotta remember is that not all of these people are bad. A lot of them appreciate the things we're doing here, they see we're here to help them." He added that insurgents often threaten many of these civilians, too.

There have been more patrols with ICDC members in the towns. They also have worked out of the local police station in Shahabi. Velarde said that he was there when insurgents attacked the station. The insurgents fired RPGs and small arms at them. The Marines had no serious casualties that day.

Velarde said that it's easy to see when an attack is coming: "Shops close, traffic stops. There are no people out. And this would be in the middle of the day." Then there would be mortar fire, or small arms fire.

Velarde was just promoted to lance corporal today. Throughout the interview, there were Islamic prayers being called over loudspeakers inside the town just outside the walls. I really noticed this later when I listened to the recording.

Velarde said that many of the Marines would not be part of this company when it returned to Iraq in the future. But the experiences of the veterans will help prepare the new Marines.

Just then:

BOOOM! BOOOOM! BOOOOOM!

There were several loud explosions that sounded as if they were landing just outside the other end of the warehouse where we were talking. They were.

I asked, "Is that incoming?"

I shut off the recorder as he looked over my shoulder at the back of the warehouse.

Velarde calmly replied, "Sir, I think you better get your Kevlar and flak on."

BOOOM! BOOOOM!

He had his flak jacket on already. Quickly I grabbed mine from the floor, buttoned up, and put on my helmet as the sound of the explosions echoed through the warehouse. A few more rounds landed, then the mortar attack was over. Lance Corporal Velarde told me that a Marine squad was already out in the town on patrol, and would be moving in the direction of the shooters.

An exciting way to end an interview.

* * *

First Lieutenant Stephen Gallagher Lewis

Platoon Commander, 1st Platoon, Bravo Company, 1/5

Now with his first rifle platoon, Lewis outlined the intense training that took place on Okinawa before the deployment into Iraq. On arrival at their first camp in Iraq, his Marines were upset that they were to serve as camp security. That soon changed as combat actions heated up at the end of March and start of April around Fallujah. His radio operator was badly wounded and evacuated to the States for treatment, and Lewis himself has been twice hit by rifle fire—one round hitting his flak jacket. He and his Marines have served in and around Fallujah on a variety of offensive actions and security patrols in the town of Shahabi.

Lieutenant Lewis is from Birmingham, Michigan, and graduated from Dennison University. He completed the PLC program and received his commission on December 18, 2001. He began TBS (The Basic School for Marine officers) at Quantico, Virginia with Fox Company in September of 2002. He completed IOC in March 2003 and was training when the invasion of Iraq began. Rumor had it was that new lieutenants were needed, but these proved groundless. He reported to 1/5 in May 2003, two days before the battalion returned from OIF1.

He was placed in command of an infantry platoon, and at the time was the only lieutenant in charge of a platoon in the company. Within a few months, Lieutenants Ayres and Palmer checked into the battalion and joined Bravo Company. Lewis said that it was pretty intense for the Marines in the company, as they had done an extensive workup prior to combat in Iraq, fought in Iraq, returned, took leave, then began another workup again.

He said, "It was a challenge keeping them focused, especially some of the Marines who had been around a little bit longer." He added, "At the time, we were working up for 31st MEU. We'd been told we were gonna deploy the 31st MEU in December of 2003. It wasn't until we returned from pre-deployment leave that we actually, in late November, that we were told we were gonna come back for OIF2."

They would go to Okinawa first, train there, then depart for Kuwait en route to Iraq.

He took me through this workup. "We started off working on individual skills, marksmanship, lotta SAW ranges, 203 ranges, things like that, to work on weapons mastery."

He said there were lots of hiking, shooting ranges, hard PT, long hours of training. Then they began to work on ranges for squad-size drills. Then they did MOUT training for a week. MEU workups came next, then a company-size training package at Bridgeport. The hard training at Bridgeport was also designed to put the Marines in a harsh environment away from outside distractions. Lewis said the result was more cohesion in the unit. Next followed mechanized training and working with the battalion to get ready to deploy to Okinawa in December.

While in Okinawa, the battalion put together its own SASO training package, and did a lot of shooting on ranges there.

In March 2004, 1/5 flew to Kuwait, spent two weeks there at a desert base. Then they moved into Iraq via a ground convoy and deployed to the MEK. Each platoon in Bravo Company was tasked out as security elements for units moving into Iraq. After a short stop at Camp Fallujah, they went to Camp Mercury.

"It was kind of disappointing, the first thing we were told is 'Tonight you're supposed to pick up security with the FOB.' We had just gotten there, and I understand Lieutenant Palmer and some captain from the Army found us and told us that. I explained to him that that was not gonna be able to take place. We just got outta vehicles. So, we weren't even aware at the time that we were going to be providing security for the FOB. We were all excited about the high-speed stuff."

Learning that they were supposed to be in charge of (camp) security was not what his Marines wanted to hear.

Within a day, the company went around with Army personnel to learn the posts. The Army left the following day, and Lewis said that it took about a week for Bravo Company to really learn the posts. He said it was a lot more work than he thought it would be. Then after about a week, they started to send vehicle-mounted patrols up to Karmah. Lewis had expected that there would be a "Left-seat, Right-seat" turnover, with Marine leaders going along on Army patrols for three days or so, and then the Army leaders going on the succeeding Marine patrols. It did not happen this way in Karmah.

Lieutenant Lewis said, "The first patrol to go out was from 2nd Platoon, they had a little trouble getting up there. Wound up not making it to Karmah. They had route trouble… the route they took was impassible."

A couple of days later, Lewis took his platoon on a vehicle-mounted patrol, taking a long route to the western part of Karmah. This was west of two bridges over a canal. The platoon dismounted and patrolled on foot. A lot of local people came out to see the Marines patrol. He showed me the route on a map. He said that they then went along a road south of a canal they called Route Santa Fe.

"There was an explosion behind us. I'd only heard one explosion, and all the reports I had said it was a mortar round." Once the platoon got back to camp, they pieced together all of the accounts, and figured out that this had probably been an RPG round that was a dud and failed to detonate on impact.

Every day a platoon from the company sent a patrol up to Karmah and the rest of the platoon did security around the FOB. The routine was to patrol, act as a React force, run security on the FOB, and get rest. Lewis said that it was pretty intensive.

At the end of March 2004, they learned about the American contractors being killed, burned, and hung up on the bridge in Fallujah. Captain Smith briefed his platoon commanders that something would be taking place, and to get their platoons ready to move into Fallujah. The company went with the battalion into Fallujah.

A cordon would be set up around the city, and the battalion (1/5) would have the southern part of the city. 2/1 would be to the north.

Within 1/5's area, Alpha Company would set up in the western part of Fallujah. Bravo Company had an objective to the east (Battalion Objective 2), that would wind up becoming the battalion COC.

At about 0100 on April 5, Bravo left the FOB. "It was bitter cold out. We drove in a long column out into the desert, just south of the city, and we kinda helped put in the cordon while we were there." They spent a day on the outskirts of the city. They continued planning what they would do when they did enter the city. Phase Lines Red, White, and Blue were established and Marines continued to be briefed.

2nd Platoon moved to just outside the Battalion Objective (2), and waited for confirmation to enter. Reports indicated that they might be able to seize it without a fight. Engineers did a demolition blast in a wall to enter the objective building, which Lewis described as "a giant warehouse." 2nd Platoon went in first, followed by Weapons Platoon that went east of this compound to clear buildings in a residential area.

Lieutenant Lewis' 1st Platoon followed 2nd Platoon in through the breach and then cleared up to Phase Line Black. They collected weapons found in the buildings and gathered some Iraqi guards into a makeshift EPW area. These guards were later released. 1st Platoon continued clearing through the industrial area into town. They expected to get a lot of enemy contact from across Route Michigan (Route 10), which runs through Fallujah. They did all of this on foot, and their vehicles were being brought up to them.

Alpha Company was south of Bravo Company during this push. Bravo pushed on line with Weapons Platoon, then 2nd and 1st Platoons moved to the west through the industrial area. Lieutenant Lewis said that this was labor-intensive, as he often had squads searching and taking out fairly big buildings. "It was tiring, it was a long night, until we reached Phase Line Orange." They then set up on top of buildings. During the day, people from the town went by, and in his opinion, they were scouting out the Marine positions in the area.

"You could tell they were tryin' to check out our lines somewhat, they knew our Rules of Engagement. So we started running some vehicle checkpoints right in front of our lines, and sending out a couple patrols, figure out who was doing what, try and limit the number of people scouting us out."

Soon they started taking small arms fire. One of his squads was at a vehicle checkpoint, and took fire from a mosque. The squad cordoned it off and made entry into the mosque. On their return, this squad took an RPG round and saw a guy who may have been the shooter running away.

During a cordon and knock, Lieutenant Lewis entered a house where the woman of the house spoke very good English. The woman said that her family liked the Marines, but in the week after this, rifle fire came from this area. Lewis said that he wondered about how the people there really felt, because they were usually friendly when they talked with the Marines. An adjoining house had men and some Iraqi police inside, but none of them said that they had seen anything.

A short time later, they again received small arms fire, and the platoon fanned out and pursued a shooter, this time the shooter ran into 2nd Platoon and was shot by them. Lewis said that throughout this time, his Marines were pretty hyped up, going after bad guys. "You didn't have to give them a lot of orders," he remarked.

When they moved across Route Michigan, there was a lot of machine gunfire directed at them down Michigan. "We had to run across Michigan with a lot of tracers skipping around." Lewis said that this is when many of the Marines realized that they were in true combat. It was not the SASO that they had mentally prepared for. Lieutenant Lewis expected some kind of enemy probe or attack onto their positions that night. "You really didn't have to work too hard to keep the Marines up, because they're pretty jacked up at this point. They're pretty attentive." But it was quiet that night.

The next morning, April 7, traffic had begun to pick up at first light. Lewis set up another vehicle checkpoint on the road. He was attempting to limit the number of people who were checking out their positions. Then mortar fire began. "You could see the people up on the rooftops, sitting there with binoculars, trying to spot us." As the mortar fire became more accurate, it became more obvious who were combatants, and Lewis' Marines started to engage these enemy spotters on the rooftops. The mortar fire decreased after that.

1st Platoon's next move was up to Orange and Michigan, on the flank to the rear of the company. Weapons Platoon left him a machine gun squad and snipers who had been attached to them. Lewis said that right down an alleyway he could see the walled courtyard of a school, and smoke from mortar tubes. However, he did not have any weapons with him with the penetrating power to get at them, and he did not have the manpower to assault the 500 meters he would have to move to get into this courtyard. He sketched out the position on a notebook page for me, and I made a quick sketch in my own notebook.

Lewis said that for the next couple of days, they took inaccurate small arms fire, along with mortar fire. When Marine tanks came up, he tried to figure out how to talk to the tanks. When he finally got comm with them, he had the tanks fire down the alleyway and hit the courtyard at the school. Marine snipers on the rooftops said that they saw men who were carrying weapons running out of the courtyard area after this. Lewis said that he hoped that the tank shot at least hurt, if not killed, some of these enemy fighters.

It seemed to Lieutenant Lewis that the enemy had a lot of weapons and ammunition stored in this part of the city. These enemy fighters continued to fire harassing small arms fire toward the Marine positions. "Little Wolf," CAAT Platoon, came to his position on April 7. Lewis was not involved in the fighting west of Phase Line Violet that day.

He said, "It was kinda tough, sittin' there listening to it, because you wanted to be there, fighting, and I'm sitting there, listening on the radio." He could hear that there were casualties and KIAs, and he wanted to bring his platoon to help them. Staff Sergeant Harrell, who was killed in that fighting, had been Lieutenant Lewis' first platoon sergeant, and many of the Marines had been close to Harrell. And Lieutenant Palmer, who was also killed, had been a buddy of Lewis.

On April 8, Lewis' platoon was still receiving random small arms fire, and mortar fire, but some enemy fighters had moved in close to them. 1st Platoon Marines on the rooftops were receiving more small arms fire, so Lewis began to look for alternate positions for them. While he was doing this, his RO (radio operator), Lance Corporal Lopez, was wounded. "We were running through an alley, trying to run around an alley, to go into a, check out a rooftop, see if we could get up on a rooftop behind us, a little bit back. We could put some guys on the deck, it'd be a little bit farther back."

Lopez was right behind him, and Lewis heard the shot that hit Lopez. "He took one wound in the femoral artery, so he was losing a lot of blood real fast, and he went into shock real quick." Fortunately, Little Wolf, the vehicle-mounted CAAT platoon, was right next to them, and Lieutenant Lewis was able to grab one of their Corpsmen. This Corpsman provided immediate first aid, and Little Wolf was able to provide a medevac vehicle to take Lopez to emergency treatment. Lopez went into a coma for five days, but was now doing better. "I've spoken to him since then, and he's doing real well," said the lieutenant. "In fact, he's back home on convalescent leave now."

Lewis himself was actually shot twice, but one of the rounds hit a SAPI plate on his back, which probably saved his life.

By the time Lewis returned to his platoon after medevacking Lance Corporal Lopez, another Marine in his platoon, Lance Corporal Cotero, had been wounded and also medevacked. His wound was not as serious as that of Lopez. He had received bullet fragments on his right arm and leg. Lewis said that Cotero's main concern at the time was whether or not the fragments hit a tattoo that he had recently had done! It turned out that the tattoo was hit, but the wounds were not serious. Cotero was back with the platoon in a few days.

Lieutenant Lewis spoke with Captain Smith about moving off the rooftops and into positions closer to the ground so they could better shoot at enemy fighters. It was also becoming more clear to him that they would be staying in this area longer than he originally thought. He found a really big building south of his position, with good observation into the city, and good-sized walls for cover. He oriented his squads towards the west (towards Orange) and north (towards Michigan). A third squad, with a machine gun, a little to the east, oriented up an alleyway. The day after this, a mortar round hit on top of the building, and two Marines were wounded: One was medevacked, the other received minor wounds. Both were now back with the platoon.

Then things got quiet for a couple of days. Curfews were instituted in the town. Lewis said that it was incredible how the people in the area continued to live in the area as if nothing was going on during all of the fighting. At the same time, some families were trying to get out of the area.

On April 12, his platoon moved west to Phase Line Violet. Lewis was on a leaders' brief with another lieutenant who was moving into his position. "I was showing the platoon commander around, with one of the sergeants. We got up onto the rooftop we had been on before, right on the corner of Orange and Michigan. And we could see some guys walking across the street with RPGs, AK 47s, RPKs. In hindsight, it was very strange, because they were just walking across the street. It wasn't like they were in an assault. They never had hostile intent, they were there to kill somebody. Just the way they were doing it was very strange. But, we shot and killed some of them. Exactly how many we got I'm not sure, because they wound up draggin' them back, the bodies. But, real shoot and kill. Some of them, I know, the weapons were left out there as well."

The Marines put together a force to go out and pick up the weapons left out in the street. "We had the [four] tracs with us, so I used two of the tracs with a squad minus in each one." One trac was set up as an overwatch, and the other to recover the abandoned weapons. "As soon as we pull out onto Michigan, we start taking lots of small arms fire. We got out onto this one alleyway directly to our west, and some RPGs came that way. It was kinda weird, I was looking right at the guy when he shot it. He was about 500 meters away. And, right when he shot it, you could tell it wasn't gonna hit us. It resembled a golf shot. A slice. Right when he shot it, it sailed towards my left. And the .50 cal [on the Amtrac] started working down the road. It suppressed pretty well. And another terrorist had been like behind a dune, we were able to see him, and kill him." The Marines were able to pick up the weapons left in the street.

Lewis also said that between the 9th and the 12th, he had a mortar team attached to him. Marine snipers on rooftops could spot for the mortar men. The tracs also fired their 40mm guns. During this time, they engaged two vehicles believed to be providing ammo to enemy fighters, and huge secondary explosions from these vehicles confirmed this.

Within an hour of this, he took the tracs back to the company CP to do some back clearing of that area. 3rd Platoon had pushed out west the previous night, so 1st Platoon went into the "back" area behind 3rd Platoon to clear these buildings. Lewis said that by now his Marines were used to hearing bullets, and could tell if the rounds were close or not. He described clearing the buildings as an exhausting experience. Not wanting to use demo on every house, there was a lot of kicking-in doors. In addition to weapons and ammo, one of the items found during these searches was a cigarette lighter, with images of the World Trade Center on it that blew up when the lighter was lit. Things like this provided motivation for his Marines.

On April 13, 1st and 2nd Platoons were co-located around a large building. Early that morning, an element from 2nd Platoon pushed out into the west of city, taking up positions in a combat outpost. 3rd Platoon had been in that area the day before. 1st Platoon moved to again back-clear the area behind 2nd Platoon. Lewis said that there were a lot of houses to search and clear, and it took most of the day. The platoon received sporadic fire the entire day. One of his Marines had a bullet that went through his sleeve, missing his arm completely but leaving two holes—one entrance and one exit!

Again, weapons like RPGs were found during the searches.

2nd Platoon had taken fire at its position throughout the day, and called for tracs to reinforce them. Lewis had just gotten back to his position and was on the radio when he heard the call that one of the tracs with 2nd Platoon had been hit.

"We didn't have an exact location where they were located, they talk about the fog of war in classes. This is my first example of real drastic fog of war."

Lewis assembled two squads, leaving a third squad on security, and pushed out. They pushed west to where 2nd Platoon had been taking lots of fire that day. "There was a big cloud of smoke to the west of it, so we assumed that was the trac. And it was in the general location of where they were supposed to be. It turned out it was a house that was on fire."

They then looked far to the south, and that was where the trac actually was. The whole time there was a lot of small arms and machine gunfire going on. Another of his Marines was wounded in the cheek by shrapnel from an RPG round. Lieutenant Lewis said that his Marines were returning a lot of enemy fire, but didn't know how many casualties they inflicted.

As Lewis began moving south, he got word that there were some tanks and vehicles moving into the city, and was asked if he could see them. He moved to a position where he could see them, and radioed to the XO who was in communication with battalion. As Lewis' Marines moved south, they began taking increased small arms fire.

The tanks had finally reached the burning Amtrac, and had another platoon (the battalion QRF) with them. Lewis listened on the radio as Captain Smith and the battalion tried to figure out where everyone was. There was talk of bringing in air support. Lewis was told to move his men back, as battalion had the damaged trac, and was withdrawing the Marines from there. He got back to his positions. He said that that day was the most chaotic he has had in Iraq.

On return to his positions, he accounted for of all his Marines. 2nd Platoon next returned to the position and also had all its Marines accounted for. There was one KIA—an Amtracker (Corporal Kevin T. Kolm), and Lieutenant Ayres had been seriously wounded. (Ayres was recovering from these wounds in the States at the time of this interview, and the prognosis was good.)

"One of the most amazing sights, though, was watching the tank dragging out that trac. It dragged it right along, in front of our position on Violet. It [the trac] was basically in half. Burned up. It was amazing to me that only one person died in that thing. When I saw that, I didn't know what the situation was gonna be, this is before the [2nd] platoon got back, and I thought for sure there was gonna be a whole lot more casualties than there were. So, once they got back and I heard the sitrep as far as who was hurt and who wasn't, it was definitely good news."

This was about the time that forward combat operations ceased in Fallujah. Lewis' platoon moved into a building on Violet and Michigan. It was an old apartment building and he had his Marines begin to reinforce positions inside the structure. Before, when they were continuously on the move, they would grab trash to make hasty positions. Here, they had a sand lot next to the building, and lots of sand bags. They built up sandbagged positions near windows and doorways. They built bunkers on the roof. The bunkers stopped sniper fire. His Marines didn't like filling the sand bags, but appreciated them when taking fire.

They stayed there for the next two weeks. The word about what would happen next continually changed. On about April 29 they pulled out and moved back to their FOB at Camp Abu Ghraib.

After return to the FOB, they straightened out gear accountability, then moved up to a schoolhouse in Karmah. It was a four-story building with great views of the whole town. They stayed there for two weeks, and used it as a base for patrols in the area. He said that they even had sources who would go to the schoolhouse and give them intel.

When they left that schoolhouse, the company began to operate out of a police station. An eight-day rotation began, with one platoon at the police station, two platoons at Camp Shahabi, and one platoon back at the FOB (Camp Abu Ghraib). Each location was a two-day stay for each platoon. They began to conduct squad-size patrols so that 24 hours a day there was a Marine presence in the area. They were continuing to do these patrols at this time. The patrols have uncovered IEDs, and learned of anti-coalition activities in this area.

Either Lieutenant Lewis or his platoon sergeant accompany these squad patrols. The squad leaders run the patrols. He related an incident where one squad was at the police station, and the station came under attack. The squad leader led a defense of the station, and called out a reaction force to drive off the attackers.

He next told of events on June 8, just three days before today. There was one platoon in the police station, along with a squad from Charlie Company, and a platoon of ICDC (who are Shiites from another part of Iraq). The Charlie Company squad was working with a Civil Affairs Platoon program to train the Iraqi forces.

This police station was attacked in a coordinated way. The insurgents had planted a video recorder to record the attack. A bunch of guys drove up in a vehicle in front of the police station. They got off the vehicle and shot off a lot of AK 47 fire, and several RPGs were fired at the station from several positions.

Bravo Company launched a React force from Camp Shahabi. The React force was Lieutenant Lewis' 2nd Squad with his platoon sergeant, Staff Sergeant Campbell in charge. As they approached the police station, they came up behind some Marines from Charlie Company who were resupplying the station.

The Charlie Company Marines moved up to the station, and took an RPG shot. Staff Sergeant Campbell took his squad off to the west and then the north. They got behind the guys shooting at the police station. These actions boxed in the insurgents there. Some insurgents were killed and others managed to begin to get away. Forces from the police station were able to pursue these insurgents and kill some of them.

Lewis came up with another squad to get any medevacs, but there were no friendlies seriously wounded. His Marines were able to kill another insurgent who had mortars with him. Lewis said that the mortars were frustrating, because it was not possible to return fire at them. There was another Iraqi that they wounded and captured. "Hopefully, they're getting some intel from him right now." He said that this was a successful day for the Marines, as they were able to kill at least five enemy, and wounded and captured one.

Lieutenant Lewis said that right now his job was to keep his Marines focused. They have been gone from home for nearly seven months. But they had to focus on the next patrol that they go out on. He expected that the company would return home sometime in mid-July 2004, but added that nothing was ever certain.

About half of the Marines in his platoon were new to Iraq and combat. He said that they did what they needed to do. When one Marine was wounded on a rooftop, other Marines moved him to medevac despite incoming small arms fire all around them. He said it was rewarding to form a tight team and see it work in Fallujah and Karmah.

* * *

Corporal Jason Charles Howell

Squad Leader, 1st Platoon, Bravo Company, 1/5

On arrival near Fallujah, Howell and his Marines were frustrated to be placed on camp guard duty. Soon, however, they would experience a full range of combat operations when they entered Fallujah. His company was supported by heavy weapons, tanks and close air support from Marine helos. His squad also did detailed searches during "back clearing" of buildings in Fallujah. He vividly recounted the sounds of combat, both on the offense and when on the receiving end of machine guns and RPG rocket grenades.

A most welcome sound was when the Air Force's AC-130 gunship would fire in the evenings. After leaving Fallujah, patrols and ambushes continued in the area around the village of Shahabi.

Corporal Howell started his Marine Corps career in Security Forces Company, and was first stationed in Washington State at the Naval Submarinc Base in Bangor. He attended some military schools while there, and after two years in this billet was sent to the Fleet. In September 2003 he went to 1/5 and took over an infantry squad during the workup to prepare for current operations in Iraq.

He said that they did some MOUT training, a raid package, patrolling, and training in Bridgeport.

After two weeks in Kuwait, the Bravo Company moved up to FOB Mercury. The company spent the first two weeks there on camp guard, then about a month in Fallujah, before going into the schoolhouse for two weeks. They then moved to Camp Shahabi where they currently operate.

Corporal Howell said that he and his Marines were frustrated at first with the guard duty assignment at the camp.

Then Fallujah happened. He said, "We got there, we ended up staging for one day and two nights, or was it two nights and one day. Seemed like eternity. We ended up laying in the outskirts of Fallujah, to the south, I believe it was." They watched tracers over at the cloverleaf outside of Fallujah, where Charlie Company was fighting. He said, "We actually sat there and said, 'Well that's it, looks like Charlie's cleaning house.' We're just gonna go clean up."

But the next night, Bravo Company ended up hitting Battalion Objective 1, where they cleared out a bunch of warehouses and buildings. They brought in some detainees and also raided the soda factory. I asked if this place looked like a soda factory. He replied, "No, when you looked at it on the map there's like quarries all around it, huge quarries in the dirt."

They moved up on foot, and Engineers used two huge charges to make a hole in the wall there. They ran through the hole and cleared the place. It later turned out that one of the warehouses was full of cases of soda. They then pushed west on the southern side of Route Michigan (Route 10), a mostly industrial area. The Marines cleared the area—they broke locks and took a lot of people's AKs. They only received fire once that night, from a shooter who was between 1st Platoon and Weapons Platoon. At night's end, Captain Smith gave the order to get up on the rooftops, and Howell said that he watched the sun come up that morning.

It was now April 6. Local Iraqis drove by the buildings. Howell said that in the early afternoon, around 1300 or 1400, they began to take sporadic small arms fire. He also said that he finally had time to heat up some MREs, the first time he had eaten in about 24 hours because of all the moving the previous night.

"And right as I go to slip it [the MRE main meal] into the heater, 'Gotta go! Gotta go!' I was more pissed at leavin' my food than anything."

"It was April 6th. Everything was happening so fast, the sitreps [situation reports] were like, 'Run over there!' And no clue what we were gettin' into. When we first got there, we were briefed: 'MSR Michigan, Route 10, we're gonna stay south of that, don't even look at it. If you touch foot on it, we got friendly units north of it. That's our control measure, don't touch it. You might get shot, blah blah, blah.'"

He said it seemed that the whole company "jetted" north, clearing houses. There were detainees everywhere. "Humvees flyin' all over the place."

Howell's squad was attached to 3rd Platoon at this time. He said that they were rushing down a wide-open street, taking lots of small arms fire. "The only words out of my mouth to my squad was, 'Keep pushin', keep pushin!' We ended up pushing pretty far. And the other platoon commander asked what was goin' on. Said, 'Who's the senior man?' 'Me, right now.' Gave a quick sitrep. Set up my guys in position, down alleys and down this major road."

Howell said that the people of Iraq seemed to like being outside and watching all of the firefights. "Makes it hard for the Rules of Engagement, who's good guys, who's bad guys, what's goin' on."

As he continued with his squad, moving west, he saw tracer rounds flying all around him. He was having his Marines leap-frog forward. "I was like, go! go!" He noticed Lieutenant Palmer behind him, waiting to be the last one to cross over the street. Palmer wanted to make sure that all of the Marines made it across the street. Howell said that Palmer was one of the Marines who wanted to take care of "his boys," and a few days later was killed while leading the clearing of a building.

Corporal Howell was in the middle of his squad. He found out that during the move, some of his Marines were separated from the squad for a couple of minutes while they had a little firefight with enemy shooters behind them. They went back onto rooftops, and the small arms and RPG fire continued. There was now also some mortar fire at them.

"You'd hear it, a huge pop, you'd say, okay, incoming! And hear the explosion somewhere near you. When we got back on this rooftop, it was such a long day, and everybody's joking. All the salty guys are like, 'Yeah, you guys are into combat!' I remember sittin' on this rooftop, and the sun's going down, we got rockets. You don't even have time to hear them. It's like 'CH-BMMMM! Totally obvious where we are. We got a small corner here, and a small corner here, with Marines trying to huddle around them trying to get corners. Got cover on one side, other side's completely exposed. Got Marines lined up on the rooftops, everybody's tryin' to figure out what's goin' on."

For the next few days they moved from rooftops to rooftops.

He described the fighting near the schoolhouse. "We're getting reports that there are Syrian snipers in town. I don't know about Syrian snipers… I figured out they're pretty decently trained, 'cause [I] had a rangefinder with 540 meters, or something like that, it was 550, 600 meters." He said that the whole country seemed to be built up in blocking positions or fighting positions. There were chunks of cinderblocks on the rooftops built up on walls that were perfect for fighting positions.

The fighters in the schoolyard were shooting mortars at them for two days. "The mortars, they were just walking onto us. [Walking-in mortar fire is when the shooter gradually adjusts the range of where the rounds land to get onto a desired target.] One would land way short, one would get closer, one would land, just past our building. Then one would get just in front of it, like five meters in front of our building. I'm just sittin' there, thinkin' they're just walkin' on us, this is ridiculous. 'Course we couldn't get air support, because we can't shoot up a school up there apparently."

Two Marine snipers on buildings were giving accurate reports about what was going on in and around the school building. They'd call in that there were enemy fighters in "man dresses" and red head scarves running across a street with RPKs and rifles, or a white pickup truck delivering supplies to the schoolhouse area. Finally, tanks pulled up and Howell said, "We were never so happy. One faced toward the schoolhouse. We had three tanks at one time, I remember. They felt safe with us, we felt safe with them. Everything was invincible when we had tanks, you know."

Howell described what it was like to have enemy rifle rounds come close: "You'd hear a snap above your head from the distance, from the schoolhouse. And then like right in front of you, like a hundred meters, you'd get some harassing fire from one of the buildings."

Then he said, "We finally got air. It was a building that was off to my right. Which would be my east." Corporal Howell said that two tanks shot at this building at the same time, Weapons Company shot a TOW missile at the building, then along came a Huey and a Cobra right over their heads and just "light the building up." He said it felt great, but when all of the attack was done, the insurgents let out "Crack! Crack!" just to let the Marines know that some of them were still in there!

A couple of days after this, Corporal Howell went down to a bunker, and an RPG hit it. "There's a Corpsman was still up against a bunker with a couple of guys and I hear him just frustrated, screaming, yelling, 'What's it gonna take to get some fuckin' air around here?' And then, so much happened."

Howell was looking for more ammo from another squad. He got the ammo and brought it back up to his Marines. The enemy was still walking in the mortar rounds close to the rooftop. He finally got the okay to pick up and move to another rooftop. The Marines had been on this rooftop too long, some 38 to 40 hours by this time, and the enemy knew their exact position.

"As I took my guys, and we went west some, south some, to where we still had eyes on some of MSR Michigan Route 10. Huge building, real nice building. It's a great position. You had corners, on the rooftop. And I ended up getting to where we could have my squad up there, a squad across the street that were in the oil [change] pits, on the ground. Had another squad that was a little further east, I believe." They were here for a day or two.

His squad had its first casualty. "I placed my guys into where they had nice dispersion, but I needed, like they were real spaced out. From one end of the rooftop to the other end it was, I think, 30 to 40 yards. It was a good distance. And I remember I had two guys down there, I had Drane, I had Brennan, two of my guys. 203 gunner and SAW gunner. And we get some sporadic mortar fire that wasn't landing anywhere near our building. We received "blue on blue" from Weapons Company, they shot at us twice. Then a mortar hit. These guys were so lucky. Mortar landed like 15, maybe 20 feet from them, tops. We hear the explosion, I look down—they were down here, I was down here [he gestured with his hands] and then it continues down this way. We hear the BOOM, and I look down, and I realize I'm not hit. I look down I see a smoke, I hear one of my guys just screamin', the worst sound in the world. Screamin'. You know, naturally, everybody wants to help, so a herd of Marines start running down here, where we just got mortared. We'd been getting small arms fire from 'em."

"So I ended up taking a couple of my guys, saying, 'Security! Security!' Some of my guys around so they don't bunch up any. I remember the Corpsman was working on him, putting pressure dressings on him. What ended up happening—one of the guys he ended up getting shrapnel in his lower back, the ass cheek. And that was pretty much it. Like it ripped right through his vest, right here, came up like this [in the] ass cheek, right into here into his lower back. He's still got some metal in the lower back." Howell said that the other Marine who was hit had a little piece of metal in his neck and some burn on his face. Howell said that this Marine looked flush in his face for a day or two.

They then got these Marines ready to be medevacked out of there. "First [the wounded Marine said] 'I'm gonna pass out! I'm gonna pass out!' Blood all over the place, and everything, screamin'. By the time the stretcher came, put him on the stretcher, and carried him down, loaded him up, he went from sayin' he was gonna pass out and looking at all the blood on him, to—somehow jokin' around, and asking where the pretty nurses were." This Marine recovered from the wounds and was with the squad for a firefight in Karmah on June 8.

After these encounters, the squad got moved back to the area where it had started on the rooftops days earlier, but took up positions in oil change pits and car garages. They did back-clearing in the area, finding lots of AK 47s and RPGs.

Marine mortars finally got the okay to fire, and Howell said that the Marine mortar men were happy about this as they set up their positions to fire into the city. Now when the Marines got mortared, their snipers on the roofs spotted the enemy shooters for the Marine mortar men. Howell said that the Marines cheered every time that their mortar men dropped rounds into the tubes.

As platoons from the company moved into forward positions in the city, 1st Platoon back-cleared the intervening buildings for couple of days. Howell said that there were still Iraqi families in this area. Many times they would bust into a house ready to kill enemy fighters, and there would be women and children inside. He said that HET [Human Exploitation Teams] were tasked out "big time" to work with the Marines to explain to the civilians what they were doing. The further west into the city they went, the more residential it got.

Other Marine units were in the city, but Howell said he didn't see them at the time. 3/4 was supposed to be north of them, and 2/1 was working in Fallujah also. 2/1 was somewhere in the northwestern corner of Fallujah. 1/5 started in the southeastern part of the city, and was now working its way across towards the western part of the city. Howell said that every day it seemed a little more hairy. He mentioned Private First Class Oswald, a Marine who "needs work" in garrison, became a stud in the field. "Out there he amazed me. June 8 as well, he was actually one of my guys who I wanted to put up for awards." He's the Marine who took an AK round through the sleeve and wasn't even fazed.

He said that one day, April 13, some of the tracs that were with 2nd Platoon ended up getting too far into the city and took some RPG fire. That day he said, "We did something like eight hours of back-clearing. This is the third day in a row my squad gets selected to do back-clearing."

He said they had just gotten back in and, "The lieutenant comes in, says, 'We gotta go! We gotta go!' 'What's goin' on?' 'We gotta go!'

"We run out, before we knew it we were runnin' out in the street, ended up linking up with somebody in 3rd Platoon. 'What's goin' on?' 'Sniper fire from every direction!'

"Sure enough, you hear the snaps and the cracks, hittin' the concrete, and I remember finally hearing that some tracs went down, we gotta link up, we gotta help 2nd Platoon, they're isolated in the building, taking heavy small arms fire. RPGs ended up lightin' up this trac."

"So we ended up goin' in. Wall hopping was like the big deal in this area 'cause it was either streets where you're exposing yourself to a shot, or hopping walls, where you're exposing yourself for a lesser amount of time. I remember, we had to keep pushing, west, I believe it was. By the time we get out there, out into the open, figure out what's going on, and start pushin', we end up, there's some houses and a lot, we end up takin' fire from every direction."

Howell hopped over a wall and was getting ready to come back over, when an RPG zipped right over. "BOOM! That's when the Corpsman ended getting a little shrapnel to the face. He's got a scar, looks like he just cut himself while shaving."

Howell ended up on another rooftop with one of his guys, and one of his buddies, Corporal Dawson, with Dawson's squad. The rest of his squad was on another rooftop with Lieutenant Lewis. Howell remembered thinking that he was dying of thirst, did not have his Camelbak with him, was pinned down on the rooftop, and did not have all of his squad with him. He looked into the distance and saw black smoke where the fight was going on, and to where they were trying to go.

Howell said that Lieutenant Ayres, who was badly wounded in that fight, was an outstanding officer. The challenge for Howell now was to get his squad together, get off the top of the building, and continue forward, all without getting shot! It was about a 20-minute process, but Howell said that, "It seemed like it took forever." When he finally got to the Marines of his squad, they were glad to see him. "They were like, 'Good to see you! Good to see you!'"

While they were on the rooftops, they got "on the hook" (radio communication) with tanks and Weapons Company, and gave them directions to get to the burning trac and the Marines who were near it. Once the rescue took place, he and his Marines had to get out of the area before air support came in and "lit up the whole town."

Corporal Howell said that the RO (radio operator) with him was "on the hook" (radio) with the Company CO and XO. There was a code word, "Slingshot," which meant that a massive air attack would hit an area. Corporal Dawson also knew what this key word meant. The CO said that they had to get out of the area because Slingshot was on its way. The two squads with Howell had to cross a big field to get out of the area.

"We ended up running. I don't know how we didn't die," Howell laughed.

"We got in, running. Taking point, I'm right behind him [Dawson]. I remember we just jet across this open field, to these other buildings. A good 200 yards, maybe. Behind us it's just a single file column, everybody's just running! The same time. Nobody's riding cover. Everybody is just like running for their lives. And we ended up just getting in this building. Busted in, cleared it out. Nobody was in there."

They posted some Marines on the rooftop, took out the GPS to learn their exact location. "We just hear air, as we're running across this field, we just hear AC-130 gunships just like goin' 'Thump! Thump! Thump!' Their machine gun makes like a burping sound, 'Brrrrrrrrrrrrr!' The nights on the rooftops, the best sound in the world!"

Howell then got word that they were "good" to come back to their temporary Firm Base. Howell said that this was a lot like a scene from the movie *Black Hawk Down* when the troop carriers were full and the soldiers had to run even though they were exhausted. He said that he and his Marines were exhausted by this time, although sporadic small arms fire would "Put a little pep in some people's step." Corporal Howell said that he still had to tell some of his boys to run. One PFC, a SAW gunner, would often break down into a walk, and Howell had to scream at him to keep running.

Next, Howell's platoon (1st Platoon) was sent to a building at the corner of Routes Violet and Michigan. This building was opposite an ICDC police station that had been taken over by insurgents. An insurgent with an RPK machine gun went out into the middle of Michigan at about 0800 one morning, and began to "light up" Marine positions.

"We got tracs with us still, at this point, so he [Lieutenant Lewis] goes in a trac, I go in a trac, we shoot out in the middle of Michigan, he hauls down on this road. I pull my trac up right here [pointing to a map he held]. Some of my boys dismount, I remember one of my team leaders jumps out—middle of Michigan. Middle of the day. Receiving small arms fire. Guy's a stud. Runs out, grabs the weapon, comes back in. While all this is happening, the lieutenant's trac's right down here, holdin' down this alley. We got small arms fire coming from all these buildings just north of Michigan. I see an RPG—'Phhhhwwww!'—right by my lieutenant's trac. My guy's still pickin' up this RPK at the time. He finally gets in. We zip our tracs around while we're still receiving small arms coming back. Somehow we retrieved this weapon. It was insane, it was, a lot we did, I guess you had to think quick."

Then, he continued to talk about the positions that they set up at the building, that he now called "Hotel Fallujah." They set up a guard rotation there with six-hour shifts: one shift on guard, one on React, and one to try to get some rest.

"That wore down the Marines real fast. They did two weeks of combat-offensive operations. Whatever political stuff was goin' on, a lot of these guys were like, 'We're gonna go home, read the papers and articles and hear about what happened.' A lot of these guys are not sure what happened."

But they had been told to stop pushing. The Rules of Engagement had been constantly changing. They spent about two weeks in a kind of guard rotation. It would be quiet for two or three days, then suddenly a round would come zipping at them. While at this building, Marines were continually filling sand bags and then forming relay chains to move the sand bags up into positions in the building. When Marines were in exposed positions outside of the building, a "guardian angel" Marine would be assigned inside a nearby position to provide covering fire for those Marines.

Howell later found out that one of his buddies he knew on Okinawa, who was with 3/4, was killed during these operations inside Fallujah.

On about April 29, they got word that 1/5 was to pull out of Fallujah, and Bravo Company was going up to Karmah. These Marines came back to Camp Abu Ghraib for about a day, got showers, put new socks in their assault packs, did a gear check, got a new SAW for one of the Marines (Brennan) who had been hit on the rooftop. Then they went into Karmah and set up in a schoolhouse there. For about two weeks they did platoon and then squad patrols to learn the area. The area was much more friendly than Fallujah had been. There was some mortar and rocket fire at the schoolhouse, but the Marines went back to filing sandbags to fortify the building. They had just gotten finished with Fallujah, and Howell said that Karmah was great in comparison—kids smiled at the Marine patrols, grown-ups wanted to shake hands.

They set up one position out on the street, Howell called it a "meet and greet post." "Then the first day it's there, it gets an RPG launched at it. We all called it

RPG bunker, they called it Post One. It's right out there on Chicago, super-exposed. At night you're the only street light that works in the city. Illuminated. Cars drive by you all the time, there's so many different ways to get attacked from."

The Marines started working with the local police at the police station across from the school. One platoon would go over at night and post on the roof of the station. By this time, the company had relocated to the food warehouse center (where I was conducting this interview). The company put the platoons on an eight-day rotation, with two days at the police station, two days here on guard at the food distribution area, two days patrolling, and two days resting. This helped to create a sense that they were getting through the deployment as weeks passed.

Occasionally mortars would hit this camp. (I had now experienced this first hand!) Corporal Howell said that the insurgents were getting more "ballsy." These insurgents used to fire mortars when it was getting dark; lately they would fire at different times of the day, often in full daylight. He said, "Now they figure out when they shoot mortars at us, we run around and react, try to find a point of origin. By the time we end up runnin' around in the middle of nowhere, they end up skirtin' away. So they're figuring out they can mortar us and shoot rockets, and it's hard as hell for us to find 'em."

He said that this pattern of harassing fire continued for a while. Then, "We're up at the police station, and we had a hole-in-the-wall out here, that we put people at stand-to from every now and then. Pretty much every night, from like 1700 to 2100. They just sit out there and get ready to run out the wall. And all the Marines think it's just pretty pointless. Then one day, these guys run out here, I don't know how they did it. But they ended running out there, they happened to find these guys in a building setting up this huge sniper rifle. Called it like a PKM, or something like that [Note: The Soviet Dragunov sniper rifle may be what he meant.] Saw it the other day when I was doing a statement from that firefight up in Karmah. Thing's gigantic. I guess they walked right in on them. There's three guys and they pretty much caught 'em with their pants down. They didn't raise a weapon at them, they detained all of 'em. They didn't kill anybody, they just grabbed them right away. They didn't grab the guys that dropped the mortars on 'em, they grabbed guys that were about to ambush them. They're very lucky they caught them beforehand, 'cause everybody knows we're here. Coulda been real bad, 'cause everybody knows we're here."

To clarify it for myself, I asked him if the insurgent plan was to have this sniper rifle set up as an ambush for when a reaction force went out after a mortar attack. He said that's what the insurgent plan seemed to be. "Yeah, they were lining them up for an ambush. Just happened to catch them beforehand."

Mostly, Howell's platoon had recently been doing a lot of foot patrols in Shahabi and Karmah. "Went on one earlier today, where the XO'd give you a patrol order, and every now and then he'd leave it real vague. It's nice, because you actually get to do some independent thinking. He said where to go, but most of the time it's, 'I want you to go here, I want you to hit this, this, and this.'"

Howell said that the patrols would leave the Firm Base, hit some parts in Shahabi, which is just on the other side of this Base's wall. Then they'll shoot up into Karmah. There were two bridges which separate the two towns. These bridges were popular for IEDs before Bravo Company got here. Now there were Marine sniper teams and engineers keeping the area clear of IEDs. Weapons Company also went through this area a lot.

Things had become relatively quiet in this area until three days before this interview, June 8.

"My guys get on post. We get off post, end up stagin'. React. We're all bitter, we're all pissed off. We get off post, we gotta go sit in some Humvees out by the main gate in the middle of the day. It's not 'stand-to' time, it's not 1700 yet, we're all wondering, 'What's going on?' Turns out, find out later, we got word there was gonna be an attack on Marines. Somebody tipped us off. We don't know this at the time. So, we're sitting there in the Humvees, pissed off, eating our chow. Everybody's zoning out, we hear some small arms fire from the north. Nothing comes over the net yet. Somebody said, 'Hey, get your gear on, get your deuce gear on, get your flak jacket on.' Throw some deuce gear on, just wait there."

They had a radio there, three Humvees, and Howell only had nine Marines in his squad. He had one fire team of three Marines and one team of four Marines, him and his Navy Corpsman. His platoon sergeant was with them, and led the react in the lead Humvee. Howell rode in the third vehicle, which was also the last vehicle.

"Hear small arms fire, jump in. My guy on the radio says, 'Blackhawk Three receiving direct contact.'"

Blackhawk was Bravo Company's radio call sign. Blackhawk Three was 3rd Platoon. Howell explained, "1/5 has this huge Indian thing going on."

Howell learned that the attack began when an SUV pulled up in front of the police station on Route Chicago in Karmah. Shooters in that vehicle started to "light up" the Marines on post there. The Marines returned fire before the SUV pulled away, and from that point on 3rd Platoon was in a firefight.

"We jump off in our Humvees. Take off, head north. Get there in a matter of minutes." His staff sergeant asked what's going on. "We pull up, we turn, just south of them. I'm in the rear vehicle, I'm in time to see an explosion. Here's an RPG shot at one of the Humvees across the street, and we hear small arms contact, like 'Crack! Crack!' and just goin' off! I look at one of my guys, says, 'Owp, here we go!' Ended up turning off, we went north to Checkpoint 6. We come up this street, and as soon as we get on this street, we hear small arms contact."

The lead Humvee driver turned left into an alley. The second Humvee stopped short, exposing Howell's Humvee to small arms fire in the street.

"We're screaming, 'Go forward! Go Forward!' His guys are getting ready to jump out, get in the fight. 'No, go forward! You're blocking us.' We ended up bumping their Humvee up, 'Go fuckin' forward!' Finally goes forward. We ended up in this street here. We're sittin' in an alley, got a house here, got a house here [he illustrated with hand movements]."

The area was a maze of alleys, streets, and buildings. The ten Marines in this alley (including the platoon sergeant) could not tell where the small arms fire was coming from. "It turned out, we ended up positioning ourselves perfectly. We come over and we were just west of the enemy. So we're west, the police station's east, and right smack dab in the middle is some of the bad guys."

"This bad guy impressed me. He was there like a good ten minutes shooting at this police station. We don't know he's there at this time, we just fire all over the place. We don't know what direction it's coming from. But as he gets ready to jet north, 'cause we ended up pushing everybody north, and then west. And as he gets ready to run north, he runs and exposes himself in this alley, and I pushed two of my guys forward. Pop these corners. And PFC Oswald, the guy that in Fallujah, he had that bullet go through his blouse, ends up raising his weapon, fires maybe like three or four rounds. One takes the guy out right in his head. He's [enemy shooter] running with an AK. Just drops him. 'Whadya got? Whadya got?' Says, 'I got that son-of-a-bitch!' I go over, sure enough, you just see feet, layin' down dead."

Howell told Oswald, "All right, good job, good job."

The Marines then popped corners, and held security. Howell had one of his teams go in and clear a house because he wanted to get a better view of the area. That house and two others were not good positions as the rooftops were too exposed. In one of the houses they detained an unarmed military-age Iraqi man. They zip-cuffed the man, told him to sit and look at the wall.

"Crazy Horse" (Weapons Company) had a small detachment in a vehicle in the street outside of this house. Corporal Howell saw an insurgent pop out from a corner, then move back. He told two of his Marines who were in an exposed position to move to cover. Howell then started to exchange volleys with this insurgent. He laughed as he recounted it.

"We're going back and forth, I'm lookin' for him with my ACOG [sight]. 'BOOM-BOOM-BOOM!' Shootin'. After about two volleys, kinda slow down, I started lookin' around, my eyes go kind of assess it. What I took cover behind, I gotta kneel, one of their trash cans which is empty. And it's like," he said, looking down at a thin metal trash can next to the cot I was sitting on. He tapped on the can: Bang, bang, bang, then laughed and continued. "What's that gonna do? What's that gonna do against a 7.62?" I laughed and said, "Make some noise!"

Howell said, "Guess what I got—just to my right? I got a Humvee!"

We both laughed as he continued. "I stand up, I open up the door. Now I at least got some steel, I got steel plate, blocking at least some of my organs. I end up kinda crouching over, and I'm still lookin' down the alley. Sure enough, he [the insurgent] pops out maybe two or three more times. Exchange of volleys back and forth. Fallujah, the whole deal with Fallujah was: 'Behind that school building they're launching mortars. Five hundred meters you got a guy running. Oh hey, one hundred meters, they're in a school, they're shootin' in that window.' Stuff like that."

In Karmah, "This was the first time I ever sat there, shot at a guy that shot at me. Watching him pop out. Shootin' back and forth. You know, it wasn't like shoot and run and suppress. Fire and move. It was… definite test. Pretty insane."

Corporal Howell said that the guy then took cover, but five or ten minutes later, a white pickup truck with two men in it came driving south towards the Marines. "And they end up pulling right in that same position that that guy was at. I let my lieutenant know what's goin on, he's like, 'Hey, engage!'"

One of his SAW gunners started shooting. "I don't even know if the kid was looking through his sights. Knucklehead. Anyway, he's shooting. I'm shootin'. Gun smoke settles, whatever, I'm looking through. Truck stopped. It no longer had the Iraqi males. Passenger door's open. It's open. And nobody's shooting at us. It's kinda quiet again."

Howell was trying to get a sitrep in over the radio, he had a combat photographer's lens in his face and his lieutenant had linked up with him along with the rest of the platoon.

Marines from 3rd Squad drove over to the shot-up pickup truck on their Humvee with a mounted 240 Golf machine gun. "They grabbed one of the guys [in the truck]. I don't know how this guy was alive. You had secondary fragmentation on the windshield, what appeared to be bullet wounds. The guy was just, the guy was a mess. Grabbed him, detaining him. As they're doing that, I send a team to go get that guy's AK that my PFC dropped [the weapon of the dead Iraqi]."

Then his lieutenant told him that there was a Humvee from Cherokee that was another block into the city. Howell could see that the Humvee was not where the lieutenant said it was, but he took his squad to confirm that the vehicle wasn't there. On the way, he saw a homemade rocket launcher. It was constructed of pipes that were crudely welded together. There was a guy there with a pickup truck, and the Marines engaged him. They killed the fighter, and grabbed his rocket system. When they brought it back to the Firm Base one Marine wiped the inside of the tube and there was fresh black residue that showed that a rocket had been recently fired through it. Howell noted, "It was a good kill."

The platoon then made plans to push west into Karmah. Howell's squad was the furthest south. His squad busted into a house that had six Iraqi men inside of it, but there were no weapons. HET guys came in to question the men. Shots cracked outside, and Howell felt that his Marines needed to be in the fight, so he left the six Iraqi men in the building with the HET team.

The fighting continued outside. "I'm super proud of my boys." They pushed north and west for another 15 minutes. Finally they turned a corner and saw 2nd Platoon, and they joined up with them. They moved to the western part of Karmah, which was more rural. A lot of Iraqi civilians were hurt during the fighting, and the Corpsmen worked on many of them.

When the fighting died down, they moved back towards the town. The Iraqis picked up the dead bodies to prepare them for burial the next day. Howell and his squad moved back to the area where the pickup truck had been shot up. They only found two dead Iraqi bodies. The Iraqi that had been shot on the pickup truck was found with a rifle magazine that was shot through by an M16 round. As they drove back to the police station with two dead bodies, many townspeople stared at them.

Howell said that the Marines later found a video camera across the street from the police station that recorded the attack. The shooting all around the city that day seemed somewhat organized.

In Shahabi there was also an orange and white taxi that was a car bomb. A small force from Crazy Horse was going around it when the car bomb was set off. Two Marines who were wounded then were currently recovering.

During the whole day of fighting on June 8, there were no friendly KIAs. Marines continued foot patrols. Howell himself had just been on a patrol this morning, and had given candy to local kids.

Corporal Howell was extremely proud of his Marines. When he joined the platoon coming from Security Forces, he bumped out another Marine who had been the squad leader. He had OIF1 veterans, new Marines, and they became tight in Fallujah. June 8 showed how much they had come together, working in a cool, calm, collected way. He was now very confident in these Marines.

June 12, 2004

After sleeping in the warehouse and getting morning chow I interviewed Bravo Company's commanding officer, Captain Jason Smith, and several other of his Marines. I was supposed to be done at 1200 to get to another interview back at Camp Fallujah, but most of the interviews lasted longer than scheduled, and I wasn't finished until about 1315.

* * *

Captain Jason Eugene Smith

Company Commander, Bravo Company, 1/5

In early April at the start of Operation Vigilant Resolve, *Bravo Company was one of the first units to enter Fallujah. Within a week, a platoon commander (Lieutenant Joshua Palmer) was killed entering a building, and another officer (Lieutenant Chris Ayres) seriously wounded by an RPG round that penetrated an AAV. A mistake made by the driver of a resupply Humvee soon resulted in a Marine squad surrounded by insurgents deep inside the city. Smith went with the battalion QRF that rescued these Marines. At his insistence, a Marine tank there hooked up a burnt-out Amtrac with a dead Marine inside, and dragged the vehicle outside of the city for recovery.*

Captain Smith's Bravo Company originally went to Okinawa with the battalion to be part of the 31st MEU. While on Okinawa they conducted SASO training similar to what the division was doing back in Camp Pendleton. They did a lot of mounted and dismounted patrolling, learned the authorized use of deadly force, how to react to IEDs and snipers. In other words, all the things that they thought they'd be doing once they got to Iraq. They were in Okinawa from December until early March 2004. They then traveled to Kuwait and spent a couple of weeks there.

When the battalion left for Iraq, Bravo Company stayed behind in Kuwait to receive gear that had been pulled from caves in Norway. Captain Smith said, "We brought up, I don't know, a hundred Humvees from the port in Kuwait up to the camps up here. So we ended up crossing into Iraq within two hours of the first year anniversary of our crossing into Iraq the first time. So it was pretty interesting. Midnight, zero one [0100] on the 20th [of March], so here we go again!"

Smith said that the Marines who were with the company last year got a big kick out of this coincidence. He added, "They were all makin' plans for next year."

Smith said that they covered the same route into Iraq that they had the year before. The countryside seemed greener to him this year, he didn't know if there had been rain, or irrigation of the areas.

Bravo Company went to FOB Mercury, then did a turnover with a battalion from the Army's 82nd Airborne, the 1st of the 504th. The Army gave the Marines what Smith called a cursory turnover.

"Really consisted of me running around with the Army captain, the Army company commander, for one day. He showed me all the places in Karmah, the cement factory, and here in Shahabi, ICDC compound, all the places that he'd been dealing with in his time here, and that we were gonna take over. They approached it a little bit differently than we were going to because they were understaffed. I think they were only runnin' about a five, six-hundred-man battalion, whereas we had about a thousand."

The Army had an enormous zone to deal with, about three times larger than the area that the Marines were now covering. As a result, the Marines could do a lot more than the Army had been able to do here. Captain Smith said that each platoon in his company had done only about one patrol each over a five-day period before the American contractors were killed in Fallujah. The focus then changed, and they went to Fallujah for April. That meant that the area around Karmah was forgotten about until the company returned in May, and a lot of time was lost there.

As to Fallujah, Smith said, "Initially, I didn't think we were gonna be involved at all. It was four American contractors killed, and bodies mutilated, but I didn't see any of the pictures. It was almost like living in a cave here, because you hear things goin' on in the outside world, but you really don't have any perspective on it." Also, Fallujah was in 2/1's zone, not 1/5's. At staff meetings, Fallujah was only mentioned in passing for the first couple of days.

Then at a battalion staff meeting on April 2, he learned about Operation *Vigilant Resolve*. The city of Fallujah was to be cordoned off, and an effort would be made to rid it of the insurgent influence. At the time, 2/1 and 1/5 were the two battalions facing this task with a city that had over 280,000 residents. Initially Smith said that 1/5 was to cordon off the southern part of the city and 2/1 the northern part. Bravo Company was given the southeast part of Fallujah, its industrial zone, and Alpha Company was to Bravo's west. Charlie Company was tasked with providing security for Abu Ghraib prison, and as such was basically lost as a maneuver element to the battalion. Squads from Charlie Company were tasked out at various checkpoints around Fallujah.

Captain Smith also explained that the thinking of the battalion was to deploy its Weapons Company assets such as 81mm mortars and TOW missiles. Before arriving in Iraq, planners had decided to reorganize these assets. Since 81s Platoon has a lot of vehicles and dismounted Marines, it was decided to turn it into a QRF. The TOW missile platoon was split in half into two smaller assault platoons. These assault platoons from Weapons Company were to be used as a screening force.

Plans for Fallujah changed several times. Finally the plan was for 2/1 and Delta Force (Task Force 626) to come from the north and do a hard hit on a photo shop along Highway 10, on the early morning of April 6. This shop had reproduced pictures of the contractors killed in Fallujah. But on April 5, word came that this would not happen. Bravo Company was told to go into the southeast of the city and hold the industrial zone. Smith said "One thing I remember, it was bitterly, bitterly, cold."

Bravo Company established positions to the southeast of Fallujah.

"When the sun came up on the 5th, we had established screening positions to the southeast. You could see into Fallujah, I mean, we were 500 meters to a click [1,000 meters] away from them. And people would come outta their houses and look around, then they'd go back in."

It appeared to Smith that people were trying to find a way out of the city. "By the end of the 5th, we had General Conway show up, had General Mattis show up, and all these generals were showing up to our pos [position]." The battalion CP was about 200 yards behind Bravo's position. Smith went back to talk with Lieutenant Colonel Byrne, his battalion commander. He learned that the plan had changed again, and that Bravo Company would be the first ones into the city.

Captain Smith went back to brief his platoon commanders on the change. Since they had been there all day, and had been under observation, the initial plan of a mounted assault to a huge warehouse was changed.

"Because we'd been sittin' there all day, we tried to deceive the people that were watchin' us a little bit. All the vehicles were lined up, and now, when the sun went down, we were gonna move away from the vehicles on foot. Keep the vehicles running. I left a small group of Marines back there, that were gonna turn vehicles on, make a lot of noise, so people would think they're there. Soon as the sun went down, I sent Lieutenant Ayres forward with his platoon, as kind of a recon element."

Ayres was supposed to figure out a route to the objective (the warehouse). At about 2300 the rest of the company was able to link up with Lieutenant Ayres and his platoon fairly easily.

They made a breach into the wall of the compound and then went in, clearing all of the buildings without any fight. They did detain seven guys there, including two Sudanese workers. Smith later found out that all of these individuals actually did work for the soda company there. These individuals unlocked areas of the warehouse for the Marines. Bravo Company was now in Fallujah, and Alpha Company came in behind them, and started clearing the southeast corner of the industrial zone. Red Cloud (the assault platoon created from the 81mm mortar platoon) tied this area in with the highway cloverleaf just east of the city. Captain Smith said that there was some confusion when they entered the city, one of his platoon commanders was in the wrong city block area. The RCT1 commanding officer, Colonel Toolan, showed up with some of his command element and got shot at. Alpha Company was to the south of Bravo, and both companies continued to push west into Fallujah.

Smith said, "It was very eerie, the whole place. A lot of low-lying buildings, lotta just cement plants and auto shops. Looked like a big junkyard, more than anything else."

They passed Phase Line Blue, moving further forward than battalion had anticipated. By now it was about 0530, and the sun was almost up. Captain Smith was not sure what kind of reception that the company would get as residents woke up and realized the Marines were inside the city, so he told his leaders to move their Marines up onto the tops of roofs.

"The battalion had decided that we were gonna go in with bayonets fixed, kinda show people that we meant business. So my thought was that well, if they see us as the sun comes up and we're standing on rooftops, with our bayonets fixed, they'll really know we meant business."

Also, his Marines could see better what was going on in the city. The company had all of its Marines on tops of buildings along Phase Line Orange, tied into Phase Line Michigan (Highway 10). His company had not slept at all for the previous two nights, and he was looking forward to giving them a little bit of rest.

The rooftops were covered with car mufflers, tail pipes, tires, and other junk that had to be moved before anyone could take up any type of position. When the sun finally came up, Smith could see that they were about 500 meters away from the residential area of the city. A vehicle or two drove by, and he decided that he couldn't have people just driving by, checking on the location of his positions. He ordered his Marines to set up vehicle checkpoints, and at the same time sent a couple of Marines to find out exactly where Alpha Company was set in.

As he was coming back from doing this, it was now about 1100, and he heard shooting coming from the north. Smith ran out into the street to where Corporal Dawson was setting up a VCP on Phase Line Orange. Dawson's team started firing at the shooters and Captain Smith started pushing Marines across the boulevard. "As soon as we cross the highway, we started taking fire from the west. So we reoriented and started pushing toward the west."

Elements from every one of his platoons were involved. They pushed into the residential area. There was a big blue mosque along Highway 10. "And we were getting fired at from that mosque." He had the area cordoned off, sent in Corporal Dawson with his team, and they detained some individuals inside the mosque, but didn't find any weapons. Captain Smith said that this was to be a continuing problem in Fallujah, where they would take fire from inside a mosque, then go into the mosque and not find any weapons there.

"We also cleared a large apartment building." It was one of the tallest buildings in the area. Smith talked to the manager of the building and explained what the Marines were doing. Then, "The mayor of Fallujah drives by at the same time. So, he stops, I go talk to the mayor of Fallujah. Explain to him, this is what's going on, he says, 'Yes, yes,' drives off. Trying to get the Iraqi police involved, they run away every time we come near 'em."

While Smith was in the middle of the road trying to figure out what was happening, some people rolled up the road in a vehicle and tried to take an RPG shot at them.

"RPG impacts in a little kiosk in the middle of Highway 10, about 30 feet away from us. And all of a sudden I hear this burst of gunfire. One of the civilians that was running across the street was shot and killed." This Iraqi died in front of the apartment building. The streets were now clear of people. Smith saw some Iraqi police down the street, and motioned to them to come over to him. They finally did, and Smith explained to them how the dead man had been killed.

Then the company started pulling back. It took longer than Smith had expected, partly because one of his platoons, pursuing some armed individuals who had gone into a building, had gone further than he had expected. Once all of the company was back at its original positions, Captain Smith started to debrief his leaders. "It was our first engagement as a company since last year, and I was the only person who had the same job through both deployments, so, it is a completely different company."

He reviewed reporting procedures and initial decisions, and basic stuff that he felt they needed to do better. Then, not 30 minutes after they had pulled back, they began to take small arms fire again from across Route Michigan. "So we deployed all the way across Michigan again, and pushed forward, and as soon as we do, we started getting' fire from the west again." The fire was coming from a school. The Marines killed a guy with RPGs there, and took his vehicle. He estimated that this firefight lasted about an hour.

Then about 30 minutes later, shooting started up again. All told on April 6, Bravo Company 1/5 had three engagements, each lasting about an hour apiece. Smith said that the insurgents didn't seem to want to fight that night. They did not have night vision devices, and may have been tired from fighting all day. Captain Smith had worked in Bahrain for a year as part of Security Forces, and in his experience there, the locals didn't want to operate at night. He was comfortable that there would not be any action the night of April 6, but maintained security for his positions. "But when the sun came up, I wanted to be in a different position than when they last saw us."

So he pushed one of his platoons a couple of blocks to the west. He did this because any time before they had pushed north, they would take fire from the west. He estimated that this preemptive move west would provide better security for his Marines should they need to move north into Fallujah again.

"We're set up in that building, and we started seeing people set up road blocks down in front of the mosque. They're pulling out tires, they're pulling out cinderblocks. A bunch of young guys, no weapons visible yet, but they're obviously doing something."

Captain Smith did not want to wait until this activity was a finished position, but he didn't have vehicles to move to them quickly, as it was about 700 meters away. He contacted Red Cloud on the radio, and the men cleared the streets when Red Cloud got there. As Red Cloud started to dismantle the road blocks, they began to be shot at. This was the start of another engagement. Tanks rolled up, Bravo Company moved up and Alpha Company got involved. Finally Bravo linked up with Red Cloud and tanks along Phase Line Violet. By day's end, this whole force was facing west on Phase Line Violet. They received fire from the north and the west for the next six days there. Smith said that now, "The people that were inside of the city was us, everybody else was on the outskirts."

"It was interesting to me to see how the Marines progressed throughout the whole week [6 through 14 April 2004]. In training it's impossible to replicate the conditions we were in."

His Marines had fired a lot of small arms rounds in training in Okinawa. His mortar men now started to calculate how to do counter-mortar fire at enemy mortar men, planning to shoot at where the enemy would move to, not where they were shooting from. He moved his Marines off the rooftops and had them improve positions closer to the ground. His Marines were learning to think more about the enemy. The harassment fire from the enemy was continuous the whole time they were in Fallujah, and Smith felt that the only reason his Marines didn't have more casualties was that the enemy couldn't shoot accurately.

On April 8 they were able to identify a sniper's location right across Phase Line Violet. He sent one platoon across to take out this sniper. They went out on two different axes (directions) and trapped him. Lieutenant Ayres caught the guy in the street in what Smith described as a Mexican standoff. "They're standing in the street, guy shoots at him, he shoots at the guy, and the guy runs back into the building."

The Marines cordoned off the building and Lieutenant Ayres called for reinforcements. Captain Smith was back at the battalion CP while this was going on. "The problem is, we had, the sniper had pretty good fields of fire from where he was… and ended up killin' Staff Sergeant Harrell, and wounding Lance Corporal Amati, as they're pushin' up."

"Lieutenant Joshua Palmer was the platoon commander who responded as the Reaction Force. Lieutenant Ayres had the sniper cordoned, and Lieutenant Palmer wanted to link up with him."

Trailed by his Marines, Palmer got to the corner of the building, and made entry into the building. There was no hesitation by Palmer, he was out to get the sniper.

"Lieutenant Palmer ran in there and started clearin' rooms. They had the sniper cornered in the room, and as Lieutenant Palmer tried to throw a grenade the sniper shot him in the chest and neck and killed him. And then the Marines just sprayed the room down, killed that guy."

Captain Smith returned from the CP and ran to the house where the Marines had continued the clearing and had detained three men. There were still women and children inside the house. The Marines continued to clear buildings in the block. They found RPGs and machine guns.

Palmer and Harrell were the first in the company to die. Staff Sergeant Harrell was still alive when they evacuated him, and Smith didn't know that he had died until five or six hours later. "It was… it was a little bit different… it was much more difficult for the Marines than I thought, they thought, and I thought it would be."

He paused. "I don't know if I could put my finger on it, other than, it wasn't like when… somebody passes away. It was just a very strange feeling. Lieutenant Palmer was there, and then he's not there." Smith didn't know if this reality had sunk in for him yet.

"I wrote a letter to the families of Staff Sergeant Harrell and Lieutenant Palmer. Staff Sergeant Harrell had a six-year-old son. It sunk in a little bit then, but we wanted to give the family something when we got back." They wanted to give the family some of the recollections of the Marines about these two fallen comrades. Marines wrote down their memories of them to give to the families.

Sniper fire continued for the next few days, and on the 11th, the same thing happened. Private First Class George D. Torres was killed during another push across

Route Violet. They started to call this general area "Shit Head Alley." All of Bravo's major firefights happened in this area of Fallujah. The enemy fighters were using the alleyways to move back and forth. Smith wanted to push across Violet and set up outposts where the Marines could observe the enemy and deny them some of their ability to move around. So, before the sun came up, they would push forward one block, then back clear the area they had advanced into.

By April 13, 2nd and 3rd Platoons had each pushed out a couple of blocks, creating a larger security area. A Humvee drove up to try to resupply 2nd Platoon. Smith described what happened as an example of what not to do: Two headquarters Marines had driven up in a single Humvee and tried to resupply the platoon, but got shot up on their way in. They returned to the company CP.

Captain Smith had just gotten four Amtracs attached to his company, and he decided to use two of these lightly-armored vehicles to do the resupply.

"So they try to conduct the resupply with these Amtracs, and, at the same time, Lieutenant Ayres knows where all the fire's coming from, it's coming from Shit Head Alley. So he comes up with an impromptu plan to ambush these guys [enemy shooters]. We're gonna drive one trac to the south of Shit Head Alley, in an ambush position. And he's gonna drive one trac to the north of Shit Head Alley, and push down Shit Head Alley and push these guys down to the south. The problem was, that as soon as his trac's south of Shit Head Alley, pulls into position, starts takin' rounds, I mean RPG rounds. And they're pretty accurate. So he pushes forward, to the west. He takes more and more fire. Immediately loses comm with the other vehicle."

While Ayres' vehicle was pushing on, the other trac circled around the block three times, got shot at, was partially disabled, and drove back to the CP. Ayres' trac pushed all the way to Phase Line Yellow, very deep into Fallujah. It was late afternoon and they saw about 100 *Fedayeen* in black pajamas, carrying AKs and RPGs. These *Fedayeen* fired many RPG shots, and several hit the trac and started a fire. Lieutenant Ayres was wounded and the crew chief of the trac was killed. The Amtrac drove away to the south, and then stopped. This Amtrac was now far away from where they had last been seen, and from where they were supposed to be, in Shit Head Alley.

Captain Smith was at the battalion CP as this unfolded. Red Cloud prepared to move out as the Reaction Force. Red Cloud had lost one of its Marines that morning. Lieutenant Glover got his guys up and moving quickly. Smith caught a ride back with Red Cloud.

"As we pulled out of the battalion CP you could see the plume of black smoke, you could see exactly where it is. As soon as I saw it, I said, This is not good. There's no way they should be where that smoke is comin' from. I go back to my company CP and talk with my XO." Smith rejoined the QRF that was waiting for tanks to join them.

"The next three hours it is just radio confusion. Because, people are just trying to help, but they're making it more difficult. I had two foot-mounted platoons, the two platoons that had been in our outpost positions."

They had gone to where they thought that the trac was, but were actually about a click and a half from the now-burning trac. These platoons were communicating with the QRF, and telling them where they were, but it seemed that they were reporting on the location of the burning trac. However, they did not know where the trac was. Smith told his two platoons to stay off the radio net for the time being.

Captain Smith estimated that there were about ten vehicles in the QRF, including Humvees and tanks. "We start goin' through these streets with tanks, Humvees, and the medevac vehicles, probably ten vehicles, part of this convoy. Of course, the vehicles bein' a big target as they were, we started takin' fire almost immediately."

They continued to look for the burning Amtrac, taking small arms fire en route. Captain Smith was receiving contradictory reports on the radio about the location of the burning trac. He finally decided to ignore them and go towards where he could see the plume of smoke from the vehicle.

Meanwhile, Staff Sergeant Sagredo who had ridden in the damaged trac was now in a building near the burning Amtrac, and didn't have radio communication. He also didn't have a map or GPS, as Lieutenant Ayres had had these, and they had been left inside the burning Amtrac. Ayres was now unconscious, having been hit in the leg by an RPG, and had lost a lot of blood.

"Every corridor we go down, we end up gettin' shot at. I'm just getting more and more frustrated the whole time. Jumping off the vehicles, trying to run up to the front, sayin', 'Let's go! Let's go! Quit stoppin'! Let's go!' You picture yourself in some kind of movie, like, 'Follow me! Charge!' and, we're at this corner, and, we're stopped, we try to take a turn to the south. We turn in south and everyone's firing at us, so we're backed up. So I'm just, all right, we'll just go one more block. So I'm trying to get people going. I jump out, run across the street. 'Let's go! Come on!' It was like, nope. All kind of debris and stuff in the road, and they can't get around the stuff. So there I am with my ass out in the breeze, getting shot at. They're trying to follow, but they can't."

Then someone broke through to the south. The tanks rolled and the QRF was going to cordon off the area around the trac.

"As we're pushing through, there's courtyards that are open and we end up taking some RPGs and RPKs, was just laying in the courtyards. We pushed through, people just picked up and left. And they were obviously firing at us, you'd see the spent brass, you could see the RPGs. We were collectin' up stuff as we moved. But we're still trying to get to where we can as soon as possible. We push up, try to cordon off the trac, and I don't know where 2nd Platoon is, because they can't get comm with us. 2nd Platoon bein' the platoon that's inside the trac. So I see a gate that's open. I see a body that's laying on the driveway. I'm like, 'Well, we gotta make entry someway, might as well make entry someplace that's open.' So we run across the street, bust through a fence. We get in there. Soon as I turn around, get into the courtyard, I got Marines yelling at me, 'Don't shoot! Don't shoot!' Just happened to be the one [building] 2nd Platoon was in. You know, we just kinda lucked out!"

As Smith began to assess the situation he saw that the good thing about the Amtrac burning was that it showed him where they were. The bad thing was that it showed the bad guys where they were, too. He said that it became a huge magnet for everybody.

"Enemy was firing at us. We were trying to get there. In the house that 2nd Platoon was in, people were throwing grenades over the walls. People were shootin' RPGs at them. They had gotten at least one assault. That's what the guy in the middle of the driveway was, he had assaulted from across the street, suicide, banzai charge."

Inside, Captain Smith got a quick verbal sitrep from Staff Sergeant Sagredo. Sagredo told him that Lieutenant Ayres was critically wounded, and they moved him from the back to the front of the house. By then the medevac Humvee had arrived, they loaded Ayres onto it and it took off with the wounded lieutenant.

"I didn't think he was gonna make it. I really did not think he was gonna make it. Barely coherent. We just got a sitrep from his wife, through battalion, he was doin' much better. That's good. He just had a daughter, too, so he was there [back in the States] for that."

Smith continued, "Then we started figuring out how're we gonna get this trac outta here. I did not want to leave the trac. I did not want to see on the news, ah, you know, the Iraqis jumping on top of the thing, 'Down! Down USA!' All that crap. Not to mention, the crew chief's body was still inside. They tried to get him out, but the fire just got out of control and they still had a lot of ammunition there, and there's still a lot of secondary explosions."

As Smith tried to get a trac or tank to hook up to the damaged trac, he said that every Tracker or Tanker had a different opinion of what could be done. (Normally a damaged trac is towed by a special Amtrac wrecker vehicle.)

Smith said, "Finally I just told the tanks, 'Hey, we got chains, link up to it, let's go.' 'Well, the chains won't work.' 'We got the chains, we got the tank, try it.'" Otherwise, the towing assets would not get there until the following day.

Once the burned out trac was linked up to a tank, it got towed out all the way to the cloverleaf outside of Fallujah. It worked. Smith said, "Score one for the chains!"

Captain Smith felt that his company was now in a good position deep in the city, but battalion gave him word to pull back to Phase Line Violet. They spent the next two weeks there. The ceasefire ended the push into the city, but Bravo Company could still engage enemy when fired upon. Most shooting ended on April 15. He said that the enemy backed off from them in Bravo's zone. "I think a lot of them went after 2/1 then, 'cause we didn't catch any fire."

On April 29 they got word to pull out of Fallujah. They heard lots of talk about the coalition trying to give the Fallujah city council some credibility, to give the Fallujah Brigade a chance to keep the peace. 1/5 left their positions, and four or five hours later, the Fallujah Brigade took over.

Bravo Company had about 12 hours in the rear, then went to Karmah, and there took over from Weapons Company, 1st LAR. Bravo was focused on Karmah and Shahabi for all of May and June 2004. "Fallujah might just as well have been the Korean War for as long ago as it seems right now."

Smith said that in their current area, they were doing what they came here to do: To act as the military portion of the coalition rebuilding effort, provide security and support, helping to get the Iraqi police and the ICDC stood up. He said that it has taken him a long time to try to figure out the relationship between the ICDC and the Iraqi police. He said it seemed that the ICDC were like the sheriff's office for a county, and the police the local police force in the city proper.

The ICDC headquarters was in the small village of Shahabi, just south of the Karmah River, according to Captain Smith. When the Army was here, they would not travel up to the bridges north of Shahabi because of the IED threat. "There's been a lot of IEDs there, but we really own this place now."

Back in March, when the company first got to Iraq, Captain Smith had gone to a meeting with the town's city council at the police station. The station had suffered several attacks before this, so Smith went into the school building, the tallest structure in the town, to get a better overview of the town. On his return in May, he knew that this would be a good building for his company of Marines to occupy. He did hesitate, however, feeling that the Marines were coming into the town to provide security and a return to normal life for the people, yet the locals would be losing control of the school building.

Captain Smith occupied the school on April 29, and the rest of Bravo Company moved in on May 1. The Marines immediately started patrols in Karmah. He tried to start work with the Iraqi police there. In the town itself, things were relatively peaceful, with people going about their normal lives, something that Smith originally expected when he came back to Iraq.

A problem was that when Fallujah happened, many of the fighters from Fallujah came into Karmah, and the local police abandoned the police station along with the weapons there. The coalition has been in Karmah from May 2003 until May 2004, and Smith said that the Iraqi police have not progressed one bit: "We're startin' over. That has been the biggest problem here in Karmah and Shahabi." He added that only just now (June 2004) have they gotten rid of the insurgent element in the local ICDC.

"We ended up arresting seven guys, one of which was the CO, and the first sergeant, and the platoon commanders. It's almost a shame, that we've been here, we being the coalition, have this long and we have achieved so little progress in this area. We're making headway, there's no doubt we're making headway. It's just, we should be much further along than what we are."

Captain Smith said that the biggest enemy contacts they currently had were mortar attacks and rocket attacks. It happened maybe every two or three days initially.

When he was here at the school in Karmah for about four or five days, he said that he was awakened when he heard a rocket fire. "I knew before I was even awake it was a rocket." They would then send out a reaction force to try to locate the shooters. Patrols in May paid off with gathering a more complete picture of the area. No Marines were killed that month. They started getting a lot of human intel. In mid-May Smith felt that this was causing pressure on the insurgents. Attacks on the Marines increased, and several local sheiks visited Smith, asking him to leave the school. Finally Colonel Toolan came and told them to leave the school. They moved from the school, and put a platoon of Marines in the police station in Karmah, while the rest of the company went down into Shahabi, its current location.

Captain Smith said that the local Iraqi police "just quit" around mid-May, and the guy running it now was "worthless." Smith would be addressing this situation at a battalion staff meeting he was going to today.

The camp here was a large area consisting of warehouses with the town of Shahabi just on the other side of a cinderblock wall. The U.S. Army occupied it during the initial occupation of the country in 2003, as it is a key location for the distribution of food in the area. A local man Smith called Hamid was in charge of the camp and worked with the Army platoon. When Smith came back down to the area, he said that Hamid was not happy that the Marines were going to occupy the camp. Over the past month Hamid and Smith developed a working relationship.

With the Marines in the area, they have shed some light on the shortcomings of the ICDC here. There was money being skimmed and suspects arrested who were let go by the ICDC. The ICDC's company headquarters was at Fallujah, and appointed a Major Fawaz as the CO of the local contingent, removing a local commander. Then all the local problems started. *Mujahideen* were freely infiltrating the area during that time. The recent arrests ended this, and the former local ICDC commander was restored to his post.

Smith said that some Marines with Charlie Company have been working with and training with ICDC units in their area, and are much further along with this than his own Marines. A platoon from Bravo Company was working with local ICDC elements, the goal being what Charlie Company had going on, a sort of a CAP (Civil Affairs Platoon). And Bravo Company should be doing its own turnover with the incoming Marine battalion, 3/1, in the next few weeks. Captain Smith felt that his company has made a positive impact on the local people. They were the first large coalition force that has stayed in this area for a long time since the invasion last year.

"We're doing what, maybe, shoulda been happening a year and a half ago, but wasn't, for various reasons."

Captain Smith felt that he had covered all of the ground that he could with me, but I asked him to give me his take on the actions around the police station on June 8, just days ago.

He began, "In the last month we've had a lot of small engagements. We've had mortar rounds land on us, we've captured guys on the way out. But there really has not been anything coordinated, from the enemy."

He said that they don't seem to really want to pick a fight with the Marines, so there has been a lot of harassing fire instead. On June 7, Bravo Company arrested seven guys from the ICDC. Smith got word from Hamid (the camp's Iraqi manager) that his workers had said that there was going to be an attack. Smith was not too concerned about this, as usually an "attack" would consist of a few mortar rounds on the camp.

Then on June 8, a white pickup truck rolled up to the police station and did a drive-by shooting on the station. RPGs followed right behind that. At the same time, guys in masks pulled up in the street in Shahabi and told the locals to get off the streets.

"They obviously had cased us out, and knew that we were gonna respond from here up to the police station. So when we ended up responding from here to the police station—BOOM! Vehicles detonated. I thought a mortar round had hit our building; it was that loud and that close. And then Little Wolf, one of the assault platoons that was the battalion QRF, took some casualties."

One of Bravo Company's platoons was already responding to the attack on the station. He sent another platoon up there, and then it became a matter of clearing the town from the western part where the station was.

"We killed a couple of guys, definitely insurgents, they were wearing deuce gear, magazine pouches, things that are not necessary for home protection. We ended up capturing a mortar system in the back of a truck, which is a big deal, we haven't done that yet. Mortars have been a huge problem for us. For the one that we captured, there's so many more out there."

They also captured some RPGs, RPKs, and AKs. The ICDC with Charlie Company shot a lot.

Smith said that the local people did not like being caught in the middle of the fight. Hamid told him that a mosque over in Fallujah was having funerals for four or five guys, and to Smith this confirmed his belief that the fighters were not native to Karmah or Shahabi. Smith also said that many of the people in Shahabi were mad at the *mujahideen* after the IED exploded, as it damaged windows and shops in their town. Smith remarked that these mujahideen claim to be fighting for Iraq, yet they cause schools to close, and damage property without compensation to the Iraqis. He remarked, "That's the Cliff's Notes version of it."

He paused for a moment when I asked him for some final thoughts. He responded, "Last year I got asked the same question. I was glad I was a part of it last year." He felt that the people of Iraq had been given a great opportunity. "It's merely a year later, the environment is much different, but I'm still glad I was a part of it. For a long time I've talked about, there aren't a lot of large, Western-style militaries to fight. The things we're going to be involved in, if we want to make a difference, are things like this. Fighting low-intensity counter-insurgencies. We took much, much more fire than we did last year. But, on a strategic level it's low-intensity." He said that last year it looked like big war, but this year is a continuation of last year. "We're making headway, but it's slow."

Captain Smith said that he and his lieutenants talked a lot and read a lot to get ready for this. They read the *Small Wars Manual*, and other military articles. He told his lieutenants that when they leave Iraq, it will feel that they have accomplished nothing, but to realize that we were making progress a little bit at a time. He said that last year, Saddam was there, and then he was not. This year, the insurgents were still there. He felt that we would be here until the people don't want to put up with the insurgents any longer.

* * *

Lance Corporal Anthony Francis Ewers

Radio Operator, 2nd Platoon, Bravo Company, 1/5

On April 13 2004, Ewers was the platoon radioman sitting next to his platoon commander inside of an AAV that was hit by RPG fire. The platoon commander, Lieutenant Chris Ayres, was seriously injured by the RPG round, and Ewers then served as radio operator for Staff Sergeant Sagredo, who assumed command of the squad of Marines who left the burning AAV and set up a defensive position in a nearby building. Without maps or GPS, he said that it was difficult for the battalion QRF to find them for a time as the heavily damaged AAV continued to burn and "cook off" ammunition inside of the vehicle. After rescue, the squad returned to the battalion CP. When Marine units left Fallujah, Ewers participated in patrols and firefights around the village of Shahabi.

This young Marine went to MCRD (Marine Corps Recruit Depot) San Diego for his recruit training in April 2001. After training at SOI in Camp Pendleton, he reported to 1/5 in mid-October 2001. The battalion was in a CAX at 29 Palms. 1/5 was supposed to be going out to Okinawa as part of the 31st MEU deployment, but that plan changed in early 2002.

Ewers went to Iraq the first time last year as a SAW gunner with 1/5. By May of 2003, he was changed to platoon radio operator (RO). He received some on-the-job training and some classes from the battalion comm shop.

He said that when the battalion returned from Iraq in 2003, the initial plan was to prepare for a workup for a MEU deployment. Once again, however, he found out on return from leave that they would not be a part of the 31st MEU, but would instead return to Iraq for the second time. "We still stayed on schedule for our deployment to Okinawa, which was, I believe, December 15th. And from there, we started training more intensely for Iraq, rather than the MEU." They went through a battalion-led SASO course, then left for Iraq in March. They flew into Kuwait first.

Bravo Company stayed behind in Kuwait and the rest of the battalion went into Iraq. Bravo provided security for a convoy of tanks and Amtracs that moved a week after the battalion's move. This convoy went to Camp Fallujah. After one night, Bravo Company went to FOB Mercury. "We were there two weeks, where we pulled camp guard, which most people in the company were upset with, because, we were considered, you know, having to stay back at the camp, the low job. Then the whole fighting in Fallujah broke out."

Lance Corporal Ewers couldn't remember the exact date that they moved to Fallujah. They left during the night, and were supposed to take down the soda factory at the southeastern edge of the town. At first they went to a field outside the town. The move to the town came a day later. Ewers said that Bravo's movement was quiet that night.

He said, "We took two shots at the compound wall." Bravo Company cleared the building and arrested a few Iraqi guards inside it. After clearing the building, they began to clear and search houses in the southeastern section of Fallujah. It was mostly an industrial area. They spent that night on rooftops, facing west. He said that a few RPGs were fired in their general direction, but there was no damage or injuries. The next morning things were relatively quiet and cars were driving near to their positions. The Marines set up some VCPs to check cars for weapons. Around noontime, they began to take fire from a mosque. They searched the mosque but didn't find any weapons.

Marine snipers saw some gunmen get out of a truck to the north. They fired and hit one of these men in the stomach. The truck drove away, and left the man there bleeding in the street. 2nd Platoon was told to go down the road and get the guy. "And as we were going down there, he opened fire on us."

Ewers continued, "He was lying behind the wall, and he knew he had no chance, so he was fightin' as hard as he could. We laid down. No one at this point had returned fire yet. And then a taxicab pulled up, two gentlemen got out, and walked directly in our line of fire between this guy that was shooting at us and us. Trying to block the shots. So none of us fired. And then the taxicab backed up and picked up the guy that was shot and sped off. At which point we opened fire on the taxicab. They got away. I don't know if either one of them was hit or not. Then we radioed it up to all the other units, we were looking for a taxicab. And then the two gentlemen left, they went to one of the houses and we lost sight of them.

"Well, we started doin' a search of the area to see if there's any weapons or any other guys around. And, we turn the corner and there were the two guys, and they started runnin' when they saw us. So, myself and another rifleman who was with 3rd Squad ran up and arrested 'em. They didn't put up any resistance, they didn't have any weapons on them, and they realized they were caught. And then later they got identified as two guys that had been shooting at 3rd Platoon earlier in the day." The two became detainees of the Marines.

Ewers said that the next day, not much happened besides an occasional exchange of gunfire with insurgents.

As platoon RO, he was normally with the platoon commander. "But, at the time, I had requested to be with 3rd Squad, because one of the NCOs there, the squad leader, is one of my best friends. Also, the lieutenant had made it clear that he was gonna be with 1st Squad, the assault squad, so. In Okinawa I had trained three different ROs as squad ROs, because I knew there'd be squad patrols when we finally got to SASO activities." Lance Corporal Adams was with the lieutenant, serving as his RO at that time.

That night (he wasn't sure of the dates) the Marines slept in oil-change pits that were in front of the auto body shops. These pits had steps and were about four feet deep, providing nice cover from enemy fire. Some Marines also manned positions on rooftops. A few random mortar shots landed nearby without injuring anyone. "The next day, we saw some Humvees pull up and they had a bunch of reporters in them, and we're like, 'Oh, no, something's gonna happen.' Whenever you see reporters you know something bad's gonna happen!"

The platoon got the word to start pushing west up the alleyways, and to leave their assault packs at the position. "The first block was easy, but we could hear shots coming from Weapons Company push farther west than us, taking heavy fire and returning heavy fire."

The platoon pushed south a block, then west a block, and started to take sniper fire. "So we started firing and maneuvering up the street." Lance Corporal Ewers and Corporal Picard (3rd Squad Leader) got pinned down behind a piece of metal in the street. SAW gunners suppressed the snipers, and Picard moved Marine snipers and designated marksmen into elevated positions to take shots. This calmed down the shooting from the enemy. Just then, an Abrams tank rolled in front of their position and started firing towards the west. There was no radio communication between the tank and the squad.

Ewers said, "Corporal Picard went up there and threw a brick at the turret, which the turret then turned on us, and we're all waving at it, telling it, 'Cease fire.' So then we moved up to the rooftops."

The enemy fired shots at them up there. After that, there was zero tolerance for anyone the Marines saw in the alleyways. If it wasn't women and children, just the men running back and forth, it was fair game at this point. "At this point, most of them did have AKs, and most of the residents had moved out." By this time the Marines were running out of clean socks, food, and water. They were there for the next few days, and it was during this time that Lieutenant Palmer and Staff Sergeant Harrell got hit and killed. Corporal Picard told Ewers about this when he had brought back some chow and bottles of water.

The squad moved into a clothes factory. Ewers described it as a nice place to stay. There were beds, and even American-style toilets. Nightly they received harassing mortar fire and small arms shots, but no one was wounded. Marines would send out squad-sized patrols to try and flush out enemy fighters. In Lance Corporal Ewers' opinion, the enemy had figured out how the Marines operated, and wanted the Marines to come out so that they (the enemy) could shoot at them.

Bravo Company decided to push 2nd Platoon out farther west into the city. First, one fire team was sent about 300 yards out onto an OP (observation post). Then all three squads were to go out. "And one morning we went out about three in the morning, and scouted out three different houses, probably a good two, three blocks up from Phase Line Violet." Each squad occupied a different house. Ewers was with the platoon commander, Lieutenant Ayres, in a house behind the other two houses, a sort of triangle of houses. They occupied these houses for the next few days, and received sporadic small arms fire. The Marines fired mortars at some enemy positions, but Ewers felt that this fire was not effective.

"This is when the whole trac incident went down.

"It started out, I believe it was the 13th [of April]. We needed resupply. So we negotiated a resupply with the CP, that was a good five, six hundred meters back. Myself and Lieutenant Ayres had pushed up where we could see the Humvee coming and call it into us."

The resupply vehicles had left too early, and as the two Marines were moving to signal the vehicles, they saw the vehicles drive past them. They overshot the platoon's positions, and were now in front of buildings holding insurgents. "There was pretty heavy fire, one guy was wounded, and they returned to the CP to take care of the medevac."

"Lieutenant Ayres called them and told them that most of the insurgents were in the one house. So, it was planned they were gonna push two tracs to us. And we were gonna use these simply as heavy fire. That's all it was gonna be. We're gonna load up. 3rd Squad was gonna go in on the trac on the northern side of the block, and 2nd Squad was gonna go in the trac on the southern side, along with Lieutenant Ayres. Corporal Picard was gonna be the trac commander of the northern trac. They were supposed to push up into a firing position, put heavy fire on the house, and we were supposed to be in a cutoff position, so as insurgents started running to the south, southwest, we were gonna run 'em down. So we got all in the tracs, and pushed up."

As Corporal Picard's trac moved west, he did not have comm with Lance Corporal Ewers. Picard had ICOM radios that would not reach that far. Picard could hear what Lieutenant Ayres was saying on the radio, but could not answer back. Ewers was right next to Lieutenant Ayres inside their trac. Ewers explained that his radio does not work unless the antenna is sticking out of the top of the trac. As he started to put up the antenna, the trac started taking fire "from everywhere." He said that the trac's .50 cals and Mark 19s were shooting, and the dismounted infantry inside the trac were shooting on both sides of the trac.

"We took, three, four, probably, RPG shots at the trac, but, I mean, it'd knock you off the side from firing. But everyone'd just get back up again and start shooting. I was told that one went through the turret, and that's what killed the gunner. The gun went silent after that. At this point, I have no clue what happened to 3rd Squad's trac, 'cause we have no comm with them."

"And, so, Lieutenant Ayres kept pushin' west. I don't believe it was in the original plan—to push west. As we kept pushing west, the firing kept getting heavier and heavier. And finally we took an RPG round straight between myself and Lieutenant Ayres. It came in and blasted out, mostly underneath him. I know I didn't catch any shrapnel from it, but then, I had the radio on my back. And it [the radio] was all charred. It hit some kind of oil line, because oil was dripping all over everybody in the back of the trac. The fire started right underneath Lieutenant Ayres, and I looked up and that was the first time I saw his leg. There was blood coming out the bottom side of his right leg. I told the Corpsman if he crawled up underneath Lieutenant Ayres' seat, and started working on his leg, do what he could, and bandage it up. I believe he had pulled out to get it out of his bag when another RPG hit the exact same spot. This time, Doc Viegas took shrapnel to his face, and his face got bloody. And then the fire got a lot worse. So he [Viegas] grabbed a fire extinguisher off the wall and started spraying the fire there that was underneath Lieutenant Ayres."

There was also a fire under the gunner in the turret of the trac.

Ewers continued: "Everyone that was in the back, started pushing back towards the back door, to get away from the fire. And Lieutenant Ayres was yelling at the driver, and hittin' him with his hands, telling him to do whatever he could to get us out of there. So the driver, I think he went one more block west, and started heading south. At this time the fire was getting really bad, we couldn't see Lieutenant Ayres anymore, we couldn't see the gunner anymore. We were just trying to push back as much as we could. Everyone was piled up against the back of the trac. Some people were still hanging out of the top, shooting."

They turned south, then east, probably about a block he estimated, then the driver told them that they would have to get out of the trac. The driver jumped out and opened up the back door. All the Marines ran out.

"The house was facing east, and there was a house directly to our south. It was in a residential area. We all jumped out, got in some bushes there that were on the north side of the house. We started opening fire on everything that was across the street, because at this point, every single building was shooting at us. RPGs, AK fire, RPK fire."

"No one was really hit at this point except Lieutenant Ayres and the gunner. So then, Corporal Garcia, he ran and just body-slammed a gate, and it opened. 'Cause houses have a gate. And then we all ran inside this house and took up positions in there. I believe it was Staff Sergeant Sagredo and Lance Corporal McCarver went back out to the trac… they had to get Lieutenant Ayres' body out of there. He was a big guy and it was pretty heavy with all his gear on and everything. Most of his exterior was burnt, part of his flak jacket was burnt, but they drug him up out of the hold and started pulling him back inside the house."

"Once they got him inside the house, um, I was on the radio the whole time, trying to tell main what was goin' on, where we're at. We had no clue where we're at. We had no grid, we looked in Lieutenant Ayres' pockets to see if he had any maps, GPS, anything, but he had nothing. I think it had already burnt up. So Staff Sergeant Sagredo, he got on the radio, was trying to tell them what our situation was, we had an emergency casualty, and we needed to get him out of there as soon as possible, we needed reinforcement, that our ammo was running low. Then they sent a few more guys back into the trac to see if they could get the gunner's body out, but it was on fire so bad they couldn't get him out. They couldn't even get in there."

"We took up positions on the house, we were on a balcony, and they were taking RPG shots at the house like it was cool. We started running out of ammo, so we started redistributing ammo. Like all the guys that were working on Lieutenant Ayres passed out their ammo to the other guys that were on the roof. The enemy moved into houses all around us, we even started taking fire from the back side [of the house]. And a grenade landed on top of the balcony, right around all the guys that were firing. It rolled inside the house, where myself and Staff Sergeant Sagredo were. We ducked around the corner and it went off, and I believe one of our guys took a little shrapnel from it, in the leg, and that was it."

"We started throwing grenades at the houses around us. Then we moved off the roof. Staff Sergeant [Sagredo] decided it was better that we come in off the balcony 'cause it was just too exposed. So we came into the stairwell and into the bottom floor. And, got in around all the windows, made sure everyone was at every window that was in the house or the front porch. Then they started shooting in the side windows, the back windows, and everyone was just shooting back.

"Over the radio at this time, everything was just going crazy. They didn't know where we were at, like, can't you see the huge column of smoke [from the burning trac] that's out there? They're like, 'There's smoke everywhere in the city.' Well this one is a huge column of black smoke, there's a trac burning out there. And then the trac's ammo started exploding. Because it had, the driver was telling us before all of this started, there was over like 9,000 rounds of 40 mike mike and .50 cal rounds. And so, the trac became just one huge explosion. Ammo box after ammo box goin' off. I think that scared the insurgents off for a little bit, because it seemed that they backed off. But then we could see ambulances in the distance, and we could see guys piling out of the back of them in ICDC uniforms and they thought for a while that ICDC had actually come to help us. But it turned out that they were insurgents, they were dressed up in the uniforms. At this point, I would have to guess there were over a hundred, because they were coming from every direction. You could actually hear them talking, in the houses next to you, you could actually hear them yelling at each other. One of the guys looked at me and said, 'Is that friendly, is that friendly?' I don't think so, it sounds like haji language to me.

"And then some of the bullets went through a propane tank. Which made matters worse. We heard propane spraying out through the rooms, so we closed the door on that room, it wouldn't get to the rest of the house and become one big bomb."

"At the same time over the radio they had called in the battalion QRF, which consisted of tanks, I'm not sure, a couple other tracs, and then, Weapons Company. They also had air on station, I guess, eventually. The first thing we that saw was an Abrams [tank], and it pulled up right in front of our house. And it was just shooting straight across from us to the north. We had to get comm with the Abrams. We had no idea what TAC [tactical radio net] he was on. Establish some sort of comm. So, Staff Sergeant Sagredo ran out in the front yard. XO's like, tell me which way you need the trac to go. I'm like, tell him to turn his turret directly south and he's gonna see us. So, the turret turned right at us! The main gun pointing at us. Staff Sergeant thinks he's gonna shoot, so he's out there yelling at him, waving at him."

The tanker saw Staff Sergeant Sagredo (see Lieutenant Adams' account). The Marines inside the building started directing the tank's fire. They told the tank that the enemy was all around them and the tank started hitting targets with its main gun. It also opened up with its .50 caliber machine guns. At about this time, Marines from Weapons Company arrived and ran into the building. Bravo Company's own QRF, the 3rd Squad, which had been in the other trac, also arrived.

"So, we loaded up Lieutenant Ayres on the medevac. At this time, I thought he looked horrible. I thought he was gonna die, 'cause he's white as a ghost. The only thing that really made him smile, we kept talkin' to him about his baby girl he had. He used to bring her to the formations we'd have, she'd run around, talk to the Marines and stuff. So we were jokin' to him about that. And that seemed to be the only thing that could keep him conscious. The medevac took off, and they were gone, and all the guys, all of Weapons Company, they just spread out all along the road. That trac showed up. And I remember that trac showed up, and that trac spraying every level of every house there. Mark 19 rounds, just one after the other."

Captain Smith called Lance Corporal Ewers to him, because Ewers had a Mark 119 radio and the captain didn't have one with him. Ewers then acted as the CO's radio operator. Smith then started calling in where he wanted air strikes to go. There were a few strafing runs, Ewers wasn't sure, but thought that they were Air Force jets making the runs. Smith wanted to ensure that the burned-out trac was moved out of the area since there was a dead Marine inside of it. Ewers estimated that it took about a half hour to get the trac hooked up for a tow with an Abrams tank. As the tank towed the trac back to friendly lines, all of the Marines in the area started moving back. There was no hostile fire as they moved.

Captain Smith and First Sergeant Van De Ven were the last ones who brought up the rear. It was now dark, and Ewers and his squad returned to the clothes factory they had been in before. They spent the night there. The other two squads from the platoon were still in the positions about 500–600 meters in front of Phase Line Violet, and he wondered about them all night. But he later learned that that was the night that a AC-130 Spectre gunship came in and blasted everything in front of 3rd Squad's position.

"They couldn't sleep all night because of the shells that were just exploding in front of them," Ewers said. In the morning, Staff Sergeant Sagredo took over the platoon, and Ewers' squad returned to the house it had held before the rescue mission. Howell was now Sagredo's RO. After a few days, the platoon was moved back to the clothes factory, and then to a cheese factory about a block away, still on Phase Line Violet. From then until about April 29, things were quiet in Bravo Company's sector. As they got ready to move out, they loaded many of the sand bags onto pallets to reuse them.

"It was like kind of depressing, while you're pulling out, kind of, you were happy you were gettin' out of there. But, you saw all the blocks you had fought so hard to take. And then, it was like, you're pullin' out, and you knew that the insurgents were gonna move right back in them. You know, it was like, what was the point? But, I guess politics is on a whole 'nother level."

They went back to FOB Mercury for a night, then moved to Karmah in tracs. They set up positions in the school there, and did patrols to suppress mortars, IED emplacement, and ambushes. They wanted to let the locals see their presence. "We never really took fire out in the town while we were on patrol that first two weeks." They did take some mortar fire at the school, and there was some IED activity. They took two casualties during a reaction to a mortar attack on the police station. When a Humvee-mounted reaction force was returning from looking for the mortar shooters, it was hit by an IED. Howell thought that the insurgents had watched the force go out, and waited until their return to set off the IED. Both Marines wounded in the attack survived, one was sent home due to shrapnel wounds.

Bravo Company then moved to its current location, the food distribution warehouses at Shahabi. Howell noted, "As you've seen, we get hit with mortars quite often. And then that firefight was the first major action that we've had in Karmah."

I asked if he was involved in that firefight, and he said yes.

"I was with 3rd Squad again, on patrol. Our patrol route was to go out past the ICDC compound to the west, up in that little village that's out there. And then back up, clear the two bridges, and then go up to Karmah. As we were in that village out to the west, we started hearing fire, RPG shots, on the police station. We weren't given orders to go up there right away, we just continued on our patrol route. We had updates on the radio, them tellin' us, 'This is goin' on, this is goin' on. They're takin' fire, we're pushin' up Weapons Company,' whatever."

When the 3rd Squad got to the southern bridge, it finally got the word to go hook up with 1st Platoon. They quickly moved across to the north side of the southern bridge, and a huge explosion went off to their south. At the time, they had no idea what it was (they later learned that it was a car bomb). Ewers laughed and said, "We had to have walked right past that car, so we were all pretty happy that it didn't happen to us." They linked up with 1st Platoon in Shahabi. There was some gunfire, but nothing like the intense shooting that they had experienced at Fallujah.

The ROEs at this time allowed the Marines to shoot at any man who looked to be a fighter, but Ewers said that they would wait until they saw an AK or an RPG before they would shoot at someone. "A couple of guys in my squad killed a couple guys in an alleyway that were runnin' out, taking pot shots, and then running back in. They were ready for them. Fallujah taught 3rd Squad a lot, and they were like, at the alleyways, had them all tied up."

As they pushed west, a Huey and Cobra came in.

They saw a car with a man dead from wounds lying in a street, a dead woman, a baby on the car hood, and a badly wounded little boy in the back seat of the car. A Corpsman started to work on the boy, and a staff sergeant started CPR on the baby.

The squad continued down the street for three or four blocks. The platoon then linked up and continued to look for weapons and wounded. The fight at the police station was well over by this time. This fight was about three days before today's interview.

"It seems that the firefight gave us some more credibility with the local people. I got the impression when we were here that they never saw us fight, so they sorta considered that we were all heart and no guns. You know, that we were just nice to them, to win 'em over and stuff. But then that day they saw that nothin' was gonna stop us from fighting back." He said that there was writing on a wall near a bridge that said that whoever attacked the Marines are cowards. He said that seeing that made him think that hopefully there were a few people who support the Marines.

I had asked him to compare last year and this year. Corporal Ewers responded:

"Last year, it seemed so much easier. Even though the conditions were a lot worse, because we were in tracs the whole time, pushing up north to Baghdad. The living conditions were horrible, like resupply hardly ever got there, so, I mean, you're down to one MRE a day. And, slept in holes every night. And you're always in MOPP suit. You're just scared of an NBC attack. Here, the living conditions are a lot better, it's more, almost, a relaxed atmosphere. But, at the same time, I say the fighting's at least ten times worse than last year, because last year you're fighting an organized enemy, you know. That recognized surrender, that, almost, followed ROEs. They weren't using ambulances and ICDC uniforms to come up close to you, to attack us. To me that's totally cowardly, it's not even, you don't even respect these people."

He said that last year there weren't people strapped with explosives or any IEDs in the roads. The Marines were fighting an army that didn't really want to fight. When that army did fight, they fought like a conventional army.

A mature overview of operations here from a very young Marine, I thought.

* * *

Staff Sergeant Ismael Sagredo

Platoon Sergeant, 2nd Platoon, Bravo Company, 1/5

A little over a year after his heroic actions in Fallujah, Staff Sergeant Sagredo was awarded the Silver Star for leadership and bravery. He saved the lives of his platoon commander and 12 other Marines who were in an AAV destroyed by RPG fire. The AAV had been hit so many times that it was bobbing before being hit by the round that killed the crew chief and seriously wounded Lieutenant Chris Ayres. After evacuating the squad's Marines into a nearby building, he returned to the burning AAV with another Marine and carried his platoon commander, Lieutenant Ayres, to safety and medical treatment inside. Eventually the battalion QRF arrived with tanks and Humvees. Once the QRF brought ammo resupply, his Marines continued to fight off surrounding insurgents until the burned AAV could be towed out of Fallujah. After this interview he learned how close he and his Marines came to death from friendly fire.

Staff Sergeant Sagredo enlisted in the Marine Corps in December 1991, and arrived at boot camp on December 7.

"I've been in for about 12 years now, my first duty station was 1st Battalion, 4th Marines, in an 81s platoon in a Weapons Company." He later served with Security Forces in Guantanamo, Cuba, then went to 2/3 as a sergeant where he became a platoon sergeant for a Weapons Platoon in Echo Company 2/3.

After he reenlisted, he served on the drill field. He left there on October 3, 2003 and checked in to 1/5. The company was training at Bridgeport at the time, and Staff Sergeant Sagredo waited for the company to finish its training there. He then trained with the company for operations with tracs, in urban warfare, and raids. He said that this training paid off during the operations in Fallujah. The original plan was for the battalion to become part of the 31st MEU in Okinawa, but soon learned that it would be returning to Iraq. This would be his first time into Iraq.

About the two months of training in Okinawa he said: "We did some training there in urban environment, and contacts, as far as what to do in case of vehicles detonated by an IED in the side of the road, or, any kind of contact, which helped out a lot out here. We've already pretty much, I would say the battalion as a whole had established a set SOP on how we were gonna conduct ourselves if we received any kind of contact whatsoever, whether it be small arms, rocket-propelled grenades, or just a device that was set on the side of the road."

He said that in training, many Marines feel that they will not need to know all of this stuff, but do the training that they are told to do. But in Sagredo's opinion this training paid off tremendously. He said that no one has yet to freeze after an IED detonation, or second detonation. They immediately respond in the way they need to.

Once Bravo Company arrived in Iraq, it was initially tasked with security for Camp Abu Ghraib. "We pretty much did this for two weeks, then our company was tasked, with the rest of the battalion, and another battalion that we were supposed to link up with, I believe it was 2/1, and we were to do a west and east push to the center of the city of Fallujah."

They had about four days to get ready for this move. They gave out more ammo and double-checked their optics, for what was supposed to be a nighttime insertion into the city. Contact began when Charlie Company was fired upon near the cloverleaf to the east of the city. Staff Sergeant Sagredo said that they could see the red tracers firing on Charlie Company, and Bravo was unable to assist them as they were preparing for their own mission.

Sagredo said on the night of April 4, 2004 they began moving into the southern sector of Fallujah. His platoon was the first platoon to make a breach and entry into the soda factory in that area. The rest of the company then filtered into the area. Weapons Platoon was assigned to the east of this compound, since there was a complex of houses nearby and Weapons Platoon could clear the area if needed. 2nd Platoon met no resistance inside the compound, and set up to the north of the soda factory. Bravo Company was not supposed to cross Route Michigan, also known as Phase Line Black at the time. The company was pretty much on line at the factory, oriented towards the west. They then pushed to the west.

"We got through the workers' shops, auto shops, and there was pretty much no resistance whatsoever, the whole way. None whatsoever. We did find a lot of weapons, at one point I had Marines carrying two to three AK 47s. I even had to use my Corpsman to carry AKs. We were just finding so many weapons. It was unbelievable that so many weapons could be in a cement factory."

It was now nearly sunrise, and the company commander (Captain Jason Smith) wanted to make sure that the Marines got to elevated positions by daybreak. Some platoons found ladders, but 2nd Platoon had to do the "hoist method" to get Marines onto roofs. There was no resistance when the sun did come up.

The platoon commander, Lieutenant Chris Ayres, wanted to do vehicle checkpoints, because there was an intersection close to the platoon's positions. There was traffic starting up from taxis and business vehicles. So the Marines set up two VCPs, one just north of them with Corporal Carnes' squad, and one further south on Route

Michigan. They used translators to tell the drivers that the coalition forces were now in the city and were looking for insurgents. By midday, the Marines started to get heavy resistance from the north in the form of a lot of sniper fire.

"We were watching insurgents running across the tops of buildings. My platoon was pretty much on the ground, being that we were the assault platoon, initiated the first move north of Michigan. So we cross Michigan, went down, received a lot of sporadic fire. We didn't know the alleys as well. Our maps weren't as great as we thought they were, and we ended up running into some dead ends, and insurgents got away a lot."

Sagredo remembered capturing two insurgents and having one insurgent KIA. There was also word that insurgents had gotten ICDC uniforms, so the Marines would have to be even more cautious. Also, the whole time during the shooting, there were Iraqi ambulances racing through the city. The whole day, the platoon would move up on Michigan, fight, reload on ammo and go out to fight again. He said that Lance Corporal Cargyle was shot crossing Michigan. (At the time of the interview, Cargyle was recovering from wounds to his right thigh.) Some type of dud round came tumbling towards Sagredo and members of his platoon. He said it might have been an RPG, a mortar round, or grenade, he wasn't sure.

The platoon was then told that it had to push to the west. "We were going parallel to Michigan, we were pretty much on the south side of Michigan." Sagredo said that either the CO or the first sergeant were pushing with another force along the north side of Michigan. They were receiving small arms fire from an apartment near a mosque. 2nd Platoon then did a cordon and knock on the apartment building to clear it. Interpreters explained to the residents what the Marines were doing in the building. They only found a rifle magazine, a butt stock, and a pistol. Captain Smith had the interpreter explain to the residents that the Marines wanted to find those who were shooting at them.

They had reached what would later be known as Phase Line Violet, when an RPG round was fired at them. The rocket-propelled grenade flew over the platoon and impacted on a center island of the street. A Marine said that it was fired from a green truck. 2nd Platoon started to move south on Violet to get closer to the vehicle, but the truck drove away.

That night Sagredo saw red tracers flying towards them. Lieutenant Ayres told him to take Corporal Garcia's squad to the top of a higher building for an OP. Before they could move to that roof, an RPG round hit it. Staff Sergeant Sagredo asked Ayres if he still wanted the squad up there, and the lieutenant said that it was a big roof, and a lucky shot, and he did want them up there. So Sagredo took the squad to the roof, and fortunately they did not receive any incoming that night. When day broke, they set up vehicle checkpoints and stayed alert.

Over in another sector, Alpha Company took contact. 1st and 2nd Platoons moved out to the west, and Lieutenant Ayres ran into the battalion commander,

Lieutenant Colonel Byrne. Byrne gave some guidance to the lieutenant as to where to go. Sagredo said it was like the movies, with tracer rounds coming towards them.

"I remember I watched Lance Corporal Gifford take a round to the left shoulder. What it was, it was a round that ricocheted off the ground, that came off, just knocked him to the ground. I thought he was shot. He just got up, he was feeling himself. 'Gifford! Gifford!' 'I'm all right! I'm all right!'"

The platoon got separated from the rest of the company during this firing. Soon all of the platoons got together as they continued to push into the city. They moved to Violet, with Alpha Company to their south. Corporal Picard's squad was in a building that continually took fire. Picard's men had to low crawl around the roof because they were being shot at. Sagredo said that he was shouting up at Picard to see if everyone was all right there. They told him that they were good, with good cover from ground fire.

Over the next few days the platoon occupied three positions, including a steel door factory (Corporal Picard), a cheese factory (Corporal Garcia), and a clothes/fabric warehouse or factory (Lieutenant Ayres). Finally, Weapons Platoon was attached out to the different platoons in Bravo Company, and Sagredo said that he felt his platoon now had a better number of Marines. The ROEs now called for firing on individuals who showed hostile intent, meaning that if they carried weapons they were considered hostile. Sagredo said, "Because at this point, the city had already had dozens of pamphlets already dropped from above, saying that bombing is going to be starting, it's in your best interest to take your families. If you're not involved with *Fedayeen*, then go ahead and take your family and get ready to leave town."

Despite these warnings, there were still houses with families and children in them in different parts of the city. Through his interpreters, Staff Sergeant Sagredo told residents to leave the city because it was getting too dangerous for them.

His Marines stayed off the rooftops during the day due to the danger of sniper fire on them. They occupied the rooftops at night to take advantage of their optics and night vision capabilities. The enemy snipers seemed to fire on regular schedules, and Sagredo said that his Marines got a couple of them.

"We got a couple of the snipers, I know that. I know we had Lance Corporal Carver had some confirmed kills. Ross, myself, and Sergeant [then Corporal] Garcia were on the high spot on top of the cheese factory, and we spotted one [a sniper], maybe a hundred, two hundred meters west of Violet, on a rooftop, moving around. Both [of us] had weapons with ACOGs, and I was the one ended up taking the shot. And Sergeant Garcia said, 'Yeah, you got him. He's dead. He's down.' We got some good kills up there."

He said that to make the foothold bigger, under cover of darkness, they put Lance Corporal Villareal's fire team forward of Phase Line Violet where they stayed for several days. They then switched out with another fire team under Lance Corporal Lukayenko. Soon Staff Sergeant Sagredo and part of the platoon moved into a building near the ICDC building. Lieutenant Ayres had had the platoon recon the area and pick the three houses that they then occupied. Sagredo described it as a triangle of houses, with Ayres in the front house. Corporal Picard's squad was to the north, and Corporal Garcia's to the southwest. "Once we were over there, we were getting non-stop sniper fire. It just did not stop. All day. All day. We could even see out there past Phase Line Yellow, insurgents running around, with rifles."

A resupply came out after about a week, and almost got ambushed. Marines with Corporal Picard identified where the fire was coming from, and Lieutenant Ayres was determined to go and flush them out.

Sagredo said, "Went ahead and went on tracs [that] were in reserve at the time. So, we went ahead, called up tracs, called higher-up, called tracs. Tracs came down, Corporal Picard's squad loaded up on one of the tracs, and Lieutenant Ayres was in the other trac. He came down and picked up Ewers and myself."

The tracs took off to the south to attempt to flush out the enemy, and the main communication between the two tracs was to be visual. Secondary comm was to be radio: Squad radios and ICOMs. The third means of comm was to be the tracs' own radio assets. Sagredo said that he was comfortable with this set-up.

"Corporal Picard's trac took heavy fire right off the bat. Lost line-of-sight, [we] tried to get radio comm with them. Then we hit a T in the road, only allowed us to go left, to the south. So we went south, we went south only about a block, maybe about a hundred yards. Then we turned back, maybe west. There was like three straight RPGs. The trac was pretty much still, and I was wondering why it wasn't moving. Could hear Lieutenant Ayres yellin' 'Go! Go! Go!' I was on the back, left side of the trac. Myself and Lance Corporal Morrow were on air watch, rear security. Trac was constantly receiving RPGs. It's like there was no small arms fire that we were getting. It was straight up, almost RPGs. We could even see the insurgents running between alleys."

Staff Sergeant Sagredo said that the alley was too narrow for the trac to turn around. "We were sitting ducks if he tried to turn around. I gotta credit that lance corporal, that driver, for the way he drove that trac. He did an outstanding job. We had no choice with the platoon, but pushing west. By that time, we were at Phase Line Yellow, and nobody had been on Phase Line Yellow yet."

There the driver headed left on Phase Line Yellow, and here, Sagredo said: "And there was nothing but insurgents. Sitting down. Drinking tea. AKs. RPGs. Propped up against the walls. And once they saw that trac, they all scattered. Jumping up, starting shooting at us. Our trac was on fire before we got off Phase Line Yellow. And, uh, it was hard to see through the smoke, to shoot at the same time. So there was times where I wasn't even shooting. I don't know about the other Marines, I can't really speak for them, but I just didn't want to shoot unless I could see something."

"I remember at one point I was shooting. An RPG struck the trac, and knocked me down into the troop compartment. And, 'Sergeant Garcia, I'll be back up.'

But while I was down, the trac was just constantly rockin' back and forth, as if it was in the ocean. Just bobbing. Just how much hits we were getting in that vehicle, I don't even know how many times that thing got hit."

The trac driver kept driving further south, to an area now called Queens. They turned east, back towards Violet about 200 meters when the trac just died. The back ramp would not open. The Marines were not waiting. They got the door opened, but the Marines were already climbing out of the open hatches on the top, and jumping onto the ground outside the trac. They did not set up a protective 360 defense around the trac, because, Sagredo said, "The damn thing was on fire!"

The Marines found positions to provide protective fire.

"The driver was staying right there, [I] asked him, where is the crew chief? And he told me, 'He's dead. I heard him screaming a long time ago and then it stopped.' So, I was like, are you sure he's dead? The hatch was buttoned down, we couldn't open it, and there was flames in the back, and we couldn't get to him. So in my mind, I'm like, he's dead."

Sagredo said, "It was hard. It was real hard for me to just leave the trac, with that Marine in there. There for a long time, I was always blaming myself. Especially with Corporal Kolm [the crew chief] being in the trac, because I was the senior enlisted, and I left a Marine behind. Did I really leave him behind? I knew where he was, the trac was right there."

Staff Sergeant Sagredo said that he often thinks about this, but I reassured him that when I earlier spoke with another trac driver, he said that there was no way to get the dead Marine out of the burning trac at that time. Normally I listened and asked only a few questions during my interviews, but I was hoping that telling him what the Amtracker said about this event would bring some comfort to Staff Sergeant Sagredo. He thanked me for telling him this.

When Staff Sergeant Sagredo sent out any patrol, he now told the patrol leaders that either he or the lieutenant wanted to ensure that they returned together. He likened it to the concern of a father.

Sagredo continued: "I asked him [the Amtrac driver, PFC Matthew D. Puckett] about Lieutenant Ayres. Did Lieutenant Ayres get out? And he's like, 'I helped him out, but I was being shot at.' He was scared, understandable. He was in a sense, out of his environment, but not really, he was used to driving, not getting shot at directly, with a weapon. I heard Lieutenant Ayres, screaming and asking where we were at, so I climbed up on the side of the trac. I reached over for him, we made eye contact, solid eye contact. But he's like, he crawled away from me. I'm like, shit, he's blind. He can't see. I don't know what it was. So I had to climb back down, and climb over to the other side, climb up behind the vehicle, the vehicle commander's hatch, where Corporal Kolm was at. The steel was hot. I climbed up, and I think I grabbed him [Ayres] just in time, because I think he was about ready to crawl into the troop compartment, directly straight into the fire. And I grabbed him."

"He was coming over towards me, I see the back of what's left, the back of his left leg was his trousers were all bloody. And then he got closer to me crawling, that's when I saw the open wound on his leg, I saw the bone, the tissue, and I was tellin' him, I don't think he could hear me or something, because I was screaming at him. 'Sir, you gotta roll off, I will catch you. Do not climb down!' Telling Lance Corporal McCarver, like, McCarver, we gotta catch him."

Sagredo was afraid of the damage to Ayres' leg if they did not catch the lieutenant. He said that Ayres tried to climb down, and he told him, "Sir, you can't climb down, you gotta roll off."

Staff Sergeant Sagredo said that he weighs about 180 pounds soaking wet, the same for McCarver. Ayres was about six foot two, and probably weighed 220. Sagredo remembers thinking that it was going to be hard to catch Ayres and to get him to a safe area. Ayres still tried to climb out of the trac, and a bolt on the cages on top of the trac got caught on his flak jacket. It finally broke loose, and Sagredo and McCarver were able to catch him so that he didn't hit the ground hard.

"Sergeant [at the time Corporal] Garcia had come back out from the house where he was at, and he took McCarver's SAW and he helped give cover fire so we could carry Lieutenant Ayres into the house. Trac was a good 50 meters away."

To carry Ayres, he and McCarver, "Pretty much did a one arm around each shoulder. We grabbed the back of his flak and one-two-three, let's go! So, we started running. We got to the house. We got him in there. Once we were in there, Doc Viegas… Marines were awesome, they went straight to Lieutenant Ayres, straight to the roof, went straight to positions they needed to go, and started laying down a good base of fire. Lieutenant Ayres, putting pressure dressings on him. And Doc Viegas, he's [Ayres] bleeding outta the right thigh. His face is burnt. Blistered."

"Sergeant Garcia's asking where the crew chief is at, and the driver was telling him, 'He's dead. He's dead. He's on the trac.' He [Garcia] wanted to make another valid attempt, see about getting him back out. So himself, Corporal Romero, and Corporal Calloway, they ran back out. And Corporal Garcia was the one that got back into the trac."

There, Garcia could hear the small arms ammo sizzling as it started cooking off inside the trac. When he got back to the house, he told Staff Sergeant Sagredo that half the ammo was already engulfed in flames and starting to sizzle. The Marines told Sagredo that they could not get the crew chief, and he told them that he knew it couldn't be done then. He told them to focus on what they had to do just now. In retrospect, Sagredo said that it was probably not a wise call to let them go back out, but at the time it did not sit right with the Marines to have another Marine in the trac and not at least attempt to retrieve him.

The house they were in was facing to the north, and insurgents were attempting to get into it. Corporal Romero took a position on the southeast corner of the house and ended up firing 9mm (pistol) rounds right out the window at insurgents there.

There were other insurgents on the west side of the house by the kitchen windows, and Marines were exchanging fire with them. One of these bullets punctured a gas line in the kitchen, which then leaked cooking gas into the house. Corporal Calloway was wounded by shrapnel at this time. They covered Ayres with blankets in case the house exploded from the gas.

Sagredo said, "At that point, I had pulled Marines off the roof, because they were lobbing grenades over onto us from roof to roof, from ground to roof from the other yards. I had Corporal Romero and Lance Corporal Gehrin who took shrapnel up on the roof. I had Ayres with me and I pulled everybody off the roof." There was also some type of fluid leaking from a car in the front yard of the house. Sagredo thought to himself that this was not good. RPGs were still hammering the house. He thought that they could not stay in this house for very long.

At that point, "That's when I heard the tracs. Corporal Pollowfox [spelling?] said, 'Hey, I hear the tracs! I hear the tracs! They're coming!' UUUHH! All right, good. Maybe we don't have to make a run for it now. During this whole time I'm trying to be calm. Talking to Lieutenant McGahee on the radio. I see Lieutenant Ayres is down, I tell Ewers, hey, from now on, I'm Blackhawk Two now. That's Lieutenant Ayres' call sign, he's the one that's in charge. My call sign was Blackhawk Two Bravo. I'm Blackhawk Two, letting everybody know right now."

Sagredo had to take the RO, Lance Corporal Ewers, with him as he moved throughout the building and areas outside. They couldn't get good comm inside the house, and couldn't go back up on the roof, so they went out into the front yard. Right after they got there, an RPG impacted just over their heads on the house. After three RPG impacts, Sagredo said to Ewers, "We're done out here. Already got communication, they know where we're at, they're coming." They went back into the house for cover.

One of his corporals then said that he could hear the tanks coming. So Staff Sergeant Sagredo went back outside with Lance Corporal Ewers to make contact with the QRF. However, the tanks ended up pushing too far west.

Sagredo said, "I'm like, great, they're gonna miss us. Go past us. So, I'm calling on the radio, calling the guy on the trac, telling him, I got one tank that's west of the house, and one tank that's now going west of my house. And that second tank needs to come back to the east at least 100 meters, and I will be directly behind him. At that point we heard footsteps and we thought it was more insurgents, like the previous ones that tried to come in. And we ended up seeing a muzzle, and we heard Captain Smith sayin' 'Marine! Marine!' Captain Smith, and then everybody was like, at ease!" Sagredo said that one of his lance corporals told him that he was never so happy to see the company commander in all his life.

Once Captain Smith got there, everyone got resupplied with ammo. Sergeant Smith was completely out of ammo. Corporal Romero had no more 9mm ammo for his pistol. Staff Sergeant Sagredo only had two magazines for his own M16. He had previously told his Marines that if they only had two rounds left, they had better have a target.

"Once we got ammo, the Marines were like, 'Great, we got ammo. Hey, Staff Sergeant we wanna go back up on the roof.' So, I went back up to the roof with them. Even once the 'cavalry' showed up, the house was still getting pummeled with RPG rounds. [Marine] snipers came up to the roof with us. They jumped on our building. 81s, Staff Sergeant Santiago showed up, with 81s. He and I were on the drill field together. It was good to see him." Santiago's Marines cleared the buildings of insurgents to the east and west of them. They now set up a good 360 defense.

Sagredo said that the biggest thing was that they were not going to leave the burning trac there with the dead Marine inside. Captain Smith was bound and determined to get that trac and the Marine out of that area, if not right then, then the next morning. Smith said, "We're gonna stay here, because there's a Marine in it. It's either coming back with us, or we're gonna wait here with it." Staff Sergeant Sagredo said that this gave him a good feeling.

Lieutenant Ayres and the Corpsman had been evacuated by this time. The other Marines, who had minor wounds, stayed there.

Marines were able to hook the trac up to a tank and tow it out of there back to Phase Line Violet. Sagredo estimated that they were about 600 meters south of Violet. Once they got back to Violet, they regrouped and got a count on all of their Marines.

"It was kind of a weird feeling, as we were walking out of there, with the trac. I've always had bad luck with the tracs. That's like the second trac I've been in that's been on fire."

He said that everyone was quiet on the return. "I honestly thought we were all gonna die in that house. Especially when the fuel was leaking, and the gas, and we were still getting RPGs coming through the house. And they were trying to throw grenades in through the windows. I thought that we might have to just make a run for it. I didn't sleep good that night, I know that. It was kind of hard sleeping. I think I smoked about a pack of cigarettes that night.

"I think one of the other hard things I had to do, it didn't feel comfortable to me, that I had to act as Lieutenant Ayres." Ayres was the leader at that level, and now Sagredo was the platoon leader. He had led before, but never in a combat situation. At 0800 the next morning, as acting platoon commander he had to go to debrief Captain Smith on what had happened. Sagredo expected that the platoon would be sent back to the cheese factory, but instead Smith told him that the platoon was going back out in front of Violet. This gave Staff Sergeant Sagredo a morale boost in that Captain Smith had that confidence in his ability to lead the platoon. "It boosted my morale, it made me feel better. I used it as a tool for the

Marines." He let his Marines know that he had confidence in them, just as the CO had confidence in him to take over the platoon. "They went back, now they're even more on their own now."

He said that Marines were always talking about going out with their small units, and he told them, "All right, you got your small unit now. Now go out and take that house!"

"I didn't realize how hard Lieutenant Ayres had it, when I took that house. I found myself constantly asking Ewers, my radio operator, and myself, from where we were at, what's the violence level? I was like, Ewers, we gotta go back, we got a fire team with us? Naw, it's just me and you. I got your back, you got my back. Let's go." Sagredo now realized how dangerous it had been for his platoon commander, Lieutenant Ayres, to move around and lead the platoon.

As the talks about Fallujah continued all of Bravo Company except 1st Platoon pulled back out of the city. 1st Platoon kept the apartment complex. The rest of Bravo occupied their earlier positions. 3/4 was coming in, 2/1 was up, and Charlie Company was coming in from the prison, all getting ready for a push into the city.

When all of the units would finally gather, there were to be four Marine battalions ready to make an all-out push into Fallujah. Sagredo's Marines spent their time filling sand bags and improving their positions in case of an insurgent attack on them. Weapons Company conducted back-clearing operations. Sagredo said, "They found ungodly amount of weapons caches." He said that they uncovered ammo buried under small trees, in the corner of offices, in paneling and in ceilings.

As a result of the negotiations, word came that the Marine units would pull out of Fallujah. "Marines are like, 'Wow, we're done, we're going home early.' But they said that they couldn't leave until they broke down these positions."

As Bravo Company moved out of Fallujah, word came that they might be moving into Karmah the next morning.

Sagredo said to me, "And guess who brought us up (to Karmah)?"

I replied, "Tracs?"

He laughed and said, "Tracs!"

Staff Sergeant Sagredo was not real excited about this, given his bad luck with tracs. He also learned that 2nd Platoon would lead the Bravo Company move into Karmah. They would occupy the schoolhouse there.

Sagredo asked, "How we getting there?" The reply came, "Your ride's waiting outside."

Sagredo saw the tracs outside: "You gotta be kidding me. Can't take Hummers? Gotta go in tracs?" He said that his Marines made the best of it, joking as they moved in the tracs. Fortunately, they met no resistance as they moved into the schoolhouse in Karmah.

There Staff Sergeant Sagredo walked through the schoolhouse, and he met his new platoon commander, Lieutenant Lynch. Sagredo saw that the position needed to be cleaned up, too. "Most Marine Corps companies, it's dirty when you got it, but it's clean while you're there, and it's cleaner once you leave." He told the Marines that when they were not on post, they were on working parties to clean the building.

Sagredo said that while in the schoolhouse, he remembered only one RPG shot, maybe three mortar rounds, and some small arms fire. No one was hurt for the three weeks they were there. They left Karmah and turned the schoolhouse over to local authorities so that kids could be back in school. They then moved to the Oil for Food camp.

"Sure enough, we left there, and we moved into here. We didn't even set up and we started getting shot at. We were receiving fire the moment we set ground in this place. We got shot at for the first four days. We received mortar fire. First four days straight."

Bravo Company began to build positions. He pointed over my shoulder outside of the warehouse to a machine gun position at the wall: Machine Gun Position Number 1. It had taken some small arms fire from the northeast, and the company continued to improve the position.

"Here lately, we've been getting a lot of mortar rounds coming in. Lot of patrolling going on out here, constant presence patrol."

When a car bomb 500 meters down the road went off, some of the shrapnel landed here at the camp. Sagredo was on a patrol with Corporal Picard at the time, and they heard the shooting going on up in Karmah. They continued their presence patrol, which was moving towards Karmah. He said that this was the first day that he and his Marines had seen a wounded woman or child. He said that it was unfortunate that there were a lot of civilians caught in the cross-fire that day.

"What hurt the Marines the most was when they saw that infant that was 19 to 24 months. That touched me, I have a son that just turned two."

He also saw a 12-year-old boy who had been shot in the shoulder, and another boy with a wound to his abdomen. In the time they had been in Karmah, they had gotten to know many of the people in the town. It was hard to see the faces of people after the fighting.

Staff Sergeant Sagredo wondered about the perception that people back home had about the war. He was curious to see this when he gets back home.

Pretty soon the battalion would be changing over with 3/1. There will be Left-seat, Right-seat turnovers. The battalion would be here until June 30. He said, "I just can't wait to get back home. It's been an experience, unfortunately, it's an experience that I hope I forget." Sagredo was good friends with Staff Sergeant Harrell, who died in Fallujah. They both had plans to do things together with their families once they got home.

Sagredo looked back on the time when he first joined the company, fresh off the drill field, and many of the Marines in the company were not happy about this. (Drill Instructors are noted for being strict and 'by the book') but he had reminded them that they were Marines, and there is a Marine way to do things. He enjoys working with all of these young Marines. They were now men. "I hope to promote some of those lance corporals to corporal." He said that many who had talked about getting out of the Marine Corps at the end of their enlistments are now reconsidering staying in.

(Note: After I finished recording this interview, I told Staff Sergeant Sagredo about my interview with Lieutenant Adams, the tank commander on the opposite side of the rescue operation. Adams had told me that he felt sick that he came so close to firing his tank's main gun at the building, and only hesitated when he saw Sagredo's Kevlar helmet appear. Sagredo's response to me was, "No shit, sir!")

* * *

Saturday July 3, 2004

I checked on email messages this morning, called Major Zeman about my upcoming visit to RCT7 at Camp Al Qaim, and then called home on an Iridium satellite phone. It was Major Piedmont's last day here at Camp Fallujah. I would be leaving for Al Assad on a helo from Camp Fallujah tonight.

Staff Sergeant Sagredo, from Bravo Company, 1/5, brought two of his NCOs to the EFCAT tent for interviews. They had both been involved in the April Amtrac rescue in Fallujah in April and also fought in Al Karmah. This was unplanned and a great opportunity to get in two excellent interviews; each interview over an hour long, and both Marines were very articulate. Good interviews about combat and SASO in and around Al Karmah. While each of these Marines waited for their interview with me, the EFCAT Marines lent him their Iridium phone so he could phone home without cost.

* * *

Corporal Jason Picard

Squad Leader, 3rd Squad, 2nd Platoon, Bravo Company, 1/5

On first arrival near Fallujah, Bravo Company was assigned camp guard duties. In early April this changed as 1/5 was sent to the outskirts of Fallujah. As Bravo Company moved into the city, it began to receive mortar, RPG, and small arms fire. A missed resupply of food and ammo eventually led to the cascade of events where an AAV assigned to another squad in the platoon would be downed by RPG fire, leading to the battalion's QRF mission to rescue that squad's Marines. His own AAV damaged by a different RPG attack, Picard and his squad rode in Humvees as part of the effort to get those Marines out.

Corporal Jay Picard sat down on a folding chair across from me for his interview in the warm shade of the EFCAT tent, covered by a camouflage net. It was cooler out here that it was inside the tent today.

Picard began: "I joined the Marine Corps September 16, 2001. Left for boot camp. The whole time in boot camp all they talked about, that was right after September 11, so, the drill instructors from the get-go were sayin', you know, 'You're gonna go to war, you're gonna go to war. If not in Afghanistan, you're gonna end up somewhere.' At the time, it was obvious America was gonna go to war."

He said that he was personally in denial about this. He graduated from boot camp in December 2001, and had ten days' leave and two weeks as a recruiter's assistant. He did SOI at Camp LeJeune, then went to Camp Pendleton and joined 1/5 during its workup for deployment to Okinawa. Halfway into the workup to deploy with the MEU, things switched up and they learned that they were going to Iraq. His first deployment to Iraq lasted a little over four months.

When 1/5 got back to the States in 2003 it had to cram a lot of training into a six-month period before it would return to Iraq again. They had to get MEU (SOC) qualified and head to Okinawa. He went to the Squad Leaders' Course for almost three months. In the meantime, many new Marines fresh out of SOI had joined the battalion. Corporal Picard did a few field operations with the company after his return from the leaders' course.

After a short block leave, the company prepared to leave for Okinawa, knowing that they would only be there for a short time before moving on to Iraq. They focused on SASO training. Picard said that he felt that the Marine Corps was better suited to "kicking in the door" rather than SASO. On Okinawa they trained hard during six-day work weeks. They left Okinawa in March 2004 and flew to Kuwait. They spent two weeks in Kuwait, doing convoy rehearsals and training.

"Cool thing about it, the exact same time on the exact same day, that we crossed the border the first time, we were driving our Humvees the second time [into Iraq]. That was pretty cool. For it to work out that way. I remember coming up, the big thing was IEDs. All we heard about on the news were IEDs." There were rumors of how many people had been hit, and the casualties on the convoys from Kuwait to Iraq. "And that ride up, I don't know if it was God looking out for us, luck, or the just bad guys didn't happen to be out there the night before, but we didn't come across any IEDs."

Corporal Picard said that a majority of the reports were based on how the Army was doing business. But as the Marines drove up, they had Marines facing outboard on every vehicle, weapons ready, looking for someone even acting like they were doing something "stupid." He said that he saw an Army convoy drive by, everybody sitting, back up against the back of the Humvees, looking inward, no rifles visible, and three or four vehicles passed before a .50 cal or 240 Golf was visible. In contrast, every Marine 7-ton truck had .50 cals and Mark 19s.

"I remember noticing that, thinking, that's gotta be a big piece of it right there. The way they're conducting business. And we just got to continue conducting business the way we've been trained the last couple months."

They got to the MEK (Camp Fallujah) and stopped for a few hours and got hot chow at the dining facility here. "We saw that chow hall over there, and compared to last year's chow, eating MREs for the whole entire time, sleeping in the trac on a good night, in the dirt on a bad night, to walk in and see there's air-conditioning systems, there's multiple food to pick from, you know, Coke machines, it was a pretty good shock. So we got a good meal there. Then we went down to what used to be called FOB Mercury, and now they call it Abu Ghraib. Not the prison, but the camp right down the road."

1/5 had Charlie Company over at the prison, training ICDC and helping out with security. They'd had Alpha and Weapons Company doing security and presence patrols in Karmah and Shahabi. Bravo wound up doing camp guard at the FOB. Picard said that in typical Marine fashion, some of the Marines in Bravo started complaining about what they were doing. The senior Marines who had been in Iraq before told the new Marines to be happy with what they were doing. They told them that this was the piece of the pie that they now had: Sleeping inside and getting hot meals. They should enjoy it while they had it, because the time would come when they would be wishing that they were back as camp guard!

Then Bravo was tasked with security patrols around the FOB, because they were getting hit with mortar and rocket fire on the camp every other day. The patrols went out day and night. Corporal Picard said that this enemy has plenty of ammo to fire, but that their aim was horrible: "I'm not gonna complain! Hopefully they don't improve." The FOB, now Camp Abu Ghraib, was not a very big place, he noted, but the incoming fire would land all around the camp.

Often on the patrols they would find locals digging in the area, allegedly to find scrap metal. There was not enough to bring them in for questioning, but enough to disrupt some insurgent activities. Patrols did find a couple of weapons caches, and one IED (a propane tank with wire coming out of it, staged for movement) was found one night. His patrol was actually standing over top of it while they determined to call EOD. EOD Marines said that it was an IED that was primed and ready to go.

Around this time, they heard rumors that 2/1 was going to cordon the city of Fallujah and do a house-by-house sweep through it. Picard noted that the city has about 250,000 people in it, and this sweep would have been ambitious for just one Marine battalion. His platoon commander, Lieutenant Ayres, got the platoon's squad leaders together and told them that they would be providing support for 2/1 if something happened. Picard said that the squad leaders all knew that they would be needed if the move into Fallujah came.

When they moved to Fallujah, word kept changing. Corporal Picard said that it was cold there the first night, and he could see Charlie Company at the cloverleaf east of the city. He went on a leaders' recon of the soda factory.

"It turned in to, 'Be ready to leave, be ready to leave. In two days, get pushed back a day. Get ready, we're leaving tonight.' You can tell as well as I can, it's pretty warm out here. But that night that we went into Fallujah, there's probably only a few times that I've ever been that cold. The temperature just dropped. And we were in Humvees. They weren't hard backs. We had extra seats in the backs, high backs with the benches. And the way our armor's set up for the doors, wind just blows straight through. There's no plastic to shut."

Picard's platoon was on a berm, and could see Charlie Company fighting over on the cloverleaf. "We could see a lot of tracers and we could hear everything going on." Marines were along the berm that ran east to west. It was so cold that they were taking turns doing push-ups and jogging around the back of the Humvees, trying to stay warm. The Marines switched off with buddies to do this. "We were told to pack for seven to ten days. Being that it's Iraq, nobody had warm equipment."

The next night, 2nd Platoon was going to go up and do a leaders' recon of the soda factory. "So we got about 800 meters off from the site. The platoon stopped—security halt. Myself and the other two squad leaders, along with Lieutenant Ayres. And I took a fire team. I took Lance Corporal Velez's fire team so they could stay back and link up with the rest of the platoon and company, once we got up there and checked everything out." He said that they walked up there and looked around. There was not much activity, just a couple of dogs in the area.

"At that time, little did we know how dangerous Fallujah was. We were at the alert, we were moving in a good formation with some dispersion. But nobody had any idea what we were fixin' to walk into.

"Got a good eye on the site. Saw where we were gonna take the SMAW shot to bridge through the wall."

When the SMAW team got there, they took a shot, but it didn't go as planned, so they shot another SMAW round. This didn't work, either. Finally, they got a hole that Picard's Marines could crawl through.

Inside the soda factory, there were only a couple of employees. Translators with a HET team began questioning these Iraqis. Then the Marines continued to push west across the southern part of the city. 2nd Platoon did not take any contact, but Weapons Company in the far north did. Marines there told Picard that one insurgent ran into the middle of the road with an AK rifle and started shooting at them.

2nd Platoon stopped when it got to the main industrial area and got up on the roofs of buildings there and waited for morning. The Marines grabbed some sleep, and in the morning started setting up VCPs in the area.

"Looking back on it, we still had no clue. We still had no clue what was coming up on us in this place. And, after we had been in the VCPs for a little bit, that's when we started taking some RPG and small arms fire."

When they received fire, the Marines would take off and try to hunt down the shooters. Picard noted that this was tough to do when you're in someone else's neighborhood and they're shooting at you, but they did it. They also used sewer ditches in the city to provide themselves cover on the ground.

Lieutenant Ayres came up to Picard and told him to be ready to have his squad (3rd Squad) ready to move at a moment's notice. "And I was like, what's goin' on? And then, he's like, 'Come on, we're movin'.' Picard got up and hollered to his Marines to start moving west. "And that's when the big bulk of the actions of the resistance came."

"We were getting a lot of rockets and mortars at that first place where we were there in Fallujah. Lot of small arms fire and RPGs. But the first time that we were actually pushing, pretty hard, to get up the street, the amount of fire that was coming down."

"Once we get up there, I look up, and there's the battalion commander, and the sergeant major. And I realize that battalion's out here. Tanks come rolling through." Counter-Mech (CAAT) Company elements were there. They stopped there and the mech elements went ahead.

2nd Platoon's squads were on top of buildings there near Route Michigan. The only cover available was from plywood RPG boxes that they found on the roofs. Some Marines joked maybe the wood could slow down incoming bullets a little bit. "Looking back on it, we were pretty lucky on that roof."

They got pulled from the roof and went into a fabric warehouse that also had apartments in the complex.

Picard said that the insurgents began a pattern of shooting at their positions. These insurgents figured out that after a while, the Marines would come out to fight. So they would have one shooter firing at a Marine position, and three or four others would wait until a Marine element came out to attack. He said that when one squad or one platoon went out like this, they could count on having to call out a QRF to help with the move back.

"If you're the one going out, you could count on having a QRF come out with you. Or, if you're the one that's QRF, you can count on going out and help bring 'em back. The worst thing about it is, the most time the QRF is called, it was because they had a casualty."

Picard rotated his fire teams, and devised a plan to leave one fire team inside of a building when the squad searched it. This way, the insurgents would not realize that a Marine element was inside of a building. Doing this, he put one fire team out as an OP for two days.

"In my opinion, the way the Marine Corps gets things done, it comes down to: What's that individual team doing? What's that squad doing? 'Cause there'll be this huge piece of pie. Of that big pie, there's this little piece that's cut out for 1st Squad, or 1st, or 2nd or 3rd Team. And that's how I explain to my guys before we came over here. Everything that's going on in Iraq is the big picture. The only thing that we need to worry about right now is that little tiny piece of the pie that they give us. We gotta eat that piece, we gotta stay alive. And then we'll come home."

Picard believed it was on April 8, 2004 that his squad's packs with the ten days of supplies finally caught up with them. The packs were at the company CP, and small groups of Marines went back to retrieve them. Picard, along with about eight Marines, got on Humvees to get their packs. He asked the driver if he knew where they were going, and the driver said yes. However, when they got to that area, it was not the CP and Picard's Marines were taking sniper fire from the west.

"They had us pinned down pretty good for a minute. We had no idea where the guy was shooting from. It's funny how that works. The crack will be so close, and you know that the guy has to be right next to you, but you can't see him. So it's kinda like when you get up to run, you just kinda expect something to happen."

When they found the CP, everyone was going crazy.

"They said that Staff Sergeant Harrell's been hit, and they had to get a medevac to him. But, couldn't get the medevac trucks in there. So there's tanks coming, and we're gonna go with them. We need you to escort the tanks to where they're at."

"So, once we got with the tanks and started heading that way, come to find out they'd already picked up Staff Sergeant Harrell. But, we had Lieutenant Palmer go down, as well. So, it was chaotic. I'd left to go for my packs, with me, six other guys that are all different squads. Yeah, we're all in the same platoon, but it's like a, uh, it's just a big mixture of different people from the platoon." Picard noted that this made accountability difficult, since he could not just rely on his own squad's team leaders.

They got into a house.

"We go in the house, and Lieutenant Palmer's laying on the floor. He had already passed away. There's a lot of Marines in the area. As I head back, there's an Iraqi man. Iraqi, Syrian, who knows? Freedom fighter, whatever they call themselves, *mujahideen*. He's dead on the floor. And then they've got another guy that is flexi-cuffed. Since we're just coming in, I'm under the impression that the people there searched him."

"Me and Lance Corporal Ross took the guy that was still alive, took him into the other room so they could finish clearing out the house. The Marines that were in there, pushed through, went around, checked everything else out. Well, in the process of doing that, they found that the guy that was dead had a vest that was packed with C4, across his chest, and a frag [grenade] dangling off his side. And that's when my lieutenant, which at the time was Lieutenant Ayres, said, 'Hey, Picard, get everybody out the house.' And, soon as I went outta the house, my old lieutenant, from my first time over here, he's now the company XO, Lieutenant McGahee. He was running by. And [he said] 'Picard, whoever's with you from your platoon, bring 'em with me.' So, off we went with him."

They were taking shots from what appeared to be a mosque. The Marines got near this mosque. They were getting spread out, so Picard said to McGahee that they better wait for everybody to catch up. The lieutenant wanted to keep moving, so they kept moving. Then Lieutenant Ayres came over the radio and told Picard to get back. But the XO said no, they had to keep going. Picard let the two officers hash it out on the (ICOM) radios that kept cutting out. Finally Ayres got it across to McGahee that the company commander, Captain Smith, wanted them back.

During this time, Lieutenant Palmer's body had been taken out of the building and Lieutenant Ayres had thrown a frag into the building when they left.

Shortly after this, word came that 2nd Platoon would move west. The platoon no longer had three squads, it was now two large squads. Picard's 3rd Squad, with attachments, now consisted of 26 Marines. It was like a little infantry platoon. As a squad leader, he found it difficult to control 26 Marines. He now had his normal three fire teams, plus another fire team, a SMAW team, a machine gun team, and mortar men attached as infantrymen.

At their new position, 3rd Squad was at the southwest, and 1st Squad was at the northwest. The headquarters element of 2nd Platoon consisted of Lieutenant Ayres, a radio operator, some mortar men, and a fire team from each squad was behind the two squads.

They did not have sand bags here, and wondered what they could use to protect themselves. Picard felt that God was looking out for them, because when they entered a house, one room was stacked to the ceiling with concrete mix sacks. So they began to build up their positions with these bags. Another room in the house was filled with concrete slabs.

"We got our positions built, and it's a good thing, 'cause soon as the sun came up, they [insurgents] opened up on us when they saw movement."

"We were out there. We were outta chow. We were real low on water. And we were told there was gonna be a resupply." Picard said that there was some miscommunication on their position somewhere along the line. They saw a Humvee go past them down the road, and then heard gunfire. This was their resupply that passed them, and they were getting shot up. That's when Lieutenant Ayres got on the radio and told him that the resupply got shot up. He also told Picard that they would push two Amtracs up to 3rd Squad.

3rd Squad was to stay put. Two houses down from them Marines were taking fire, and beyond that was an open courtyard. Picard was to get into the trac, push south and west and move the enemy away with the Amtrac's .50 caliber machine gun. However, the .50 cal and the Mark 19 on the trac jammed up.

"Now, we're sitting ducks, with nothing but our riflemen. We had a 240 [Golf] on the top, and then all our SAWs and sixteens [M16s] on the air watch at the back of the trac. But as far as the .50, the muscle on [it], the main reason you would even want a trac given to you, it doesn't work. The guns are down."

"We drive through, thinking, okay, we'll link up with 2nd Squad over here. Tell them what the situation is. Whole time, rounds are firing. RPGs are being shot. I think we [in the Amtrac] took three RPGs, but then, a couple of the guys say four. The first time we went through, and we didn't see 'em. I was like, where the hell are they? So, I'm like, I'll try my comm again. If it didn't work the first time, maybe something's going to change. So now, we don't have our guns: We don't have our .50s, we don't have our Mark 19. We have no communication with anybody in our company. We don't have comm with the other trac, we don't have comm with Blackhawk main, or anything.

"We turned down the road where we expect them to be at, and they're not there. I'm like, what the hell's goin' on?"

They drove through again, then pushed through a road further south. They continued to take more rounds and RPGs, but could not find 2nd Squad. The Amtrac driver (see interview with Sergeant Gilbert Guadalupe Alcantar) told Picard that they needed to go somewhere to fix the guns, so they went back to the company CP. The whole time Picard could hear 2nd Squad on the radio saying that they needed support, and to look for the smoke. He did not know what had happened to 2nd Squad yet. Picard could hear the rest of the company on his radio, but they could not hear him. The Amtracker told Picard that his vehicle's guns were now good. However, when they got to the area a third time, the guns still did not work.

"Finally an RPG penetrated where the gunner was sitting, and caught the back of the trac on fire. I pull my seat down from the TC (Trac Commander hatch). I'm looking back. I see my team leader, Lance Corporal Vasquez, just flat on his back. I thought for sure he was dead. Marines are just layin' on top of each other. Looking dead. And then, I see all this smoke. I'm talking to the gunner, I'm like, look, what did we get hit with on that side? I remember his exact words, was, 'Yeah, we're fuckin' hit. And I'm on fire.' I was like, holy shit! I look back in the back again in the trac, and that's when I see the fire just blazin' up."

"I didn't want to dismount right there. I didn't see us making it out alive, dismounting a burning trac with no guns. And bein' surrounded." Picard wanted to take the trac back to Route Violet, drop the back hatch, and get the Marines out there instead.

By now, the fire in the Amtrac was going good. PFC Switzer was in the back, he had the fire extinguisher. "He was trying to put it out. Which I later found out, he's in the States now. The blast, he lost his vision, in his left eye. That's his trigger, shooting eye. But, [the] Marine kept goin'. Didn't even tell me. He wasn't like, 'Hey, Picard, can't see.' 'Cause I know he never told his team leader. Never said anything to me about it. Just kept goin'. He was the one back there trying to put out the fire.

"I came out the top. And at this time, I'm telling the driver, open up the back hatch. I'm thinking, all right, Marines are getting out the back. Meet up once we get out there. So I get on the ground. It's funny, one of those tracs seems really high.

Everybody wants to climb the ladder when things are going good." He laughed. "Soon's that thing's on fire, you just roll right off the top of that son-of-a-bitch. As soon as I hit the ground, I looked over, and the door's still shut. And there's just smoke, raring out the top. And about that time, it was like a waterfall of Marines coming out the top of that thing."

"We were fortunate. The [trac] gunner, he had some pretty bad shrapnel, and some burns on his legs. Which as soon as we got out, my first sergeant [Van de Ven], that was in charge of the medevac, came right around the corner. We got him there, took the tracker back to the cloverleaf. Dropped him off. Came back. Then, started the process of tryin' to, trying to get in there and get these Marines out [of Fallujah]."

"The first medevac attempt I was on, and the second medevac attempt I wasn't on. The first one, it was just amazing. I had no idea there were that many people inside that city." Before this, Picard had only seen insurgents in ones and twos, moving ammo. The Marines would shoot at them when they could from inside of the houses.

He continued, "But they came outta the wood work. We tried going south, cut west, thought we'd come up on them. Couldn't do it. RPGs, RPKs, AKs, firing from everywhere. So, was like okay, let's go north. Shoot up north, trying to cut in there. Can't do it. Okay, let's go down the middle. Get all the way in there, to where we can almost see the people. And we're right out in that courtyard again. And, they were just coming from everywhere. They were just, RPGs flying. So, swung the medevac around again and went back. Everybody got out, and I went down to the corners 'cause the trackers got back to the trac."

The Amtrackers were on their way back into the city for a medevac using their Humvees. Picard linked up with them and they took off.

Picard found out that 2nd Squad had gone west into the city on a trac that had gone down inside Fallujah. Corporal Picard knew that I had previously interviewed several Marines from 2nd Squad when I visited Bravo Company at Camp Shahabi. Once Lieutenant Ayres and Doc Viegas finally got medevaced out of Fallujah, the Bravo Company Marines tried to get some rest.

"It was just one of those nights. You know, Marines didn't really want to talk about it, just relax. Trying to get some sleep. Trying to get some water and food in us. Told, the next morning we were going right back out, to those same houses." He paused.

"So, re-upped on ammo, re-upped on all our 203 rounds, five-five-six, linked, make sure everybody still had smoke [grenades]. Good on water, good on chow. And, uh, off to our house again. We had left a skeleton team out there. They actually stayed out there and spent the night. Lance Corporal Luhinko's team, Villareal's team. They stayed in the house. So we went back the next morning. Linked up with them. We got in fine. Everything was good. And that's when we sent our resupply out. Fire team. To link up with Staff Sergeant Sagredo. Well, on their way back, they couldn't get back in, because of all the fire [shooting]."

Picard's squad was getting ready to go out and help the team get back in. Lance Corporal Howard, a SAW gunner, jumped over a wall when they got there. They needed a ladder to climb over the wall at this house. After they were at the house for about an hour, they got word on the radio to pull back. They had planned to exit via the front of the patio area wall. But they began to take AK and RPK fire. Picard called Staff Sergeant Sagredo and told him, "We can't get outta this house right now." He said that if one squad came out and faced north, and another squad faced south, then Picard could get his Marines out the back of the compound. Sagredo told him to throw a smoke grenade into the middle of the road when he was ready to "rock."

Corporal Picard had one Marine at each position inside the house, and got ready to throw the smoke grenade into the road.

"Our Corpsman, he's a hard-charger. He had a [M]16 with him. Navy Corpsman, first one over the wall." The Corpsman then held security as the rest of the Marines there trickled over the wall. They ran back to the house that Staff Sergeant Sagredo was using as his headquarters.

"From there, together as a platoon, we just bounded back. Covering the alleys. Watching each other's back. Back to our original position at that warehouse."

Picard had a hard time remembering exactly what happened then. He said that this is when things seemed to die down a little bit in Fallujah.

I asked him if this is when the big ceasefire (in late April 2004) took place. He said it was often confusing: "We had ceasefires going off and on the whole time. It's like, excuse me, could someone please untie my hands from behind my back, so I can fight? 'Cause these people, they're not stopping. You got all these sheiks that wanna come and talk about how they want peace. You know, Marines want a ceasefire. And I'm sure they're running right back to the *mujahideen* at that area. And they're like, 'Look, they're not gonna be shooting at you today. Move your weapons around.'"

Corporal Picard knew that this type of decision was not made anywhere near his level, but said that it made it difficult for his Marines to fight a war. "Because that's what this was. We were no longer in Security and Stability Operations in Fallujah. We're trying to fight a war, and we've got people in certain ties, back at the Pentagon. That's what I'm assuming. Maybe I shouldn't say this on tape, I don't know for sure." Picard felt that someone was making this call who wasn't in Fallujah.

Picard said that after the last ceasefire, things really did start to settle down in Fallujah.

"They had a lotta air campaigns in that place. I think that had a lot to do with it. They had dropped flyers, sayin' that we were gonna have a big offensive move. And that if you wanted to live, get out of the city. Because they were gonna just be annihilated. Artillery was supposed to hit them. Fixed wing was supposed to come through and hit 'em. And they'd been hittin' them pretty much every night. And we got to where we just love the sound of those AC-130 Spectre gunships. The first time I heard those things going it scared me 'cause I didn't know what it was. But then as we got used to them, that's something that's easy to go to sleep to. Because you know they're out there, doing their thing. Likelihood of somebody coming to mess with you, pretty small."

For his Marines after this it turned into standing posts, and doing back-clearing from Route Violet back to the outskirts of Fallujah. "Going through every one of those shops. Looking for weapons, looking for ammunition. We found a lot of it, too. We found a lot of grenades, a lot of RPKs, AK 47s. Lot of stuff was in there." Marines also filled a lot of sandbags and improved fortified positions. They did this for about two weeks. It was good news for them when they learned that they were pulling out of Fallujah.

The company went back to FOB Mercury. They only stayed there for one night, and were told that they would be heading up to Karmah. The next morning after breakfast, they loaded up on Amtracs and went up to a school in the northern part of Karmah. 2nd Platoon was the advance platoon for Bravo Company. They got preparations started there. The rest of the company got there the next day, and they soon began running patrols in Karmah.

"About the only thing we ever received up at the school was just mortars. Occasional mortars. Rockets." Picard said that the longer they stayed there, the more *mujahideen* came. IEDs in the area increased, too. The company spent about a month in Karmah, patrolling out of the school and running night ambushes.

Corporal Picard said that during the original turnover, Army units that had been operating in the area had told them to stay off Route Chicago, and that things were bad in Karmah. But the Marines had gone out and done a mounted patrol along Route Chicago (before going to Fallujah).

Bravo Company also put a Marine squad in the local police station in Karmah. Some mortars landed near them, and some RPGs were fired towards them. The squad reported this to Blackhawk Main. The Marines were told to take a fire team with a translator and three or four Iraqi police and walk the area to see if there was anything suspicious.

"So I go into the police office, and I'm telling them, you, you, and you. Well, they're no idiots. They heard the RPGs. They've heard the mortars goin' on. And they just all cowered in the corner. They wouldn't look up, each one was tryin' to hide behind the other one. Because, they didn't want to be the one to get picked. Translator came over, talked to 'em. 'No, no, no.' They just weren't coming out. So, we went out, did a walk around. Came back. City's so big, and there's just so many places. You know, take a left, and you're gone. Nobody's gonna see you. Just stick out, shoot an RPG, and they're outta there."

"The people of Karmah, at first, seemed pretty nice. Everybody was friendly, lots of wavin'. Then I think they started gettin' upset, at, we were in the school. So, [I] believe they had a meeting. Cause something came down from higher. Said, we're moving from the school. That's when we moved down to the food plant [Shahabi]. Started rebuilding positions there."

Bravo Company began to patrol in Shahabi and up into Karmah. Picard said that mortar and IED attacks on them increased. "It seemed like every day." He added that the longest that they went without being mortared was nine days. When the mortar attacks were coming, they seemed to come between 1600 and 1800 in the late afternoon. Then they started from 1100 to 1300. The times got consistent, but the shooters constantly changed their shooting positions around Shahabi. QRFs from the FOB at Shahabi would try to locate the shooters, but never could. Picard said that by the time the insurgents shot at them with their 60mm mortars, they were probably a couple of clicks away and already packed up and moving by the time the rounds hit near the Marine camp.

"The people in Shahabi were a lot like the people in Karmah. They're nice, but yet they're not willing to help. They'll smile, they'll wave, they'll offer you a Pepsi. They'll offer you some water. Some tea. But, ask them about some *mujahideen*. Ask 'em who put the IED out in the road. They don't have a clue. It's almost that they lived under fear for so long under Saddam Hussein, that they're just used to it. They've just accepted the fact that they want to live under fear of the *mujahideen*."

"On a positive note, though, about two weeks before we left [Shahabi], the police station got attacked. Small arms fire, RPGs. 3rd Squad, we were actually about a click and a half, two clicks, south, when it all started. So, we started moving pretty quickly. Get up there. Try to support any way we could. Once we got up there, we linked up with Charlie Company. Their CAAT platoon had been working with the ICDC out of the police station. Which, they really did some work with these ICDC. They were pretty impressive, out there on patrol with us. Walking at the ready, covering each other, moving around. Talking, back and forth. You could just, I was impressed. It was the first Iraqi military service that I've actually been impressed with, for any type of service group. These ICDC guys were pretty good. They pressed through there with us, as well.

"Throughout this whole process, there's casualties. There's rounds flying, there's casualties. It's just how it goes. Well, the next day, I'm in Shahabi, on a patrol, and I'm talking to a guy. And he's telling me he's upset because his cousin got killed in Karmah yesterday. And how angry he is, at the *mujahideen*. And I gave him like a double-take. And I look at the translator, I was like, 'Ask him what he just said. Make sure.' He was like, 'Yes.'"

Picard came across three Iraqis that day who said that it was the fault of the *mujahideen* that people had died in Karmah, not the fault of the Marines. Picard said that this was a sign for the better in that area around Shahabi and Karmah.

At the food warehouse at Shahabi, there was an ICDC unit operating right across the street from the Marines. This was a different unit than the one up near the police station, but Picard said that they too had definitely made a turn-around since the Marines had been there working with them. They went on patrols with the Marines. Also, the HET team did a lot of investigation of members of this ICDC unit, and discovered that seven of them were *mujahideen*. One of these individuals was an ICDC major.

"There was this one translator who would always come with me. And always had these ICDC guys come up to him and, 'Like look, the major's crooked. The major's crooked. He's *mujahideen*.' And I'd come back, report it to higher. I didn't know if anything'd ever come of it. Maybe it was just ICDC who didn't like their command."

Corporal Picard said that for instance, when he asked for four ICDC, he would often be told that they could only send him two. After the *mujahideen* were brought to the Marine FOB at Shahabi, he recognized some of these uncooperative ICDC/ *mujahideen* now in custody. "I didn't do what I (really) wanted to do, but I did get to laugh and wave at the flexi-cuffs on 'em, looking like they had gotten caught with their hand in the cookie jar!"

Picard and his squad got to do regular patrolling in Shahabi, talking with the locals and giving soccer balls to the kids. He established good relationships with several families in the area. In one instance, a little Iraqi girl had fallen down during some of the fighting in Karmah. Her grandmother was carrying her to the house and fell. The grandmother now could not get out of the house, and the little girl had a broken arm. "So we started making it a point to stop by there as often as we could. Doc ended up putting a splint on the little girl's arm. And he would give that older lady some type of anti-inflamatory."

Corporal Picard said that one time he, Lance Corporal Villareal, and the Corpsman, were leaving a house that had some older women and a young girl in it. One of the women stopped them. She asked if any of them wanted to marry the older woman, covered with tribal tattoos, who was sitting on the floor. "I showed her my wedding band, and I pulled my wallet out, showed a picture of my wife. I was like, 'No, no, I already have a madam.' Then they asked about my father back home. 'She can marry your father.' I was like, he has a madam, too! It was pretty funny."

He continued with a story about a guy who owned a chicken store on the other side of Route Chicago. Picard said that this man would often give them tea. Accepting tea or food showed the locals respect. Later on, a car bomb blew all of the windows out of the chicken shop. Picard told the man to go to his local city council and tell them that he needed money to replace his windows. Then, "If they don't work for you, just come to where the Marines are, and you tell them. And see to it that we get you some money. This guy actually told me, tells the translator, translator relays it to me. 'Look, the Marines are doing enough for us in the community. I'll do my part and I'll pay for my own windows.'"

Often, people would come up to the Marines with a small ricochet mark on a window asking for money. "This guy had all his windows blown out, and he's just grateful somebody's there helping him." Picard said that this kind of thing, the progress that is being made, would not be shown on CNN.

What Corporal Picard did not know at the time was that the Marines in the area had stopped giving out money because a translator had been abducted up in Karmah. Picard went to his CO (Captain Smith) and told him about this storekeeper's windows. He told Smith, "'Look, you know me. I'm not big on giving any of these people money, because they could be helping out a lot more than they can. But this guy actually told me he didn't want the money, that we do enough. I think it's important that we get something to him.' Next day, took a truck out there with the legal officer. And hooked the guy up. I think they gave him $500. I came back three days later, guy had new windows up. Smilin'. It was good to be able to see something positive like that."

Since then, 3/1 showed up at 1/5's position, and they have just started the changeover.

I asked, "How did that go? Relationships you had with these people there? Like, introducing them to locals there? Patrols?"

Picard responded, "When we're doing the changeover, they didn't wanna see, they didn't want the Iraqis to see a turnover going on. Instead of crawling across the finish line, they wanted to run across. So we boosted our patrols up. Instead of doing four-a-days, we're doing six. Well, our platoon only has two squads. So, for the changeover, we pretty much took guard, at the food plant. And, 1st Platoon, since they had three squads, they did all the patrolling with 3/1."

He said that 3/1 shadowed 1/5 for one night and one day, by platoons. Once the changeover was complete, 1/5 moved back to Camp Fallujah, which Picard called the MEK. They were told that they were going to start their transitional period to get ready to leave Iraq when they got to Camp Fallujah. However, RCT1 needed them for more missions after handing the power over to the Iraqi government. Bravo Company started doing security patrols with tracs, on the roads going out to the cloverleaf outside of Fallujah. They ride out, dismount the vehicles to check trash heaps for IEDs, and also set up VCPs.

Corporal Picard said that besides that, they are now "living the life." They have hot chow and showers here at Camp Fallujah. They can get PT in, go to a gym, get to sleep on a rack (cot) with an actual mattress. The tents have air conditioning. He said that the chow hall is open about 23 hours a day and is "awesome."

"Things go right, we should have four, five, more days here, before we move over to where we're gonna fly out. It's definitely been a trip. We were talking about it a couple of days ago, if we had to pick one. Would we pick this deployment, or last deployment. On which one we thought we'd rather do. And, we all said, this one."

I responded, "Really?"

Picard said, "Surprisingly, because this one, the intensity level, of the fighting, was upscale, extremely. From this time to last time. Last time, we were just pushing up the highway. Anybody got in our way, you know, we had artillery preppin' everything right before we got there. If anything was left, we just drove right over it. If they didn't have a white flag, we'd kill 'em. If they had a white flag, we'd get out, you know, tag 'em, flexi-cuff 'em." The Marines in 2003 traveled up in tracs, wearing MOPP suits the whole time. There were fears of gas attacks.

In Baghdad in 2003, they went through "RPG alley." This year (2004), they did squad patrols. They were not in MOPP suits. They were not in tracs for the whole trip up from Kuwait.

"This time, being able to operate at the squad level has been nice. Get out, do what Marine Corps infantry squads do. It's been good.

"We're all looking forward to go home. And we're saying we're on standby, for March, maybe, coming back. If not, we'll go to Oki [Okinawa] in July." Picard said that he just planned on being back in Iraq in March (2005). "The way it's gone the last two times, I just count on being here." He jokingly referred to Iraq as a "home away from home."

* * *

Sergeant Ronnie Garcia

Squad Leader, 2nd Platoon, Bravo Company, 1/5

Sergeant Garcia enlisted on October 2, 2000, with a guarantee for infantry or Security Forces. For the first half of this enlistment he served in King's Bay, Georgia. He wanted to obtain a security clearance to have better job prospects when he left the Marine Corps.

He received orders to report to Bravo 1/5 in the April/May 2003 time frame. The unit was returning from OIF1, so Garcia helped with the advance party to bring them back to the U.S. He said that there was then a leave period, so for him it was almost like a big vacation when he joined 1/5.

1/5 then began to train for a MEU deployment, doing MOUT and mountain warfare training. Bravo Company did a hike every Friday to earn liberty. They deployed to Okinawa, Japan, and there learned that they would be going to Iraq. In Okinawa they began to do lots of SASO training. At Camp Hansen, Okinawa, there were areas set up with simulated IEDs so they could rehearse immediate actions during patrols. But at that time everyone still expected only low-level threats in Iraq.

Bravo Company arrived in Kuwait for OIF2, then convoyed into Iraq in Task Force Gypsy up to what was then called FOB Mercury. There they learned that they would be operating in the area of Karmah. They attempted to get there without using the main roads due to the IED threat. However, he said that they tore up some of the vegetable fields of local farmers on that move.

Sergeant Garcia said that there were rumors that 1/5 was going to be sent to the aid of a Marine unit in Fallujah. He used the term "Lance Corporal Hotline" to describe the way the rumors flew. "I went ahead and believed it," he said.

"I was on a security patrol one day, I was taking the XO of H&S Company. And, while we were doing that, we got pulled back from our patrol early, for the simple fact that he [H&S Company] was taking over guard." That's when Bravo Marines figured out that they would be going to Fallujah. Sergeant Garcia went into a company meeting with their CO, Captain Jason Smith, who said that they would be going to Fallujah within the week. The Marines in Bravo were told to pack for three days, but most of them guessed that they would be out longer than that, "So we packed for at least a good week."

Garcia said that they rode into the outskirts of Fallujah at the beginning of April 2004, about the third or the fifth. "I remember that night, because I don't think I've ever been that cold, any of the training that we've done. The worst thing I can say, is I just wanted to get moving!" They stayed put for 24 hours before making a raid to a warehouse. They took the soda warehouse and captured the five civilian guards in the warehouse and his Marines wanted to know what they would do next.

Garcia said, "Finally, the word came down to push forward. So we started pushing forward, clearing out the industrial area." They were clearing out houses and seizing weapons, and their ISRs (Integrated intra-squad radios) were reaching their range limits because the company was so spread out. Sergeant Garcia could hear Marine .50 cals firing at a firefight somewhere to their rear. He said a man came out of a house that they were searching, and walked into the open area with rounds whizzing overhead. He said that this man's unworried attitude opened his eyes to the level of violence in Fallujah. The man was very friendly to the Marines, and his wife even prepared some food for the Marines while they were there. As the push continued, Garcia said to his Corpsman, "This isn't what we planned to do in SASO!"

They were in a section of the town that was full of auto shops and restaurants. They then went onto the rooftops of the buildings. He set the watch, with one Marine on watch while another slept. Garcia wondered how he would be able to sleep with RPGs and small arms fire going on, and then he dropped right off to sleep.

The next morning, they were told to set up VCPs to stop Iraqi vehicles from free access to learn about Marine positions. His squad set up on a choke point on the road. They ran the VCP until about 1530 that day. On the second day of VCPs they took their first contact in Fallujah. Garcia and his squad had just pulled off a VCP, and he was talking with his Corpsman, joking about how he couldn't read any of the signs in the city as they were written in Arabic. Then a mortar round landed about 10 feet from some of his Marines! He ran over to them to check them out. He was next to the impact crater when another mortar round landed so close to him that it knocked out his hearing.

"I couldn't hear when it hit. I grabbed my SAW gunner, made sure he was all right. My Wiley Xs that were supposed to have the ballistic sunglasses, broke. I guess a piece of shrapnel caught the side of it. Next thing I know, I'm wearing Wiley Xs flopping around." He estimated that this mortar round had hit on top of the roof of the next building over, and showered the shrapnel down onto him. He said he was kind of worried about the broken goggles because he didn't have another pair to protect his eyes.

Once he and his SAW gunner got into the middle of the street, they began taking small arms fire. The SAW gunner broke towards a concrete barrier, while Garcia ran behind a tin sign lying in the road. "It was a blue tin sign, I'll never forget it. I took cover right behind it, and as I hit it, it made that 'doooing', that tin sound. And out of all the Arabic writin' on it, the only letters I could point out was 'KIA.' And I was like, wow, that's cool."

He then went to hide next to his machine gunner. "I coulda swore, by the way the bullets were whizzin' around, it was like right behind us. It was in a warehouse that was right behind us." He said that the shooting was coming from an elevated position. Garcia gave a sitrep to Lieutenant Ayres and Ayres gave him the go-ahead to clear that building. "That building was like a maze." They cleared out the building and then he saw the rest of his platoon pushing out, going north on Route Michigan.

Sergeant Garcia said that the Marines were chasing after the bad guys. He said that he grew up in a bad neighborhood back home, but now he was chasing after someone who was shooting at him. After a while they were able to sit down for a rest.

He said, "I remember when I first enlisted, first came in the Marine Corps, I hope something happens. Because I wanna have something to talk about, coming out of the Marine Corps. After that first firefight, we sat down, and I was like, 'Wooh! I didn't think it was gonna be like that!' My Corpsman asked, 'You hate being out here?' And I was like, well, to be honest, I asked to come out here. It's like they said, be careful what you wish for, you might get it. This is everything I asked for."

And as they were talking, AK 47 fire on them resumed.

I interrupted him and said to Sergeant Garcia, "You gotta stop talking to the Corpsman!"

He laughed. "Sir, basically yes!"

He said that Lieutenant Ayres told him to take his squad and start pushing north on Route Michigan again. Garcia said, "You know, if we didn't get any good PT in, past couple weeks, you know, we're running with 80 pounds of gear on, my Doc, of course, two times our load 'cause he's got his medical bag. If we weren't getting good PT in, we're getting it now. Getting fired at. Believe it or not, I've seen some of my slowest PT runners pass me!"

They did not find any enemy fighters. And then they started taking fire again. They went back into the building that they had cleared earlier. His platoon then pushed up towards a mosque. Garcia and his Corpsman hopped a fence, and took off running. When he got to Lieutenant Ayres, he looked back and saw his squad strung out at about 15-meter intervals. Shortly after they moved away from this position, an RPG round hit it. He moved his squad back to set up VCPs.

"We're sitting there, laughing and joking about our near-death experience. We're like, 'Aw man, that was close.' They were like, 'I saw you die!' 'No, he tripped me.' So we're sitting there making fun of each other. 'Aw, you died!'"

Garcia then got a little serious and said that they could have all lost their lives, but they didn't. And now they were joking about it. He said that he joked with the SAW gunner, and that they could joke because they were all alive. "So for another ten minutes it was a good joke about who 'died,' who's scared, this happening, who's running slow. It was good to get your mind offa that. Once that hit again, of course, we got shot again!"

He said that Route Michigan was a big road, with a median in the middle. Lots of the firing at them came from Michigan.

By late in the day, his Marines were getting tired and moving slower. "Any of the training that we did, did not compare to what we were doing at the time. 'Cause we were chasing bad guys. Weren't using any kinda skill, or we didn't know where they were coming from, so we couldn't use any kind of technique, maneuvers, we didn't know how far we could go, and things. We just had one up and down area.

"They say, being a leader is getting your Marines to do what you need them to do when they don't want to do it. And this is the fourth firefight we're gettin' in. The fourth time we've ran, sprinted, like all out, to get to where we're going."

He ran and led his squad to link up with the platoon sergeant, Staff Sergeant Sagredo. As he approached the Sagredo, the platoon sergeant picked up and moved. Garcia described the movement as a dog chasing a rabbit as he tried to do a link-up. "By that time, my legs and my thighs were giving out." For a brief time he felt how tired he was at this point. He caught up with Lieutenant Ayres and got a good sitrep from the officer.

Garcia said that one of his marksmen now sighted an enemy fighter. The marksman said to him, "'I got the guy, and he's getting in the cab!' And then we all looked, and it was the first time we actually, you know, that's the shooter! That's who we were looking at. And he got in the cab and he [the Marine marksman] was like, 'I got a shot!' Garcia said that on practice shooting ranges on Okinawa they would often see who had the most hits. His squad always had the most hits. The marksman took the first shot, and then several other SAWs and M16s fired at the taxi. The insurgent dropped to the ground and the taxi sped off. Weapons platoon recovered the enemy KIA body. This was the first confirmed enemy killed for his squad.

Sergeant Garcia said that they had done five attacks that day, and he was exhausted. "And then we knew, the next day we were gonna be running the same way. Once again, go here! Go there! We need you now! We need you now! And the next day, it was the same thing. Small arms fire. Go get 'em." He said that they would get attacked at the same time, and were starting to figure out when they could take a break to eat and take care of hygene. He remembered, "Say 1130 we'll get attacked. Sure enough, at 1130. Like 1600, they'll probably stop, probably be over with. Sure enough, at 1600 they'd stop."

On one occasion as he and one of his Marines were about to run across a street, the Marine grabbed Garcia and yelled "Stop!" Just then Garcia saw the vapor trail of an RPG round blaze right in front of him. He said that there were many occasions like this when rounds just missed by a matter of split seconds. He also said that sometimes he tried to move his Marines without drawing attention to himself as the leader. But often he just had to stand in the middle of a street and direct his Marines where to go. During one movement in the town, he realized that he was missing one of his fire teams. As he did, he heard someone shouting that they were running to join them.

Garcia got into an argument with Lieutenant Ayres at one point, when Garcia had just moved his men up, and Ayres wanted for Garcia to move them to a new position. "I'm moving them as best I can."

As rounds were snapping over his head, the lieutenant yelled, "Corporal Garcia, get over here NOW!" Garcia then realized that he was standing in the middle of the street, and he better get over to his lieutenant for his own safety. "And that's the only time I think I really worried about getting hit." As Ayres told him to get Marines to certain positions, Garcia told him that his Marines were already there.

By this time, there were Marine tanks in advance of them, and these had moved up to a main road a block or two ahead. They then began to set in. And they were now five days into the operation, but had only brought three days of supplies with them. They did not have any running water there, and Garcia said that he could go about two weeks without shaving, but some of his Marines would shave in the morning and by the next morning have a good beard going on. Everyone was getting "scrufty" with dirt and grime. "We're just nasty looking!"

They had set up in a cheese factory, which he said stunk. But it was better than sitting on the top of a rooftop getting sniper and mortar fire, or running across Route Michigan five times a day. They had a working stove in the building, some Marines found eggs, and made omelets for breakfast. Even though they were still getting shot at, many of them said, "This is the life! This is the life!"

Then Lieutenant Ayres came up to him and told him to take some Marines onto a rooftop where he was pointing. As Garcia was asking if that was the rooftop, a mortar round hit it! Ayres said that was the rooftop where he wanted him to take his Marines. Garcia noted to me that the mortar rounds seldom hit the same spot twice. Garcia gathered up his Marines and brought them to the building. Once they got on top, one of his Marines picked up the fins from the mortar round and said, "This is bullshit!" as he tossed the fins towards Garcia. They all realized this is where the round hit. Garcia told them that this was the spot that they got. He said,

"'Look at it this way, mortars never land in the same spot twice.'" He continued. "They couldn't do nothing but accept it."

After getting intel that they would be attacked again at night, they got pulled off that building.

"As soon as they pull us off, next thing I hear is chrrrrrrrrr, BOOM! I was like, you know what, mortars do land in the same spot, 'cause it got hit on that rooftop. Not the same area, but that same rooftop."

When his Marines questioned him about what he had said about mortars not landing in the same spot, he told them that he thought that it was a rocket, not a mortar. "At least we didn't get hit with that one, right?"

He said that they got used to hearing the sounds of RPGs, rockets and mortars. Some mortars hit pretty close to his Marines, but an individual had to be pretty much directly hit by one to get killed. Garcia joked to some of his Marines that the next time he was back home on a mortar range, he was going to sleep downrange.

They had MREs and water. When they would go to back-clear some areas looking for weapons, they found RPGs, AKs, RPKs, and lots of other weapons in the buildings right behind their position. After these were loaded up onto a Hummer, they would go back into the same buildings and find more bags of weapons! When they checked restaurants, they found weapons, and ammo, and grenades, and rockets. After securing the gear, they would sometimes find soda or eggs. This enabled them to have the omelets in the mornings. Finally their packs were brought up to them.

After a while, they continued to move west, and the Marines joked about not wanting to go west ever again, even when they got back home. But finally Garcia went to his squad when they got word to push west. He said that some heads went down, and some wondered how close they were to getting killed.

"How close we gonna get today?" It was an everyday thing. "How close? Who, if anybody, is gonna get hurt today?"

Sergeant Garcia now got more serious. "I know, myself, just being a squad leader, I came out, and maybe four, five, six, in a day, near-death experiences. And that's me, as a squad leader, where I'm able to take cover whenever I can, wherever I'm at. I'm not the Marine that's providing the security. I'm not the Marine that's looking down that road. I'm not the Marine that's got no other choice but to sneak out and not be under cover. And God knows how many times these Marines keep going."

Garcia said that it was fun moving out at night with NVGs on. At one point, one of his Marines came over the ISR (squad radio) in a whisper, telling him that he had just stumbled over an RPG round. Garcia told him to bring it back to their position. This became a trend during that night with other Marines tripping over rockets.

Garcia explained that the original Rules of Engagement for Fallujah were to fire on suspected enemy only if they showed hostile intent. Otherwise, if they saw Iraqis carrying AK 47s or RPGs, they were not to fire on them. They had seen guys casually walking around with rockets, mortar tubes, and AKs. He had a conversation with Staff Sergeant Sagredo about the fact that they were now behind enemy lines.

Sergeant Garcia discussed at length the fact that it was fun to be in combat, as long as he was not hit. It was what he joined the Marine Corps for, even though he did not fully know what it would be like. He was wondering what would happen each day, and each part of each day, with the possibility of an enemy fighter being in the next house or behind the next door. He said that he and his Marines learned to get used to it and accept it. When his Marines went to the rear to get mail, they reported back that the Marines in the "rear" were not really doing anything out of the ordinary, and were not worried about being shot. "That really brought the Marines down," he said. The Marines in the rear were getting the same pay as the Marines on the front lines. Garcia said he had to use leadership to keep up morale.

Now that he was a sergeant, he noted that even though he was only 21 years old, he was responsible for 13 lives, along with the equipment and weapons for his Marines. He said that when his enlistment was up in October (2004), he planned to get out into the civilian world to see what it's like. "I just wanna get out and be young." He can then make mistakes when he is a civilian and be relaxed. He cannot make mistakes as a sergeant. He described the round-the-clock responsibilities of leading his Marines.

We then talked about April 13, 2004—the day of the trac. Sergeant Garcia said that a resupply Hummer passed by one of the houses where part of the platoon was set up. The Hummer got shot at. He said that the rounds were kicking up dirt all around the vehicle. Then Lieutenant Ayres came up on the radio and said that he was getting two tracs up to those Marines in the house. One trac would pick up Corporal Picard's squad and the other would pick up Garcia's squad. Ayres said that he would go with Picard's squad to flush out the enemy and have them run towards Garcia's squad so that they could finish off the enemy fighters.

Garcia asked if his squad was going to walk alongside the tracs or get inside them. Ayres responded, "I wouldn't be sending you tracs if you wouldn't be getting in them."

Garcia went to his Marines and asked for some teams to go with him. "Everybody got hyped up when they heard the word tracs. They got a Mark 19, they got a .50 cal on there. They're mobile, they're faster than when we're on foot. They got a little bit of armor. So everybody was like, 'All right, let's go!' Everybody was pumped up to go. And it was a drag when I said [to some of the Marines], you stay here. Everybody's like, 'Man, this sucks.' Everybody got all pumped up."

Garcia asked Staff Sergeant Sagredo if he wanted to ride in the TC (trac commander's) hatch. Then they heard the tracs getting close. "It looked like a football game getting ready to go. Everybody's getting pumped, everybody's excited. Everybody's checking their weapons real quick. Quick check on them. Loading them up. Stretching, popping their necks, adjusting their gear, like real quick. Everybody's getting excited. And we see one trac picking up one squad, and we're like, okay, they're going. And we're like, where the hell's our trac? I hope they don't pick us up at the wrong spot. And then, here comes our trac. We see Lieutenant Ayres in the TC hatch. [I] look up, see Staff Sergeant Sagredo, say, 'Looks like we're both on air watch [observing out of the top of the opened vehicle]!' It's funny, to add insult to injury, Lieutenant Ayres was in the TC hatch, and the Amtrac hit the brakes, hard as he could, comes the TC hatch. It landed on Lieutenant Ayres' head pretty hard!"

The ramp opened up, and his squad ran onto the Amtrac and immediately posted themselves on air watch inside the vehicle. They knew what they had to do right away. As Garcia got inside the trac, he thought to himself that they had the platoon's whole chain of command in one trac—the platoon commander, the platoon sergeant, and a squad leader. He thought that somebody's got to get out. But they all stayed.

Garcia said that this trac had trouble getting comm with the other trac. He was listening on a handset inside the trac. The other trac was making loops inside the city to try and get back and get visual contact with their trac. While this was happening, Lieutenant Ayres told the trac driver to push forward to try and get visual link-up with the other trac. "And once he did that, pushed forward about one block, that's when the Marines started unloading [firing their weapons]."

Garcia was sitting down inside the trac, and saw the brass shell casings showering down on him. He could hear rounds pinging off the Amtrac. "There's explosions, people throwing grenades. But, you know, the trac would hit the brakes, the Marines would fall down. And then I'd help everybody get back up. And it sucked, because then we get an RPG shot at us. And they would blow up right on the trac. And I saw Staff Sergeant [Sagredo] fall down. Couple others fall down. And then the quick thought, if they're hit, where are they hit at? If it's a head wound, all the first aid, all the training that comes, that we get, is like, when I saw them fall after that big explosion, it's like, you know, what do they look like, are they all right?"

Garcia said that the RPG blast knocked them down, but didn't wound them. They got up and all said that they were fine. The Marines continued to shoot from inside the vehicle. "Marines were falling down 'cause of the explosions again. Next thing I know, I look over to the right, and the trac got hit. And… it was the biggest puff of white smoke. And my Corpsman and some of my other Marines are over there. And that's all that I could do, 'cause there's so much chow, and water, and rounds, you know, all kinds of ammo everywhere."

Garcia continued: "So I'm inside the trac, and my head's like crushed in by the explosion. So I'm sitting there, my head's hurting, my Marines are down, and I'm like, 'We're still moving! We're still moving! We're still all right!' I'm hearing everybody yell, 'I'm okay, I'm okay!' So they get back up, put their weapons back in action."

He was still trying to get his head back to normal when another RPG round hit the trac. He said it was an RPG 7, and it penetrated into the vehicle. This round pierced the armor, went through the engine cover, and set off a fire in the gunner's compartment. Garcia saw the fire inside the engine cover. The round "took out"

Lieutenant Ayres. Garcia said that a chunk of the lieutenant's leg was carved out. Garcia worried if all of his Marines were okay at this point. A whole range of thoughts raced through his head at this time. When he saw the fire in the gunner's compartment, he yelled for a fire extinguisher. He handed the extinguisher to Lance Corporal McCarver, who then tried to put out the fire. The Corpsman, Doc Viegas, went up to tend to Lieutenant Ayres. After applying a pressure bandage to the officer's leg, he came back through the fire in the trac to get his full medical kit. The Corpsman then tried to go back through the fire to get to the lieutenant. Then the trac began to move forward again and threw Doc Viegas back towards Garcia. Carcia saw second degree burns on Viegas' face.

Sergeant Garcia described the situation: "I got my Corpsman in my hands, second degree burns. I got some of the Marines down. I got a fire going in this trac. It's getting hotter and hotter, and all we're doing is driving and driving. We're still driving. We're still taking rounds, we're still getting blown up. They're shooting RPG 7s, they're still shooting this and that."

Garcia said that the RPG round that hit the gunner's compartment went through the armor there like warm butter. He thought that a round like that near him would go right through the vehicle. He felt that they should stop and find a safer place. There were two SMAW rockets and a thermal round rocket inside the trac, and he worried about them "cooking off" due to the fire there.

Then the Amtrac stopped, and the Marines yelled to get out. Insurgents continued to fire at the trac. Sergeant Garcia opened the door to let the Marines out. He was the last Marine out, and he immediately looked for some concealment or cover from the shooting. He ran to a small bush. Then he saw Staff Sergeant Sagredo go back to the trac to get Lieutenant Ayres. Sagredo climbed onto the top of the trac to pull the lieutenant off, and Lance Corporal McCarver ran to help Sagredo.

Garcia then ran to find a house or building for the Marines to use for defense. He said that there was this house with a metal door on it. Usually the Marines would have to shoot off the lock on this type of door. "I looked at the door, and thought, 'Ooh, a door!' That's the only thing I thought."

He didn't think twice about having to shoot it to get inside. As he ran to the door, he could hear the small arms rounds whizzing and snapping all around him, some of it kicking up dirt onto his ankles. Other Marines had told him that the snapping rounds were closer to a Marine, while the whizzing rounds were a little bit further away.

As Sergeant Garcia ran to the door, he worried that he might not be able to crash through it, that he might bounce off of it, or have to stop and shoot the lock off. As it was, he ducked his head, and hit the door with his shoulder and knocked it right open. His momentum carried him right into a car that was parked inside. He yelled to the Marines to get inside. By this time, Staff Sergeant Sagredo and Lance Corporal McCarver were coming back with Lieutenant Ayres.

Garcia was using McCarver's SAW gun to give them cover fire as they got to the building. He ran out of SAW ammo: "I remember shooting, shooting, shooting, then I hear 'click!' and I'm like, shoot, then pushing them in, shutting the door behind them."

Lieutenant Ayres' wounds had left a blood trail where he had been dragged across the street into the building. The Marines took position inside the house to fire at the surrounding insurgents. The enemy fighters had not stopped shooting from the time the trac was first hit, and this shooting continued. Some Marines went onto the rooftop for better positions, and also for security.

The trac commander was saying that his crew chief was still inside the trac that was burning in the middle of the street. Garcia told Sagredo this, and that he was leaving to get the Amtrac Marine. Corporal Calloway volunteered to go with Garcia, and when they got to the door, another Marine said that he would go, too. When they got to the gate outside the building, Garcia took off towards the Amtrac and again heard rounds snapping at the ground around his feet. They were snapping and whizzing by his head, too.

He said that he knew what it felt like to have an enemy in his sights and fire at him. Now he knew that enemy shooters had him in their sights and were shooting at him! "And that kind of freaked me out a little bit!" He reached the trac, and fell down as he got inside of it. There were rounds for the 203s, grenades, and .50 cal rounds all over the floor of the vehicle. And the fire inside was getting bigger and bigger. As he reached for the engine cover, it burned right through his glove and burned his hand. He tried and failed again to get the engine cover off. He realized that he could not get to the Marine in the burning compartment. Garcia ran back to the house and told Staff Sergeant Sagredo that there was no way to get the dead Marine out of the burning compartment in the vehicle.

Sagredo was on the radio trying to get comm up and get a medevac for Lieutenant Ayres. Garcia checked to see that all of the Marines were stationed at firing positions throughout and on the house. The Corpsman was also wounded. Garcia started to give first aid to Lieutenant Ayres. He changed the pressure dressing, and gave him water.

Then the Marines yelled, "They're throwing grenades at us! They're throwing grenades at us!" Marines began to throw their own grenades at the enemy fighters.

A grenade came into the kitchen and a Marine shouted that the grenade had hit a propane gas line there. Garcia could hear the hiss of the gas now. Afraid that the gas would blow up, Garcia covered Lieutenant Ayres with his body. Corporal McCarver tried to turn the gas off, but couldn't because of shots being fired into the room. Then Corporal Calloway went into the room. Garcia heard Pop! Pop! Pop! Corporal Calloway yelled, "I'm hit!" It turned out to be a graze wound, but he had turned the gas line off.

Garcia told Lieutenant Ayres that he had to take him into a room without windows. It was painful for Ayres to be dragged into the room. Garcia said that most of the

Marines were now down to their last magazine of ammo. Staff Sergeant Sagredo called this in to the company commander, Captain Smith. Ayres told them that he had five magazines on his vest and these were distributed to the Marines. Garcia gave his M16 to his SAW gunner, who was out of ammo for his weapon. The only weapon that Garcia now had was his K-Bar knife.

His Marines saw insurgents walking around outside. Then they saw an ambulance pull up and Garcia said that the Marines breathed a sigh of relief. It looked like an ICDC ambulance, and they thought it would be help. But instead they saw *mujahideen* getting out of the ambulance! Now the Marines were running out of ammo and were pinned down. Garcia took one last look at everybody and thought that this was going to be "it" for everyone.

Then they heard the rumbling of an Abrams tank approaching.

"Everybody's outta ammo. Nobody's firing. We're getting shot at like it's cool. And nobody's firing back, they're waiting for them to come inside the house, before they start shooting. And while that's going on, Staff Sergeant's getting sitreps, who's hurt, they're taking grenades on the rooftops, you know. Not everybody had major wounds. Doc Viegas. The lieutenant. Fistful of shrapnel."

Now Garcia heard jets flying over. The Abrams tanks were coming in, tracs and Hummers were approaching, and the Marines were feeling relieved. First Sergeant Van De Ven and other Marines now came into the building. Garcia said that Van De Ven always seemed to be everywhere, and sometimes in too many places. However, when he came into the house and asked where Lieutenant Ayres was, Garcia felt good to see him: "I've never been so happy to see First Sergeant." He gave Van De Ven an update on Ayres' condition. Afterwards, Van De Ven told Garcia that he looked as if he was going to fall asleep during this break.

Outside, other Marines were trying to hook up the burned Amtrac to an Abrams tank in order to retrieve both it and the Marine who had died inside of it. When the trac began to get moved, the Marines from his squad began to run out of the house. The company used the radio call sign "Blackhawk," and some of them said that this running reminded them of the ending of the movie *Black Hawk Down*.

Garcia said that his ISR radio had been keyed throughout the day, and Marines in other squads heard everything that was going on: Yelling that the lieutenant had been hit; the enemy approaching; the yelling inside of the house. Garcia got on his ISR and asked another squad leader if his Marines were okay. That leader replied that Garcia should be the one being asked the question instead.

"I've seen Marines tired, we've hiked every Friday. But I've never seen Marines drained out." He then did an ammo count. Everyone started out with 180 rounds. His Marines responded with numbers: "Three." "Two." "One." One Marine said zero, and then when he pulled back the bolt of his rifle, his last round popped out.

Garcia asked, "AT rounds? Frags?"

"We're outta ammo."

Now when they do operations around tracs, they look at them and know what can happen to them. "Can't even look at 'em. 'Cause we saw that trac melted, whole melted, gone." Garcia said that 2nd Squad was lucky on April 13. No one died. But on May 13, they lost two Marines (wounded in action) to an IED while operating in Karmah. One was a Marine who had had trouble in another unit, and Garcia had been working with him. This Marine's helmet was shredded from the IED, and the wounded Marine apologized to Garcia for causing him trouble. He survived, as did Garcia's radio operator who got shrapnel wounds to his shin.

Once in Karmah, he said that they did a lot of SASO patrols in and around the town. They got to know faces of the adults and children. He said that he met one Iraqi boy who had a red eye infection that Garcia kept tabs on as the eye healed over several days.

Garcia said that he was getting tired of dealing with the feelings of the locals who seemed to blame the Marines when anything bad happened, even if it was instigated by *mujahideen*.

His squad has been near many IEDs that have been detonated. He has gotten jumpy from this.

On a patrol on June 3, they found two African-made artillery shells that were primed and ready to blow up. They cordoned off the area and called in EOD to destroy this IED.

Another squad was needed to patrol into Karmah. Garcia said that he and another squad leader yelled over their ISRs, "Not it!" Corporal Calloway was late on his call, and said that his ISR didn't work. They told him that his squad had the patrol. Garcia's squad took the cordon of the area near the IED, while Garcia took his squad into the town.

"Next thing you know, we hear a big explosion, BOOOM! Comin' from the north. It's, where the rest of the patrol went. So my RO's like, 'They got casualties.'"

Garcia listened up on the radio.

Calloway's squad had medevacs: One priority, one urgent. Calloway was walking right on top of the IED when it blew up. What saved Calloway was that the IED was dug into the side of a little hill and it blew out to the side instead of up. Calloway got shrapnel through his forearm. Garcia was upset at seeing his best friend laying in the back of the Hummer waiting for medevac and blew up at a Marine who asked him if he was okay. He yelled at them, but knew that they still had a mission to do. He told them, "I'm not the one that's hurt, so don't ask me if I'm okay!" He then got mad at himself for losing control for this short time.

But by the time Calloway had been taken to Baghdad, he was moving his fingertips. Calloway was now on convalescent leave. He went to the States unable to move his right hand. Both he and Garcia ride motorcycles back home, and the right hand operates the gearshift.

Garcia said that later today his squad had a patrol going out from 1400 to 2200, and the Marines were very cautious. Before Fallujah, his SAW gunners carried 300 to 400 rounds, now they carried 600 to 900 rounds. Instead of six magazines, Garcia now carried 12. When they kidded each other about looking so motivated with all of this ammo, the response was that they ran out of rounds the last time, and would not run out again.

Garcia said that as a squad leader he would not be able to aim and shoot at enemy because he will probably be too busy calling in sitreps on the radio and directing his Marines, but he will have extra rounds to give out to his squad. "So it's not a big deal to carry them."

He had mixed feelings about being out here. He was getting tired. Today's patrol was going out to the cloverleaf and back. It seemed that word from "up high" changes. Life on Camp Fallujah now was relaxing compared to the constant state of alert when they were outside in Fallujah and Karmah. On the camp they could walk around without wearing helmets or Kevlar vests.

I told him that when I asked Staff Sergeant Sagredo when he would relax, Sagredo told me, "Sir, not until the wheels are up on the plane!" Garcia laughed at this. But he said that he won't relax until gets to March Air Force Base. Bravo Company was supposed to be leaving here (Camp Fallujah) in about one week, and then return home. He said that Iraq could turn into the next Okinawa if things calm down here.

Final Thoughts

"Sir, what's gonna happen with this interview?"

Almost without exception, junior Marines who I interviewed wanted to know what would happen with the interviews that I did with them. I explained that they would be sent to Washington, DC, location of the Marine Corps History Division at the Washington Navy Yard at that time. Eventually they would be made available to researchers, as digital recordings. Some would be transcribed. The History Division moved to Quantico, Virginia during the mid 2000s, and is now part of the Marine Corps University system.

After finishing up my interviews with Sergeant Garcia and Corporal Picard, I went back to my quarters and packed for a night-time flight to Camp Al Assad. I would soon meet with officers and Marines from 2/7 at that large base, and later take a ground convoy to FOB Hit for interviews with the Marines of Echo Company, 2/7.

Travel throughout Al Anbar province in 2004 required a lot of coordination. My approach was not to investigate particular incidents, but to attempt to meet with Marines from as many deployed units as possible. To make the most of my time at different camps, I first made email contact with key leaders at units so that Major Piedmont and I would maximize our time at each unit. As conditions on the ground changed, so did the locations of Marine units. A company might be at a large camp such as Camp Fallujah for a short time, then be sent into the outskirts of Fallujah, or be tasked with anti-IED patrols. Several interviews scheduled with various staff officers never took place as events took over.

Several times I was on the official schedule for an interview with Colonel John Toolan, regimental commander of RCT1. Even though I operated out of Camp Fallujah where his regiment was headquartered, and Toolan wanted to sit down for an interview, developing operations always got in the way. Unplanned meetings with MEF staff or local Iraqi leaders made his schedule fluid at all times. I was fortunate to get to sit down for an hour-long interview with one battalion commander, Lieutenant Colonel Gregg Olson of 2/1, and also with two staff officers of 2/2: Majors Dixon and Neil.

The interviews in this volume are solely from those that I conducted. Major John Piedmont met with an equal number of Marines for his own interviews when we traveled to each unit.

This approach paid off, as every unit made key Marines available for us to interview. We met with Marines from private first class up to brigadier generals. We kept the interviews on the unclassified security level for ease of reporting and transmission. The challenge was to keep our own situational awareness in order to ask cogent questions that would create interviews that will be useful to researchers in the future.

The collection of interviews in this volume covers several significant events in and around Fallujah, mostly during the April–May 2004 period. I have grouped the interviews as they were completed at each unit, to show how a big picture of an event can be drawn from the perspective of many participants. The rescue of the Amtrac in Fallujah is a perfect example. The words of the tankers, Amtrackers, and infantry Marines clearly create this picture: the initial plans, the problems faced, the view from inside a tank, a stricken amphibious vehicle, the surrounded Marines in a building, and the other Marines in the infantry company who came to the rescue. All of the Marine units in this volume were involved in operations in and around Fallujah during the spring of 2004. The Glossary was updated in August 2022 to more clearly explain both general military and Marine-specific terms in use during 2004.

The chapter on Marine Aviation outlines the planning and operations of the elements of the 3rd Marine Air Wing, and some of the helicopter units it deployed to support operations on the ground. Several crew members described the feeling of being shot at by ground fire, and in one case, an emergency landing.

In reviewing my notes and listening to the interviews, I noticed that oftentimes I did not get the spelling or full names of Marines mentioned by Marines being interviewed. This shortcoming is on me. After completing an interview, I documented it with a summary and finding aids that I included in a folder recorded onto a CD. Sometimes I was able to process interviews in the same day, other times I was not able to do this until returning to my operating base at Camp Fallujah. While doing this, I would be planning another trip to another unit, and then conducting a series of new interviews there. It was not until later years as I attempted to transcribe some of the interviews that I noticed that I often did not have names that were mentioned in interviews spelled correctly. I apologize to those Marines and sailors, and ask that if possible they contact me so that I may give them the recognition that they deserve.

The actions described in this volume occurred during the build-up of tensions in the April 2004 period, after the killing of civilian contractors inside of Fallujah. I arrived at Camp Fallujah in mid-April as events seemed to be pointing to a huge military attack on the insurgent forces in that city in Operation *Vigilant Resolve.* Marine units and attachments had been moved into the outskirts of Fallujah, and many Marines had fought inside the city limits as they encountered opposition forces believed to be a combination of local insurgents and outside fighters. Just as events seemed to be reaching a tipping point in favor of a full-scale attack by the Marine forces arrayed around Fallujah, an attempt at a peaceful, Iraqi-flavored settlement was made.

Once Marine forces got orders to move away from Fallujah and allow a "Fallujah Brigade" to assume security for the city, the Marines responded quickly and maturely. Even the most junior Marine I met with felt that it was worth the chance to put an Iraqi face on the situation. The Marines knew that they had fought well, doing all that was asked of them. Unfortunately, over the summer and into the fall, the hopes for a long-term peaceful Fallujah turned out to be unrealized. Fallujah became the center of continuing insurgent trouble, requiring the Marines and U.S. Army units, along with trained Iraqi forces, to storm into the city in November 2004 for weeks of intense fighting in Operation *Phantom Fury*, causing destruction and death for friend and foe.

In looking back on the Marines I met and interviewed, I continue to be impressed with their dedication, professionalism, and attitude. Most had been in multiple situations that required focus and teamwork. They were all proud of what they were doing every day. Every day they spent doing very important things. They made decisions that affected the lives of their fellow Marines. For many young men, these events may be the most important achievements that they will accomplish. I hope that by writing their stories here, they may have a tangible piece of their accomplishments to share with family and neighbors.

Semper Fi!

Lieutenant Colonel David Kelly, USMCR (Retired)

Glossary

0311	Military occupational specialty (MOS) of a Marine rifleman
1/5	1st Battalion, 5th Marine Regiment
2/1	2nd Battalion, 1st Marine Regiment
2/2	2nd Battalion, 2nd Marine Regiment
29 Palms	Marine Air Ground Combat Center in California
203	M203 single-shot 40mm grenade launcher, under barrel attachment to a rifle
240 Golf	M240 belt-fed, gas-operated machine gun firing a 7.62mm belt-fed round. Rate of fire 650 to 950 rounds per minute
.50 caliber machine gun	Browning M2 machine gun
7th Marines	7th Marine Regiment, also Regimental Combat Team 7
7-ton	MTVR or Medium Tactical Replacement Vehicle. Tactical truck with a 7-ton capacity
81s	81mm mortar system, range up to 6,000 meters
82mm mortars	Soviet-designed mortar system, range up to 3,000 meters
9999	Military Occupational Specialty code for a sergeant major or first sergeant in the Marines
AAA	Anti-Aircraft Artillery (also "Triple A")
AAV	Amphibious Assault Vehicle, LVT P 7 (Landing Vehicle Tracked). Fully tracked amphibious landing

	vehicle. Armament includes M19 40mm automatic grenade launcher, and M2 .50 caliber machine gun. See "Amtrac"
Abrams	M-1 A1 Main Battle Tank
ACE	Marine Air Combat Element. Its size and number of aircraft depend on the mission of the supported Ground Combat Element
ACF	Anti-coalition forces in Iraq
ACOG	Advanced Combat Optical Gunsight for the M16 and M4 rifle
AIF	Anti-Iraqi forces
AK 47	*Avtomat Kalashnikova*. Soviet-designed assault rifle firing a 7.62mm round. Commonly called Kalashnikov
Amtrac	Nickname for Marine Amphibious Assault Vehicle (AAV)
AO	Area of Operations
AO	Aerial observer. Enlisted aircrew/aerial observers/aerial gunners are flight crewmembers that perform duties incident to the operation of Marine helicopters and tilt rotor aircraft
Apache	Boeing AH-64 helicopter of the U.S. Army
APC	Armored Personnel Carrier, a broad type of armored, military vehicle designed to transport personnel and equipment in combat zones
Arbaeen	Annual festival that commemorates the martyrdom of the prophet Mohammed's grandson Husayn ibn Ali. Millions of pilgrims make the trip to the city of Karbala, Iraq. Celebrated on April 10–11 in 2004
ASE	Air Survivability Equipment to detect and defeat incoming missiles. An array of related electronic devices and systems designed to protect aircraft and crews by detecting and defeating threats from infrared (IR) guided (heat-seeking) missiles, laser-guided RF missiles, and unguided munitions

ASR	Alternate Supply Route
AT4	84mm unguided, portable recoilless smoothbore rocket. Common anti-tank weapon
AWS	Amphibious Warfare School. A 41-week resident course for company-grade officers at Quantico, Virginia. In 2003, reorganized into Expeditionary Warfare School (EWS)
BAS	Battalion Aid Station. Medical section within a battalion's support company. Led by battalion surgeon, a Navy medical doctor, and staffed by Navy nurses and medical corpsmen
BCT	Brigade Combat Team of the U.S. Army. Composed of one combat arms branch, one maneuver brigade, and assigned support and fire units
Bird	Nickname for any helicopter
Blackhawk	UH-60 medium-lift helicopter of the U.S. Army
Bradley Fighting Vehicle (BFV)	Family of U.S. Army armored fighting vehicles with a crew of three and room for six soldiers
Bronze Star	Medal awarded to members of the United States Armed Forces for heroic achievement, heroic service, meritorious achievement, or meritorious service in a combat zone
Brooklyn	Nickname used by RCT1 for southwest portion of Fallujah
C-130	Marines often referred to both the AC-130 and KC-130 Hercules by this term. The AC-130 is a heavily armed Air Force version of the KC-130 Hercules fixed-wing transport aircraft
C4	Variety of plastic explosive
CAAT	Combined Anti-Armor Team. A platoon from a Weapons Company task-organized to support infantry operations in Iraq during 2004. Employed armored vehicles with heavy machine guns and TOW missiles
CAG	Civil Affairs Group. Marine reservists who provide specially trained, organized, and equipped civil affairs

	personnel in order to plan, coordinate, and conduct Civil Affairs operations
Camelbak	A commercially available water bladder in a backpack with a tube for drinking. Holds several quarts of liquid
Camp Abu Ghraib	Name for camp initially called Camp Mercury by the U.S. Army, later renamed by the Marines Camp Abu Ghraib (not the infamous prison of the same name)
Camp Mère St. Église	U.S. Army name for camp later renamed by the Marines Camp Fallujah (see MEK)
CAP	Combat Air Patrol; also, Civil Affairs Platoon that works with local forces
CAS	Close air support by fixed wing or rotary wing aircraft for ground actions in close proximity to friendly forces
CASEVAC	Casualty evacuation
CAX	Combined arms exercise. A live-fire training exercise conducted at Marine Corps Base 29 Palms, California
CFACC	Combined Forces Air Coalition Command. Controlled all air assets for Operation *Iraqi Freedom*
CG	Commanding general
CSH	Pronounced "cash." Combat Support Hospital. A U.S. Army field hospital
CH-46	Boeing CH-46 Sea Knight medium lift helicopter. Used by Marine forces to provide combat service support lift in Iraq during 2004 (see "Phrogs"). Beginning in 2007 it was replaced by the V-22 Osprey tilt rotor aircraft
CHOP	Change of operation control. A temporary assignment for a unit or individual to serve with or under a different command
Chopper	Nickname for any helicopter
Click	1,000 meters on a standard military map
CMO	Civil-Military Operations

CO	Commanding officer
Coax	Short for coaxial 7.62mm machine gun on M1A1 Abrams tank. Pronounced "co-ax"
Cobra	Bell AH-1W SuperCobra attack helicopter. Weapons systems can include 20mm M197 3-barrel Gatling gun, 2.75mm Hydra 70 rockets, 5-inch Zuni rockets, TOW missiles, AGM 114 Hellfire missiles, AIM-9 Sidewinder anti-aircraft missiles. Nicknamed "Snake"
COC	Combat Operations Center
CONUS	Continental United States
Corpsman	Enlisted Navy hospital corpsman, serving with Navy and Marine units
CP	Command post
CSS	Combat service support
CSSB	Combat service support battalion
CWS	Commander's weapon station
Daisy-chained	Multiple IEDs wired together to detonate at the same time
Deck	Naval term that Marines also use to describe a level floor or section of land
Det cord	Detonating cord. A thin, flexible tube filled with PETN that detonates at a rate of 6,400 meters per second, used to detonate high explosives and multiple charges
Deuce gear	Slang term referring to field equipment issued to individual Marines. Refers to the form DD 782, signed when gear is issued
DOD	Department of Defense
Dragon	M47 Shoulder-fired, wire-guided, man-portable anti-tank missile system. It was phased out in favor of the Javelin missile
Dragunov	SVD Soviet sniper rifle. Effective range of up to 800 meters. Fires a 7.62 round

EAS	Expiration of active service, when a Marine leaves active duty obligation
"Easy" Company	Honorific title used by Echo (E) Company, 2nd Battalion, 2nd Marine Regiment
EFCAT	Enduring Freedom Combat Assessment Team. In 2004 based at Quantico, Virginia. Sent teams to Iraq and Afghanistan to collect Lessons Learned relating to Marine Corps participation in Operation *Enduring Freedom* and Operation *Iraqi Freedom*
EOD	Explosive Ordnance Disposal
EPW	Enemy prisoner of war
EWS	Expeditionary Warfare School. A 41-week resident course for company-grade officers at Quantico, Virginia. Formerly AWS (Amphibious Warfare School) until 2003
F-16	U.S. Air Force's "Fighting Falcon" single-engine multi-role fighter jet
FAC	Forward air controller. Marine aviator officer deployed with an infantry company to coordinate close air support
Fallujah	City in Al Anbar province about 43 miles west of Baghdad. Estimated population in 2004 was between 250,000 and 300,000
FARP	Forward arming and refueling point. Provides fuel and ordnance necessary for highly mobile and flexible helicopter and fixed wing operations. Used extensively in 2003 during Operation *Iraqi Freedom 1*
FAST	Fleet Anti-terrorism Security Team. These Marines usually guard a variety of installations like naval bases and others too sensitive to leave without an armed presence
Fedayeen	Arabic term used to refer to various Islamic military groups willing to sacrifice themselves for a larger campaign

Firefight	Exchange of gunfire between opposing forces
Fire team	Marine infantry organization of 4 Marines. Part of a 13-man infantry squad
Firm Base	Small, austere outpost. "Going Firm" is creating a hasty defense when stopped for a short time
Fixed wing	Jet aircraft
Flak (jacket)	Sleeveless jacket reinforced with Kevlar, protects against bullets and shrapnel
Fleet/FMF	Fleet Marine Force. Operational forces of the U.S. Marines
Float	Marines' nickname for the forward deployment of a Marine Expeditionary Unit on Navy amphibious shipping
FOB	Forward Operating Base
FPAC	Fallujah Provisional Authority Council. Organized by U.S. Army Lieutenant Colonel Brian M. Drinkwine in early 2004. Composed of sheiks, business leaders, and imams in Fallujah
Frag order	A hasty order for an action. To be "fragged" is to receive such an order
Frag wound	Wound caused by shrapnel fragment(s)
Frock	Temporary promotion to higher rank before normal promotion date to fill a billet
FSSG	Force Service Support Group. Provides combat service support for a Marine Expeditionary Force (MEF)
Fujahideen	Term used by Captain Timothy Bairstow (Fox Company, 2/2) to describe local fighters in Fallujah who joined with the *Mujahideen* fighters
G3	Operations officer at Division, Wing, or higher command
Gatling	See "Mini gun"
GAU-17	See "Mini gun"

GBU	Guided bomb unit. Also known as a smart bomb, a precision-guided munition designed to achieve a smaller circular error probable (CEP)
GPS	Global Positioning System, satellite-based radio-navigation system
Grid	Refers to the six-digit location on a military map
Grunt	Nickname for a Marine infantryman
Grunt phone	Tactical wired phone mounted onto the back of an M1A1 tank for communication with infantry
Gunner	Nickname for non-technical Marine chief warrant officer (CWO-2 to CWO-5)
Gunny	Nickname for a Marine gunnery sergeant (E7)
Harrier jet	McDonnell Douglas AV-8B vertical takeoff and landing (VSTOL) jet attack aircraft. Will be phased out of Marine Corps use by 2029, being replaced by the F35-B VSTOL variant jet
HD	History Division of Headquarters Marine Corps
Hellfire	AGM-114 Hellfire air-to-surface missile (ASM)
Helo	Short term for helicopter
HEAT round	High-Explosive Anti-Tank round fired from M1A1 Abrams tank
HESCO barrier	A barrier made of collapsible wire mesh filled with earth, gravel or rock, to create a defensive position
HET	Human Exploitation Team that includes translators, provided by the U.S. Army
HETS	U.S. Army Heavy Equipment Transporter System. A tractor and trailer system that can carry up to 140,000 pounds on or off road
HMLA	Marine light attack helicopter squadron. Aircraft includes UH-1N "Huey" and AH-1W SuperCobra attack helicopters
HMM	Marine heavy helicopter squadron. Flew CH-46 Echo helos until these were replaced by MV-22 Osprey tilt-rotor aircraft in 2006

HMX 1	Marine Helicopter Squadron One. U.S. Marine Corps helicopter squadron responsible for the transportation of the president and vice president of the United States, heads of state, Department of Defense officials, and other VIPs as directed by the Marine Corps and White House Military Office
Huey	Nickname for the Bell UH-1 series of twin-engine helicopters
Humvee (Hummer)	The High Mobility Multipurpose Wheeled Vehicle (HMMWV, nicknamed Humvee) is a family of light, four-wheel drive, military trucks and utility vehicles produced by AM General
H&S Company	Headquarters and Service Support Company of a battalion
ICDC	Iraqi Civil Defense Corps, became the Iraqi National Guard after the turnover of sovereignty at the end of June 2004
ICOM	Brand name of a commercially available two-way radio.
IED	Improvised explosive device. Hidden explosives assembled by insurgents, grew increasingly sophisticated during 2004
IMEF	1st Marine Expeditionary Force. Includes ground, aviation, and combat service support elements
Intel	Intelligence
IO	Information operations, and public relations
IOC	Infantry Officer Course, at Quantico, Virginia. Challenging course to screen Marine second lieutenants seeking the infantry MOS 0302
IP	Iraqi Police
Iridium phone	Commercial satellite phone
ISR	Integrated intra-squad radio, AN/PRC-343. Developed in Britain and variants used in many countries. Also: Intelligence, surveillance, reconnaissance capability

Javelin	FGM-148 Javelin. Fire-and-forget anti-tank medium-range (about 3 miles) missile
JDAM	Joint Direct Attack Munition. A guidance kit that converted unguided bombs into all-weather precision-guided munitions
Karmah	City of around 90,000 people located about 10 miles northeast of Fallujah
KIA	Killed in Action
LAAD	Low Altitude Air Defense. Responsible for providing short-range air defense using the Stinger missile system
LAR	Light Armored Reconnaissance. Armored mobilized land reconnaissance unit, used to gather intelligence and for screening. Marines use the LAV 25 as its main vehicle
LAV	Light Armored Vehicle 25, an eight-wheeled armored reconnaissance vehicle
Left-seat, Right-seat	Technique used to familiarize incoming military units with an area. The combat veteran would take the left seat of a vehicle at first. Within days the new arrival would take charge in the left seat
Leupold	Commercially available brand of rifle scope
Litening Pod	An electro-optical infrared sensor system for targeting and surveillance that enables aircrews to detect, acquire, identify and track targets at long ranges
LOD	Line of departure. A line established to coordinate attacking units when beginning the attack
LP	Listening post. A manned position beyond the main lines of a Marine unit
LZ	Landing zone, area set aside for helicopter landings
M1A1	Abrams Main Battle Tank. In use by U.S. Marines and U.S. Army. Armed with 120mm smoothbore cannon, 7.62 coaxial machine gun, .50 cal M2 machine gun
M4	The *M4 carbine* is a 5.56×45mm NATO, gas-operated, magazine-fed, carbine assault rifle

M16	M16 A4 was the standard-issue infantry rifle for Marines in Iraq during 2004
M203	Single-shot 40mm grenade launcher, under barrel attachment to a rifle
MACG	Marine Air Control Group. Its mission is to coordinate all aspects of air command and control defense within a Marine Air Wing
MAG	Marine Air Group. MAGs consist of a MAG headquarters, a Marine Aviation Logistic Squadron (MALS), a Marine Wing Support Squadron (MWSS), and from two to ten aircraft squadrons and/or detachments
Mahdi Militia	Shia militia group formed in 2003 and led by cleric Muqtada al-Sadr, that attacked Sunni Iraqis and coalition forces
Mark 19	A 40mm belt-fed automatic grenade launcher
Mark 82	An unguided, low-drag general-purpose 500-pound bomb
MARPAT	Marine pattern camouflage combat uniform first introduced in late 2002
MAW	Marine Air Wing. Aviation unit of a Marine Expeditionary Force
MCRD	Marine Corps Recruit Depot. The Corps has two: One in San Diego, CA, and one in Parris Island, SC
MEF	Marine Expeditionary Force. Largest Marine air-ground task force. Includes a command element, a ground combat element (Marine Division), a Marine Air Wing, and a Marine Logistics Group
MEK	Mujahedin-E Kalq. Training camp near the city of Fallujah. Taken by U.S. Army forces in 2003 and renamed Forward Operating Base St. Mère Église. Renamed Camp Fallujah by the Marines in 2004 (See Camp Mère St. Église)
Meritorious Mast	A formal and ceremonial acknowledgement recognizing an enlisted person being awarded a Letter of Appreciation for noteworthy performance

MEU	Marine Expeditionary Unit. Smallest Marine air-ground task force. Usually based around a reinforced infantry battalion and attached elements
MEU (SOC)	Marine Expeditionary Unit, Special Operations Capable. Such units were expected to be able to respond to a variety of crises, most notably incidents that conventional units may not be able to properly handle. A MEU (SOC) was also expected to be capable of providing various forms of security or a military presence to any region worldwide, within 24–72 hours of receiving orders. As of 2013, the term is obsolete
MHG	Marine Headquarters Group of a Marine Expeditionary Force (MEF)
Mike mike	Slang for millimeter
Mini gun	The M134 mini gun is a six-barrel rotary machine gun with a high rate of fire. Used by the Marines on helicopters. Can fire at a rate of 2,000 to 3,000 rounds per minute
MOPP suit	Mission-oriented protective posture equipment. In the 2003 invasion of Iraq, this included gas mask, protective suit, gloves and boot covers
MOS	Military Occupational Specialty
MOUT	Military Operations in Urban Terrain
MP	Military Police
MPAT	120mm tank round used in the M1A1 Abrams tank
MPF	Maritime pre-positioning program. Strategic power-projection naval capability to provide most of the combat equipment needed for two Marine Expeditionary Brigades (MEBs)
MPS	Maritime Pre-Positioning Ship (see MPF)
MREs	Meals ready to eat. Rations for operations in the field
MSG	Marine Security Guard. The primary mission of the MSG is to provide security, particularly the protection of classified information and equipment vital to

	the national security of the United States at American diplomatic posts
MSR	Main supply route
Mujahideen	Muslim guerrilla forces
MWR	Morale, welfare, recreation
Navy Comm	Navy Commendation Medal. Awarded to an individual who distinguishes himself/herself by heroic or meritorious achievement or service
NBC	Nuclear, biological, chemical weapons. Also CBR: Chemical, biological, radiological weapons
NCO	Non-commissioned officer. In the Marines, enlisted member ranking from corporal (E4) and higher
NEO	Non-Combatant Evacuation Operations
NROTC	Naval Reserve Officer Training Corps. College program to prepare undergraduates for commission as either Navy or Marine Corps officers
NVGs	Night vision goggles
OCS	Officer Candidate School. A ten-week screening and selection program for college graduates to obtain commissions as Marine second lieutenants. Most Marine officers are obtained through this program. Also OCC (Officer Candidate Course)
OIF	Operation *Iraqi Freedom*
OP	Observation post
Op Con	Operational Control of a unit. Usually a temporary control measure
Operation *Vigilant Resolve*	Combat operations in and around Fallujah, April 4 to May 10, 2004. Began with RCT1 deploying two battalions to block all access roads and conduct raids into the city
Pack 2	Infrared laser night sight for the M16 rifle
PFC	Private first class. Enlisted rank (E2)

Phase line	Military control measure for units. Often designated on a road or easy-to-identify geographic feature
Phrogs	Marine nickname for Boeing CH-46 helicopters
PKM	A Soviet-designed machine gun firing a 7.62mm round with an effective range of 800 meters
PLC	Platoon Leader Course. A screening and selection program for college students. Held each summer at Quantico, Virginia. Successful candidates receive Marine officer commissions after college graduation
PSYOPS	U.S. Army Psychological Operations. Specialists who assess the information needs of a civilian population and craft messages to influence them
PT	Physical training
PX	Post Exchange. A base retail store. In remote FOBs, often offering toiletries and personal items for sale
QRF	Quick Reaction Force. Any task-organized unit ready to respond to another unit in contact with enemy forces
Queens	Nickname for southeast section of Fallujah used by RCT1
RCT	Regimental Combat Team. Marine infantry regiment with attached and supporting elements that allow it to be self-supporting in the field
RCT1	Regimental Combat Team 1. An infantry regiment based at Camp Pendleton, California, under the command of the 1st Marine Division
RO	Radio operator
ROEs	Rules of Engagement in a conflict
ROTC	Reserve Officers' Training Corps. Provides training to prepare college students to become officers in the U.S. military
RPG	Shoulder-fired rocket-propelled grenade

RPK	Soviet-designed light machine gun, fires a 7.62mm round
SAFIRE	Surface to air fire
SAM	Surface-to-air missile
SAPI plates	Small Arms Protective Insert. Placed into ballistic vests (flak jackets) to intercept projectiles and some explosive fragments
SASO	Security and Stability Operations
Satellite patrol	Urban patrolling technique with the command element of a unit on a primary axis, with teams moving in front of, behind, and parallel
SAW	Squad Automatic Weapon. M249 light machine gun. Belt-fed, firing a 5.56mm round, has a quick-change barrel
SIPRNET	Secret Internet Protocol Router Network, used by Department of Defense to transmit classified information
Sitrep	Situation report of an ongoing action
Six	Six o'clock direction, directly in the rear of personnel or vehicle
SMAW	Mk 153 Shoulder-Launched Multipurpose Assault Weapon. A rocket used primarily to destroy bunkers and fortifications
SMCR	Selected Marine Corps Reserve, the reserve force of the U.S. Marine Corps
Snake	Nickname for a Marine Cobra helicopter
SOC	Special Operations Capable Marine Corps unit
SOI	School of Infantry. Second stage of military training for enlisted Marines who have completed Basic Training
SOP	Standard Operating Procedure
Spectre	U.S. Air Force's AC-130 H gunship. Primary missions are close air support, air interdiction, and force

	protection. Armed with 40mm cannon, one 105mm M102 howitzer
Squad	In 2004, a Marine rifle squad was 13 Marines: A non-commissioned officer leader (sergeant or corporal), and three fire teams of four Marines each
STA	Surveillance and Target Acquisition. Provide surveillance and scout-sniper teams
Staff NCO	Staff non-commissioned officer. An enlisted Marine with rank of E6 or higher
Staff Organizations	S1 Personnel/manpower S2 Intelligence or security S3 Operations S4 Logistics or supply S5 Plans S6 Communications
Stage	To prepare personnel, weapons and equipment for a military action
SUV	Sports utility vehicle
TAC	Tactical Operations Center. A mobile command post with the battalion commander, where the majority of planning takes place
TAC radio	Tactical radio
TBS	The Basic School at Quantico, Virginia. A 26-week course. Provides training for all newly commissioned Marine second lieutenants prior to further MOS training
TC	Amtrac "Trac" vehicle commander
TCP	Traffic control point, used to control civilian traffic
TF	Task Force. A unit or formation established to work on a single defined task or activity
TRAP	Tactical recovery of aircraft and personnel
T/O	Table of Organization and Equipment. Personnel or weapon designated to a unit

TOW	Tube-launched, Wire-guided missile (BGM-71 TOW) with a range of 3,700 meters
TQ	Slang term for Camp Al Taqaddum
Trac	Nickname for a Marine AAV (see AAV, Amtrac)
Triple A	Slang term for anti-aircraft artillery (see AAA)
UH-1N	A twin engine medium military helicopter designed and produced by the American aerospace manufacturer Bell Helicopter. Nicknamed "Huey"
USNA	United States Naval Academy at Annapolis, Maryland
UXO	Unexploded ordnance
VBIED	Vehicle-borne improvised explosive device
VCP	Vehicle checkpoint
VMFA	A Marine Fighter Attack Squadron (fixed wing)
WESTPAC	Western Pacific area
WIA	Wounded in Action
Wiley X	Commercially produced sunglasses that provide some eye protection against sand and rocks. Provided to most Marines in Iraq during 2004 operations
Wing	Element of Marine Aviation, fixed wing or helicopter
Winthrop Method	A counter-terrorism technique develop by the British army in Northern Ireland to locate certain hidden sites
WTI	Weapons tactics instructor. The WTI course is an advanced, graduate-level course for select fixed wing, rotary wing and tilt rotor pilots and enlisted aircrew from the Marine Corps aviation community
XM 908	A 120mm round fired from an Abrams tank that can effectively destroy concrete obstacles. Used for the first time in combat in 2003–2004
XO	Executive officer in a military unit of company size and above

Sources and Further Reading

Field History Journal of Lieutenant Colonel David E. Kelly, March–July 2004 (On file with US Marine Corps History and Museums Division)

Interview Notes of Lieutenant Colonel David E. Kelly (Author's collection)

Field History Interviews by the Author

Colonel Mant Campbell Hawkins II, USMC, Camp Al Assad, Iraq, 05/18/2004
Colonel Jon G. Miclot, USMC, Camp Al Assad, Iraq, 05/19/2004
Colonel Gerald Allen Yingling, Jr., USMC, Camp Al Assad, Iraq, 05/18/2004
Lieutenant Colonel David William Coffman, USMC, Camp Al Taqaddum, Iraq, 05/02/2004
Lieutenant Colonel Gregg P. Olson, USMC, Camp Bahariyah, Iraq, 06/15/2004
Major Christopher Dixon, USMC, Camp Fallujah, Iraq, 04/22/2004
Major Kevin John Lee, USMC, Camp Al Taqqadum, Iraq, 05/01/2004
Major Brian Warren Neil, USMC, Camp Fallujah, Iraq, 05/23/2004
Captain Timothy Michael Bairstow, USMC, Camp Fallujah, Iraq, 04/22/2004 and 05/24/2004
Captain Samuel Lee Meyer, USMC, Camp Al Assad, Iraq, 05/20/2004
Captain Michael Dale Skaggs, USMC, Camp Fallujah, Iraq, 05/12/2004
Captain Jason Eugene Smith, USMC, Camp Shahabi, Iraq, 06/12/2004
Captain Kyle Marvin Stoddard USMC, Camp Bahariyah, Iraq, 06/15/2004
Lieutenant Benjamin Scott Adams, USMC, Fallujah, Iraq, 05/12/2004
Lieutenant Joshua B. Jamison, USMC, Camp Bahariyah, Iraq, 06/15/2004
Lieutenant Walker Clark Koury, USMC, Camp Fallujah, Iraq, 05/23/2004
Lieutenant Stephen Gallagher Lewis, USMC, Camp Shahabi, Iraq, 06/11/2004
Lieutenant Brandon McDaniel, USMC, Camp Fallujah, Iraq, 04/22/2004
Lieutenant Ilario G. Pantano, USMC, Camp Fallujah, Iraq, 04/23/2004
Lieutenant Troy M. Sayler, USMC, Camp Fallujah, Iraq, 05/12/2004
Lieutenant Brandon Stibb, USMC, Camp Fallujah, Iraq, 04/22/2004
Lieutenant Edward Minnich Trainor, USMC, Camp Fallujah, Iraq, 05/23/2004
Lieutenant Anthony Triviso, USMC, Camp Fallujah, Iraq, 04/22/2004
Warrant Officer Thomas Ray Smith, USMC, Camp Al Taqaddum, Iraq, 05/02/2004
First Sergeant Scott Aldan Van De Ven, USMC, Camp Shahabi, Iraq, 06/11/2004
Master Sergeant Gregory Scott Staggs, USMC, Camp Al Assad, Iraq, 05/20/2004
Staff Sergeant Thomas L. Reynolds, USMC, Camp Fallujah, Iraq, 05/24/2004
Staff Sergeant Ismael Sagredo, USMC, Camp Shahabi, Iraq, 06/12/2004
Staff Sergeant Jason M. Velez, USMC, Camp Bahariyah, Iraq, 06/15/2004
Sergeant Gilbert Guadalupe Alcantar, USMC, Camp Fallujah, Iraq, 05/11/2004

Sergeant Edgar D. Aguilarvaldizon, USMC, Camp Abu Ghraib, Iraq, 06/15/2004
Sergeant John Jeremy Belcher, USMC, Camp Al Assad, Iraq, 05/20/2004
Sergeant Jeffrey S. Duarte, USMC, Camp Bahariyah, Iraq, 06/15/2004
Sergeant Heriberto Escamilla, USMC, Camp Fallujah, Iraq, 05/12/2004
Sergeant Ronnie Garcia, USMC, Camp Fallujah, Iraq, 07/03/2004
Sergeant Kevin S. Keeley USMC, Camp Bahariyah, Iraq, 06/15/2004
Sergeant Todd Lewis Luginbuhl, USMC, Camp Bahariyah, Iraq, 06/15/2004
Sergeant Michael Wayne Rinehart, USMC, Camp Abu Ghraib, Iraq, 06/15/2004
Sergeant Michael Thomas Vollmer, USMC, Camp Abu Ghraib, Iraq, 06/15/2004
Sergeant Prince Witty, USMC, Camp Fallujah, Iraq, 05/12/2004
Sergeant Judd Anthony Word, USMC, Camp Fallujah, Iraq, 04/23/2004
Corporal Michael Edward Cazzola, USMC, Camp Fallujah, Iraq, 05/23/2004
Corporal Michael J. Fiscella, USMC, Camp Fallujah, Iraq, 05/12/2004
Corporal Jason Charles Howell, USMC, Camp Shahabi, Iraq, 06/11/2004
Corporal Ernie Moreno, USMC, Camp Shahabi, Iraq, 06/11/2004
Corporal Jason Picard, USMC, Camp Fallujah, Iraq, 07/03/2004
Corporal David Thomas Silvers, USMC, Camp Abu Ghraib, Iraq, 06/15/2004
Corporal Tyler Steven Trenda, USMC, Camp Abu Ghraib, Iraq, 06/15/2004
Lance Corporal David Graham Braun, USMC, Camp Fallujah, Iraq, 04/23/2004
Lance Corporal Anthony Francis Ewers, USMC, Camp Shahabi, Iraq, 06/12/2004
Lance Corporal Fue Lo, USMC, Camp Abu Ghraib, Iraq, 06/15/2004
Lance Corporal Angel Quiles, USMC, Camp Abu Ghraib, Iraq, 06/15/2004
Lance Corporal Delphine Philberto Velarde, USMC, Camp Shahabi, Iraq, 06/11/2004
Private First Class Richard Eric Speir, USMC, Camp Bahariyah, Iraq, 05/23/2004

Further Reading on Conflict in Iraq

Camp, Dick, *Operation Phantom Fury: The Assault and Capture of Fallujah, Iraq*, Minneapolis, MN, Zenith Press, 2009

Estes, Kenneth W., Lieutenant Colonel, USMC (Ret.), *U.S. Marine Corps Operations in Iraq, 2003–2006*, Washington, DC, History Division Marine Corps University, 2009

Estes, Kenneth W., Lieutenant Colonel USMC (Ret.), *US Marines in Iraq 2004–2005 Into the Fray*, History Division Marine Corps University, 2011

Lowry, Richard S., *New Dawn: The Battles for Fallujah*, New York, Savas Beattie, 2010

O'Donnell, Patrick K., *We Were One*, Boston, Da Capo Press, 2006

Reynolds, Nicholas E., Colonel, USMC (Ret.), *Basrah, Baghdad, and Beyond—The US Marine Corps in the Second Iraq War*, Annapolis, Maryland, Naval Institute Press, 2009

Schlosser, Dr. Nicholas J., *US Marines in Iraq 2004–2008: Anthology and Annotated Bibliography*, History Division Marine Corps University, 2010

West, Bing, *No True Glory: A Frontline Account of the Battle for Fallujah*, New York, Bantam Books, 2005

About the Author

Lieutenant Colonel David E. Kelly had retired from the Marine Corps Reserve in 1999 after a 29-year career, both active and reserve. His last assignment prior to military retirement was as operations officer for the Marine Corps Field History Detachment that operated out of the Washington, DC, Navy Yard. In that billet he planned training for Marine Corps field historians, and also contributed to the Marine Corps' 1998 commemorative anthology, *Marines in the Spanish American War.*

In late 2003, he agreed to return to active duty in order to deploy to Iraq as one of only two Marine field historians there. That year, the 1st Marine Expeditionary Force (IMEF) planned and trained for security and stability operations, but events would overtake this planning as a full-scale insurgency in Iraq began in the spring of 2004. During a five-month deployment, Lieutenant Colonel Kelly and Major John Piedmont traveled to interview Marines in most areas of Iraq.

Upon completion of the deployment, all oral interviews, photographs and documentation were downloaded onto CDs and filed at the Marine Corps Oral History department. The collection is now located at Quantico, Virginia. Several of the interviews have been transcribed there.

Lieutenant Colonel Kelly "re-retired" on the completion of his deployment, and returned to civilian life in the fall of 2004. He then began to review his copies of these interviews to create this book. He plans to continue to use many of his other interviews for upcoming books.

He retired in June 2017 as high school history teacher at Cardinal O'Hara High School in Springfield, Pennsylvania.

His first book *Hell in the Streets of Husaybah* was published in March 2022.

Index